HISTORY OF BRECHIN

THE
HISTORY OF BRECHIN,
TO 1864

DAVID D. BLACK

FACSIMILE EDITION

The Pinkfoot Press
Brechin
2009

Facsimile edition published 2009 in Scotland by
The Pinkfoot Press
1 Pearse Street, Brechin, Angus, DD9 6JR

The History of Brechin was first published in 1839, followed by
a revised and updated second edition in 1867, *The History of
Brechin, to 1864*, published by William Paterson, Edinburgh,
and Black and Johnston, Brechin. The facsimile is of the second
edition, and the illustrations on pages 375–394 are reproduced
from a further printing of 1902.

ISBN 978 1 874012 51 1

Printed by The Cromwell Press Group, Trowbridge

This facsimile edition
is respectfully dedicated
to the memory of the author
David Dakers Black
1797–1875
and to the inspiration
of another Brechin historian
David Gordon Adams
1940–2002

ACKNOWLEDGEMENT

The publishers gratefully acknowledge the co-operation of Angus Council Cultural Services, who kindly made available an original copy of the work for digitisation. In particular we wish to thank Norman Atkinson and Gavin Hunter for their assistance.

HISTORY OF BRECHIN.

HIGH STREET AND TOWN HALL OF BRECHIN.

CHURCH STREET, HAVING MECHANICS' HALL IN THE DISTANCE.

Page 1.

THE

HISTORY OF BRECHIN,

TO

1864:

BY

DAVID D. BLACK, F.A.S., Scot.,

LATE TOWN-CLERK.

"Breathes there the man with soul so dead,
Who never to himself hath said,
This is my own, my native land!"
–Scott.

Second Edition.

EDINBURGH:
WILLIAM PATERSON, 74 PRINCES STREET.
BRECHIN: BLACK & JOHNSTON.
1867.

ORIGINAL PREFACE

PUBLISHED IN 1839.

"ALTHOUGH THE PUBLICATION WILL HAVE NO PRETENSIONS TO
RANK WITH HISTORY, ACCORDING TO THE PROPER INTERPRETATION
OF THAT WORD, YET, FOR WANT OF A BETTER NAME, THE PUB-
LISHERS PROPOSE TO STYLE THE WORK 'THE HISTORY OF
BRECHIN.'"

PROSPECTUS.

PREFACE TO THE SECOND EDITION.

WHEN this book was originally written in 1838, the Author
was immersed in business, and could not bestow time on verify-
ing all the statements in it by reference to authorities. He has
now more leisure, and has employed it in examining every
authority he could find bearing on the statements made. He
cannot hope to be free from error; but he trusts this enlarged
edition will be found to contain fewer mistakes than the previous
publication. He meant to have quoted his authorities, and the
manuscript was prepared with that view, but as it was found to
be troublesome in the printing, and of little moment to the

general reader, the references are only given in particular cases. The list of Bishops, however, in the Appendix, is supported by references to the authorities, warranting the insertion of their names in that compilation. The original publication was no source of emolument to the Author—the reverse; but it brought him the acquaintance of noblemen and of gentlemen, with whom he has had much pleasant intercourse. He has now and formerly been greatly indebted to many parties for hints and information; and while he feels it impossible to select particular individuals, he finds it would be tedious to give a list of the whole, and he therefore confines himself to tendering general thanks to his numerous friends, and to living authors from whom he has freely borrowed when he found anything in their works to answer his purpose, as some of them had borrowed from him previously.

The first volume of the records of the Town Council commences with *Laus Deo*, and the Author of this book desires to finish his labours in the same spirit, for he cannot be too thankful that after having completed his seventieth year he is enabled to finish this work.

CLERK STREET, BRECHIN,
3rd July 1867.

CONTENTS.

CHAP.   PAGE

I. THE HISTORY OF BRECHIN TO THE YEAR 1250, ... 1

II. THE HISTORY OF BRECHIN FROM 1250 TO 1560, ... 16

III. THE HISTORY OF BRECHIN FROM 1560 TO 1600, ... 39

IV. THE HISTORY OF BRECHIN FROM 1600 TO 1670, ... 53

V. THE HISTORY OF BRECHIN FROM 1670 TO 1700, ... 82

VI. THE HISTORY OF BRECHIN FROM 1700 TO 1727, ... 114

VII. THE HISTORY OF BRECHIN FROM 1727 TO 1760, ... 137

VIII. THE HISTORY OF BRECHIN FROM 1760 TO 1800, ... 154

IX. THE HISTORY OF BRECHIN FROM 1800 TO 1838, ... 180

X. THE HISTORY OF BRECHIN FROM 1838 TO 1864 INCLUSIVE, . . 213

XI. THE CHURCH, STEEPLES, AND ROUND TOWER OF BRECHIN, . . 230

XII. BRECHIN IN 1864, ... 258

APPENDIXES.

NO.   PAGE

I. CHARTER BY WILLIAM I., ... 293

II. INQUIRY INTO THE ORIGIN OF THE WORD "BRECHIN," . . . 295

III. LIST OF THE BISHOPS OF THE SEE OF BRECHIN, ... 298

IV. EXTRACTS FROM THE ACCOUNTS OF WALTER JAMESON, CHURCH-
MASTER OF BRECHIN, 1684, ... 326

V. CENSUS 1841-1851-1861, ... 329

VI. INVENTORY OF ARTICLES FOUND IN THE ROUND TOWER, 1842, . 330

VII. LETTER BY MR BLACK TO WILLIAM HACKETT, ESQ., REGARDING
EXPLORATIONS IN THE ROUND TOWER, ... 330

VIII. LIST OF THE TOWN COUNCIL OF BRECHIN, ... 334

IX. TABLES OF WAGES AND PRICES OF OATMEAL COMPARED, . . 361

LIST OF WOODCUTS.

Page no. this editi

I. HIGH STREET OF BRECHIN, ... 1 *Frontispi*

II. VIEWS OF MAISONDIEU CHAPEL, ... 16 *Opposite*

III. THE CATHEDRAL FROM THE EAST, ... 39 *Opp. 38*

IV. THE CATHEDRAL FROM THE NORTH, ... 48 *Opp. 39*

V. GROUND PLAN OF CATHEDRAL, ... 230 *Opp. 136*

VI. THE CATHEDRAL FROM THE WEST, ... 234 *Opp. 137*

VII. DOORWAY OF ROUND TOWER, ... 249 *Opp. 212*

VIII. CARVED STONE, ... 254 *Opp. 213*

LIST OF ILLUSTRATIONS

(ADDED IN 1900).

		PAGE	Page no. in this edition
I.	BRECHIN FROM THE SOUTH	*Frontispiece*	375
II.	THE CATHEDRAL FROM THE WEST	45	376
III.	LIDDLE'S CLOSE, BISHOP'S CLOSE, MAISONDIEU LANE	51	377
IV.	BRECHIN IN 1600	53	378
V.	VIEWS OF CATHEDRAL	59	379
VI.	BRECHIN CATHEDRAL—RUINS OF OLD CHANCEL	77	380
VII.	BRECHIN BRIDGE	98	381
VIII.	THE CATHEDRAL FROM THE EAST, ROUND TOWER, BRECHIN FROM THE BRIDGE	133	382
IX.	RIVER STREET	148	383
X.	ST NINIAN'S SQUARE	203	384
XI.	MARKET STREET, HIGH STREET, BRECHIN CASTLE FROM THE INCH	206	385
XII.	'PRENTICE NEUK	208	386
XIII.	MONTROSE STREET IN FORMER DAYS	224	387
XIV.	BRECHIN CATHEDRAL (RESTORED)	240	388
XV.	BRECHIN CATHEDRAL—NEW AISLE	242	389
XVI.	DEN BURN WORKS	271	390
XVII.	GARDNER MEMORIAL PARISH CHURCH	278	391
XVIII.	PUBLIC LIBRARY	280	392
XIX.	MECHANICS' INSTITUTE	283	393
XX.	BRECHIN CASTLE	286	394

EXTERIOR VIEW.

INTERIOR VIEW. *Page* 16.

HISTORY OF BRECHIN.

CHAPTER I.

THE HISTORY OF BRECHIN TO THE YEAR 1250.

The origin of the city of Brechin, like that of most other burghs, is involved in much obscurity. The oldest document belonging to the burgh, of which we have the exact words, is a charter by William the Lion, who reigned between 1165 and 1214, *confirming* to the bishops and Keldeis of the church of Brechin a right of market on Sundays, as formerly granted by David I., and that "as freely as the Bishop of St Andrews holds a market." The original of the charter by King William is lost, but the precise words of it are found in various attested transumpts, and we give a copy of the deed in our Appendix, No. I. Now, as David I. died in 1153, we may fairly infer that Brechin was a place of some note, if not a royal burgh, as we think it was, in the twelfth century. Authorities differ considerably as to what constitutes a royal burgh. The late Mr Thomas Thomson, advocate, the famous antiquarian, Deputy-Clerk-Register for Scotland, and to whom mainly we owe our present excellent arrangements for the keeping of the public records, in his introduction to the report of the commissioners appointed to inquire into the state of municipal corporations in Scotland in 1835, says, (page 9): "The origin and state of the burghs of Scotland, in common with those of our other political establishments, are unfortunately involved in all the obscurity arising necessarily from the absence or loss of contemporaneous and authentic

A

documents." And again : " David I., whose reign of nearly thirty years terminated in 1153, has been commonly regarded their chief, if not their first founder." " And although there is not now to be found any charter of erection granted by that monarch in favour of any burgh royal, there exists in the chartularies of religious houses, and in other authentic records, numerous grants of property to bishops and abbots, which are described as situated in particular burghs." Mr Cosmo Innes, advocate, one of the principal clerks of the Court of Session, and Professor of History in Edinburgh College, in his preface to the first volume of the folio edition of the Scots Acts, page 6, says : " Among the marks of rapid improvement and civilisation which distinguished the reign of David I., the most important was the recognition of the privileges of free burghs. There can be no doubt that communities existed in the towns of Scotland, supported by mutual confederation, at a much earlier period ; and indeed here, as in other countries, a part of our burghal institutions can be traced up, with much probability, through the free towns of the Continent, to the *Municipia*, which survived the downfall of the empire. But it was under this wise prince that the burghs of Scotland took their place as recognised members of the body politic of a feudal kingdom. Their voluntary incorporation was legalised. They became tenants *in capite* of the Crown, and from that period yielded a large proportion of the revenue of the country, whether as rent of the tenements within burgh, or as custom levied on their merchandise. Their increasing consequence was aided by the organisation of an assembly for treating their common affairs. Long before the principle of representation can be distinguished elsewhere, the burghs of Scotland sent delegates to a court of their own, where they framed laws for their common government, and reviewed decisions of individual burgh courts ; a burgher parliament, which, though now become insignificant, long continued under its successive characters of the Court or Convention of Burghs, one of the most remarkable of the peculiar institutions of Scotland. In that assembly probably were voted and assessed the taxes which the burghs contributed to the necessities of the state. We know, indeed, that they joined in the aids and public contributions from a very early

period; and it seems more probable that the burgesses met for
that purpose in their own court, than that their attendance in
the national councils during a whole century should have been
unnoticed by the contemporary chroniclers, and in all the vestiges
of parliamentary proceedings that remain to us." The regular
series of the records of the Convention of Royal Burghs does not
commence till 1552, and even then the records are very incomplete; but we find Brechin represented at a meeting of the Convention held at Dundee on 18th September 1555, and although
Brechin, like many other burghs, was negligent in sending
representatives regularly to the Convention, and in October 1572
was, along with other absent burghs, fined in £10 for contu-
macy in not attending a meeting held at Stirling, still Brechin
continued from time to time to send representatives to Convention,
as the volume of records of that body, edited by Mr J. D.
Marwick, the learned town-clerk of Edinburgh, and lately published by the Convention, proves. Brechin also was regularly assessed in its share of the public assessments; thus in 1535,
Brechin has to pay £56, 5s. as her proportion of the 5000 merks
allocated on the burghs of the extent of £20,000 granted by the
three estates for sustaining James V.'s expenses in France, and
so on downwards, as is shown by extracts from the Council
Records of Edinburgh, printed by Mr Marwick in the Convention volume alluded to. A *royal* burgh, then, does not appear
to have been a corporation constituted by any special grant raising it to that dignity, but a place of some importance in itself,
recognised by a royal grant of some peculiar right, as the right
of market granted by David I. to Brechin. Previous to 1153,
Brechin was undoubtedly a place of some importance. Kenneth III. is said in 990 to have given Brechin to the Church,
and is described as " Hic est qui tribuit *magnum civitatem*
Brechne domino." Hector Bœce, under the reign of Malcolm
II., (1001–1031,) represents the Danes as assailing " Brethenum
vetus Pictorum oppidum," and states that their leader, having
failed in taking the citadel, " infesto agmine in oppidum et
sanctissimum templum ruit; quæ cœde, ruinis ac incendijs ita
diruit, ut oppidum exinde pristinum decus nunquam recuperarit.
Veteris vero fani præter turrim quandam rotundam mira arte

constructam nullum ad nostra secula remanserit vestigium."—
Scotorum Historiæ, lib. ix. All this, we think, warrants our
assertion as to the importance of Brechin in the twelfth century,
if not earlier, and we are decidedly of opinion that Brechin was
one of the royal burghs recognised as created by David I. in or
about 1150, as has been generally reported.

The Keldeis or Culdees referred to in the charter by King
William were Christian pastors brought into Britain in the
sixth century by St Columba. Of their origin, of their name,
their doctrine, or their church government, we know extremely
little on any authority. Dr Reeves in his essay on the Culdees, exhaustive and learned, but possibly prejudiced, published in the volume of the Transactions of the Royal Irish
Academy for 1864, derives the name from Servus Dei, the
Servant of God, translated by the Irish into their Celtic
compound of Céle Dé and re-Latinised into Caledeus and Kele-
deus. In Gaelic, Gille Dhé means Servant of God, and is just
as likely, we think, an original for the word Culdee, as the twice
Latinised words of Dr Reeves. The learned doctor contends that
the Culdees of Scotland were no particular body, but clergy generally; the name " sometimes," he says, (page 120,) "borne by her-
mits, sometimes by conventuals ; in one situation implying the
condition of celibacy, in another understood of married men ;
here denoting regulars, there seculars ; some of the name bound
by obligations of poverty, others free to accumulate property ; at
one period high in honour as implying self-denial, at another
regarded with contempt as the designation of the loose and
worldly-minded." Be all this as it may, it is certain that the
Culdees did not use images in their worship, and that their
practices did not accord with those of the Church of Rome.
The Culdees are stated to have had a convent in Brechin, and
to have got a grant of the town of Brechin from King Kenneth
III., A.D. 990. We never saw the grant, nor any satisfactory
evidence that it ever existed ; but we find that " Leod, Abbe de
Breichin," is witness, along with bishops and other great
officials, to a grant made by King David I. to his new Abbey of
Dunfermline, and it is thus inferred that the Culdees had an
establishment in Brechin at or prior to 1150. This convent is

believed to have stood a little to the west of the present parish church, in the gardens now belonging to the kirk-session, still called the "College Yards." A small well of delightfully pure water in these gardens receives the name of the College Well, and is reported by tradition to have been the well of the Culdee convent. The last mention of the Culdees in Brechin is in a deed granted about 1218 ; but Mr David Miller in his "Arbroath and its Abbey" tells us, (page 32,) that in 1219, "John Abbe, the son of Malise," (whom he infers to be a direct descendant of Abbot Leod,) "made a grant to Arbroath of firewood from his woods of Edzell, for the salvation of himself, his ancestors, and heirs,"—rather an ominous gift. We may mention that the Latin word translated "salvation" by Mr Miller is by some held rather to mean "safety." Leod, the Abbot just alluded to, appears to have left his property and his office (and probably the sur-name of Abbot) to his descendants; for Donald, grandson of Leod, gifted certain lands to the monks of Arbroath for the good of the souls of his father Samson, and of himself and his heirs, while the prior of the Culdees is a witness to the grant.—Miller, page 32. Mr Cosmo Innes, in his "Sketches of Early Scottish History," says, page 156,—"Towards the end of the reign of William the Lion, we find an infusion of other clerks in the chapter, (of Brechin,) the prior of the convent of Culdees, however, being still the president. In 1248, the last year of the reign of Alexander II., the Culdees have disappeared altogether, and the affairs of the cathedral are managed in the ordinary modern form by the dean and chapter." Dr Reeves states that the Culdees disap-peared from history in 1332. The Church of Rome was too strong for the Culdees. David I., under the influence of Robert, the English Bishop of St Andrews, gave to the canons of St Andrews the Culdee island of Lochleven, that they might establish canonical order there ; and declared that the Keledei who chose to live as regulars might remain, but that should any of them resist, his will and pleasure was that they should be expelled from the island—an injunction which the bishop was not slow in carrying out ; for he immediately placed the Keledei in subjection to the canons regular, and took possession of their vestments and library, of which a list is given in the Register of the Priory of St Andrews, page 51. The persecution thus begun at Lochleven seems to have been systematically continued throughout Scotland, till the Culdees disappear altogether. In Brechin, by 1248, as stated by Mr Innes, we find the affairs of the diocese managed in the usual Episcopal form by dean and chapter, and the Keldeis altogether gone out of view.

It has been generally reported that the Episcopal see of Brechin was endowed by David I. in 1150, but Dr Reeves is of opinion that he merely added a bishop to the existing society of Culdees, and that previously the country was wholly monastic, and dioceses and parishes unknown. Mr Cosmo Innes is of the same opinion; and in his "Sketches of Early Scotch History" says, page 86,—"It was the fate of the ancient Columbite foundations in Scotland to disappear under the reforming vehemence of David I., the most zealous of Romanists, who raised on the ruins of many a primeval monastery his grand establishments of Augustinian canons or benedictines, or converted their convents into the chapters of his new Episcopal dioceses." It is certain, however, that Samson, or rather Sansane, was bishop of the city of Brechin during the reign of Malcolm IV., (1153–1165,) for the name occurs frequently in charters granted by that monarch. Pope Honorius III. in a bull dated in 1218, arranges the Episcopal sees of the Scottish Church in this order, —"St Andrews, Dumblane, Glasgow, Dunkeld, *Brechin*, Aberdeen, Murray, Ross, and Caithness." (See Chalmers's "Registrum Episcopatus Brechinensis," vol. ii. page 387.) We give a list of all the bishops of Brechin in our Appendix, No. II.

Of the Druids, who preceded the Culdees as the ministers of religion in Scotland, and who are said to have had an establishment in Brechin, little is known that can be relied on, and that little merely from the incidental mention of these priests by the Roman generals in their Commentaries on the Roman Wars in Britain. The Druids were of various ranks and orders, and over the whole there was one supreme head or arch-Druid. They were not only the priests but the judges and physicians of the people. They had two sets of religious doctrines; one known to the commonalty, the other only to the initiated; and it is supposed that they taught the immortality of the soul. The word

Druidh in Gaelic means wise man or magician, and this character they appear to have kept up by all means in their power. Considerable doubts now exist, whether the religion of the Druids was of the bloody character once imputed to it, and whether the circles called Druid circles—the immense one at Stonehenge in England, the large one called the Standing Stones of Stennis in Orkney, and the smaller ones found in almost every district of Scotland—were really temples, or in any way connected with Druidical worship. Till within the last fifty years, there was a circle of the description alluded to in the Muir of Leighton-hill, the vestiges of which are still to be discerned from the surrounding heath, by the smooth grass and wild flowers growing on the gently rising slope, which overlooks a great extent of ground around, and commands a splendid view of the Grampians and adjoining country. At Colmeallie, in Edzell, there is such a circle, and at Gilfumman of Glenesk there was a rocking stone, all imputed to the Druids. But whether these stones and circles were connected with the worship of the Druids, or whether the larger enclosures were not rather courts for the administration of justice, and places of assemblage of the people when framing new or altering old laws, like the Tings amongst the Norsemen, it is certain the Druids had places of worship in groves, chiefly planted of oaks, and that they paid great veneration to the mistletoe, a parasitical plant that fixes itself on many trees, but was only respected by the Druids when found growing on the oak.

The Culdee teachers brought to Scotland by Columba succeeded, in process of time, in expelling the Druids, the priests of the ancient Scots ; and if we allow ourselves to believe that the Culdees did to the Druids, their predecessors, as was done to the Culdees by their successors, the priests of the Church of Rome, and subsequently to these priests by the teachers of the reformed doctrine, then, without much stretch of imagination, we can conceive that the site of the present Presbyterian church of Brechin was the place of worship successively of Druids, Culdees, Romanists, Episcopalians, and Presbyterians. Nor is there anything in the situation of the church of Brechin opposed to the idea that it was originally a Druidical temple. The church

stands on a sandstone rock, the sides of which are precipitous
on the south and east; and while the western side slopes more
gently, the northern side appears to have been a deep ravine;
for every excavation made on that side proves that the earth, to
a very great depth, is forced or artificial. Such an isolated rock
presented a fit site for the worship of the Druids; and the dells
around may then have been clad, as some of them still are clothed,
with umbrageous trees, the castle and town of Brechin being, in
the days of the Druids, both alike unknown. Whether such a
succession of religious orders did or did not occur on the little
mount which for ages has been the burying-place of the inhabitants of Brechin, it is impossible positively to say; but there is
nothing in the supposition inconsistent with what has occurred
amongst other nations which have undergone changes in their
religious dynasties—the newly established order having generally selected the places of worship of the expelled party for the
site of the new churches or altars.

The derivation of the name of the town, like the origin of the
burgh, is the subject of much doubt. In the oldest document
which we have seen, the name is spelled exactly as it is now
written—Brechin; and the various orthographies of Brychine,
Brechyne, Breychin, Brechyne, Brychin, Brichein, Brichine,
Brechyn, Brechene, Brechine, and Brichen, which may occasionally be found, do not throw any additional light on the origin of
the name.

From the connexion which existed between the Culdees and
the town of Brechin, and the probability that this body succeeded a Druidical establishment at Brechin, an opinion has
been hazarded that the name of the place is to be looked for
from some such source; and as it appears that in the days of St
Columba there was a noted Druid of the name of Broichan or
Bœrchan, it has been suggested that probably the Culdees, when
they expelled the Druids, bestowed on the place the name of the
chief person previously connected with it. The Druids have
furnished another theory equally plausible for the name of our
burgh, and it is this:—The island of Anglesey is well known to
have been the principal station of the Druids in the southern
part of Great Britain, but from this island the Druids were ex-

pelled by the Romans in the year 61, while Nero was emperor.
The Druids, who were thus driven from their principal station,
fled into Caledonia, Ireland, and the lesser British isles, carrying with them, of course, the rites and ceremonies of their
religion, as well as the laws and customs of their community
which they had formerly used. In Anglesey there are yet the
remains of a rude throne or tribunal, composed of earth and
stones, which belonged to the arch-Druid, and which is called
Bryngwyn or Breingwyn, that is, the Supreme or Royal Tribunal.
The analogy of this word Brein-gwyn to Bre-chin, leads the supporters of this theory to assert that either the arch-Druid expelled from Anglesey had taken refuge here, and hence given
the name of a royal tribunal to this place, or that Brechin was
always the supreme tribunal of the Druids in North Britain—
Anglesey being their capital in South Britain, and Dreux the
capital of the sect in Gaul. Pretty nearly allied to this is still
another theory, that Brechin was the principal seat of justice to
the Druids, and thence called Brehon, or the Judger, a word
identical with the name of those judges and laws so often mentioned in the histories of Ireland. Certainly the numerous
Druidical remains still to be found in the vicinity of Brechin—
the circle at Easter Pitforthie—the temple at Barrelwell or Pitpullox, of which only one stone now stands—the erection at Vane
of Fearn—the *Law* or Mound on the farm of Hilton of Fearn,
and several other similar structures—go to prove that the Druids
were a powerful body in this quarter—independent of the conclusions arrived at by Mr Huddleston in his edition of Toland's
History of the Druids, that the three farms close upon Brechin
called Pittendriech, are identical with Pit-an-druach, the burial-
place of the Druids.

The apparent similarity of the words Brechin and Brein-gwyn,
royal tribunal, has given rise to another speculation regarding
the name of the town, founded upon a tradition—for it scarce
deserves a better name, if it is even entitled to that appellation—
that Brechin was the capital of Pictavia and the seat of the
Pictish kings, the round tower, so conspicuous an appendage of
the church, having (as this tradition bears) been built for *a look-
out* by this nation, while the hill of Caterthun, about four miles

to the north of the town, surrounded with an immense coronal of loose stones, is reported to have been a fortification belonging to that ancient nation; and hence called Caither-Dun, the City Hill or Fort. The same tradition states that the parish of Menmuir, in which this hill is situated, derived the name of Mainmuir, the Stone Wall or Fort, from the erection on Caterthun, and that Stracathro, the parish immediately adjoining to Brechin on the east, was called from its locality Strath-Cath-rach, the City-Strath. In the oldest charters the name of this parish is spelt Strathcatherach, which some hold to imply Strath-Cath-Re, that is, the Field or Valley of Slaughter of the Kings. Our Gaelic friends, however, with whom we have advised, will not recognise any of the translations we have given, except that of Strath, a valley, generally taking its name from a river that runs through it; and we therefore dismiss this Pictavian theory as altogether fanciful.

Other antiquarians pretend, and certainly with as much apparent authority, to deduce the word Brechin from a Gaelic term signifying a sloping bank, and descriptive of the site of the town, which is placed on the face of a brae, and they give us Brica as the Gaelic word which is thus so descriptive; but for our own part we must admit we have never been able to find any Gaelic scholar who knew the word Brica as a Gaelic term.

In the "Historical and Descriptive Notes of the City of Cork," published by J. Windele, Esq., in 1840, we find mention of a property called Ballybricken belonging to D. Connor, Esq., and on page 329 we have this paragraph, "Brickeen Island, *i.e.,* Bric-in, the place of small trout, lies between Dinis and Mucross." Our piscatory friends, we have no doubt, will adopt the Irish gentleman's Bricin, and contend that Dinis is just Dun, and Mucross, Monros or Montrose, and that Brechin derives its name from the par in the South Esk.

Amidst these contending authorities, we think ourselves warranted, if not indeed bound, to offer a theory of our own. Brechin lies on the banks of the Esk, where that river is confined between the high grounds of Burghill on the south and the high grounds of Brechin on the north and west. To the east the land on each side of the river presents a gradual slope or fall with some excellent carse ground close on the banks of the river. Looking from Brechin down the Esk towards Montrose, the observer has before him a beautiful little strath or valley, of which the high grounds of Brechin are the head or western end. Brecon in Wales is, we have been informed, similarly situated at the head of the vale of the Usk after it is joined by the river Hondey. Most readers are aware that Usk, Uisk, Uisge, and Esk signify the same thing in Gaelic, namely, water. Every person, we think, must be struck by the fact of two towns so remote from each other, and yet approximating so near in name, being so similarly situated as are Brecon in Wales, at the head and on the sloping banks of a valley through which runs the river Usk, and Brechin in Scotland, at the head of a strath through which runs the river Esk, and on the side of a brae sloping towards it. Now we find that in Gaelic Bruach Abhainne means the bank or brink of a river, and hence we are inclined to infer comes the words Bruchaine, Brechin, and Brecon. We state this not on our own authority, but on that of an old friend and shopmate—a true-born Gael, and a person of education, having been intended for *The Church.* In the parish of Livingston and county of Linlithgow there is a small river called the Breich, with sloping banks, which would go still further to confirm this theory of the origin of the name of Brechin. Mr Andrew Jervise, in his able work the "Memorials of Angus and Mearns," published in 1861, says, in a note on page 129,—"The Gaelic Braigh-chein signifies a Hilly Brae, and is quite descriptive of the situation of the town of Brechin."

Some of our readers may be inclined to cry with the love-sick Juliet, "What's in a name?" but if these will take the trouble to read the ingenious "Inquiry into the Origin of the word Brechin," furnished us years ago by a learned friend, and which is subjoined in the Appendix, they will find that there is much in a name; and if they are not instructed, we think they will be amused by the speculation to which the name Brechin has given rise.

The town of Brechin was burned by the Danes in 1012, during the reign of Malcolm II. Of course no traces of this conflagration now exist, and little is known of the mischief then done except the simple fact that the town was burned by the Danes.

But a natural inference arises that the place was then of some consequence, otherwise the Danes would not have wasted their time and attention upon it. In this view, it may not be uninteresting to remark on the circumstances which led to this early conflagration of the burgh. Sueno, son of Harold king of Denmark, being banished from home, came to Scotland, where, having become, or pretended to become, a convert to Christianity, he received a few forces, with which he returned and regained his kingdom. Reinstated in power, Sueno immediately invaded England ; and because his old friends and allies the Scots opposed this invasion, he sent Olave and Enick, two of his generals, with a powerful army into Scotland. After various battles, in which sometimes the Scots, sometimes the Danes, were victorious, Enick was slain, and Olave with the remainder of his troops was driven into Morayshire. Upon the news being carried to Sueno in England, he despatched a reinforcement under the command of Camus, who landed his troops at the Redhead, and pitched his camp at Panbride or St Bride. There he was attacked and defeated by the Scots. The Danes then attempted to retreat in three divisions to join their friends under Olave in Moray. One division under Camus was cut off, and he and all his followers were destroyed near the village of Carnoustie, where an obelisk still serves to preserve the memory of this victory, called Camiston Cross ; and where the traces of a camp may yet be seen on the side of a burn, by some called a Roman camp, by others a Danish camp, but popularly styled " Norway Dikes." Another division of the defeated army retreated by Brechin, and in their progress northward burned that town, but they too were attacked and cut off, and the " standing stones," as they are called, in the parish of Aberlemno, are supposed to record this event, and to mark the grave of the general who led this second division. The third division, again, which had retreated to their ships, landed on the coast of Buchan, where they also were destroyed by Mornan, Thane of the county. Sueno, not disheartened by his repeated calamities, sent his son Canute with a new army into Scotland, who, after fighting a severe battle in Buchan, concluded a treaty with Malcolm, the conditions of which were that the Danes should leave Scotland, and that neither of the nations should make war on the other, or give assistance to the enemies of the other, during the lives of Malcolm or Sueno. One most important result seems to have attended this contest. Upon its conclusion, Malcolm divided all the royal lands amongst his nobles, and established various new titles of nobility,— "magis ad vanam ambitionem quam ad ullum usum," Buchanan observes.

This digression may be pardoned, because slight as the connexion of Brechin is with this Danish invasion, it is an important era in early history. Perhaps it is only continuing the digression to add, that Malcolm, as alleged, was afterwards murdered in the castle of Glammis, in consequence of his avarice and unjust exactions from the nobles he had created, and that the murderers flying, during a snow-storm under night, became bewildered and were lost in the loch of Forfar, the ice on which broke beneath the weight of their horses. In the castle of Glammis, the room where Malcolm was murdered is still shown, and the attention of the visitor is regularly called to the stains of blood on the floor, although, if we mistake not, when Malcolm died, the tree was not planted out of which the boards thus stained are made, nor was the castle built for three hundred years afterwards.

Tradition also points out Brechin and its vicinity as the site of the contest between the Romans under Agricola, and the Caledonians under Galgacus. The South Esk, which passes Brechin, is said to have been the Æsica of the Romans, upon which they had a station, mentioned in the Itinerary of Richard of Cirencester as being in the province of Vespasiana, twenty-three miles distant from the Tay. In the parish of Oathlaw there are the remains of a Roman camp at Battledikes, on the side of the river Esk, supposed to have been the principal station alluded to by Richard of Cirencester; and at Keithock, near Brechin, there were, some fifty years ago, the remains of another camp supposed to have been connected with the former. In the woods of Slateford are still to be seen marks of what are supposed to have been a Roman camp; and on the farm of Eastertown of Dunlappy, immediately adjoining Slateford, a Roman sword was dug out of a moss in 1838; while near the railway station there were found

in 1853 two bronze swords and scabbards, now in the Antiquarian
Museum of Edinburgh, and marked E 137, 138 in the catalogue
of the museum, which are exactly identical with those described
by Dr Daniel Wilson, in page 228 of his " Prehistoric Annals of
Scotland." Indeed some of our friends are clearly of opinion that
the battle between Agricola and Galgacus must have been
fought on the sloping ground immediately south of the two hills
of Caterthun. We are told by a popular rhyme that

> " Between the Killivair and the Buckler Stane
> There lies mony a bluidy bane;"

or, as another edition of the same rhyme has it,

> " 'Tween the Blawart Lap, and the Killivair Stanes,
> There lie mony bluidy banes;"

and as the " Killivair Stane " is on the farm of Barrelwell, and
the " Blawart Lap " on the farm of Langhaugh, something more
than half a mile north, and both are opposite the western hill of
Caterthun, our antiquarian friends presume that the principal
struggle had taken place at these points, where the Romans,
being defeated, had been driven eastward on their camps at
Keithock and Slateford, from which they retreated to the
Mearns. The " Killivair Stane " is a plain upright stone, without any trace of the hands of a mason having touched it, exactly
similar to those used in Druidical structures; and most probably the stone is the remains of a Druidical temple, at which
place, it may naturally enough be concluded, the onset of the Scots
had begun. The " Buckler Stane" is said to have been a large
broad stone lying in the muir on the farm of Langhaugh, near the
Blawart Lap, about half a mile east by north of the Killivair
stone, but removed by the farmer of Langhaugh when the
ground was improved some forty years ago. Other antiquarians would have all these traditions and monuments to apply to
the Danish expeditions just noticed. On a subject like this,
which Monkbarns has left undetermined, and which has divided
antiquarians for ages, it would be presumptuous for us to hazard
an opinion.

Our friends possibly may think we have bestowed too much
time on these ancient matters; but we cannot imagine we have

done so when we find our researches so far behind those of David Mitchell, Esq., A.M., who, in his History of Montrose, published in 1866, states (page 95) that, " In the year 156 B.C. the mariners of Montrose were a daring set of savages, who in their prows put to sea, and robbed the Fife shore. They lived on shore in rather a primitive state,—just dug a hole and shoved in. Only think of a family or tribe lying on the ground to rest all night ! Brechin at this period was the hunting ground of the ancient Celtic marauders"!! The learned author does not quote his authority, and we own we have been unable to discover it.

CHAPTER II.

HITHERTO we have been dealing chiefly with romance and conjecture, and little that we have said is absolutely certain, except
that Brechin was the seat of a bishop in the reign of David I.
previous to 1153. Perhaps the world might have moved on in
its usual course although this *important* fact had not been so
distinctly established as it certainly is. Connected thus early
and thus closely with the Church, Brechin seems to have derived
its chief importance and support, for long after, from the same
source. We have made up a list of the bishops of Brechin, and
have collated the list with various histories and other documents ;
but as it is a record chiefly of dates and names, we think it
better to throw it into a section by itself, than to interrupt the
flow of events by discussions here on the subject of the succession of these dignitaries, and accordingly it will be found in our
Appendix, No. II.

Amongst the earliest grants to the Church of Brechin extant,
is a charter, without date, but believed to have been given about
the year 1222, granted by Randolph " de Strathphetham," supposed to be equivalent with Strachan, of the lands of Brectulach,
understood to be Brachtullo in the parish of Kirkden, "pro
anima mea et animabus omnium antecessorum meorum." The
chapel of " Messyndew," still so pronounced, but now written
Maisondieu, was founded by " Willelmus de Brechine, filius Domini Henrici de Brechine filij Comitis David," that is, by William
of Brechin, the son of Lord Henry of Brechin, who was the son
of Earl David ; hence the chapel was founded by Sir William of
Brechin, grandson of David Earl of Huntingdon and Garioch,

Lord of Brechin and Inverbervie, and brother of King William the Lion. The charter, which is witnessed by Albin, who was Bishop of Brechin from 1247 to 1269, is understood to have been granted about 1256. By it William de Brechin gave the mills of Brechin and other lands to God and the Chapel of the Virgin Mary, by him founded, and to the master and chapter and poor of the same, and that, as the charter bears, for prayers for the safety or good estate of William and Alexander, kings of Scotland; " Dominis Johannis Comitis Cestrie ; " of Lord Henry his father, and Lady Juliana his mother; and of his own soul; and of the souls of all his predecessors and successors and of all the dead in the faith; a sufficiently long but not uncommon catalogue in those days of parties to be remembered in prayer. In 1267, William again gives a right of a road to his favourite chapel, and the charter says the grant is made to God and the blessed Virgin, " et Domui Dei de Brechine." A precept of sasine of Easter Dalgety in the charter-room of Kinnaird, granted in 1549, is thus styled on the back,—" Factum per Dominum Wuillielmum Carnegie de Messindew, Roberto de Kennaird," while in the body of the deed Mr Carnegy is styled " Preceptor Domus Dei sive Hospitalis dive Virginis Marie infra Civitatem Brechinensem ; " thus showing the identity of the hospital of the Virgin Mary and the preceptory of Maisondieu. William de Brechin was one of the regency favourable to England appointed during the minority of Alexander III., as mentioned in Rymer, Fœdera, i. 563. Robert I. seems to have been a great friend to the church of Brechin. In 1308 he prohibits the people of Forfar from interfering with the bishop and canons of Brechin ; and two years after, by a charter dated at Brechin 4th December, in the fourth year of his reign, he relieves the church of Brechin of all secular services. The same King Robert, by a charter dated at Scone, 10th July 1322, in the sixteenth year of his reign, gave to John, Bishop of Brechin, and to the chaplain and canons of the cathedral church of the Holy Trinity of Brechin, the privilege of having a market within the city on Sundays, the same as had been formerly conferred upon them by the former kings of Scotland, and as had been possessed by them in the time of Alexander " of good memory," his pre-

B

decessor; and to that effect Robert commanded all justiciaries, sheriffs, provosts, and their bailies to defend the bishop therein. This John was of the family of Kinnymond of Fife, and appears to have been a decided friend of King Robert Bruce; for in 1309, he is one of the bishops who solemnly under their seals recognise Robert's title to the throne of Scotland. The revenues of the see at this time were £416, equal to £2000 at least of the present day. Bishop William, who was in the see previous to John, was a man of a different stamp, for he was one of the few Scots clergy who, in 1290, addressed Edward I. of England, entreating that monarch to marry his son to Margaret, "the Maiden of Norway," heiress of the crown of Scotland. It is comfortable to reflect, however, that if at this period there was a servile bishop, William, of whom little more is known than the circumstance just noted, there was also one generous spirit connected with the burgh, the noble and independent Sir Thomas Maule, governor of Brechin Castle, whose name is immortalised by the check he gave to the troops of Edward, and by his gallant defence of the castle for three weeks in 1303. Against this castle Edward brought a then famous engine of attack called the War Wolf, which discharged stones of two or three hundredweight. Sir Thomas Maule is reported to have stood on the walls of Brechin Castle wiping away with his handkerchief, in derision of the besiegers, the rubbish caused by the War Wolf, till the engine swept him away. Tradition has it that Sir Thomas was slain on the bastion still existing at the south-east corner of the castle wall, and that the stone which killed him was thrown from the high ground to the east of the ravine running between the castle and the town of Brechin. Some years ago, when the earth was *tirred* from the garden on the top of the bank alluded to, a skull was found buried, having a nail in it, supposed to have been one of Edward's soldiers, killed by some instrument fired from Brechin Castle—for gunpowder was partially in use by this time. Perhaps it is to Edward's invasion of Scotland that we are to attribute the want of documents connected with the earlier history of Brechin, and the necessity for King Robert renewing the right of market; for Buchanan tells us, so inveterate was Edward's hatred to Scotland, that when he returned to England after this invasion, "historias, fœdera, monumentaque vetusta, sive a Romanis relicta, sive a Scotis erecta, destruenda curavit; libros omnes, literarumque doctores, in Angliam transtulit." Edward is said to have come to Brechin on the 6th, and to have obtained from Baliol the surrender of the Scottish crown and kingdom at Brechin on the 10th July 1296, in a very humiliating manner, in the castle of Brechin, where the Great Seal of Scotland was broken to pieces. Sir David de Brechin, nephew of King Robert the Bruce, an accomplished knight, and who had signalised himself in the Holy War, suffered the punishment of treason in 1320, in consequence of having joined William de Soulis and others in a treasonable conspiracy against King Robert. Sir David appears to have long tampered with King Edward I. of England, and to have been opposed through life to Bruce's pretensions, although often receiving pardon and favour from the king his uncle. Yet on 10th March 1354, King David, son of Robert Bruce, grants to " Alexander de Berkeley et Catarine sorori mee spouse sue," the lands of Wester Mathers, by a charter quoted in the Miscellany of the Spalding Club, vol. v. p. 248; thus showing the reconciliation of the families of Bruce and Berkeley.

The induction of Bishop Adam into the see of Brechin in 1328 displays the grasping spirit of the Church of Rome. There is a bull by Pope John, dated 31st Oct. of that year, printed by Mr Chalmers in his Register, vol. ii. p. 389, apparently confirming Bishop Adam in the see, but in reality claiming the right to nominate the bishop, and the same Pope by subsequent documents claims the same right in regard to the canons. Pope Clement VI., following up the tactics of Pope John, by a bull dated 20th Feb. 1350, states that he had reserved for his own disposal the provision to the church of Brechin on the decease of Bishop Adam, but that in ignorance of this reservation the chapter had unanimously elected Philip, dean of the church, to be bishop; and that Philip, in like ignorance, had consented to the election, but on being informed of the reservation had come to Rome and explained the matter, and therefore the Pope had of *new* appointed him to the office. Previously, in 1320, Robert Bruce, in a Parliament held at Arbroath, had asserted

the freedom of Scotland in opposition to the claims of Popedom.
Theiner, in his "Vetera Monumenta Hibernorum et Scotorum,"
gives, p. 306, a bull by Pope Innocent VI., in 1354, dispensing
with the objection to the marriage of John Mongombry and
Elen More because they were cousins; and p. 312, another bull
by the same Pope dispensing with a similar objection to the
marriage of David de Berclay and Elizabeth Countess of Fife,
both bulls being addressed to the Bishop of Brechin.

The privilege of market renewed by Robert I. was confirmed
by David II., who, on 26th October 1359, was pleased to grant
a charter stating that "for the fear and reverence of God, by
whom kings reign and princes govern," and in respect of the
troubles and dissensions throughout the kingdom, by which the
monuments of the church had been lost, therefore he confirmed
to the cathedral church of Brechin the whole privileges formerly
granted by his ancestors, and especially by his father, to the
cathedral church of the Holy Trinity of Brechin. The bishop
of this period was Patrick de Leuchars in Fife, a favourite at
court, and one of those who took an active part in the redemption of David from the English. Still the right of market, thus
guaranteed by repeated royal grants, seems to have been dis-
puted from some quarter or other—by Montrose, we believe,
for we find "Ane Inchibitioun for halding off mercats of
Stapillhand at Brechine and Fordoune" to the prejudice
of Montrose, issued by King David II. in 1352. However,
there is a "cognition" taken regarding the Brechin market in
1364 by Walter de Biggar, chamberlain of Scotland, John de
Rossy, John Lamby, David de Foulertoun, John de Allardice,
and other gentlemen; and thereafter we find David, in 1369,
giving a new charter to Bishop Patrick, stating that the whole
merchants inhabiting the city of Brechin had free ingress and
egress to the waters of Southesk and Tay for carrying of their
merchandise in boats and ships, upon paying duties accustomed,
and that notwithstanding of any grants to the burgesses of Dundee and Montrose, who are strictly prohibited from troubling the
merchants of Brechin. This grant was confirmed by Robert II.
in 1372; and the same prince, in 1374, addressed a precept
to his justiciaries, sheriffs, and provosts, charging them to de-

fend the Bishop of Brechin and the canons of the cathedral church of Brechin in all their lands and privileges. James II., by a charter dated in September 1451, again renews at great length the rights of trade granted to Brechin; but Dundee, alarmed at the growing importance of Brechin, enters a protest against this and the previous charters, "purchased of false suggestion by information of partial persons," as a document quoted by Mr Chalmers proves.

The earls of Crawford were great benefactors to the church of Brechin in the fifteenth century; and some grants or charters are still preserved having the arms of that family attached, impressed in a bold and handsome style. The members of the family of Dun appear also to have been zealous supporters of the cathedral. The church having acquired right to the lands of Eaglesjohn for payment of certain quit rents to Sir John Erskine of Dun, that knight, in 1409, mortified these rents to the bishop, from reverence to the Holy Trinity, and from the more secular feeling of affection to Walter, then bishop of Brechin. The lands thus conveyed to the church in 1409 are at present called Langleypark and Broomley, the latter now again belonging to the laird of Dun. The Duke of Albany, while governor of Scotland in 1410, granted a precept to Alexander Ogilvy of Ouchterhouse, Sheriff of Forfar, for examining into the marches of certain lands belonging to the bishop; and thereupon the sheriff gives a decree in favour of the bishop addressed "tyll all yat yir letters heirs and seis," "gretyng in God aye lestand," and stating that "Walter, throu Goddis sufferance Bischope of Brechin, fand ane borch in our hand as schref," which the lairds of Kinnaird "recontret." There is still extant amongst the papers of the burgh a curious precept by James I., in 1427, by which, for the growth of grace, and various other ostensible reasons, he grants different sums to the cathedral, payable out of his annual rents of the city of Brechin; and amongst the individuals from whose lands these sums are payable, we find the names of William White, Richard Lindesay, possessor of the "Forkit Akir," David Garden, John Durward, Laurence Smith, John Guthrie, proprietor of certain lands between the two vennels; John Tindall, James Myres, James

Potter, John Saddler, and John Walker, names still common in Brechin. But the chief friend to the church of Brechin at this early period, was Sir Walter Stewart, Knight, Palatine of Strathearn, Earl of Athole and Caithness, and Lord of Brechin and Cortachy, which latter title and property he assumed, together with the lands of Brechin and Navar, &c., on marrying the heiress, Margaret, only child of Barclay, Lord of Brechin. On 22d October 1429, by charter dated " apud Castrum nostrum de Brechyn," he gifted £40 Scots, payable annually, to the church from his lands of Cortachy, and failing thereof through war, poverty, or other cause, from his lands and lordship of Brechin, for the maintenance of two chaplains and six boys to perform divine service within the choir of the church. He also in the same month bestowed the patronage of the church of Cortachy on the cathedral ; and, further, he gave a piece of land lying on the west side of the city of Brechin, adjoining to the Vennel, for the residence of the boys and chaplains. In these grants, and in a relative obligation by the bishop, there are long directions about the clothing of the boys, and in regard to their education and demeanour. In particular, the lads are prohibited from going to the fields without one of the chaplains, and they are ordered, on these occasions, to be clothed in open coats, purple or white, and to *have their hair neatly dressed.* In regard to the chaplains, again, it is provided that one of them shall be instructed in music and the other in grammar, which branches of education they are to study in the hours when they are free from spiritual duties. It is curious to find the bishop, so early as 1435, backing out of his part of the obligation, and upon various pretences reducing the two chaplains to one, and of course reducing the duties to be performed ; and the duties thus reduced seem to have been but indifferently attended to, for, in 1524, there is a decree of the bishop of that period deciding various differences which had arisen between the chaplains and the chapter of the cathedral for non-performance of duties. It is no less curious to remark, that Walter, Earl of Athole, who made these liberal grants to the cathedral of Brechin, was the son of Robert II. by Euphemia, daughter of Hugh, Earl of Ross, and was suspected, from a desire to ascend the throne, of having been the means of procuring the deaths of most of his own relations. Ultimately, he was himself put to death by lingering tortures protracted for three days, in consequence of being the principal instigator of the murder of his nephew, the courtly James I.

The bishop who was so particular about the exterior and interior of the heads of the chaplains and of the boys, was a John Carnoth, a gentleman and a courtier, for he was selected to accompany Margaret, daughter of James I., to France, when she was espoused to the Dauphin, afterwards Louis XI. In the chronicle of the reign of James II. kept at Auchinleck, there is an entry bearing that John *Crenok*, Bishop of Brechin, died there in August 1456, "that was callit a gude, actif, and vertuis man, and all his tyme wele gouvernande." Apparently this bishop had gone more than once to France, for amongst the records of Brechin there is an instrument bearing that Bishop John, in a synod held on 14th April 1434, narrated that in his *last* voyage from France, probably a stormy one, he had vowed to give to the church of Brechin two silver candlesticks, in acquittance of which vow he then delivered to John Liall the treasurer of the church six silver cups, gilt on the edges, and also a silver gilt cup with cover, the cover having the rays of the sun engraved upon it, this last cup to be for the exclusive use of the dean and canons at their common festivals. Judging from the documents left, we would say that there was more business done during the reign of this bishop than during that of any other bishop. He it was who, in July 1450, obtained an inquisi-tion by which it was ascertained that the inhabitants of Brechin had a right of market on Sundays, and liberty of trading between the waters of Southesk and Tay. Amongst a variety of other grants obtained by this bishop to the church, we may notice that by Alexander Cramond, laird of South Melgund and Aldbar, of an annual rent of £26, 8s. Scots, payable from a tenement called Lammyslande ; a similar grant by John Sievwright, citizen of Brechin, and a conveyance to the cathedral by Robert Hill of a tenement lying near to that of John Tod, and an acre of arable land in the Crofts adjoining the land of Patrick Guthrie and John Masson. We may also refer to a charter by Mr Thomas

Bell, vicar of the parish church of Montrose, of some property
in Murray Street of Montrose, witnessed on 20th June 1431
by Patrick Barclay, then provost of Montrose, and John Niddry,
bailie, names still to be found amongst the municipal rulers of
that burgh.

Besides acquiring property for the church, bishop Carnoth
seems to have acquired property for himself. Thus on 13th
February 1444, David Conan conveys to the bishop the Templehill of Keithock, to be held of the master of the hospital of St
John of Jerusalem, for payment of a yearly feu at two terms,
Pentecost and St John in summer; and this property is ratified
to the bishop in 1450 by brother Henry de Livingston, a knight
of the order of St John of Jerusalem, commendator of the preceptory of the same, and " Magister de Torfechyn." If we mistake not, these lands are now known as the Templehill of Bothers,
and form part of the estate of Cairnbank.

A dispute appears to have arisen during this bishop's reign
which may afford evidence for fixing the period when either the
steeple or the round tower of Brechin was erected. Mr David
Ogilvy, rector of the parish church of Lethnot, having failed to
pay a sum of 28 merks, said to have been due from the income
of the church of Lethnot to the bishop and chapter of Brechin,
was repeatedly cited to appear before the consistorial court. He
treated the summonses very lightly, and neglected to appear;
but a court was held by Robert Wyschart, rector of Cuykstoun,
in the diocese of St Andrews, as substitute of the bishop, at
Brechin, on the 9th of February 1435, when, after the examination of a variety of witnesses named, it is recorded as having
been proved that Lethnot was liable in 28 merks annually to
the church of Brechin; and that in part payment of this debt,
Henry de Lechton, vicar of Lethnot, had delivered to Patrick,
Bishop of Brechin, (1354-84,) a large white horse, and had also
given a cart *to lead stones for the building of the belfry of the
church of Brechin* in the time of Bishop Patrick, and which cart
was made by Elisha Wright, then residing at Finhaven. These
are the words of the decree:—" Quarto, Ponit et probare intendit
quod quondam nobilis vir Henricus de Lechton arrendator dicte
ecclesie pater Johannis de Lychton soluit et cum effectu realiter

deliberauit reuerendo patri domino Patricio episcopo Brechinensi et capitulo eiusdem unum magnum equum album in partem solutionis dicte pensionis. Quinto, Quod idem Henricus de Lechton ad ducendum lapides ad edificationem campanilis ecclesie Brechinensis tempore quondam domini Patricii episcopi Brechinensis realiter et cum effectu dedit unum currum quem fecit Elisius Wrycht tunc commorans apud Fynnewyn super le bank de Lymyny in partem solutionis dicte pensionis."—R. E. B., vol. i. page 74.

During Bishop Carnoth's reign, and on 28th May 1445, King James II. gave to John *Smyth*, citizen of Brechin, the hermitage of the Chapel of the Blessed Mary in the forest of Kilgerre, lying in the barony of Menmure, with three acres of arable land which had formerly belonged heritably to Hugh *Cuminche.* This hermitage is understood to have been somewhere on the south face of the hill of Caterthun, and the prayers which the hermit was bound to offer for the king and the other duties of the office likely had not been severe.

Bishop Carnoth himself seems to have been a builder, but to what extent we cannot say, only we find, in 1579, a grant by the then bishop of a piece of ground " tending along by the wall and street onward to the gate of the tower called *Carnock's* Tower," being, as the document leads us to infer, the gate or entry now called the Bishop's Close, on the west side of the High Street.

The reign of this bishop, good and worthy as he is reported, appears to have been rather stormy, for, in 1439, we have an instrument bearing that Mr Thomas Lang, chaplain of the choir, protested against the bishop's bailie for having given possession to William Foote of a tenement on the west side of the High Street, belonging to the chaplains, and asked if, by securing the tenement and *putting out the fires thereof,* he could interrupt the possession ; and upon these threats he takes instruments in presence of Alexander Fotheringham, John Forrest, Walter de Craig, and a variety of others. Again, there is a protest in 1439 by the bishop against certain convocations alleged to have been improperly held in his absence, in one of which it is said the chaplain had been removed from the prebend's stall in the

church of Lethnot, and a boy put into the chaplain's place.
There are also a variety of documents bearing upon a claim
which this bishop had, or pretended to have, upon the lands of
Marytown, occupied by William Fullarton. In this dispute,
Janet Ogilvy, widow of Fullarton, just does as the bishop bids
her ; but her son Patrick takes a different course. While in
August 1448 the bishop is engaged in a dispute with his dean
and archdeacon about taxes that ought to have been recovered
from the canons for repairs of the choir.

Besides being thus actively engaged, Bishop Carnoth procured
transumpts or authentic copies of all the royal grants in favour
of the town and cathedral, and obtained ratifications of them by
James II., on 1st September 1451, a most important document
for the burgh. Indeed, the only thing this active man left
doubtful is his own surname, which is variously spelled Carnock,
Crenok, Carnoth, Crennach, Crannoch, and Crenuch, now commonly said to be equivalent with the surname of Charteris.
But the history of the incumbency of this bishop would be incomplete did we not notice that, during his reign, the boundaries
of the muir of Brechin were first ascertained. By the bishop's
influence, James II. was induced to direct a precept to the
sheriff of Forfarshire for the purpose of ascertaining the marches
between the lands of Menmuir, belonging to John de Collace,
and those belonging to the church. The sheriff accordingly
chose an assize, consisting of Sir John Scrymgeour, constable of
Dundee, Richard Lovell of Ballumby, William Lyell of Balna-
gerro, Patrick Rind and James Rind of Carse, Robert Fuler-
toun, Henry Fethy of Balyesok, John Carnegy of that Ilk,
Walter Carnegy of Guthere, William Guthere of Lownan,
Walter Carnegy of Kynnarde, David Walterstoun of that Ilk,
and Thomas Lamby ; and this inquest report, on 13th October
1450, that the town's property began at the east at Threiphaughford in Cruik, extended towards the west, according to
the ancient course of the water of Cruik, by the lands of " Bal-
zordy," and went as far west as the lands belonging to John de
Colless of Balnamoon went. The inquest also state that they
had caused make a large ditch as a fence between the lands of
Balyeordie and of the burgh, and that right upon the water of

Cruik they had placed a cross with a large stone under it as a march. John Collace, however, does not seem to have tamely submitted to this marching of the lands, for, in May 1451, we have an instrument bearing that John, Bishop of Brechin, and Walter de Ogilvy, Sheriff of Forfar, compeared upon the water of *Cruock* at the Threiphaughford, and protested for remeid of law in consequence of the march stones having been removed from the situations in which they were placed, and thrown into the water. And in 1458 there is a precept by James II. directed to the Sheriff of Forfar charging him to command Thome of Cullaiss to abstain from annoying the community of Brechin in the possession of the lands decreed to them by the perambulation. This document directs the sheriff to "summonde and charge ye foresaid Thomas to compeir before ws and our counsaile at *Dundee* ye secund day of ye next justice aire of Anguss;" so Dundee had been the site of a circuit court previous to the recent Act of Parliament for the holding of courts there. Notwithstanding of all this, however, the family of Collace and the inhabitants of Brechin, as the records of justiciary prove, had battlings till the Collaces sold their lands to Sir Alexander Carnegy, brother of the first earls of Southesk and Northesk, in 1632. This Thomas Collace was a favourite at court, for on 23d March 1499 he got a charter from James IV. confirming to him a right of vert and venison in the forest of Kilgarry.

It was during the Episcopal reign of Bishop Carnoth that the battle of Brechin, as it is called, was fought at Huntlyhill, in the parish of Stracathro, about three miles north-east of the city. The historical reader will recollect that the Earl of Douglas was murdered by James II. in Stirling Castle, in February 1452, because he refused to break a league which he had formed with the earls of Crawford and Ross. In consequence these noblemen joined the Douglases in open rebellion to the royal authority. Alexander Gordon, Earl of Huntly, was advancing with a body of troops consisting of his own vassals, and of the clans Forbes, Ogilvy, Leslie, Grant, and Irving, with the intention of joining the royal standard, when he was encountered, on 18th May 1452, at the Hair Cairn, near Cairnbank, by the Earl of Crawford, surnamed " The Tiger," from his fierce temper, and " Earl Beardie," from his immense hirsute appendage. Crawford was in command of the " bodies of Angus," and of the adherents of the rebels in the neighbouring counties, headed by foreign officers. An engagement ensued, and the centre of the royal army began to give way, when John Coless or Collace of Balnamoon, who bearded the bishop about the marches of the muir, and who hated Crawford in consequence of some dispute regarding property, deserted to the royalists with the left wing, which he commanded, and which was the best equipped part of the troops, being armed with battle-axes, broadswords and spears. The royal army being thus enforced, and the rebel party so weakened, Huntly, contrary to expectations, gained the victory, and gave his name to the hill where the battle was fought. The Earl of Crawford retired to his castle at Finhaven, about six miles west of Brechin, and is reported to have declared, in the frenzy of disgrace, that he would willingly pass seven years in hell to obtain the glory which fell that day to his antagonist, or as tradition has it, " that he wad be content to hang seven years in hell by the breers o' the ee "—the eyelashes. After his defeat Crawford turned his vengeance from the royalists towards those who had deserted him, wasting their lands and burning their castles, and he was left at liberty to do so, as Huntly was obliged, immediately after the battle, to return home to protect his own lands from the ravages of the Earl of Moray. In 1562, we notice that David Fenton of Ogill sold to Robert Collace of Balnamoon, and Elizabeth Bruce his spouse, the lands of Findoury, which lands they transferred in 1574 to Robert Arbuthnott. Balnamoon and Findoury are once again united under one worthy proprietor in the person of James Carnegy Arbuthnott, Esq. In March 1625, we find John Collace, fiar of Balnamoon, witnessing a charter by David Ramsay, younger of Balmain, to John Moncur of Slains, of the lands of Cossins and others in the barony of Mondynes and parish of Fordoun, while between that date and the period of the battle of Brechin, the name of Collace occurs frequently in connexion with properties in the town and neighbourhood of Brechin, but of the traitor John Collace himself we have no further notice. Of Crawford, again, we aer told by Buchanan that soon after the battle of Brechin he took the opportunity of the king passing through Angus to submit himself to the royal authority, and to make his peace with King James, to whom he remained firmly attached for the remainder of his life, which was of but short duration, for he died in 1453. The succeeding Lord, David Earl of Crawford, seems to have been a man anxious to be on good terms with the church, for, in the year 1472, he burdened his lands of Drumcairn, " lying in his lordship of Glenesk," with £3 annually to the cathedral of Brechin.

The stormy reign of James II. did not prevent peculation in the church: at least a precept by James III. in 1463, states plainly that through the profligacy of the bishops and canons of Brechin, the revenues of the cathedral had been greatly reduced by frequent alienations of its property, so that it was then suffering under great deficiency of its resources, and therefore his Majesty exhorts the bishop (then Patrick Graham, cousin of the king) to revoke the whole of such alienations as were made without just cause, and his Majesty orders all judges to assist the bishop in the recovery of the property, whether lands, movable goods, or effects. This precept was not allowed to remain a dead letter. In 1464 a decree of the Lords of Council and Session was issued, decerning Walter Dempster of Ochterless to reconvey to the church the lands of Ardoch, Adicate, Bothers, and Nether Pitforthie, alleged to have been surreptitiously obtained by him; and Dempster, in 1468, implements the decree by resigning the lands to the bishop " upon his bended knees, and having his hands closed and within those of the bishop." Other documents import that Mr Dempster, being reconciled to mother church, got back his lands for payment of an annual feu to the cathedral. The family to which this gentleman belonged took their surname from the fact of having been appointed by Robert II. to the office of heritable Dempsters to the Parliaments, or readers of the doom or sentence pronounced against criminals in the courts of the kingdom. Patrick Graham was afterwards translated from Brechin to St Andrews, and died archbishop in 1479—a prisoner in the castle of Lochleven, broken-hearted by court intrigues, although a man of

strict morals and considerable learning. Previous to his removal
from Brechin, however, he had the influence to obtain from
King James III. a charter, dated at Linlithgow 29th June
1466, changing the weekly market day from Sunday to Monday,
and of new conferring upon the bailies and citizens of Brechin
all their former privileges. The same monarch, shortly before
his decease in 1488, granted a charter in favour of the bailies
and community of the city of Brechin, by which, in respect of
the income of the city being small, and of the faithful services
of their predecessors rendered to the king in times of trouble,
he gives and confirms to them the right of levying for every
horse-load of goods brought to the town, "unum oblum," or
obolus, which originally was a small Athenian coin of silver
weighing about twelve grains, worth three halfpence at the
ordinary price of silver in the present day, but in the fifteenth
century of much more value, and the charter authorises the
magistrates to employ one or more officers to collect the tax.
This charter was produced by the town clerk as a witness before
the House of Peers in 1853 in the case regarding the original
dukedom of Montrose, and is, with the clerk's evidence, printed
in the folio volume published by Lord Lindsay on that case,
(page 404–6;) the charter is also printed by Mr Chalmers in
his "Registrum Episcopatus Brechinensis," vol. ii. page 122.
We thus refer particularly to the charter as it is a most important one for the burgh.

James Stewart, second son of James III., was at his birth
created Duke of Ross, Marquis of Ormond, Earl of Edirdale,
and provided with the lands and lordships of Brechin, Navar,
Ardmanach, and Nithsdale. In 1497 he was made archbishop
of St Andrews. With Brechin he appears to have had no connexion further than in drawing revenue from it.

The register of the burgh of Aberdeen gives the taxation laid
on the burghs beyond the Forth by the commissioners of the
burghs in the Parliament held at Edinburgh in 1483, when we
find the Angus burghs rated thus:—" Dundee, £26, 13s. 4d.;
Forfar, £1, 6s. 8d.; Montrose, £5, 6s. 8d.; Arbroath, £2;
Breching. £4." Aberdeen is then rated the same as Dundee.

The year 1481 was one of those years of so frequent occurrence in the fifteenth century, when poverty perished, and even riches scarce supported itself; it was a " dear year"—and Brechin, like other burghs, suffered severely.

We cannot tell whether it was the grant of right of custom given by James III., or what it was, that involved our citizens of Brechin in a dispute with the burgesses of Montrose, but we find, in 1508, that there was a contest between the two towns regarding the market, and that the Bishop of Brechin, then William Meldrum, granted authority for defending the interests of the city of Brechin, and of the church of Brechin, in an action raised before the Lords of Council and Session at the instance of the *aldermen*, bailies, and burgesses of Montrose, against the citizens of Brechin, for vexations and hindrances alleged to have been given to the community of Montrose in their use of the market of Brechin. How this dispute terminated, or whether it is still in ccurt, we do not know.

In the charter chest of Viscount Arbuthnot, there is a discharge by this Bishop Meldrum " of the teind-penny for James Arbuthnott's waird and marriage," dated the "penult Maij 1511 ;" owning receipt of 35 merks, "gude and usual money of Scotland," of composition for what would now, at least, be thought a strange demand ; and amongst the documents belonging to the burgh of Brechin there is an instrument dated in 1508, bearing that John Carnegy of Kinnaird had delivered a horse, "grosij coloris," as the *Herzeld* of the late John Carnegy his father for the lands of Little Carcary, held of the Cathedral of Brechin. " Herrezelda" (says Skene, in his " De Verborum Significatione") "is the best aucht ox, kow, or uther beast, quhilk ane husbandman possessor of the aucht pairt·of ane dauach of land, (four oxen gang,) dwelland and deceasand theirupon, hes in his possession the time of his decease, quhilk oucht and suld be given to his landislord or maister of the said land." Probably this language of Sir John Skene of 1681, our readers may think requires interpretation itself. The substance of all this however is, that Bishop Meldrum looked carefully after all the property belonging to the see of Brechin, and indeed added considerably to it.

Lord Gray preserves in his charter-room a document, which

is a curious specimen of the numerous hereditary offices that
existed in feudal times, being a retour of the service of Alexander
Lindsay, as heir of his father Richard Lindsay, in the office of
blacksmith of the lordship of Brechin; it is dated 29th April
1514, and is published in the Miscellany of the Spalding Club
for 1853. By it the inquest selected from the barons of the
shire report on oath that the late Richard and his forefathers
were common smiths of the lordship of Brechin, and received
hereditarily nine firlots of good meal of every plough and mill
of the tenants of Balnabriech, Kintrocket, Pitpullocks, Pittendreich, Hauch of Brechin, Burghill, Pettintoscall, Balbirnie,
with the mill of the same, Kincraig, and Leuchland; and one
fleece of an old sheep yearly of every one of the tenants of the
said towns; and also common pasturage in the Long Haugh of
Brechin for two cows and a horse. No bad berth this of the
blacksmith of the barony of Brechin. We trace the office
further down. On 5th October 1605, in the Speciales Inquisitiones
for Forfarshire, published by order of Parliament, there is recorded the service of David Lindsay, as heir of Robert Lindsay,
in the office of common blacksmith of the lordship of Brechin,
and his right as such to two bolls one firlot of meal, and pasturage, like his predecessor, with the fleece of a sheep and a lamb,
as his payment for making wool scissors, we suppose, or " tonsules
lanæ" as they are called here; while in the previous retour they
are termed "forcinij." The Richard Lindsay first mentioned
is, we presume, the proprietor of the Forkit Akir of which we
spoke under the date of 1427, and which is understood to have
been a part of the lands now known as the Latch. The name
of Lindsay, as a blacksmith, occurs for the last time in the
records of the hammermen trade of Brechin in the year 1616.

John Hepburn, who succeeded to the see of Brechin about
1517, seems, in reference to the property of the burgh, to have
pursued the course of Bishop Carnoth. In 1524 he gives out a
long decree finding that the chaplains of the chaplaincy founded
by the Palatine of Strathearn were neglecting their duty, and
ordaining them to build and repair, and to provide proper
vestments, and he gets this decree confirmed by a charter
granted by James V. in 1528. On 25th May 1535, Hepburn

procured a cognition by the sheriffs-depute of Forfarshire, James Gray and David Anderson, regarding the common muir, so full and particular, that we shall take leave to lay it before our readers. This cognition states that "in the matter and cause pursued by a reverend Fader (father) in God, John, Bishop of Brechin, the dean, chapter, and citizens of the same, by our sovereign lord's letters direct to my lord sheriff of Forfar and his deputes, purporting in effect that where they have the muir of Brechin with the pertinents pertaining to them in commonty and their predecessors, and they have been in possession thereof as common past memory of man, whilk now, lately, William Dempster of Careston, Janet Ochterlony, his mother, George Falconer, her spouse, William Marshall, David Deuchar, David Waterstone, portioner of the lands of Waterstone, Matthew Dempster, and James Fenton of Ogil, has stopped the said reverend father, dean, chapter, and citizens of Brechin in casting of peats, turfs, and fuel upon the said commonty, and to pull heather thereupon, and has riven out, tilled, and sawn a part thereof, and built houses upon another part of the same, tending to appropriate the said common muir to them wrongously, and to call both the said parties, and take cognition in the said matter upon the ground of the said lands, as in our sovereign lord's letters, direct to my lord sheriff and his deputes foresaid, at more length is contained. By virtue of the which David Lokky, one of the Mairs general of the said sheriffdom, by the sheriff principal's precept direct to him thereupon, charged and required the said reverend father, dean, and chapter, and citizens of Brechin, followers on the one part, and the said William Dempster, Janet Ochterlony, George Falconer, William Marshall, David Deuchar, David Waterstone, Matthew Dempster, and James Fenton of Ogil, defenders, on the other part, to compear before my lord sheriff foresaid or his deputes, one or more, to this said court, day, time, and place in the hour of cause to hear and see a cognition to be taken in the said matter, and justice equally ministered to both the said parties, after the tenor of our sovereign lord's letters foresaid. At the which day, and in the said court, the said sheriffs-deputes caused call the saids parties, followers, and defenders, to compear before them the said day

C

and place, to hear and see a cognition taken in the said matter, as they that were lawfully summoned thereto. Both the said parties compearing personally, their rights, reasons, allegations being proponed and shown, together with the depositions of diverse famous witnesses produced and admitted, and sworn in presence of parties foresaid, and their depositions, the said sheriffs-deputes being ripely advised therewith, finds and declares, by cognition taken in the said cause, that the said reverend father, dean, chapter, and citizens of Brechin, and their predecessors, has been in peaceable possession of their muir of Brechin foresaid, with their pertinents pertaining to them, in commonty in time bygone, past memory of man, bounded on all the parts about as follows—1*st*, Beginning at the gallows of Keithock at the east; from that west to the Muirfauld dyke, and from that Muirfauld dyke to the Bog dyke, and from the Bog dyke, extending west to the Park dyke, at the south, extending west to the south side of Montboy, the Myre of Montboy there along, and from thence extending west to the gallows of Fearn; and from the gallows of Fearn, east at the north part to the Qualochty, and from thence east to the gallows of Kethock foresaid; and decerneth the bounds before expressed: The whole muir to be commonty to the said reverend father, dean, chapter, and citizens of Brechin: And anent certain lands and houses that are called Todd's houses, and lands lying within the bounds betwixt the gallows of Fearn and the gallows of Keithock, pertaining to James Fenton of Ogil, pertaining to the lands of Fearn, which has been occupied these twenty years bygone, without impediment of Brechin, but bruikit (enjoyed by) them peaceably, as it is clearly proved before the said sheriffs-deputes; therefore the said sheriffs-deputes excepts that lands and houses in this their process, nought (nothing) hurting the property of the superior, nor yet the commonty of the same lands and occupiers thereof, but Brechin to have commonty over all the muir; and the said reverend father, dean, chapter, and citizens of Brechin, shall be kept and defended in such like possession of the said muir as said is, in time coming, ay and while they be lawfully called and orderly put therefrom; and also finds, because the said muir is found that it has been used and holden as common in times bygone past memory of man, therefore the said sheriff should cause it to be held common such like in time coming, according to justice, after the tenor, form, and effect of our sovereign lord's letters foresaid, and doom given thereupon ; and precepts decerned hereupon, according to justice." We have modernised the spelling and phraseology a little. The cognition thus formally taken was ratified by the precept of Lord Gray, sheriff of Forfar, in a court held by him at Forfar, within two days after the perambulation of the muir by his deputes. On the back of the original cognition, which is an excellent specimen of the writing of the sixteenth century, we find this docquet engrossed, "23d January 1769, registered by Mr David Rae, conform to the probative act, and presented by Charles Guthrie, writer in Edinburgh, to whom the same is returned without receipt, G. O."

Hepburn, who took the trouble of thus fixing the boundaries of the common muir, was descended of the powerful family of Bothwell, and is reputed to have been a man of great abilities. He died in August 1558, and Keith says that Listacus *de rebus gestis Scotorum* gives the prelate a very *large* character. But if he was, as we conceive he was, the John Hepburn who was abbot of St Andrews in 1513, and who competed with Andrew Foreman for the Archbishopric of that see, after the death of Alexander Stewart at the battle of Flodden, then he scarce deserves the very large character here spoken of ; for, if Buchanan is to be believed, Hepburn was a factious plotter, a greedy, ambitious, and intolerant priest, and the cause of much trouble during the regency of the Duke of Albany. The documents still in existence in Brechin prove that he was an active and an intelligent man. As to his moral character, these documents afford no information. In 1543, during the minority of Queen Mary, and in the first parliament held after her father's death, an Act was passed ordaining that " it shall be lawful to all our sovereign lady's lieges to have the Holy Writ, viz., the New Testament and the Old, in the vulgar tongue,"—an enactment that sounds strange in our ears, more especially when it is added, " they shall incur *no crime* for the having and reading of the same." The Archbishop of St Andrews, Chancellor of the kingdom, entered a protest against this enactment, "for himself, and in name and behalf of all the prelates of this realm present in Parliament," including the then Bishop of Brechin. Hepburn is the last Roman Catholic bishop who has left any documents connected with the town ; for although after his death, and previous to the Reformation, there was one, and some authorities will have it two, bishops in the see of Brechin, namely, Donald Campbell and John Sinclair, there are no writings in existence in Brechin connected with the Episcopal reign of either of these gentlemen. It is curious enough to observe that the last document by a bishop of the Church of Rome, remaining amongst the records of Brechin, is a charter granted by Bishop Hepburn at request of Sir John Erskine of Dun, the great reformer of the Church, then the patron of the chaplainry of the Virgin Mary, in the church of Brechin, founded by his progenitor, Sir Robert Erskine of Dun, whereby the bishop, in consequence of the incomes of the two chaplains being insufficient for their support, unites the two chaplainries into one, and appropriates the income for the support of one chaplain only.   This charter, bearing date 18th and 27th June 1556, is signed by Erskine, in token of his consent to the arrangement, and completed at Farnell, which then belonged to the bishops of Brechin as a *grange* or country residence.   The chaplainries being thus united, "Joannes Dominus de Erskyn" appoints Nicolas Thomson to the office of chaplain.

Campbell and Sinclair just alluded to, although they have left no traces of their reigns in the records of Brechin, appear both to have been men of considerable eminence.   Campbell, who was of the family of Argyle, but whose induction into the see of Brechin is doubtful, died invested in the office of Lord Privy Seal to Queen Mary in 1562.   Sinclair was the fourth son of Sir Oliver Sinclair of Roslin, and younger brother of Henry Sinclair, Bishop of Ross, and had the honour, while dean of Restalrig, to join Queen Mary in matrimony to Lord Darnley.   Bishop Sinclair was first an Ordinary Lord of Session ; and afterwards, on the death of his brother Henry, president of that court, he was promoted to that important office. By the constitution of the Court of Session at that period, seven of the members behoved to be laymen, and seven clergymen, be-

sides the Lord President, who was also required to be a churchman. Sir Thomas Erskine, Lord Brechin, proprietor of the
lordship of Brechin and Navar, was one of the lords of Session in 1533. He was secretary to James V., and was uncle of,
and tutor to, John Erskine of Dun the famous reformer, mentioned above. In 1584, *parochial* clergymen were declared incapable of exercising any office in the College of Justice, that
their minds might not be diverted from their proper functions ;
and Cromwell, with that strong spirit of common sense which
was exhibited in most of his measures, by act in 1650, debarred
all clergymen, without distinction, from sitting on the judicial
bench of the Court of Session. After the Reformation of 1560,
several parsons and rectors were lords of Council and Session,
but John Sinclair, Bishop of Brechin, was the last churchman
who was president of that court.

The records of Brechin are altogether silent on the events
which occurred in the burgh when Romanism was abolished and
Protestantism established, and neither tradition nor general history gives any information on the subject. We therefore infer
that this change in the religion of the state had created little
disturbance in the city of Brechin.

We have mentioned previously that Brechin was regularly
assessed along with the other royal burghs for the maintenance
of royalty, and in 1525 contributed £56, 5s. towards the expenses of King James V. in France. In the division of the
money granted for the defence of the Borders about the same
period, Brechin paid £45. During Mary's minority the Lord
Governor, in 1550, desired a sum to purchase peace with the
emperor, and Brechin gave 40 crowns. In 1556, Mary got a
donation from the burghs, and Brechin contributed £11, 5s. ; and
towards the expenses of her marriage with the Dauphin of
France in 1557, the burgh gave £168, 15s. ; while in 1563,
this small city contributed £32, 13s. 11d. in part of the expense
of an ambassador to Denmark. But it is perhaps more worthy
of remark, that of the extent of £4144 odds, levied from the
burghs in 1556 to defray the expenses incurred by Gawin, commendator of Kilwinning, and James Maxwell, " burgess of
Rowane, for the down getting of the xvj deniers of ilk frank

wairing of guids coft be Scotts merchants in Rowane and Diep by the four deniers payd by them," Brechin is assessed in £36, 11s. 3d. These extracts are taken from the records of the Town Council of Edinburgh, preserved in the Advocates' Library, Edinburgh. The records of Convention in March 1575, show Brechin to have been then assessed in £55 towards defraying the expense of sending men to Flanders "for tryell of falis cunzie." The records of the Town Council of Aberdeen in 1483, give the tax-roll of the burghs north of the Forth, as modified by the Convention of Burghs, in which Brechin is put down for £4, and Montrose for £5, 6s. 8d., so Brechin must have been a place of some trade long previous to the accession of James VI.

But this chapter would be incomplete, did we not mention that, in 1503, the courtly James IV. appears to have visited Brechin on some of his missions of peace amongst his troublesome subjects. The books of the Lord High Treasurer, preserved in the General Register House, bear that there were paid " the xv day of October, in Brechin, to the foure Italien menstrals, and the more tanbroner to thar hors met, x lb. v s." James seems to have been on his way north at this time, for on the 11th October there is an entry of a payment of 14s. "to Mylson Harper in Scone ;" and immediately after the Brechin entry there is this entry, " Item, that samyn nijcht in Dunnottar to the cheld playit on the monocords be the king's command, xviij s." The fondness of James for music and mirth is matter still of popular tradition, as well as of authentic history, and on this his journey north he seems to have gratified his taste to the full. It will not be forgotten that it was in consequence of the marriage of James with Margaret Tudor, daughter of Henry VII., in the August of this year, that the Stuarts came to the throne of England, and through them the Guelphs, the present reigning family.

CATHEDRAL OF BRECHIN.

VIEW FROM THE SOUTH-EAST.

BRECHIN CATHEDRAL.

VIEW FROM THE NORTH-EAST.   *Page* 48.

CHAPTER III.

WE come now to treat of a period which produced changes on every burgh in Scotland, but more especially on those burghs which were the seats of Episcopal dignitaries, we mean the Reformation in 1560. The Earl of Argyle, who was then the most popular and most potent nobleman in Scotland, had the influence to introduce into the see of Brechin Alexander Campbell, a son of the family of Ardkinglass, who, at the period of his induction in 1566, appears to have been a mere youth ; for we find that, the year after his induction, he got liberty from Queen Mary to go abroad for his education ; and in the Book of Assumptions of 28th January 1573–4, it is noticed that he was then at Geneva at the schools. As there are no documents with Campbell's name existing in Brechin from 1569 to 1579, we are inclined to suppose that he had been abroad between these periods ; and we adopt this opinion the more readily, because we find that, although his licence to go abroad for seven years was granted in 1567, he was present with Regent Moray in the convention at Perth in July 1569. During the absence of the bishop for the period alluded to, David, archdean of Brechin, commendator of Dryburgh, managed the temporalities of the bishoprick of Brechin. Alexander Campbell, as we have said, was inducted into the see in 1566, and he died bishop of Brechin in 1610, so that he filled the Episcopal chair for forty-four years, from which circumstance, independent of other authorities, it might fairly be inferred that he was not a very old man when he was elevated to the dignity of a bishop. But the most remarkable circumstance connected with this gentleman, was the terms of

the grant in his favour of the bishoprick. By this document
Campbell was empowered to sell, for his own benefit, all the revenues and properties belonging to the see then vacant, or when
they should become vacant. Of this power the young bishop
availed himself, or was obliged to avail himself, by making
large grants to his patron the Earl of Argyle, who was not without strong temporal reasons for supporting the Reformation.
At the period of Campbell's accession, the see of Brechin was
possessed of a revenue of £410 in money, 11 bolls of wheat, 61
chalder 5 bolls of bere, 123 chalder 3 bolls meal, 15 bolls of
oats, 11 and a half dozen of capons, 16 dozen and ten poultry,
18 geese, and 9 barrels of salmon annually. But although
Argyle swept off the greater part of these good things, Bishop
Campbell made some grants and sales for his own especial
benefit. Thus, immediately on his accession, he dispones the
Little Mill of Brechin, with the acre of land and other rights
thereto pertaining, to William Kinloch, burgess of Dundee, and
Janet Lindsay his wife, in liferent, and to Alexander Ramsay in
fee, and that for payment of a price of £30, and an annual feu
of 3s. 4d. The property thus sold passed from Ramsay to
William Fullarton of Ardo, who transferred it to the town of
Brechin in 1695 ; and by that corporation the Little Mill was
converted into a waulkmill in 1693, and afterwards disannulled,
the Muckle Mill having swallowed up the duties and properties
of the Little Mill. However, if this was then the practice of the
Church, it is but justice to say that there were also many grants
made by the Crown of Church property for the promotion of
education at this time. Thus in 1575, according to the records
of the Privy Seal, printed by Mr Chalmers, the teinds of Bonnyton, not exceeding £20, which had previously belonged to the
canons of the Cathedral, are given to James Small, son of George
Small, saddler in Edinburgh, who " being puire, fathirless, and
destitut of all support of parentis or frendis, is of convenient
aige to entir in the studie of grammer, and apt and disposit
thairfore, and promist to be subject to discipline," and the master
of the Grammar School of Edinburgh is ordered to receive
Small under his charge for seven years, and thereafter to report
that another may be appointed to the scholarship ; and we ob-

serve, accordingly, that this grant was renewed in 1581 for
other seven years, after which these teinds were gifted for a
similar purpose to Henry Sinclair, son of the deceased Henry
Sinclair, writer. A similar gift is made in 1576 of the emoluments of Kilmoir to James Cokburne " brother-german to
Johnne Cokburne of Clerkingtoun," who might have been fatherless, but certainly had not been poor. There are many other
grants of a similar kind, but we shall only further notice that of
the teinds of Middle Drums in 1577 to " Mr John Nicolsoun,
who has been brought up at the schools since his youth, and has
completed his course of philosophy, and intends to pass beyond
sea for his further exercise in good learning, so that he may
return again a more profitable member to serve in this common-
wealth."

The family of Erskine appear now, as at other times, to have
got their share of Church property ; thus, James Erskine,
vicar of Falkirk, on 14th March 1585, obtained a grant for his
life of all the annual rents which had been bestowed on the officials " for celebrating of messis, singing and saying of dirigie,
and doing of utheris ryteis, ceremonies, and papisticall services,
whilk now be the Word of God, and laws of his Hienes realm,
are *damnit* and altuterlie abolischit," and for which grant Mr
Erskine was to pay yearly to the collector of the alms for the
poor within the city £6, 13s. 4d. Scots. And John Erskine of
Dun, for his " lang, ernest, and faithful travellis," " in the suppressing of superstitioun, papistrie, and idolatrie, and avance-
ment and propagatioun of the evangell of Christ Jesus, the tyme
of the reformatioun of the religion, and in ydnt and faithful per-
suerance in the samin," has a grant for his lifetime, on 5th November 1587, of various sums from the abbeys of Arbroath and
Cowper, from Jedburgh and Restennet, the bishoprick of Brechin,
and other places ; and this grant is renewed in 1589 to John
Erskine of Logy, grandson of Dun, for the lifetime of Logy.

Bishop Campbell married an Helen Clepan or Clephan, and
of course was the first bishop of Brechin who had a lawful wife.
George Wishart of Drymine, by a charter dated at Findowrie
23d March 1583, conveys to Mr and Mrs Campbell that estate, so
they appear to have trafficked in Church lands to some account.

James VI., after the Act of Annexation of the bishops' temporalities to the Crown, granted those of Brechin to Campbell in
1588 for his lifetime, for payment of 40 merks Scots to the
Crown ; and this grant seems to have been renewed and ratified
in Parliament in 1597, for Campbell makes his right good
against the King's collector-general by a Decree of Council and
Session, dated 1st Feb. 1603.

The example of spoliation set by the highest dignitary of the
church of Brechin was quickly followed by the smaller powers.
The archdean sold his mansion ; the presbyters constituted by
the Palatine of Strathearn disposed of their house; the chancellor
conveyed away his manse, and every one was more active than
another in converting the property of the church to his own
private use. It is amusing to notice the various pretexts fallen
upon by these churchmen for this general spoliation. The
bishop found that the piece of ground from nearly opposite the
tolbooth to the present Bishop's Close had, for many years, been
a receptacle of filth and nuisance, so that not only the citizens of
Brechin had contracted disease and infirmity thereby, but the
bishop himself had not been able to walk in his own garden in
safety by reason thereof, and therefore, being anxious to remove
this nuisance, (so the charter bears,) the bishop and chapter sold
the property to James Graham. The archdean, again, discovered that his mansion was in a ruinous state, and having of
purpose to build a new one in lieu thereof, he sold the old, with
the houses and yards pertaining thereto, for a certain sum of
money, to Mr Thomas Ramsay, commissary of Brechin. The
chancellor, in like manner, conveyed a *piece of waste ground*
upon which *formerly* stood his manse, with the garden thereof,
to Mr Paul Fraser : and the presbyters of Strathearn found that
part of their residence and habitation was in a like dangerous
and decayed situation, and that there was no cure but a sale.
These and other similar grants are all ratified by James VI. ;
and thus a great part of the property belonging to the church of
Brechin passed to lay hands. If we are to believe the reformed
clergy of this era, the manses, houses, and hospitals of the
Roman Catholics had been contrived to last only during the
continuance of the papistical dominion ; for, at the period alluded

to, the buildings are all found ruinous, while the lands, formerly
so fair, are declared to be pieces of mere waste ground. But
there is one redeeming fact connected with this exhibition of
worldly-mindedness—not, however, emanating from churchmen,
but again from the Crown. James VI., by a charter dated at
Leith, 20th June 1572, and granted with consent of John Earl
of Morton, regent, instituted the hospital of Brechin. The charter
narrates that His Majesty, in consideration of the duty incumbent upon him to provide for the comfort of the poor, the lame,
and the miserable, orphans and destitute persons, grants that
there be an hospital founded within the city of Brechin, into
which persons of the above description shall be admitted and
properly accommodated; and because of there having been diverse annual rents within the city, which, in former times of
ignorance, were mortified to presbyters and chaplains for the
performance of masses and anniversaries, therefore the king appropriates these annual rents to the more useful purpose of supporting the poor in an hospital, and appoints the bailies, council,
and community of the city of Brechin, and their successors, to
be patrons of the hospital, and ordains that all the lands and
annual rents appropriated for papistical purposes, shall pertain
to the bailies, council, and community for support of the hospital.
The chanter's manse, a house in the Lower Wynd—now called
Church Street—was bought for an hospital in 1608; and in
1688, there is a minute of council strictly prohibiting any person
from receiving any benefit from the hospital except they "keep
the house and wear the habit;" but what that habit was we
have not been able to discover. This injunction seems soon to
have fallen into abeyance, for, in 1689, we find a minute of
council dispensing with the pensioners living in the hospital,
there called the Bede House, upon account that it was then
neither wind nor water-tight, but continuing to them their pen-
sions notwithstanding. The revenues thus gifted by King James
have always been applied by the town council of Brechin for the
maintenance of poor people within the town; in 1864 they
amounted to £51, 5s., besides £66 obtained for entries from
vassals; and twenty-two pensioners had £51, 10s. divided
amongst them; the property being estimated at £1456. The

gift was ratified by James upon his attaining majority in July 1587. The original grant in 1572 is witnessed by "Mr George Buchanan, pensioner of Corsragwell," then keeper of the Privy Seal, the celebrated historian, and the tutor of James VI.

The Hammermen Incorporation are possessed of a thick octavo volume, which contains the minutes or scroll minutes of the Bailie Court of Brechin for 1579-80. The subsequent part of the book is filled up with the minutes of the incorporation, some of which indeed, of a comparatively late date, 1770, are intermixed with those of the acts of the bailies. The only explanation of the matter is that the Messrs Spense of those periods were, at the same time, the town clerks and trades' clerks, and that paper being then an expensive article, the book which had ceased to be used for the Bailie Court was found handy for the hammermen trade when it was constituted into a corporation in 1600. Be that as it may, the book is anterior to any in possession of the town council, and contains some entries worth extracting, as indicating the state of society and the price of articles towards the close of the sixteenth century. Thus several parties are punished for using unlawful measures ; breaches of the peace are as numerous as at present, and offenders are punished by fines just as in the present day. John Hutton is ordained to pay Richard Thomson 30s. for the hire of a mare for seven days ; David Watson claims £3 of Thomas Liddle for his fee for three half-years' service ; decrees are given for the prices of malt at 5 merks and 6 merks, and at £3 the boll ; for 13s. 4d. as the price of a hide ; for 18s. and 40 pence for 100 calf skins and a dozen of kid skins ; for 30 pence for a leg of mutton ; and for £4 as the price of 4 ells of gray cloth. One decree is against John Thomson for 40s. resting of £8 due James Watt for sybees, that grew in his yard—rather a large quantity of the onion species ! John Hamilton and James Strachan apprehended with flesh, wool, and other property in their possession, are banished the town, and if found therein afterwards are to be hanged without process ; and William Skinner, for stealing leather meets with a similar sentence. But the bailies are not always so bloodthirsty ; for in the action at the instance of Thomas Bellie, cutler, against George Meldrum, a burgess of Crail, they postpone

giving sentence for a month, in hopes of the parties agreeing.
Query, Had the magistrates doubted their authority over the
Crail burgess ? The Muckle Mill and weigh-house are exposed
for let in a way continued down to a much later period, the
rouping being from day to day, and the lease for one year only.
In January 1580, however, the Muckle Mill is agreed to be let for
100 merks of grassum, and £50 of yearly rent, for nineteen years,
to defray the great expenses incurred at law and by taxation;
but this plan having failed, the mill is let in May for one year,
and part of the profit ordered to be given towards building a
school; and Alexander Knox then becomes tenant at 103 merks.
Mr Andrew Leitch, in Nov. 1580,—who, we believe, was the
schoolmaster of the period,—agrees to serve the council for 40
merks yearly, notwithstanding of their first agreement for 50
merks, and that during their pleasure—not a very comfortable
position for a man of letters. About the same time the bailies
appoint William Thornton, procurator in Dundee, to be their
procurator before the sheriff of Forfar, and grant him a yearly
salary of £5 to attend to their lawsuits. In the same year John
Schewen, baker, is admitted freeman, paying 20s. for "spice
and wine as accords;" and in subsequent minutes it is ordered
that no unfreeman bake within burgh, and that no baker, although a freeman, shall bake any bread under the size formerly
directed, while a committee is appointed for proving the butcher
meat. In May 1580 the bishop and council order a contribution of 100 merks to be applied for the repairs of the tolbooth,
and 80 merks for the repair of the church; but an obstreperous
councillor, David Dempster, in a few days after, has the hardi-
hood to enter a protest against the order for the repair of the
church, to the no small annoyance, no doubt, of Bishop Alexander Campbell. But the mighty affair seems to have been in
June 1580, when the great man of the time, and the principal
proprietor in the neighbourhood, John Earl of Mar, Lord of
Garioch and Erskine, and proprietor of the lordship of Brechin
and Navar, makes his appearance. On 4th March 1579, the
whole inhabitants had been ordered to meet in the churchyard
in array of war by six o'clock next morning, to proceed with the
bailies in affairs of the city; but in June 1580 all actions,

civil and criminal, are put off for some days; all persons named in a list are ordained to compear well mounted, and in their best apparel, on two hours' warning, to meet the King's Grace, while the Earl of Mar and his servant Thomas Windygates are made burgesses. The order for the assemblage of the citizens is on 21st June; the admission of the Earl of Mar, and the adjournment of the Bailie Court, are on 28th June; so we infer his King's Grace, the sapient James VI. of Scotland and I. of England, had been in Brechin on that day, although we have no record of the event.

Disputes and battling amongst the noblemen were frequent during the unhappy reign of the beautiful, the learned, the unfortunate, the ill-treated, but we fear the highly culpable, Queen Mary; and *raids* in the neighbourhood of Brechin, involving the peace of that and other burghs, too frequently occurred. The burgh records of Arbroath have this entry under date "4th March 1568-9," (that is, March 1569 according to our mode of beginning the year in January):—" The qlk day, for divers causes concerning the common weill and relief of the taxation fra the rayd of Breichin, it is concludit and decernit be the bayleis and counsall that the haill common gress be devydit and partit, and set to every man, puir and rich, that plesses to tak part of it:" and again in June 1572, "Thir persons are chosyng to ride with my lord, (the abbot, we presume,) to the raid of Breichin—John Akman, James Pekyman, Wm. Bardy, Andro Dunlop, James Ramsay, Nyniane Halis; and all the rest of the honest men of the town oblisit tham to ryid thair tym about when requirit, or ony of the said persons war chargit thereto in time to come." There is in the register of the Privy Seal a remission to John Cockburn, citizen of Brechin, of the crime of being art and part with Adam Gordon, brother of George Gordon, Earl of Huntly, and others, in seizing, in August 1570, the "pyramidis" of the steeple of Brechin—the Round Tower, we presume—and maintaining it against the peace of the king during one of the raids of that unhappy time.

In 1573 a rencontre took place between the supporters of James and the Earl of Morton, then regent, and the friends of Queen Mary. This engagement is known by the title of the

" Bourd of Brechin," and was fought by the Adam Gordon of Auchindown just named, the brother of Lord Huntly, for the queen's party, and by the Earl of Brechin for the regent. In the previous year Gordon had gained a considerable advantage over his opponents at Craibstane in Aberdeenshire, and, emboldened by that victory, he entered Angusshire. The regent's party resolved to stop Gordon, and for this purpose they assembled all the forces of Angus at Brechin. But Gordon, being apprised of their proceedings, left the siege of Glenbervie, with which he was then engaged, came to Brechin overnight with the most courageous of his troops, knocked down the watch, surprised the town, fell upon the gallant lords, drove them from the city, and took possession of the town and castle of Brechin. Next morning, the lords of the king's party, being informed of the few troops which Auchindown had with him, collected their scattered forces and marched to Brechin to give him battle. Gordon courageously met the lords, routed them, and slew about eighty of their troops, but generously dismissed, without ransom or exchange, nearly two hundred prisoners, most of them gentlemen.

Alexander Scott, who wrote in 1562, is said to have been a native of Brechin. Of this there may be doubt, but it is probable he was in some way connected with the burgh, for we have heard his poems recited by individuals in the town, who represented that they had the verses handed down to them by tradition. One of these poems struck us as particularly plaintive. It is entitled " An Address to the Heart," and runs thus :—

> " Return thee hame, my heart, again,
> And byde where ye war wont to be;
> Thou art ane fule to suffer pain
> For luve o' ane that luves no thee.
>
> " My heart, take neither strute nor wae
> For ane, without a better cause;
> But be thou blythe and let her gae,
> For feint a crum o' thee she fa's.
>
> " Ne'er dunt again within my breast,
> Nor let her slights thy courage spill,
> She'll dearly rue her ain beheist,
> She's sairest paid that gets her will."

As the close of the sixteenth century is the close of the connexion of the Popish hierarchy with the cathedral church of
Brechin, we may here take a hasty glance at the constitution
of the chapter, and at the altarages and chaplainries connected
with the cathedral during the time of Papacy, as stated in the
documents still existing. The charter by Robert I., in 1322,
granting a right of market on Sundays, is addressed to the
bishop, chaplains, and canons of the cathedral church of the
Holy Trinity of Brechin. Amongst the old records there is an
apostolic declaration dated on the Monday of the Holy Trinity
in 1372, issued by Patrick, Bishop of Brechin, and the canons,
rectors, vicars, and elders of the diocese, for the purpose of ascertaining the number and quality of the benefices belonging to the
church, and the dignities, offices, and prebendaries belonging to
the cathedral. By this writ it is declared that there are eleven
benefices belonging to the church, four of which have the dignity
of dean, chanter, chancellor, and treasurer, and the fifth has the
dignity of archdean, which five benefices are incompatible with
other offices. Then it is declared that there are six benefices,—
viz., vicar, pensioner, subdean, Kilmoir, Butergill, and Guthrie,
all of which are simple prebends, and are compatible with other
offices ; and it is further stated that although two of these prebends are commonly called vicar and subdean, yet they have no
care of souls, nor prerogative of dignity, nor office, nor administration, within or without the cathedral, but only that, as already
said, they are simple prebends compatible with other offices.
The witnesses to this letter are described as Fergus de Tulach,
præcentor ; Richard de Monte Alto, chancellor ; Matthew de
Abirbrothoc, treasurer ; Stephen de Cellario, archdean ; William
de Dalgarnock, vicar ; Radulph Wyld, subdean ; John de Drum,
prebend of Butergill ; Thomas de Luchris, prebend of Guthrie ;
John Wyld, rector of Logie ; John de Gaok, rector of Monzeky ; and
Alexander Doig, vicar of Dunnychtyne, canons of the church ; the
dean and the pensioner, dwelling at a distance, and the prebend of
Kilmoir, being only absent. In the park of Burghill, not far from
the keeper's house, there is a round knoll planted with trees, where
it is understood the chapel of "Butergill" stood, and where yet the
remains of humanity may be found, indicating that a graveyard

had surrounded the chapel, while a well of excellent water near at hand proves that the comforts of the living had been provided for, and that the mansion of the priest had not been far distant. John of Drum, we presume, had his dwelling, if not his church, on the farm of West Drums, on the estate of Aldbar, where the remains of buildings and enclosures are still to be seen in a field called the chapel field. Kilmoir, or the church of St Mary, is understood to have been within the policies of Brechin Castle —not far from the castle itself, and only at a short distance from the cathedral. A few years after the date of this famous "declaratio,"—that is, in 1384,—the church of Lethnot was created a prebendary of the cathedral of Brechin, at the request of Sir David Lindsay of Glenesk, the patron of the parish of Lethnot; and the prebend of Lethnot was declared a canon of the cathedral church of Brechin, with a stall in the choir, and a place in the chapter. In 1429, we find a decree of the bishop and chapter, by which, amongst a variety of other matters, it is again declared that there are four dignities in the church, here called the dean, præcentor, chancellor, and treasurer, who have the precedence of all other canons. In August 1435, the bishop and chapter enter into a curious agreement amongst themselves to keep the ornaments of the church in suitable condition, under the penalty— the bishop, as a prebend, of ten merks; the dean, præcentor, archdean, the vicar, and the ministers of Lethnot and Glenbervie in five merks each, and every other canon in forty shillings. In 1474, the parish church of Finhaven was, at the request of the Earl of Crawford, erected into a prebendary of Brechin, and, of course, the clergyman would have a prebend's stall in the cathedral.

With the eleven benefices declared in 1372, and the additions of Lethnot in 1384, and Glenbervie, as just mentioned, in 1435, and Finhaven added in 1474, and of the bishop himself as a prebend, claiming we believe to be rector of Brechin, the chapter of the cathedral church of Brechin consisted in all of fifteen canons.

In a charter dated in 1469, there is an allusion to a tenement commonly called "Cattiscors," lying at the south end of the city of Brechin, on the west side of the road leading to the bridge of

D

Brechin, and situate between the lands of John Cockburn and the north brow of the brae towards the south gable of the Little Mill of Brechin. This Cattiscross had stood somewhere near the present South Port, but what description of a cross was so named cannot now be known.

Connected with the cathedral, there were several chaplainries. A writing dated September 1630, makes mention of the chaplainry of St James the Apostle, and this is the only time we find that chaplainry alluded to, except in a grant for life in 1588 to David Balfour of the "chaplainry of St Ann, founded at the altar of St James within the cathedral kirk of Brechin." "St James' land," however, is mentioned in 1491 in the Acta Dom. Concilij as being within the city, and in the title-deeds of a property lying on the east side of the High Street and south side of the Blackbull Close, the subjects are described as belonging "to the Chapplenary of the altar of St James, situate within the cathedral church of Brechin." This property now belongs to Mr Lawson, baker. The chaplainry of St Mary Magdalene undoubtedly belonged to the cathedral of Brechin. This chapel was situated on the lands of Arrat, between Montrose and Brechin, close by the present turnpike road, where a burying-ground still exists, known as "Maidlen Chapel." In old writings the chaplainry of Mary Magdalene is called sometimes the Chapel of Arrat, and sometimes the Chapel of Caldhame, from lands adjoining Brechin on the east side of the town which belonged to the chapel, and on part of which the railway station now is, and a new town is fast arising. These lands were *thirled* to the Little Mill of Brechin, and the chaplain was obliged to aid in upholding the mill, cleaning the dam, and bringing home the mill-stones. The origin of the chapel is unknown, but it was repaired during Bishop Carnoth's reign, 1429-56, and the revenues were augmented about that time by the addition of the revenues of the Holy Cross founded by Dempster of Carreston. The chapel, together with the other property belonging to the altarage, was gifted by James VI. to John Bannatyne in 1587, for his maintenance "at the sculeis," and subsequently the emoluments were drawn by the Hepburnes and the Livingstones. To the cathedral of Brechin also belonged the Maisondieu chapel, situated in the lane running west from the Timber-market—now called Market Street—the property of which was managed by a person styled "the master of the hospital of the Virgin Mary of *Mazendeu.*" It is said there was a monastery of Red Friars or Trinitarians in Brechin, so designated from part of their garb, but whose correct name was Ordo Sanctissimæ Trinitatis ad Redemptionem Captivorum, hence sometimes called Trinitarians. The Society for Promoting the Fine Arts in Scotland, published in 1848 a plate representing Italian peasants entertaining a brother of this order. We never could trace out any property which had belonged to such a body, nor is the slightest allusion made to them in any writing that has come under our notice. We have, amongst the papers of the town, allusions also to the chaplainries "Nomine Jesu," St John the Evangelist, and St Laurence, although probably the different names might have been given occasionally to the same chapels.

The altarages within the cathedral were still more numerous. There was the altarage of "our Lady," where mass was ordered to be said daily at the second bell in the morning, "at all seasons in the year," for the souls of Walter, Palatine of Strathearn, and his successors; and to this altarage several properties in the vicinity of the present Mill Stairs belonged, as well as certain subjects in Montrose, and some property in Dundee. In 1537, James Leslie, chaplain of the chaplainry commonly called "Berclay Stall," grants 13s. 4d. to the church from his lands in the town of Brechin, which we presume to be the same as the altarage of the Virgin Mary founded by the Barclays. There was also the altar of St Thomas the martyr, founded by Sir John Wishart of Pitarrow, Knight, about the year 1442, to which certain revenues belonged, payable out of the lands of Redhall, Balfeich and Pittengardner. There was likewise the altarage of "the blessed virgin Katherine," to which a worthy citizen, Robert Hill, in 1453, gave an acre of land at the Crofts, and a tenement within the town; which example is subsequently followed by other citizens, no doubt no less worthy in the eyes of the church. There was further, the altar of St Christopher the martyr, to which a John Smart left certain lands and annual

rents in 1458. And there was the altarage of St Ninian, to
which considerable property within the burgh belonged. We
likewise have mention made of the altars of St Nicholas and
St Sebastian, the martyrs, in 1512, and that of All Saints in
1537, of which latter Sir Thomas Finlayson was chaplain in
1547, and which is then described as having been founded by
Mr William Meldrum, archdean of Dunkeld, and to have had
belonging to it, amongst other properties, the land's called
Scale's Acre, where the Crofts markets were formerly held, now
the principal sites of Panmure Street and Clerk Street. The
altarage of the "Holy Cross" is mentioned in 1435, and there
are allusions likewise to those of St Duthoc, St Magdalene, St
George, and others incidentally. A piece of ground termed
"Kirk Dur Keyis,"—Kirk Door Keys,—is described in a
charter of 1578 as lying between the lands of Unthank and
Caldhame, on the east side of the road leading to Unthank,
being, as we understand, the first field of that property on the
east side of the Toll Road, going northwards from Brechin.

The records of the burgh contain no reference to the existence
of the plague in the town about this time, but in the accounts
of the burgh of Aberdeen we find this entry on 18th August
1597, "Given to Michael Fergus, poist, for careing of a letter to
the baillies of Brechin anent the plaig, 1lb. 10s."

CHAPTER IV.

THE year 1600 was the first which was held to be commenced in Scotland on the 1st day of January. Previously, the year was understood to begin on 25th March, or Lady Day. This alteration in the style was enforced by an Act of the Estates, and requires to be kept in view in regard to the precise date of any document executed between January and March before 1600. The beginning of this century was also remarkable in Scotland by the accession of James VI., in 1603, to the crown of England, and the consequent transference of the seat of royalty from Edinburgh to London. Before leaving Scotland James took a personal interest in a trial before the High Court of Justiciary in 1601, wherein Thomas Bellie, burgess of Brechin, and his son were accused of " having and keeping of poison, mixing the same with daich or dough, and casting down thereof in Janet Clerk's yard in Brechin for the destruction of fowls, by the which poison they destroyed to the said Janet two hens." The accused were banished from the kingdom for life, as recorded by Burton in his Criminal Trials,—no great punishment, perhaps, some of James' English courtiers thought. This change of the seat of government was at first detrimental to Scotland, as it drew off the rich nobles to the court in England, where they spent the ready money which Scotland so much needed. The change was the more felt in consequence of the policy adopted by both nations, which, although then made one kingdom, so far as the title of Great Britain, bestowed by James, could unite them, still remained as hostile and distinct in reality as any two nations could be, each showing its jealousy of the other by enacting that sheep, black cattle, wool, hides, leather, and yarn, should be prohibited from exportation and reserved by both nations for internal consumption. The families of Panmure and Southesk seem to have followed the court party at this period, and to have added to their titles of honour in consequence.

Patrick Maule of Panmure, who was born in 1603, was on 3d August 1646 created a peer by the title of Earl of Panmure, Lord Maule of Brechin and Navar. This noble family has been long and closely connected with Brechin ; and, after ranking five earls in succession, is now represented by the Right Hon. Fox, Lord Panmure of Brechin and Navar, the title having been renewed to his father the Right Honourable William Ramsay Maule, the representative of the ancient family, through a female, by William IV. in September 1831. Patrick, the first earl, was much attached to Charles I., and was present with him at all the battles fought by the king during the civil wars. His Lordship died on 22d December 1661, and was succeeded by his son George, who was an equally keen royalist, and was present at the battles of Dunbar, Inverkeithing, and Worcester, in 1650 and 1652. George, the third earl, succeeded his father in 1671. He was a privy councillor to Charles II. and to James VII., and lived till 1686, when he was succeeded by his brother James, the fourth earl. This nobleman had a very checkered life. He was a privy councillor to James VII., but was removed from that office in consequence of opposing the abrogation of the penal laws against Popery. In 1689, however, he strenuously supported the cause of James VIII., and he was present, with his brother, Harry Maule of Kellie, at the battle of Sheriffmuir in 1715, having previously proclaimed James at the cross of Brechin as King Regnant of Great Britain. After this battle he escaped abroad. He was then attainted of high treason, and by Act of Parliament deprived of his lands and titles. His honours and estates were, however, twice offered him if he would take the oaths to the house of Hanover, but he conscientiously declined to do so, and died in exile at Paris on 11th April 1723. His brother, Harry Maule of Kellie, was a man of a similar stamp, noted for his goodness of heart, and marked by all the characteristics of a cavalier and high-bred gentleman. The fifth earl was William, son of Harry Maule of Kellie. William was born about the year 1700, and was created an Irish peer in 1743 by the title of Earl Panmure of Forth and Viscount Maule of Whitechurch. He represented the county of Forfar for forty-seven years, and was a general in the army in 1770. In 1764, he purchased the estate of Panmure from the York Buildings Company for £49,157, 18s. and 4d., and died in 1782, leaving his estates to his nephew, the eighth Earl of Dalhousie, with reversion to William Ramsay, the second son of Lord Dalhousie, who died, universally lamented, on 13th April 1852, having been long known as the Honourable William Ramsay Maule, subsequently as the Honourable William Maule, and finally as Lord Panmure, and who through life made it his study to patronise every plan calculated for the benefit of Brechin. The present representative of the family is the Right Honourable Fox, Baron Panmure of Brechin and Navar, and Earl of Dalhousie, well known for his energetic services as Secretary at State for War during the Crimean contest, as well as his labours in other public situations. The late Lord Panmure represented the county of Forfar in the successive Parliaments from 1796 to 1832 ; and the present Earl of Dalhousie sat in Parliament, first for the county of Perth in 1835, next for the Elgin burghs in 1838, thereafter for the town of Perth in 1841, and sat for that city till 1852, when he became a peer, having been returned by that community for four successive Parliaments, and elected in 1846, 1847, and 1852 by the unanimous voice of the electors. Lord Dalhousie was created a Knight of the Thistle in 1853, and on the fall of Sebastapol in 1860 he had conferred on him the honour of Grand Cross of the Bath ; his lordship is Lord Lieutenant of Forfarshire, Lord Privy Seal for Scotland, and a member of Her Majesty's Privy Council. The family of Panmure is of French extraction. The progenitor of Maule of Panmure came over with William the Conqueror in 1066, and from various chartularies and other documents, the genealogy of the family can be traced downwards from that date to the present time.

The family of Southesk was also ennobled during the seventeenth century, and took an active part in the eventful affairs of
that period.   The progenitors of this family were anciently
proprietors of the lands of Balinhard ; but in the reign of David
II. John de Balinhard obtained a grant of the lands of Carnegie,
in the barony of Panmure, and from thence he took his surname.   From John descended Duthac de Carnegie, who, in
1409, by a charter from Robert, Duke of Albany, obtained the
lands of Kinnaird.   He was succeeded by his son Walter, who
joined the Earl of Huntly, on behalf of James II., against the
Lindsays at the battle of Brechin, for which he had his Castle
of Kinnaird burned to the ground by Earl Beardie and his
followers.   John, the grandson of Walter, was slain at the
battle of Flodden in Northumberland, fought by James IV. in
1513.   This John left a son, Robert Carnegie, who was in
great favour with Regent Hamilton, and was by him promoted
to be one of the judges of the Court of Session, then to be ambassador to England, and subsequently to be ambassador to
France, previously to which last embassy he was knighted.   He
was esteemed an excellent lawyer, and was the author of a work
on Scots Law, entitled " Liber Carnegij."   Sir Robert Carnegie
died in 1565, leaving by his wife, Margaret Guthrie, six sons
and seven daughters, and from some one or other of these sons are
descended most of the numerous families in Angus-shire bearing the surname of Carnegie.   This Sir Robert Carnegie was
succeeded by his eldest son John, a great friend to Queen Mary ;
and John again was succeeded by his brother David, a favourite
with James VI., who promoted him to be one of the Lords of
Session, a Privy Councillor, and a Commissioner of the Treasury.
Sir David left four sons, David, John, Robert, and Alexander.
David, the eldest son of Sir David, was created Lord Carnegie
of Kinnaird by King James VI. on 14th April 1616, and Earl
of Southesk by Charles I. on 22d June 1633.   From the other
sons of Sir David are descended the families of Northesk and
Balnamoon.   David, the first earl, who was buried at Kinnaird
on 11th March 1658, left four sons, David, James, John, and
Alexander of Pitarrow, whose son David was created a baronet
of Nova Scotia in 1663.   Earl David was succeeded by his son

James, who was a Privy Councillor to Charles II. Robert, the third earl, succeeded his father in 1669. Before his succession he resided for some time in France, and was captain of one of the companies of Scots Guards to Louis XIV. He again was succeeded by his son Charles in 1688, and upon his decease, James, *his* son, took up the title as fifth Earl of Southesk. This James was attainted of high treason, being concerned in the rebellion of 1715, and having gone abroad, he died at a convent in France in 1729. Sir John Carnegie, second baronet of Pitarrow, grandson of Sir Alexander, fourth son of Earl David, then became head and representative of the family, the other sons of the earl having left no male descendants. Sir John was succeeded by his son Sir James Carnegie, a man of great abilities, who purchased the forfeited Southesk estates from the York Buildings Company, and was very active in making like purchases for other noblemen similarly situated, and who sat in Parliament for Kincardineshire for many years. This Sir James was succeeded by his son Sir David Carnegie, who for some time represented in Parliament the Aberdeen district of burghs, then comprising Bervie, Montrose, Arbroath, and Brechin, along with Aberdeen. Having left the burghs, he was called to sit for the county of Forfar, which he continued to represent till his death in 1796. Upon the decease of Sir David the title and estates devolved upon his son, the late Sir James Carnegie, the fifth baronet of Pitarrow. Thus, Sir Alexander Carnegie of Pitarrow (fourth son of Earl David) was succeeded by his son Sir David Carnegie of Pitarrow, who again was succeeded by his son Sir John Carnegie of Pitarrow, who came to be of Southesk, and was followed by his son Sir James Carnegie, who was succeeded by Sir David Carnegie, the father of the late Sir James, who died in 1849, and was then succeeded by his son James. The late Sir James Carnegie began the prosecution of the claim to the earldom, which claim was followed out by his son. The committee of the House of Lords in July 1855 found the claim proved; and the attainder being reversed, Sir James Carnegie, sixth baronet of Pitarrow, was restored, with the original precedencies, to the dignity and titles of Earl of Southesk and Lord Carnegie of Kinnaird and Leuchars, in the peerage of Scotland, which had been forfeited by James, the fifth earl, in 1716.

It was in 1600 that the trades of Brechin were first incorporated. The seal of cause was issued on 3d October 1600 by Robert Kinnear and Robert Rollock, bailies; David Lindsay, Thomas Lyall, Thomas Ramsay, Matthew Dempster, David Dempster, John Mortoun, George Ferrier, John Leich, Thomas Liddel, elder, Alexander Gellie, David Noray, David Carnegy, and Alexander Clark, councillors; on the petition of David Noray, skinner; Alexander Gellie, cordiner; John Daw, smith; John Adam, tailor; Thomas Schewan, baxter; William Bruce, webster; John Langlands, bonnet-maker; and James Fairweather, flesher; and these tradesmen state that, notwithstanding of Brechin being a royal burgh infeft and established with right of guildry and deacons of crafts, yet, partly from oversight, and partly from want of sufficient numbers of master tradesmen, the election of deacons of crafts had been pretermitted, to the great hurt and decay of the crafts, and also to the prejudice of the lieges, by insufficiency of work through lack of trial; therefore, these tradesman desire the town council to fortify and maintain the crafts in their rights; and in consequence the bailies and council, with consent of the " greatest multitude of the commons convenit," grant the prayer of the petition, and ordain that the freemen of the crafts enumerated should yearly, twenty days before Michaelmas, choose a deacon from each craft, with collector or deacon convener, officers and other members requisite, and that, " in the election of magistrates, the vote of the deacons of the crafts shall be sufficient for the haill members." The bonnet-makers and fleshers have long ceased to be corporations in Brechin. The bonnet-makers, indeed, do not appear ever to have taken up the privileges conceded to them by the seal of cause, and the fleshers, although they formed themselves into a craft, took no part in municipal matters. The other six trades, however,—namely, the hammermen, glovers, shoemakers, bakers, weavers, and tailors,—proceeded, in virtue of this seal of cause, to choose deacons from each craft, and the six deacons annually elected a deacon convener, and the whole subsequently took an active, and often an important part in the muni-

cipal government of the town. It is interesting to observe that
the copy of the seal of cause engrossed in the record of the hammermen trade bears to be signed, " Rot. Rollock, baillie, be the
clerk, *because he could not subscribe."* The crafts thus incorporated in 1600 were very zealous for the religion and morality
of their members, as became the craftsmen of an Episcopal city.
The hammermen, the principal or first in rank of these incorporations, may be taken as an example of the whole trades.
Immediately on being incorporated they enacted that the whole
members, with their servants and apprentices, should keep the
church on the Sabbath and three week days—viz., Monday and
Saturday to the lecture, and Wednesday to the sermon ; that
the masters should have family worship morning and evening ;
that if any be seen drunk or using unlawful pastime during the
hours of worship on the Sabbath-day, he should pay a fine to the
craft, besides the kirk's punishment ; and masters were enjoined
each to have a whip in his house for punishing his servants and
apprentices that took the Lord's name in vain. Any apprentice
who broke the seventh commandment was to double the years of
his apprenticeship, and pay 40s. to the poor, " by and attour the
penalties and punishment belonging to the kirk." Masters were
to pay *each* time of their marriage 6s. 8d., likely to defray the
cost of a little feast to the trade on the occasion, but certainly
not a provocative to matrimony, although immediately after this
enactment we find it ordained that it shall in no wise be
"leisum" for an unmarried master to take an apprentice. All
members of the craft were strictly prohibited from using improper language, and some are fined for misconduct in this
respect. To secure a respectable attendance at funerals a fine
was imposed for absence. An attempt seems to have been made
to raise a fund something like a friendly society, but to have
failed. The grand affair, however, always appears to have been
the church ; a list is given of the twelve persons who contributed
in the erection of their loft in the cathedral in 1608, each of
whom paid 250 merks ; " therefore, *with the arms* of the trade,"
which, if we mistake not, remained on the front of the loft till
the church was repaired in 1806 ; and a list is also given of the
seven persons whose wives were to be admitted, by the unani-

mous consent, to sit in the front seat, likely as much a matter of ambition as the right of entry of a duchess to the royal presence. In November 1687 a letter is read by His Majesty's command, King James II. of England, ordaining the continuance of all magistrates and office-bearers until further orders, with which illegal order of the foolish Stuart the officials readily complied; but in October 1689, during the interregnum, the craft, in obedience to the Act of His Majesty's Council, makes a new election of deacon, treasurer, and other office-bearers. A law plea occurs in 1752 in regard to the gate penny, a tax of a penny exacted by the hammermen from every stall at the markets in the town on which was found anything of iron work, understood to have been originally an allowance made to the trade for keeping the gates of the town at market times. The result of the plea is not mentioned, but we presume it had been favourable, as the trade continued the exaction till very recently. The mode of electing the office-bearers of all the trades was regulated by a minute of the Convenery Court in 1742, and, we believe, continues to be the rule to this day.

The bakers of the burgh had surely been in repute at this time, for in the accounts of the town of Aberdeen there is this entry: "1603–4.—Item, to the post that brocht hame thrie loodes of quhyt breid fra Edinburgh, Donde, and *Brechin,* to try the baxteris with, 6s. 8d." But the next year the same accounts have an entry of a different kind, still, however, showing the intimacy between the two burghs; it is this, "To Caddell the post to gang to Brechin at command of the Provost for inquisition of the *pest* at Killimuir, 1lb. 10s." The plague did not become serious in Brechin till more than forty years after this. The Brechin bakers do not appear to have been the only tradesmen from that burgh held in repute in Aberdeen, for in the accounts already alluded to we have, under date "1626–27.— Item, at command of the magistrates, given to ane calsie maker (paviour) that cam to this town from Brechin for undertaking the bigging of the town's common calsies, for making his expensiss forth and hame, 6lb. 13s. 4d."

A few years afterwards, in 1629, the guildry incorporation was *commenced,* for this seems the proper term for a body whose records begin thus: "The said day and several days before, these persons undernamed, who were then actual merchants, traders within the burgh of Brechin, taking to their consideration, that for themselves and their posterity, and for respect and love that they have to the welfare of the burgh wherein they were living and residing, they should lay out and improve themselves to their utmost, to be example to those who should survive them, to advance the interest of merchandising, and for that end, the surest mean so to do was, that they should incorporate themselves into a body who were to keep order and rule, and with common consent to make such laudable acts as should be performed by them so convened, and obeyed in all burghs for the weal of each other and the common good of the whole body, ay, and until they should attain to that perfection that other royal burghs do brook and possess of late, that is, to have a dean of guild established, under whose jurisdiction they were to be, and to be governed by the laws of the guild." This preamble is followed up by a statement that a loft in the church had been bought for the use of the guildry, and mortcloths (palls) provided to be used at the interment of members and their families, and then a list of the contributors to the guildry is given. For many years afterwards, nothing is entered in the guild records but simply the names and contributions of persons admitted; but, in 1666, there is a long decree engrossed from which it appears that the merchants had applied to the convention of burghs, and that that body had appointed commissioners, who met at Brechin on 5th September 1666, and, after hearing parties, ordained " that at the next election of the burgh of Brechin, and yearly at elections, in all time coming, in the said burgh, there shall be strictly kept and observed, without the least change or seeming alteration, these rules following: to wit, that the whole number of the council, magistrates, and others who shall have voice, shall consist of the number of thirteen only, whereof there shall be still eight of the said thirteen such as either has been or are actual trafficking merchants or maltmen who are not incorporate with any other handicraft; and if any be presently on the council under the name of merchants or maltmen, or yet incorporate in any of the trades, or meets with them, that they are hereby obliged, before

they can be leeted as councillors for the merchants, to renounce
the said trade both before the collector at the meeting of trades,
as also in presence of the council, and that the said thirteen shall
not leet any to be magistrates but those who are merchants
traffickers, and that at the said next election, and in all time
coming, there shall be chosen out of the said merchant councillors
so leeted, their magistrates, conform to their ancient custom, with
ane dean of guild and treasurer, with ane master of the hospital ;
and the said dean of guild is hereby declared invested and empowered as fully and freely in all respects as any royal burgh of this
kingdom, with all the power, rights, and privileges that is or can
belong thereto in any other royal burgh, as said is ; and that of
the said thirteen of the council in all time coming, seven shall
be a quorum, the haill councillors being always cited either personally or at their houses, to keep each council day, with this
provision always, that the said dean of guild and his council
shall not have power to quarrel, stop, or impede any burgess residing within the town, and bearing burden with the rest of the burgh,
whether merchants or tradesmen, already made, in their privilege,
that is. cannot challenge them, nor force them, or either of them,
to enter of new as burgesses, or pay anything to the guild box."
John Donaldson, who was the first contributor, in 1629, to the
voluntary association then formed, was the first dean of guild of
Brechin.   His election is entered in the record on 8th October
1669.   Probably some delay had arisen with the convention, and
the guildry had not been brought into play till that time.   Like
other corporations, the guildry is now on the wane.   The maltmen have long ceased to exist.

The authority of the bishop, though considerably abridged,
was sufficient to constitute him the principal man of Brechin for
the greater part of the seventeenth century.   Andrew Lamb was
bishop of the see from 1606 to 1619, and was one of the bishops
sent to England in 1610 by King James for the purpose of receiving Episcopal Ordination from the English bishops, as some
doubts existed regarding that of the Scottish bishops.   The Bishop
of Brechin was accompanied by the Bishop of Galloway and the
Archbishop of Glasgow, so we may infer that Lamb was considered a man of some importance.

David Lindsay held this diocese from 1619 to 1634, when he was translated to Edinburgh. He is not more indebted to the popular rhymes of the day than are his brother bishops; but, notwithstanding of the insinuations of the reformers and bards of that period, Lindsay appears to have been a man of unspotted virtue, and he certainly was a man of undoubted ability. Bishop Lindsay was one of the most spirited of all the prelates, and hence drew upon himself the especial hatred of the Covenanters. It is related of him, that being one time threatened with personal violence in case he should read the service-book in his cathedral, he went into the pulpit with a pair of pistols in his belt, and resolutely read out the liturgy; and his minister having become recusant, and refused to read the prayers as appointed in the service-book or Scottish edition of the liturgy, the bishop caused his own servant ascend the desk and read the service regularly. It would appear that King Charles held Lindsay in high estimation, for he selected this bishop to act when he was crowned King of Scotland, at Holyrood House, on 18th June 1633. The ceremonies on this occasion are described with great minuteness, and seem to have attracted no little attention from their near resemblance to Popish practices.

Bishop Lindsay, when translated to Edinburgh, met with ruder treatment than he had ever experienced in Brechin. On the Sabbath of 16th July 1637, an order was promulgated from the different pulpits in Edinburgh, for the introduction of the Scottish liturgy on the Sunday following. Accordingly, on 23d July 1637, the dean of St Giles' appeared in his surplice, and began to read the prayers, when an old woman, named Janet Geddes, rising with the tripod on which she had been seated, exclaimed, " Villain, dost thou say mass at my lug ! " and made the stool fly at the clergyman's head. All was immediately confusion; Bishop Lindsay, who was present, ascended the pulpit and endeavoured to allay the ferment; he was answered by volleys of sticks, stones, and stools; and had it not been for the assistance of the magistrates and influential nobility who attended this cathedral, in all probability the bishop would have been killed. As it was, Lindsay was much injured, and being then "a corpulent man," and not able to defend himself as he had done in his earlier days, he was carried off with great difficulty in the coach of the Earl of Roxburgh.

The great bell, as the session-house tablet informs us, was recast during Bishop Lindsay's incumbency. The session records state, that on 17th August 1630, " there was no session, because the minister was in Dundee agreeing with a skipper to take the great bell to Holland and found her of new, because she was riven." Immediately following this entry we find it recorded that James Peires left £300 to the kirk-session, " £200 thereof to the poor, and the third hundred to help the bell."

In 1629 there is a disposition by John Mortimer of Craigievar to Robert Arbuthnot of Findowrie of his desk and seat in the kirk of Brechin, which sometime pertained to Symer of Balzordie, *with the ground whereon the same stands,* but reserving the life-rent use thereof to Craigievar and Helen Symer his spouse ;—so the conveyances of seats in the church, whether legal or not, had commenced at an early period.

Bishop Whiteford, who succeeded Lindsay in the diocese of Brechin, met with pretty much the same treatment in the kirk of Brechin, in November 1637, as Lindsay had done under Mrs Geddes in Edinburgh ; and in consequence of the irritation of the inhabitants, and the pugnacious spirit displayed by them, Whiteford was obliged to flee from his see, his palace having been plundered, and his wife and children threatened, if not ill-used. The burgh records contain no account of these transactions, but we observe that for several weeks about the end of the year 1637, there was no session, " because the minister was in Edinburgh." In 1638 Whiteford fled the kingdom and went to England, where he obtained, in 1642, the see of Waldegrave in Northamptonshire, from King Charles, to whose person and fortunes he appears to have been decidedly attached. Whiteford died in England.

A curious agreement is extant, dated in 1637, between Bishop Whiteford, " with advice and consent of the chapter of the said bishoprick, on the first part," the Right Honourable Patrick Maule of Panmure, " one of his sacred Majesty's bed-chamber, on the second part," and the bailies, dean of guild, and town-treasurer, " with the advyce and consent of the counsell " of Brechin, on the third part. This document states that Mr Maule stood heritably infeft, "by his sacred Majesty" Charles I., with whom he was a great favourite, in the heritable offices of justiciary and constabulary within the city of Brechin, with power and liberty of election of one of the bailies of the burgh, "upon the resignation of Umquhile John, Earl of Mar, who was infeft therein, upon the resignation of Umquhile David, Earl of Crawford, authors to the Laird of Panmure;" but that disputes having arisen about Mr Maule's right, the king had, in 1635, directed a commission to the archbishop of St Andrews, and other prelates, for settling of all controversies, and that, in terms of the recommendation of these commissioners, it was agreed, in 1635, that, for the future, one bailie should be chosen by the bishop, one by the Laird of Panmure, and one by the town of Brechin, and that the Laird of Panmure should give a deputation of the offices of justiciar and constable to the bailie whom he named, "by doing whereof, all controversie betwixt the depute of the justiciar and the town, anent the jurisdiction therein, will be removed, whereas of before there has been still debait and contention, in matters of riot or bluid, the justiciar and his deputes claiming the samen to them, and the bailzies of the town also pretending right thereto." The charter chest of Panmure contains some long processes, in reference to the right to judge and punish in matters of "riot and bluid," claimed by the town and by the justiciar. The present magistrates, we daresay, would be most happy if Lord Panmure would relieve them of the trouble of deciding such "bluid wits" occurring now-a-days. This agreement, with some partial interruptions, was acted upon till the forfeiture by the Panmure family in 1715.

The disturbances in Scotland during the reign of Charles, have afforded materials for many volumes. It is not our province to detail these civil wars, but we must glance at them in so far as Brechin was affected by them. Suffice it for us to say, that the despotic attempts of James, and the still more despotic attempts of Charles, to force upon a rude people a mode of worship which certainly bore, in some of its forms, a likeness to the Roman Catholic ceremonies, led to serious wars between the king and the people, which finally terminated in the

E

decapitation of Charles, and the establishment of a miscalled republic, under the dictatorship of Oliver Cromwell. Many and severe were the struggles of parties before matters were thus settled. In March 1638, the solemn league and covenant was subscribed in the Greyfriars Church of Edinburgh, by the great majority of the barons and leading men of Scotland. Copies were immediately transmitted through the land, and were received with exultation in almost every quarter. The Bishop of St Andrews is reported, on hearing of these proceedings, to have exclaimed, " All we have done these last thirty years is at once undone." At this time a Committee of Estates, as it was called, assumed the temporary government of Scotland. In 1643 this body raised a regiment of horse, and "appointed 140 to come out of the sheriffdom of Forfar." Most likely these men were furnished by the landed interest ; but subsequently—as we are informed by Spalding, in his "History of the Troubles in Scotland and England "—there were " lifted out of the town of Edinburgh 1200 men, out of Dundee 180, out of Brechin and Montrose 110 men ; " and these assuredly were raised by the burgesses. Presuming Montrose and Brechin to have borne to each other the relative proportion of inhabitants which they now do, this would give about 36 men for Brechin ; and holding again that the proportion was just between Brechin and Edinburgh, it would show that the inhabitants of Brechin were then as one to thirty-one of those of Edinburgh, while at the last census they were about as one to twenty-three. " Ilk soldier (of this period we are told) was furnished with twa sarks, coat, breeks, hose and bonnet, bands and shoon ; a sword and musket, powder and ball for so many, and others, some a sword and pike, according to order ; and ilk soldier to have six shillings (sixpence sterling) every day, for the space of forty days, of loan silver ; ilk twelve of them a baggage horse worth £50, (Scots,) a stoup, a pan, a pot for their meat and drink, together with their hire or levy, or loan money ; ilk soldier estimate to ten dollars."

In 1644, Brechin was made the place of rendezvous for the Covenanters, and the Marquis of Argyle is said to have been joined in the September of that year, by the Earl Marischal, the

Lord Gordon, Lord Forbes, Lord Frazer, Lord Crighton, and other noblemen who met him at Brechin. In the following years the Covenanters again made Brechin their rallying-point, and Hurry and Baillie, the covenanting generals, assembled their troops at Brechin, in January 1645, with the view of intercepting the Marquis of Montrose in his descent upon the low countries. Hurry, who was a man of considerable abilities, left Brechin, with six hundred horsemen, one morning early in March, to reconnoitre the royal army, then lying at Fettercairn, but was led into an ambuscade and defeated by Montrose at the planting of Haulkerton, a little beyond the North Water Bridge. The covenanting army, although superior in numbers to the royal army, was deficient in training, and its generals were obliged to waive a battle, and to allow Montrose to proceed westward by the ridge of the Grampians; the Covenanters keeping between the Marquis and the low country. The covenanting and royal armies thus both marched westward at the same time, in parallel lines, but at a respectful distance from each other. Montrose, however, proved himself a second time an overmatch in policy for Generals Hurry and Baillie. By a stratagem, he passed the Covenanters, came down upon Dundee, sent his baggage and part of his troops on to Brechin in the end of March; and, after plundering Dundee, came with the rest of his army, by forced marches, to Arbroath, and then up to Careston, and so away into the Highlands over the Grampians, where he was joined by the baggage and the party which he had despatched to Brechin; and thus he eluded General Baillie, who was again in full pursuit after him. The citizens of Brechin are alleged to have been not a little alarmed when the royal troops came to visit them, and apparently they had too much reason, for Montrose is said to have burned and destroyed some fifty or sixty houses in the burgh. The kirk-session records state, that on 23d March 1645 there was "no preaching, neither collection, by reason of the enemies being in the town;" and on 31st March, there is an entry to the same effect. On 29th July 1645, a similar entry is repeated; and on 16th November of that year, we are informed there was no session in consequence of the absence of the ministers, "and of the enemie, Lodovick Lindsay, approaching near to the town." A minute under the date of

28th June 1647, is still more graphic: "No session, neither collection, by reason the sermon was at the Castle of Brechin for fear of the enemie." Another equally graphic entry occurs in November 1646: "Taken out of the box, (says the record,) to buy a mortcloth, £80; the first mortcloth was plundered by the common enemy and taken away." This "common enemy" seems, however, to have had some friends in Brechin, at least the session records insinuate as much, for on 28th February 1647, "the minister demands of the whole elders if any of them had drunken James Grahame's good health," which, of course, they all denied. Spalding, in reference to the visit by Montrose's troops in 1645, says, "The town's-people of Brechin hid their goods in the castle thereof and kirk steeples, and fled themselves, which flight enraged the soldiers; they herried their goods, plundered the castle and haill town, and burned about sixty houses." In the Balnamoon charter room there is a list of the losses sustained by the Laird of Findowrie and his tenants, through the Marquis of Montrose in 1646, and "by burning of his Ludging in Brechine," so that lairds as well as burgesses had suffered from the great marquis. General Baillie, however, having returned and again made Brechin his rendezvous, the courage of the people was somewhat restored, the more especially when they saw the covenanting general joined in Brechin by the Earl Marischal, the Viscount Frendraught, the Lord Frazer, the Master of Forbes, the Lairds of Boyne, Echt, Craigievar, Leslie, and most of the gentry in the surrounding country. Fortune was at this time against Montrose and the royal troops ; and the glorious victories of the Covenanters were unfortunately tarnished by the delivery of Charles I. to his English subjects in 1647 ; a transaction which reflected small credit upon either the buyer or seller, for, disguise it as we may, the delivery of Charles was little else than a money bargain between England and Scotland ; although we Scotsmen are fond enough to think that our ancestors were misled by the Southerns. Against this transaction, we are happy to say, the commissioner for the burgh of Brechin stood out, along with the commissioners for Forfar, Ross, and Tain. We regret we cannot record the names of these worthies, who showed themselves persons of sense and deliberation, when overzeal seems to have blinded the feelings of most men. Montrose, although defeated in 1647, was not a man to be easily put down. In 1650, he again raised the civil war in Scotland for behoof of Charles II., who then claimed the throne of his ancestors, but the Covenanters met Montrose with spirit, overcame him, and finally beheaded him. No sooner was it known that Montrose was in Scotland for another campaign, than the Estates, the covenanting party, directed David Leslie, their commander-in-chief, or as Father Hay, a keen royalist, was pleased to designate him, "Argyle's Postilion," to gather together, at Brechin, all those parties of horse and foot which, since the termination of the first campaign, had been dispersed over the country for its protection. During the wars of Montrose, therefore, it would appear that Brechin was esteemed the key of the covenanting army, and its situation immediately on the line between the Highlands and Lowlands, and commanding the only bridge then in existence over the South Esk, seems to have rendered it of importance in such a civil warfare. The burgh was much annoyed by this distinction, which rendered it an object to both parties. For several weeks in the end of August, and during the months of September and October 1651, there were " no sermon, collection, nor session, by reason both the ministers were absent, the English forces lying in garison round about this town and a garison in the Castle of Brechin," so the kirk records bear ; and they further inform us, that on 2d July 1651, there was " no session, neither sermon this Wednesday, by reason all within this burgh was called to go to Aberbrothock to assist them against the pursuing enemy by *sea;*" although in what manner the landsmen of Brechin were so to assist is not explained. Again, in November, we are told there was " no sermon this Wednesday, be reason twelff hundreth English were in the town, Tuesday all night, and on Wednesday till the time of Divine Service was past."

The country in the seventeenth century seems to have been much infested with vagrants. In 1615, John Mill, kirk-officer, and bailie John Liddle, are enjoined by Bishop Andrew Lamb and his session to go daily through the town and expel the " vagabonds and stranger beggars ; " and in subsequent years, these enactments are renewed in the records of the session of Brechin. Similar proceedings were adopted in most other parishes. The natural consequence of this state of things was, that the poor were compelled to feed on filthy garbage, and became infected with disease, which rose from the lowest to the highest, and raged in various shapes in different parts of Scotland, for several years, about this period. In 1604, the Scottish Parliament was obliged to meet at Perth to avoid the plague then raging in Edinburgh, and the disease seems to have gone on increasing and travelling northwards for many years afterwards. Great frosts and snow, which occurred in the seed-time of 1640, still further tended to increase the evil. Brechin was visited with the pestilence in 1647. The session records, after informing us that there was a public fast on 4th April, state " there was no session, neither collection, from the 4th April, by reason the Lord inflicted the burgh of Brechin with the infecting sickness until the 7th November ; " and even on the 7th November, when a collection is made, there is no session, by reason the minister and elders are afraid to keep company, or, as the records of the *Landward* session bear, " be reason the moderator and remanent sessions feared to convene under one roof." Indeed, the regular meetings of the session scarce seemed to have recommenced till 26th December 1647, although all business was not interrupted, for the records inform us, that " when it pleased the Lord that the sickness began to relent there were some persons contracted and married ; " such is life. *Cleansers* were at this time brought from Edinburgh, who, if we may judge from some of the entries in the session records, were not men of the best character, but what these cleansers did we have no means of ascertaining. Other parts of the session minutes show, that amidst this scene of death, there were scenes of folly. The terror of the disease seems to have extended to the country. The records of the parish of Menmuir of 11th April 1647, bear that " because of the forthbreaking of the plague in Brechin, the minister preached in the fields, therefore no collection ; " and from that date till 26th September, a similar entry is made every Sabbath. A stone built into the wall of the churchyard of Brechin, records that in 1647, no less than six hundred died of the plague in Brechin in the course of four months. The inscription is comparatively modern in point of workmanship, but most probably has been copied from an older stone. It runs thus :—

> "1647.
>
> Luna quater crescens,
> Sexcentos peste peremptos,—
> Disce mori,—vidit.
> Pulvis et umbra sumus."

Close by the stone is another, placed between double columns, supporting a Saxon arch, and recording in bold *alto relievo* lettering, the death in that year of Bessie Watt, spouse of *bailzie* David Donaldson, and their daughters, Elspet and Jean, all of whom most probably also died of the plague. The inscription is in very simple language: " Heir lyes Bessie Watt, spovs to David Donaldson, bailzie of Brechin, and Elspet Donaldson, and Jean Donaldson, their Dochters, 1647." From a sasine found amongst some old papers belonging to the town, it appears that, in 1633, Bailie Donaldson and Bessie Watt were owners of the house now belonging to Mr Thomas Ogilvy, on the High Street, the adjoining house, on the south, having then belonged to Lord Airly, the head of the clan Ogilvy, to whom it yet pays feu-duty.

The plague seems to have continued in and around Brechin for the greater part of the year 1648, for in January the treasurer of the session takes credit for thirty shillings, (Scots of course,) " given to William Ross lying in ane hutt ; " while in August it is twice recorded there was " no sessiòn be reasen the infection was begun again in the toun; " and finally, in October £3, 12s. additional are given " to buy malt and meall to those in the *hutts.*" These huts are said to have been erected in the Glen of Murlingden, and before the present garden of that property was made out we remember small mounds at different places which were reported to have been huts or houses pulled down over the inmates who had died there of the plague. It is to the honour of the then inhabitants of Brechin that amidst their own troubles they did not forget those of their neighbours, for in October 1648, no less than £42, 14s. 2d. (Scots we believe) are collected for the "distressed people in Montrose," where by this time, we presume, the "infecting seekness" had been worse than in Brechin.

In 1634 the South Esk suddenly subsided, from what cause was not known, at least is not reported ; but the fact is recorded and imputed as a sign of the troubles which then hung over the kingdom. Tradition has it, that the bed of the river was wholly dry for twenty-four hours, except at the Ee-o'-the-weil, and Stannachee, and that the water gradually subsided, and as gradually returned. Most probably the circumstance had arisen from a great drought. The subsequent winter was one of severe storm, and the greater part of the shipping on the east coast of Scotland was destroyed.

The town council possess few records of this period, but the kirk-session have several old volumes relating to this time. On the fly-leaf of one of them, there is the following note : " The town register evidencing that, in James Watt, reader and session-clerk, his time, the town and landward kept session weekly ; and for the landward collections an elder was appointed, for receiving and keeping the same, which was distributed by the direction of the minister and remanent elders, to the landward poor. Upon the 20th June 1624, the minister and landward elders, taking into their serious consideration, that the landward elders could not conveniently attend the town-session weekly, by reason of the distance of place, and their urgent and necessary labour and affairs at home, particularly in the oat and bere seed time, in summer season for casting, winning, and leading eldon, and in the harvest time : Therefore, after mature deliberation, resolved, and thought it expedient and most necessary to separate. Whereupon, it was condescended and agreed by the minister and elders, to keep the landward session on the Sabbath day, betwixt sermons, and to have a box for keeping the collections, and a register containing their acts, collections, penalties, and processes, and distributions. The book from the year 1624, containing these particulars above expressed, was taken away by the *common enemy,* and this book, de novo, begun on the 3d of March 1644." The sessions thus disjoined, continued separate till about 1708, when Mr Willison, then clergyman, seems to have taken considerable trouble in getting the

burgh and landward sessions again united. The session have
another volume, commencing in 1615 and ending in 1677, containing the "acts and ordinances of the kirk and session of
Brechin," and thus, amongst the different volumes, there is a
pretty correct report of the proceedings in the session. In these
volumes there are many curious entries. John Duncanson,
baxter, in 1619, applies to have "an act of slander against all
such as should object anything to him concerning Marion Mar-
now, a witch, that was burnt, which the session refused, till
further advisement." The same year the session resolved that
for every burial in the body of the church between the pillars,
there should be paid £20, and in the aisles and toofalls £10,
"all to the use of the kirk." On 13th December 1620, we
have this entry in the records of the church, "Given to the
session by John Donaldson and his brother, David Donaldson,
at their return from their sea voyage, £4, 4s., to be bestowed on
the poor." From similar subsequent entries, we learn that the
voyage was to London. In the same year, 1620, application
is made for assistance in building a bridge over Noran water, at
Courtford, when the session appoint a collection to be made
through the town, " both to help that bridge, and the Pow Bridge
betwixt Kinnaird and Auld Montrose, which our sovereign, King
James the Sixth, caused lay over for leading of his Majesty's
provision to Kinnaird, in 1617." Hence we might infer, what
we find elsewhere to be a fact, that James that year visited
David Carnegie at Kinnaird, whom he had the year previous
raised to the peerage, by the title of Lord Carnegie of Kinnaird.*

* James was a mighty hunter, although a most awkward horseman, and was
fond of pursuing the game in the muir of Monroumonth or Montreuthmont,
adjoining Kinnaird. In "Adamson's Muse's Welcome," printed at Edinburgh in
1618, there are some curious addresses presented to the king on his visit to
Scotland in 1617. One says :—

> " Stay then, (dread Leige,) O stay with us a while,
> With pleasing sports the posting time begyle ;
> Thy fynest hawks and fleetest hounds shall finde
> Of fowls and beasts, a prey of everie kynd.
> For morning both and evenyng flight, each day
> Each hawk thou hast, shall have her proper prey :
> Each fowl that flies shall meit thee in thy way,
> And in their sorts shall *Ave Cæsar* say."

These events are all during the time that Episcopacy was the form of worship recognised by the state.

The session records of 15th April 1650, state that the town and landward elders being convened after sermon, and it being shown by the minister that Mr John Fyfe refused to take the charge, to be an actual minister in this congregation, " they all being inquired whom they would nominate to that charge, they all, *una voce*, after due deliberation, nominated Master Laurence Skinner, to be conjunct minister with Mr William Raitt." We have not observed any previous mention of Mr Fyfe in the records, but whether there is such entry or not, this minute proves that the session then exercised the right of choosing the minister. The volume of records, commencing in 1615, gives a somewhat different version of the matter. There it is stated, " that on 13th March 1650, the minister, provost, bailies, council, and others within the burgh, and commissioners direct from the landward session, being convened for nominating and calling ane actual minister to this vacant kirk, and that be reason Mr John Fyfe refuses to embrace the charge, all in one voice did nominate Mr Laurence Skinner, minister at Navar, to be their minister, and colleague with Mr William Raitt;" and on 24th May, the same record tells us Mr Skinner " was heartily received by the magistrates and others of the parish, as their minister." The magistrates appear always to have formed constituent members of the session at this time, and every two or three years a list of the elders and deacons is made up, commencing with the provost and two bailies. Hence, the acts and ordinances of the session have much the character of the proceedings of a lay court, the magistrates carrying with them to the session their magisterial powers, and sending to *ward*, or jail, persons who did not implement the orders of the session. On the one hand, the session then assumed powers which are now vested wholly in the town council, and we find them repeatedly admitting individuals to the benefit of the hospital, and making a regulation, that applicants for this privilege shall be both examined and catechised publicly before the session, and that the person who has best insight in the grounds of religion shall be preferred: this entry is dated 24th November 1646. On the other hand, the absence of the magistrates was deemed sufficient reason for not holding a session ; thus 21st May 1662, "No session holden this day, by reason the magistrates went, immediately after sermon, to bring in the Trinity fair; " and similar entries frequently occur. Amongst other crimes which then engaged the attention of the dignitaries of the kirk, Sabbath-breaking frequently occurs ; some are punished for selling *ale*, others for winnowing corn, a few for frolicsome behaviour, and a good many for "yolking their carts, both in the burgh and landward," and going "to the moss." Where this moss was situated is not mentioned ; but apparently it had been at some distance, as the offenders are occasionally accused of commencing their labour before twelve o'clock of Sunday night; and it may thus be inferred, that they wished to have a long day for bringing home their *eldon*. A serious discussion is entered upon the minutes of the session in December 1649. One woman complains to the session against another for scandalising her, by calling her a witch ; and the party complained upon undertakes to prove that the complainer is actually a witch. Witnesses are called. One person swears that the suspected witch rubbed the witness's side, and then followed such a pain, that the witness could not bow herself for weeks; another, that his mother having refused to give the witch a little butter, could make no more butter that season ; a third, that the witch spoiled her *brewsts ;* and others, that a suspicious dog kept company with the witch, who was over-kind to the animal. The session sent the matter to the presbytery, and as we hear no more of it, we flatter ourselves that they gave the silly affair the go-by. The trial of witches was, however, common in this part of the country; and the minutes of the kirk-session of Menmuir, of 2d and 23d December 1649, tell us that there was "no lecture this week, because the minister was attending the committee appointed by the provincial assembly, for the trial of witches and charmers in their bounds." Tradition also informs us that unfortunate beings did suffer in Brechin for this imaginary crime ; and the hollow where the gas-work is now erected, bears the name of the Witch Den; digging in which, some years ago, a gentleman found a quantity of ashes mixed with human bones, and a piece of iron chain, tending to confirm the tradition, that witches had been burned in this place. Amongst the *archives* of the town is preserved an instrument called the witch's branks, an iron frame made to embrace the head, with a piece shaped like an arrow contrived to enter the mouth and prevent the criminal from speaking, and the whole fastening behind with a padlock, which might have been easily attached to a stake or a building. We should be truly thankful that the march of intellect has now banished such superstitions from Brechin. Amongst other minutes in the records of the session of 1650, there is one illustrative of the price of books in these days; stating that the session had " given to Catherine Williamson, to buy a New Testament, 16s."—Scots of course, but almost then equal to sterling money of the present time. In October 1654, there was a collection "for helping to build the bulwark of Aberbrothick;" and in October 1657, a similar collection for building the shore of Montrose; while the bridge of Tayock got an aid in October 1660.

All these events, for the proof of which we are indebted to the kirk-session records, being subsequent to 1640, of course, took place while Presbyterianism was predominant.

On 26th January 1662, the records of session state, " This day it was shown by the minister, that it is appointed by authority, that no session be keeped within this land till afterwards a way and liberty be opened and granted by authority hereafter; but only to keep session for writing up the collection and distributing charity to the poor." This entry is explained by another occurring on 3d August 1662, which says there was " no session holden this day, by reason it was the first Sabbath of the bishop his entry, and preached this day." This was Bishop David Strachan. Episcopacy was thus again re-established by Charles II.; and the ministers and elders went on under the bishop, in pretty much the same style as they had done during his absence. An elder is punished and deprived of his office, for permitting piping and dancing in his house on a Sabbath, and "having many more at his daughter's marriage than was appointed;" others are punished for less peccadilloes; and in April 1670, there is a collection made to assist the inhabitants of Dundee in rebuilding their shore.

The different clergy of the period embraced in this chapter seemed to have vied with each other in gifts to the church, probably with the view of purchasing the good opinion of their hearers. In 1643, as a tablet affixed to the wall of the session-house informs us, " Mr Alex. Bisset, minr. at Brechin, gifted a silver cup for the communion table; " and in 1648, " Mr Wm. Rait, minr. at Brechin " made a similar gift. These silver cups, presented by Presbyterian clergymen, are still in use. The same authority tells us that in " 1655 Mr Laurence Skinner, minister at Brechin, gave the church's great Bible; " and that in " 1665 Dauid B. of Brechin gifted the orlidg on the steepel," a clock which, we believe, continued to mark time to the people of Brechin till pulled down, when the cathedral was repaired sixty years ago. But the greater dignities of the church were not the only benefactors of it. The tablet referred to informs us that in " 1660, John Mil, church-officer, gave three tinne basins for serving in administration of the sacrament," which basins continue to be so employed at the present time, and are interesting as illustrative of the state of popular feeling in 1660, each having a pretty good likeness of Charles I. embossed in the centre. Round the margin of each plate or basin, there is an inscription to this effect:—" Pelvis Ecclesiæ Brechineensi Dedicata Ut Eeidem In Administratione Sacramentorum Inserviat, Anno 1660." The inscription varies slightly on the different plates. A rose, impressed on the margin of each basin, would lead us to infer that the basins are of English workmanship.

The records of the burgh for this period, as already said, are extremely scanty, arising no doubt from the unsettled state of the times ; but amongst the few records which do exist, we find one dated 26th June 1656, " By his Highness' council in Scotland," bearing that the council having received good information that the town of Brechin was, in former times, the seat where the commissary court for the shires of Forfar and Kincardine respectively were kept, and that it is the most convenient place for the two shires ; therefore, the council directed " that from henceforth the commissary court of the said shires respectively be kept at Brechin, aforesaid, until further orders." This document is signed " Broghill, president; " and was issued during

the protectorate of Oliver Cromwell, when the civil administration of Scotland was committed to a council of state, composed
of nine persons, seven Englishmen and two Scotsmen, of which
council Lord Broghill was president. The name of the commissary of this period is not extant; but as most of the com-
missariots were then filled by English military officers, very
likely the commissariot of Brechin was put under similar command. When the commissary court of Brechin was abolished in
1824, and the duties of it transferred to the sheriff, the parishes
of Strachan, Glenbervie, and Caterline were the only places in
Kincardineshire which were connected with the commissariot
of Brechin. But, curiously enough, Michael Hill, within the
policies of Brechin Castle, was understood to be in the diocese
of Dunkeld, while part of Aldbar was in the commissariot of St
Andrews. All these anomalies were corrected in 1824, by making each sheriff the commissary within his own county.

During the seventeenth century, the exports of Brechin consisted chiefly of malt and half-tanned hides ; and to almost every
property in the burgh belonged either a kiln and coble, or a tan-
pit. The other manufactures were few, and such only as supplied the most pressing wants of the immediate neighbourhood ;
bonnets, shoes, blankets, and coarse cloth. Altogether the state
of the people seems to have been very uncomfortable, deprived
of the support which they formerly received from the church,
distracted by civil wars, and without manufactures, and on many
occasions without food.

We must, however, bring this long chapter to a close. The
period of time embraced in it is not great, but this period, from
1600 to 1670, witnessed events of no small importance to Scotland : the accession of James VI. to the English throne ; the
succession, dethronement, and death of his son Charles I. ; the
protectorate of Oliver Cromwell ; the succession of Cromwell's
son Richard to, and retirement from, the same proud eminence ;
and the recall of Charles II. to the throne of his ancestors ; the
abolition of Episcopacy ; the establishment of Presbyterianism ;
and the restoration of the authority of the bishops. It was
during the currency of the time embraced in this chapter, also,
that a very melancholy event occurred in Brechin. Robert

Symmer, son of the Laird of Balzordie, having quarrelled with David Grahame, son of James Grahame of Leuchland, the two met on the "Hauche of Insche,· neir to the Meiklemylne of Brechin," on 30th April 1616, when Symmer struck Grahame "throw the body with ane rapper-sword; quhair of sex or seven days thereafter he decessit." For this crime Symmer was tried before the High Court of Justiciary on 18th March 1618; found guilty by the verdict of assize, and sentenced "to be tane to the mercat-croce of Edinburgh, and thair his heid to be striken from his body, and all his moveable guidis to be escheit,"—forfeited to the Crown.

The most remarkable literary character of this period was Thomas Dempster, who by one author is said to have been born of a family of little note in Brechin, and by another to have been the son of the Laird of Muiresk in Aberdeenshire, where he was born in 1579. He was educated first at Aberdeen College, and afterwards became a student at the University of Cambridge. Being a zealous Catholic, he went to France about the time of the Reformation, and obtained a professor's chair at Paris, "when," says Boyle, "though his business was to teach a school, he was more ready to draw his sword than his pen." In conse-quence of his quarrelsome disposition, he was obliged in a short time to return to England, where he married Susanna Waller, a woman of uncommon beauty, with whom he soon after went again to Paris. Here the lady, vain of her charms, while walk-ing the public streets, exhibited more than an ordinary portion of her breast and shoulders, which attracted such a mob, that she and Dempster were both nearly trodden to death. Dempster obtained, by competition, a professorship in the university of Nimes, and soon after a vacant chair and a large salary in the University of Pisa. But here his comfort and usefulness were suddenly marred by the conduct of his "beautiful wife," who eloped with one of his scholars. Leaving Pisa, Dempster pro-ceeded to Bologne, and was appointed professor of Greek, in the university of that town, in which situation he continued till his death, in 1625. Chambers describes Dempster as "a learned professor and miscellaneous writer, born at Brechin, in the county of Angus." During his life he enjoyed an extensive reputation;

his published works were many and various; but the principal
of them was an "Ecclesiastical History of Scotland," in "XIX
beuks." Speaking of him as an author, an eminent critic says,
"It would perhaps be difficult to point out another Scottish
writer of his time, who had the same intimate acquaintance with
classical antiquity." King James, in 1615, appointed Dempster
to the office of Historiographer Royal.

Another literary man of this period connected with Brechin
was William Guthrie, a person of a very different character from
Dempster. William Guthrie, author of the well-known work,
"The Christian's Great Interest," was born at Pitforthy, near
Brechin, in the year 1620. His father, who was proprietor of
that estate, had five sons, four of whom devoted themselves to
the ministry. Of these William was the eldest, and to qualify
himself for the profession he had chosen, he acquired a very
superior classical education, studied divinity at St Andrews
under Mr Samuel Rutherford, received licence to preach in 1642,
and in 1644 was ordained minister of Fenwick in Ayrshire.
During the "troublesome times" that followed, Mr Guthrie was
by no means an idle spectator. When not engaged in his
parochial duties, he was with the army as a chaplain, or assist-
ing in conducting the business of church courts. At the restoration of Charles II. and re-establishment of Episcopacy, he was
ejected from his living, and returned to Pitforthy, where the
affairs of the family required his presence. He had only been
there a short time when a complaint which had preyed upon his
constitution for many years, rapidly increased. After some days
of great pain, in the intervals of which he cheered his relations
with his prospects of happiness in another and better world, he
died in the house of his brother-in-law, the Rev. Lawrence
Skinner, at Brechin, on the 10th of October 1665, and his body
was interred in the cathedral church, below the pews belonging
to the estate of Pitforthy.

Various donations were given to the church during the period
we have been considering, as recorded on a board in the session-
house, which, as stated in the session minutes of 1683, was then
put up to record the mortifications that till then had been made
to the church, and those which might *afterwards* be made;

showing a grateful sense of favours expected, a gratitude still existing. In 1680 Walter Jameson, bailie and kirk-master, gave two quart stoups for the communion table, which are still in use; Bishop Strachan's widow, Mrs Anna Barclay, gifted £33, 6s. 8d. in 1682; and in 1690 Mr John Glendei, dean of Cashels and prebend of St Michael's, Dublin, who had likely been a native of Brechin, gave £40.

CHAPTER V.

OUR further labours will be so far lightened, that we have now
the council records of the burgh to refer to for our guide. The
earliest existing volume of these records commences in 1672, and
is thus titled by the clerk: " Heir followis the acts off the Toun
Council off the Citie off Brechin, begun ano 1672 : Balyiess then
Geo. Steill, Da. Donaldson, Da. Liddell." This is succeeded by
the following pious inscription : " Incepto Libro Sit Laus et
Gloria Christo, Gloria perpetua sit tribuenda Deo, (signed) Jo.
Spence." The tradition is, that in 1745, the Highland troops
used the council-room and court-room as guard-rooms, broke
open the presses, and destroyed all the books and papers which
they found there ; and that the books which do exist previous to
that date, were only saved by being in the town-clerk's private
house, while the other documents saved were preserved by being
deposited in a press in the church steeple. Certain it is, that ·
the oldest *book* of records belonging to the burgh, is a record of
instruments of sasine commencing in 1648.

The town-clerk of the period was John Spence, who signs the
pious inscription quoted ; he was of a family who long held this
office. A mortuary stone in the churchyard of Brechin records
that John Spence, merchant in Brechin, who died about 1640,
had a son John, who was town-clerk of Brechin, and died in
1689, being the gentleman who commences the first existing
volume of our records. In 1678 Mr Spence's salary as town-
clerk was fixed at one hundred merks Scots, and in 1679 all
investments within the town are ordered to be given by him.
Previously the clerk seems to have drawn the feus and mortifi-

cations payable within the town.as a recompense for his labours. In October 1681, George Spence is nominated clerk with his father, in a well written minute, which is signed by the bishop and all the councillors in a very neat manner, and the office is given to them jointly and to the survivor. George died in 1717, having previously, in June 1713, commenced the second volume of the council records with the same inscription as his father had begun the first, and in November of that year his only son John is appointed helper and successor. This John, as the stone in the churchyard tells us, died in 1773, having been town-clerk for fifty-six years; and he again was succeeded by his only son John, who was made conjunct with his father in 1748, and died in 1790, after holding the office for forty-two years. It is worthy of remark that a John Spence was also town-clerk of Montrose in 1736, for in that year we find a charter in his favour of the Chanory House. Most likely he was a cousin of the John Spence who died in 1773, for he could scarcely be the same person monopolising the same office in both burghs. In 1788, John Spence, elder and younger, had been appointed conjunct clerks, with right to the office to the survivor, and this last John Spence died in 1817. Mr Alexander Ritchie, who had married his cousin, Miss Spence, was appointed depute-clerk to his brother-in-law, John Spence, in 1790, and having apparently managed the whole business after that, he was, in June 1796, conjoined to the office with John Spence. Thus the family of Spence were continuous town-clerks of Brechin for more than one hundred and fifty years. We were conjoined in office with Mr Ritchie in Nov. 1825, and he died in Nov. 1826, and as he was in a measure a Spence, it may be said we were the first stranger in the office, which we resigned in 1864, when the present official, Mr James Loudon Gordon, was appointed town-clerk.

This first volume of the town council records alluded to, commences with a minute, intimating that the convention of royal burghs had resolved to protect Brechin against certain encroachments on the Common Muir, made by the lairds in the neighbourhood. The entry almost immediately following this, is one appointing a committee of the council to go to Arbroath, and there to treat with the other commissioners from Dundee and Montrose, "for a settlement with Robert Carnegy of Newgate, anent his encroachment on their common lands." The lands of Newgate still continue as much a subject of debate to the good folks of Arbroath, as the lands of the Common Muir do to the citizens of Brechin, and one hundred and ninety years do not seem to have much changed the tempers of parties interested in these respective lands.

A minute of rather an inhospitable nature is found amongst the first records in the volume. It is entitled "An act against keeping of strangers by the inhabitants;" because, as the act states, "vagabonds and outcountry people" came in their poverty to reside in the burgh, and swallowed up the charity which properly belonged to the poor of the place. It is to be feared that Montrose's wars had sent too many poor vagabonds to wander the country at that time.

About the same period, there occurs an act of the town council, curiously illustrative of the then state of the country. This act bears that the magistrates and council, finding it has proved greatly to the disadvantage of the town of Brechin, "and has ruined the change-houses," and prejudiced other trades, in this, that strangers have not been encouraged these many years past, to frequent this place on their road south and north for the want of horses to furnish them with; therefore the council ordains a postmaster to be chosen yearly, who is to be bound to keep two horses of "furtie punds price the piece," and who is to be allowed "twelve pennies of ilk pund of hire from everie other person who shall hire horses within the town," and have also the privilege of pressing horses accustomed to be hired for the use of strangers. John Hall is immediately after named postmaster. The office appears to have been profitable, for, in 1674, it is exposed for sale by public roup.

The first election of councillors, of which there is any record, is that of 26th September 1673. The council then proceeded, according to the practice of the *good old times*, first to elect themselves, then to set a leet of six persons for bailies " of the whilk number (the record bears) my Lord Bishop of Brechin has named and appointed David Donaldson, younger, to continue and officiate as his lordship's bailie, from Michaelmas ensuing, 1673, to Michaelmas 1674, and have referred the remanent five persons to ane noble earl, George, Earl of Panmure, to nominate and choose one of the saids persons as his lordship's bailie and justiciar." A treasurer is then elected, and the minute of that day closes. On 30th September the council are assembled, when there is presented a commission and presentation granted to John Liddell, by Mr Ersken, factor and commissioner for the Earl of Panmure, nominating Liddell to be "the said noble earl his bailie and justiciar-depute the said year." By "pluralitie of voices," the . council then "nominated and appointed David Liddell to continue and officiate as town's bailie; "and (as the minute records) the bailies, council, and dean of guild, have nominated Andrew Allan as dean of guild for said year." Thereafter, an hospital-master is elected, and the minute closes by a statement, that "the said day the court being fenced, the bailies for the last year did demit their office." Upon the 3d October following, a head court of the burgh is held, and the following entry made: "The roll of the whole inhabitants being called and diverse being absent, therefore unlawed ilk absent in the sum of five punds money, and ordains letters and executorials to be direct against them therefore." No other business *ever* appears to have been done at the annual head court of the burgh of Brechin, which was thus nothing more than a mere formality; for as the names of the absentees were never entered, no fines could be enforced against them.

The guildry record of the same period, 13th October 1673, bears that "Andrew Allan, of new chosen dean of guild, did compear and did accept of his office;" a treasurer is then elected by the guildry from a leet of two persons named by the guildry, and the minute closes thus: "Nomina Concilij Gildi, John Liddell, late dean gild, James Henderson, treasurer, David Donaldson, younger, David Liddel." It will be remarked that Donaldson was the bailie named by the bishop; John Liddell the bailie named by Lord Panmure, and David Liddell the town's bailie, while James Henderson was a councillor of the burgh; so that the town council seem to have had the whole sway in the guildry at that time, although by act of the guildry in October

1671, it was specially appointed that the council should consist of five members, the dean of guild, the box-master, and other three persons, "who shall be nominate, with common consent, by plurality of voices out of the said fraternity" of guildry. The same influence predominates during the whole period embraced in this chapter of our history ; in 1683, Robert Strachan is received brother guild, gratis, at the request of my Lord Bishop, then provost of Brechin ; and in 1698 the provost and bailies are named *before* the dean in his own court. The proceedings of the guildry, during the period alluded to, are chiefly confined to the regulation of their own internal affairs. On the 9th February 1676, Christian Wilson, daughter of Charles Wilson, was admitted a guild *brother*, or as the minute more properly phrases it, "a free person" of the guildry. In 1697, this lady got a husband, John Guthrie, and he was gallantly received a member of the guildry in respect of the payment formerly made by his wife. The right of sitting in the front seat of the loft in the church of Brechin occupied no little of the time of this incorporation. In October 1676, the guildry "have thought fit that there be one nominate to sit in the principal place of the loft in the church, and for that end, John Skinner is appointed, and failing of him, John Allan, to sit in that seat *for the year to come*,"—a pretty long sederunt. Three years afterwards this is remedied by appointing the treasurer to enjoy that proud eminence " ilk Lord's-day," but the treasurer is enjoined to " come in timeously before the last bell rings." If we may trust the church records of this period, the sway exercised gave a man little choice whether he should go to church "timeously" or not ; for it would appear, if he had not attended, he would have been exposed both to the spiritual ban of the clergy, and the temporal power of the civil magistrate. At the beginning of the volume of records of the session commencing in 1678, are engrossed the " acts, statutes, and ordinances, according to the rules set down in the old register, anno 1615, and others added." Some of these acts are severe enough. " Imprimis, (says the record,) it is statute and ordained that all, both in town and landward, shall repair to the church on the Lord's-day to hear God's Word ; whosoever shall be found absent without a relevant excuse, shall pay for the first fault 5s. Scots, and so *toties quoties* doubling it, with their *public* repentance." It is also ordered that all within the town shall repair to the "hearing of sermon on the week day, and on Thursday at the exercise, under the penalty of 40 pennies, dispensing with the servants their absence on these days." To enforce these rules, the collectors of charity were to go through the town during the time of service and take down the names of offenders. Many other rules equally severe are enacted, and amongst the rest, "It is statute and ordained that whosoever shall be found drunk shall be admonished by the elders *pro primo*, and if they continue in that sin, shall be delated to the session, and then to be charged to appear there to acknowledge their offence, and shall be punished according to the discretion of the minister and elders, both in purse and private repentance ; and if they continue in that sin, they shall satisfy publicly." These enactments, be it remembered, were made during the prevalence of Episcopacy, for it was not till 1640 that Presbyterianism was predominant, and Episcopacy was restored in 1662.

Brechin was burned in 1672. The presbytery records of 21st March 1672, have this entry on the subject : "This day the magistrates of the burgh of Brechin appeared, presenting the sad and deplorable condition of the distressed people in this town through great losses by a devouring fire on the third of this instant, betwixt one and two after midnight, whereby their dwelling-houses, insight plenishing, corn in barns and barn yards, were destroyed, and supplicated a recommendation to the several kirks within the presbytery for charitable support, which was granted." Subsequently, these records tell us that the sums collected were as follows :—" Marietoun, £8, 10s. 6d. ; Craig, £13, 6s. 8d. ; Montros, £66, 13s. 4d. ; Logie, £10, 13s. 4d. ; Dun, £9, 6s. 8d. ; Stracathro, £17, 1s. 6d. ; Edzell, £10 ; Lethnot, £8, 8s. ; Navar, £4, 10s. ; Menmuir, £20, 1s. 6d. ; Fearn, £12, 13s. 4d. ; Othlo, £5, 10d. ; Carrotstoun, £3. No collection at Farnell, by reason there is no minister there ; Kynnaird only deficient.' These collections serve to give an idea of the respective wealth of these different parishes in 1672. The council records give no direct account of this fire. On a loose slip of paper, now bound up with the council book, there is an entry under date 6th November 1672, bearing that "the council taking to consideration the condition of those who had the loss by the late fire, and that there are some that have lost all their subjects," therefore ordered an accompt to be taken of the money collected and distributed ; "and ordains that yet there shall be the sum of four-score punds distributed amongst those who have not houses burned, at the distribution of the bailies and council, and the superplus to be bestowed for rebuilding the houses." On 18th May 1674, we find an entry in the council book renewing the order for an account of the money " given for charity by this burgh and parish, and several other of our good neighbours, for the help of those who were sufferers in the late sad accident of burning ; " and in June following, the accompt is given in, bearing that there had been collected from the burghs of Dundee, Forfar, Arbroath and Montrose, and the presbyteries of Dundee, Forfar, and Brechin, and the presbytery of the Mearns, £479, 6s. Scots. The session records of Arbuthnott state that, on 2d June 1672, a sum of £6 Scots had been collected at the kirk door of that parish for the benefit of the persons in the town of Brechin who had suffered by fire. From these entries we may conclude that the fire had been purely accidental, but that it had done considerable damage. And as we find the council employed at different times down to 1676, in regulating the distribution of the money collected, it would appear that they had found no small difficulty in pleasing all parties in regard to it.

Brechin sent a representative to Parliament in 1585, and continued to do so till the Union.

A number of the entries in the burgh records of the seventeenth century refer to the expenses which the burgh incurred by sending a commissioner to Parliament; and occasionally differences seem to have existed between the representative and the constituents, as to the sufficiency of the sums remitted for his support. Other matters, however, also engrossed the council, matters which would now seem as strange as paying a salary to a member of Parliament; and not a few acts and ordinances were then made by the town council of Brechin, which would scarce be observed by the burgesses of the present day. Thus, in 1674, it is enacted that no person shall put any of their male children, above ten years of age, to any school without or within the burgh, except the grammar-school, under the pain of £20 Scots.

The gentleman whose school was thus fostered by a penalty was Mr John Dempster, a great favourite with the then town council. In September 1674, Mr John Dempster was appointed by the bishop to supply his charge as minister, upon which the council nominated Mr James Dempster assistant schoolmaster ; and, in the June following, Mr James Dempster is promoted to be principal schoolmaster ; Lord Panmure, then patron of the præceptory of Maisondieu, having presented him to the emoluments arising from that endowment.

But while matters went on thus smoothly with the heads of the church, one of the inferior officers gave the council no small annoyance. Robert Strachan, kirk-officer, presumed to " vilipend and abuse the bailies," and to declare that he cared not a —— for all the bailies in Brechin. An act of council is therefore made on 22d March 1675, embodying all this in the *plainest* language, and a copy of the act is sent to the bishop, Mr Robert Lawrie, who lived in Edinburgh, and officiated as one of ·the ministers of Edinburgh. My lord bishop immediately writes back to his " much honoured and very good friends, the magistrates and town council of Brechin," condoling with them on the enormity of the offence committed, and authorising them to dismiss the offender. The council accordingly nominated James Liddell, and presented him as kirk-officer to the session ; when the minister, Mr Laurence Skinner, declared his willingness to receive Liddell, if it was the bishop's pleasure, upon seeing a confirmation of the nomination under the bishop's own hand ; and yet, withal, he declared that he could not receive him presently as kirk-officer, because it being a church office, he humbly conceived that before Liddell be actually admitted to officiate, it was expedient that his election be authorised by some one clothed with church power for that end ; and in this resolution Mr Skinner is confirmed by the " commissioners direct from noblemen heritors, and other inferior heritors ; " but on 28th April, a very tart letter, written by the

bishop " with his own hand," is produced, confirming all that
the magistrates had done, "whereupon Mr Laurence Skinner
protested against the sudden procedure of the bailies and town
council," &c., which protestation, however, " the bailies prohibited the clerk of the session to insert in the town session book,
and that under the highest pains ; " but Mr Skinner " commanded
the clerk to insert it, the next Lord's day, in the landward session
book, which was done accordingly, and there it is extant," says
that record.   We suspect Mr Patrick Brokas the session-clerk,
who appears to have been an intelligent and pains-taking man, had
also been a prudent one, and while complying so far with the in-
junctions of the minister, had had the terror of the bishop before
his eyes, as he cuts short Mr Skinner's protest with an " et cetera."
Strachan was accordingly discharged, but behold ! in July my
lords of the Privy Council take a different view of the matter, and
Strachan is then restored by the town council, "conform to the will
of the foresaid decreet of the lords of the Privy Council, letters of
horning following thereupon and charge given to the magistrates."
Strachan is mentioned as continuing kirk-officer in 1684.

The tolbooth of the burgh has always been a source of annoyance to the council.   In October 1675, one debtor escaped, and
the council were in fears about other two.   They therefore appointed the jail to be watched night and day by two " armed
able men," to be furnished alternately by the incorporations of
the smiths, glovers, bakers, shoemakers, weavers, tailors, merchants, maltmen, and wrights.   In 1683, a debtor of some note
is recorded as offering the town-officers considerable sums to let
him go free ; and therefore the council very wisely apply to have
him *transported* to some other burgh.   Besides the town-officers,
the magistrates of that time possessed an official who has since
been dispensed with—the town's-piper—and to that office we
find a John Wyslie admitted on 20th June 1688, to whom there
is assigned a salary of ten merks yearly, " by and attour the
good will of the town's-people."   Wyslie was discharged in
January 1691, because he did not perform the duties of his
office, in going regularly through the city morning and evening,
but in 1698 he is again restored, likely upon promise of better
behaviour.   The person who held this office of town's-piper

about 1750, was wont, after his perambulations through the town to rouse the inhabitants from their couches, to terminate his journey opposite the White Swan Inn, then the principal inn of the burgh, on the site of which the Union Bank is now built, in what was then called the Meal Market Wynd, now denominated Swan Street, and where the piper blew his chanter till mine host of the Swan gave him a " mornin'," which, we have understood, was generally ample, and the glass was duly emptied by the piper with a significant nod to the landlord, and a hearty " heer's till him "—both gentlemen were out in the " fourty-five." The office seems gradually to have fallen into abeyance, the town withdrew the salary, the incorporations withheld their grants, the inhabitants became chary of giving money for such music, and towards the close of the eighteenth century the piper ceased to play ; the latest notice which we find of the musician being the grant of a coat for him by the guildry in 1796. This last of the pipers was named Low. He lived at the Gallowhill, or where the North Port Distillery is now situated. He discharged the duties of his office by playing through the town in the morning at 5 o'clock, and in the evening at 7 o'clock, while then, as now, the great bell was rung during summer at 6 o'clock morning, and during the winter at 7 o'clock morning, and each evening at 8 o'clock ; the piper serving as the precursor of the bellman, or a warning for those who preferred early hours.

The crop of 1674 appears to have been deficient. In March 1674, the session records tell us there was " intimate a day of humiliation to be keeped through the whole presbytery the next Lord's day, by reason of the great storm of snow and frost lying on the ground in the spring time of the year, when the seed ought to be sown in the ground." In 1675, there appears also to have been a bad harvest, for on the 25th July of that year, a fast is proclaimed, "first, to mourn for the contempt and disobedience of the gospel and holy ordinances; second, for the great increase and prevalence of aitheism and profanity in the land ; third, for the sinful undervaluing the great blessing of peace so long enjoyed under his Majesty, (the *pious* Charles II. ;) and fourth, because the Lord is angry with this land, threatening the destruction of the fruits of the ground, necessary provision for man and beast, and

that by a long continued drouth, threatening the plague of famine." In November 1675, the town council approve of a de-
duction from the treasurer's account of £52 Scots, lost by the sale
of 24 bolls of meal " that was bought up by the town, and was
sold out to the poor people the last summer, during the time of
the scarcity of victual." The price of the meal is not mentioned.
The crop of 1681 was also deficient, if we may believe a proclamation issued by the Privy Council, and noticed in the session-book,
enjoining a fast, because, " first of abuse of peace and plenty, and
contempt of the gospel ; next, because many have departed from
the communion of the national kirk ; thirdly, because the Lord's
wrath is manifested by afflicting the land with a long scorching
drought, making the heavens as brass, and the earth as iron,
binding up the clouds, threatening thereby to consume the
fruits of the ground, necessary provision for sustaining the life of
man and beast ; lastly, to pray for a blessing to the ensuing
Parliament, which is to sit down at Edinburgh, 28th July next."
This proclamation was issued by Charles II. ! Mr Laurence
Oliphant, writer in Edinburgh, was then agent for the town ; and
in August 1681, that gentleman craves the council to send him
eight or ten bolls meal, in part payment of his account—the
scarcity in Edinburgh probably having reduced Mr Oliphant to
this necessity.

Amongst other devices fallen upon by Charles II. for raising
money, was the farming the duties then imposed as excise. The
records of Brechin state, that on 13th May 1676, bailie David
Donaldson was authorised to offer for the excise of the burgh for
that year, the sum of a thousand merks Scots, " and if he find
it convenient to go the length of twelve hundred merks," equal
to £66, 13s. 4d. sterling. It is not stated whether the offer of
the burgh was accepted ; but for that year, and for some years
afterwards, " a month and a quarter's supply " is ordered to be
raised "in lieu of excise," from which we conclude some arrangement had been made to save the burgh from the gaugers
of that period.

In 1676, for the first time, we find the collector or convener,
and the deacons of crafts, called to vote on the election of the
town's bailie. When the council became possessed of the right

to elect all the magistrates, the trades also had the privilege to vote on the leet set by the council for provost and bailies, a right which the deacon convener and deacons enjoyed till the reform act of 1833 threw the election of the whole council into the hands of the ten pound voters, and since then the council thus elected choose out among themselves the magistrates and office-bearers.

However much the body of the inhabitants of Brechin may have been inclined to Presbyterianism, the ruling party seem, after the restoration of Episcopacy in 1662, to have gone hand in hand with the court. Defection in high places was not much to be wondered at during a time when men's minds were so unsettled. Nay, defection seems to have gone down to the lowest classes, for we even find that the renowned Jenny Geddes, who first put out a hand against Episcopacy in 1637, gave all the inflammable materials in the booth where she carried on the trade of a green-grocer, to raise a bonfire in honour of the coronation of King Charles in 1661. It is not to be wondered at, then, that the magistrates of Brechin of 1678, cheerfully sent Mr David Donald-son as commissioner to the Parliament summoned " in order to the levying of forces for defence of the kingdom from foreign invasion *and for suppression of field conventicles,*" a mode of preaching in wilds and glades, resorted to by the persecuted Presbyterians, who were prohibited under severe penalties from worshipping God according to the dictates of their own conscience. As we find no mention of conventicles in this neighbourhood, and as there are not, so far as we know, any memorials of Cove-nanters in the town of Brechin or surrounding country, we presume that the spirit of the people, like that of their rulers, had now readily bent to Episcopalian sway. At any rate, Bishop Hali-burton, who was inducted into the see of Brechin in 1678, seems to have been determined to assume all the temporal, as well as all the spiritual power, attached to his office ; for the minute of the annual election of councillors in September 1678, commences by declaring that there were " convened personally, the Right Reverend Father in God, George Lord Bishop of Brechin, as also," the bailies and councillors; and frequently afterwards, when any business of importance fell to be transacted, the bishop took his place at the council board. Haliburton's attention to civil matters does not appear to have interrupted the proper discharge of his ecclesiastical duties, for he often presided at meetings of session, frequently preached during week-days, and was always present at Christmas, although, as we believe, he did not generally reside in Brechin. After his translation to the see of Aberdeen, we find it stated in the session records of Brechin, that on 20th September 1683, " Bishop Haliburton preached on the Lord's day, forenoon text, Matthew, 5th chapter, 7th verse," it being then the practice to enter in the records of the session, not only the names of all the preachers, but the respective texts from which they preached.

The arbitrary proceedings of Charles II. and his advisers produced as much discontent as the despotic proceedings of his immediate predecessors, and the kingdom was kept in a ferment during the whole of his reign, which closed in 1685. In 1679 occurred the battle of Bothwell Bridge, between the Presbyterians and Royalists, and in the same year Archbishop Sharpe was murdered by a party of the Noncomformists in Fife. In consequence a general arming of the kingdom was ordered, and the council of Brechin named David Donaldson, younger, then dean of guild, to be captain on the east side of the town, James Cowie to be lieutenant, and Francis Molison, ensign ; and for the west side of the town Laurence Skinner, late bailie, was appointed captain, William Gray, lieutenant, and Alexander Millar, ensign; the captains being authorised to choose their inferior officers. The valorous deeds of these heroes are not on record. Probably their labours were confined to pretty much the same duty as was discharged by the constables, who, till the establishment of a regular police, were annually elected, and who were governed by officers bearing the same high-sounding titles of distinction which were given to the military gentlemen of 1679. The arms belonging to the burgh are subsequently stated to be twenty-seven halberts, ten muskets, nine pairs of bandiliers, " and ane pudder horne," five pikes, two half pikes, and five swords, "by and attour the three swords which the officers have." A quarter of a month's cess was also levied at this time for payment "of the militia at the rendezvouse," a body of troops differing from the burgh soldiers in the same respect that the modern local militia differed from the volunteers. The number of militiamen raised by the burgh is not mentioned; but in 1685 John Strachan, William Crabb, and George Scott, shoemakers, along with a James Tindall, and a person bearing the appropriate name of David Cadger, fishmonger, are all admitted burgesses gratis, because they undertook to go out as militiamen from the burgh for seven years.

These warlike preparations, however, seem not to have altogether abstracted the attention of the council from municipal affairs, for in October 1679 the passage, as it is termed, at the North Port, is ordered to be made up "for convenience of passage of carts over the burn and up to the Port;" the Port being then situated at what is now the point of junction between the dwelling-house belonging to the North Port brewery and the house immediately south of it. Good drink also seems to have been worthy of notice about this period; at least in May 1680 this "David Donaldson, younger," so often mentioned, and whose death is recorded as having occurred in 1684, is commissioned to go south, and endeavour to obtain a remission of the excise fines then imposed upon the malsters in the burgh, for "nonconformity" to laws which have often been evaded by the inhabitants of Brechin since that period.

In 1681 an Act of Parliament was passed, ordaining all persons in public office to take a certain oath to Government; and at the annual election of that year we find this oath recorded as sworn by the councillors and deacons of crafts of Brechin. The form is very solemn, though the right of the king to impose such an oath may be doubted by many in the present age. The swearers declare in presence of the eternal God, whom they invocate as judge and witness, that they profess the true Protestant religion, contained in the Confession of Faith recorded in the first Parliament of King James VI.; that they will adhere thereto, and will educate their children therein; that King Charles II. "is the only supreme governor of this realm over all persons, and in all causes as well ecclesiastical as civil;" that it is unlawful for subjects, upon pretence of reformation or any other pretence whatsoever, to enter into covenants and leagues, or to assemble to treat of any matter of state, civil or ecclesiastical, without his Majesty's special command or express leave; and that there was no obligation on them by the Solemn League and Covenant. The council of this period do not seem to have been of the same mind with the English gentleman, Richard Rumbold, who, when on the scaffold for rising in arms against James II., declared that "he never believed the generality of mankind came into the world bridled and saddled, and the rest booted and spurred to ride upon the multitude."

Mr Robert Douglas was appointed bishop in 1682, when the council created him, "Silvester Douglas his lawful son, Alexander Douglas, writer in Edinburgh, Mr Silvester Lammie, minister at Eassie, and James Lamb," the bishop's servant, burgesses. This was in August, and in the September succeeding, Mr Alexander Gardiner, minister at Girvan, and James Douglas, another of the bishop's sons, were received to the same honour. On 5th November 1683 the head of the Little Steeple was "blowen ower," as the kirk-session records bear, and it was repaired at an expense which was equivalent to the price of twelve bolls of meal, as we show in an appendix, where we give the details of the curious expenses incurred. The injury done, therefore, had not been very serious. Bishop Douglas was succeeded in 1684 by Bishop Cairncross, an able man of peculiar fortunes, who does not seem to have met with the same respect from the council as Douglas; at least we see nothing said about him in the council records, except the fact of his having attended the head court, and taken the oaths to the king, in 1684, and he only remained in the see a few months, having been then promoted to Glasgow.

Andrew Wood of Balbegno, incarcerate in the jail of Brechin in February 1683, gives the magistrates much trouble in consequence of having several times offered to the officers considerable sums of money by way of bribe to set him free; and, therefore, the council write their agent in Edinburgh to endeavour to have Andrew removed to another town, and meantime they get the town-officers to renew their oaths of fidelity. The imprisonment of parties for debt in the jail of Brechin has given much trouble to the council since 1683; but, happily, there is little of

that sort of imprisonment now; and in Brechin there is no
prison either for civil debtors or for criminals—the *accommodation* in the police cells being merely for temporary customers.
Every one who has witnessed the fairs held on Trinity Muir
has noticed the array of halberts with which the council are
guarded to the markets, and by means of which, when necessary,
the decisions of the magistrates, given in the markets, are enforced. This guard is furnished by the incorporations of the
town, each sending two men at Trinity fair, and one man at
Lammas fair. The weapons with which the men are armed belong to the respective incorporations. The array yet bears a warlike, although rather a burlesque appearance; but in the period
to which this chapter alludes, these men-at-arms were considered
as strictly under martial law; for it is solemnly recorded that
two of the guard, in May 1683, "did mutiny under their arms,"and
disobey the magistrates' orders, in consequence of which an Act is
made to prevent the like in time coming. One of these mutineers,
named David Duncanson, seems to have given the magistrates
no small annoyance on different occasions, and he ventured even
to meddle with the bishop; for, on 3d September 1679, it is
stated by the session that they had received a letter from his
reverence, complaining of Duncanson " for uttering imprecations
against him and his family;" but whether Duncanson was
troublesome from political or clerical reasons, or from the pure
spirit of mischief, is not recorded, although it would rather appear
that he was merely a roving blade. Duncanson was, on the occasion of the mutiny, the guardsman sent out by the baker trade,
and a baker himself—a craft which is severely censured in the same
year for the insufficient bread offered to the public; the craft
then consisting of only "two baxters," who are strictly prohibited
by the town council from meeting together to cheat the community. The other trades, however, come in for a share of the
ban of 1683. The minute of council immediately following
that regarding the mutiny, states that the town was then very
ill served for want of good craftsmen, by reason of the exorbi-
tant entry fees demanded; and enacts that, in time coming, the
full fees of admission to the hammmerman, glover, shoemaker,
and weaver trades, should be £20 Scots; and to the baker and

G

tailor trades, twenty merks; and that any sufficient craftsman tendering the entry-money then enacted, should be entitled to exercise his trade, though his craft refused to receive him a member of their body. It is melancholy to observe that, in July 1684, Walter Jameson, "church-master," as the treasurer was then designated, is directed to give David Duncanson a boll of oatmeal, and that in 1685 the children of Duncanson are admitted to the benefit of the hospital as a fatherless family left in want. This is generally the result with persons of such character as Duncanson.

The bridge of Brechin was repaired in 1684, chiefly at the expense of the council, who were obliged to borrow money from the kirk-session to meet the heavy disbursements. The extent of the repair is not mentioned, but the record bears "that the workmen have been at it for a long time," and the voluntary contribution expected for the defraying of the expenses not being come in, the money was borrowed "lest the work should be delayed, and therethrough miscarry." The session minutes state that on the 19th January 1684, there were collected at the church of Brechin £31, 13s., Scots of course, "to help to repair the bridge of Brechin;" while the presbytery records of the same year bear that the clerk was instructed to deliver to the town treasurer of Brechin the money collected by the "several ministers and sessions" for repair of the bridge, the amount not being mentioned. The repair, however, then made was not complete, for, in December 1686, the council state "that the rail of the bridge of Brechin has been this long time in an ill and dangerous condition both to strangers and others, being broken down and fallen to the ground by the violence of the wind in November 1683, which is a great reproach to the town;" and, therefore, for removing of this reproach, Thomas Scott is ordained to repair the bridge, and "to have thretty punds for his pains, and his freedom to the town." Again, in 1691, the bridge is appointed to be put to rights; but the work must have been executed in a very slovenly manner, if executed at all, for in 1695 the "east ravell," (eastern protection wall) is found to be very ruinous, and ordered to be repaired; and in 1707 the whole "ravell" is directed to be amended. A property at Meikle Mill which belonged to the late Mr John Symmer, dyer, was held in feu of the town council for payment of a small sum annually, and under the obligation of keeping the *caulseway* (roadway) of the bridge in repair; but this latter obligation was taken out of the last charter granted to Mr Symmer in 1833. Amongst the records of Arbroath there is a disposition granted by Stephan, son of Stephan of Kinnardesley, about 1220, in which he dispones to Gregory, Bishop of Brechin, for the sustentation of the bridge of Brechin, and the maintenance of the chaplains praying for the dead, his lands of Drumsleed, with all the pertinents particularly enumerated. The bridge of Brechin was not the only public work to which the attention of the inhabitants of Brechin was directed. In 1661 a collection was made for the erection of "two necessary bridges to be built over the waters of Esk and Prossin;" on 24th June 1668, the session of Brechin gave £4 to help to build the bridge of Idvie; in April 1670 a collection was made to assist in repairing and rebuilding the shore and harbour of Dundee, "which was destroyed and ruined in one night by a stormy tempest of the sea;" in January 1673 a collection was made "for the burning in Coupar of Fife;" the sum of £38, 4d. was raised in 1679 for the burning there was at Glasgow, although, from various causes, the money was not paid over till 1682 to "David Rose, collecter of the general contribution throw the whole kingdom for building the bridge at Endersonne;" and on 6th June 1680, the bishop ordered a collection to be made "through the *presbytery*," for repair of the bridge of Stracathro, to which the Brechin session willingly assented and appointed £6 Scots to be given "as their proportional part." But these were not the sole purposes for which collections were made. Although the spirit of the times ran hard against liberty of conscience, yet the impropriety of slavery and the right of the liberty of the person were fully admitted, abstractly at least, and the sufferings of those in bodily captivity met with Christian sympathy. On 6th March 1678, the sum of £64, 14s. 4d. Scots, no mean sum, was collected in the cathedral church "for the use of the prisoners of Algiers;" and again in March 1682, were gathered for " Francisco Polanus, a Grecian, his brethren and sisters in Turkish captivity," £22, 10s. 4d.   Indeed, during the Episcopal reign of Bishop Haliburton, we meet with many liberal collections for the like generous purposes.

The discipline of the church appears to have been very severe and strict about this time, for one woman is ordered to stand all night in jail for scolding an elder, and another is recorded as having occupied the " place of public repentance" no less than fifteen times successively before being " absolved." The offenders nevertheless continued numerous, and no small portion of the income of the session was derived from fines.   Another source of revenue, and a far pleasanter one, was the contributions made by parties when the nuptial knot was tied.   In July 1685, the kirk-session enacted that the elder who collected on the Sabbath should attend all the marriages of the week " for gathering the collections," an appointment which would be very agreeable to those members of session who liked good cheer.   Numerous Acts were also made about this period by the bishop and town's session in favour of individuals for the erection of desks or pews in the cathedral, all of which were specially directed to be wainscot.   It will be observed that cathedral churches originally were open to every comer, and that there were few or no permanent seats in the church, each person being content to stand or bring his seat with him, and assume such place as he could find unoccupied.   This is yet the case with the cathedrals in England and on the Continent.   The setting aside of special seats in the body of the church to individuals is first mentioned, so far as we have noticed, in the records of the landward session, on 10th February 1658.

The oath we have alluded to, commonly called the test oath, was sworn in Brechin for the last time in 1685; and it then, for the first and last time, contained the name of James VII.   In 1686, the election of any new magistrates or council was discharged by a letter from the Earl of Perth, Lord Chancellor of Scotland, and the existing office-bearers were directed to continue their functions.   The same arbitrary measure was resorted to by the infatuated James in 1687 and 1688; but in the end of that year, this monarch, the last of the long line of Stewarts, was dethroned, and William Prince of Orange, and Mary his wife, the daughter of James, were called jointly to the crown of Great Britain under the title of King William and Queen Mary. A minute of the town council of Brechin of this period is so characteristic of the state of the kingdom, that we prefer copying it verbatim to giving any abstract of its contents. The minute thus proceeds :—" Brechin, the 28th December 1688 years ; convened in the town council of the said burgh the persons after named—viz., James, Lord Bishop of Brechin ; James Allan, Laurence Skinner, and James Cowie, bailies ; Francis Moleson, dean of guild ; David Liddell, James Henderson, David Gray, Alexander Young, David Stewart, John Hendry, Alexander Dall, Alexander Jamieson, John Low, councillors : Who taking to their consideration heretofore and at this time, how frequently the whole kingdom is alarmed by the noise of invasion of Papists from France and Ireland, and of assaults and insurrections by Papists within this kingdom, have, conform to the practice of other burghs of the kingdom, put this burgh under arms, to be in a posture and condition of defence to join with the rest of the shire if they should be called. And by several proclamations through the town, ordered all the fencible men, free and unfree, within the town, to keep their several rendezvous well armed. And as it is known and complained of by several who gave due obedience that there were several persons able of body and means who made no appearance, and some others does appear in the fields but had no arms ; therefore, for their contempt, and in example to others to disobey in time coming, ordains them to be poinded to the value of ten pounds Scots money for ilk day's contempt. Whilk sum, so to be poinded for, is to be employed and bestowed for buying of powder and lead, to be distributed by the magistrates to those in the town who have muskets and firelocks when occasion shall offer. And it is further enacted, that whoever shall be convicted of being absent at any rendezvous without a good and lawful cause to be allowed by the town council, shall amit, lose, and forfeit the privilege of a burgess until he buy the same anew at the highest rate used within this burgh ; and besides to be poinded for the said ten pounds for ilk day's contempt. And further, it is enacted for the better and easy convening and rendezvousing, that the town

be divided in four companies under the command of four captains, who are to choose their under officers, for whom they
will be answerable, to which captains afternamed the rolls of
their several companies are delivered, who are to take care of the
particular arms of ilk man under their command, and to report
the same to the bailies and council; and if any person or persons
be deficient any day without a lawful and good excuse when the
company is called or convened by authority, the several captains
are hereby warranted to poind for the said sum of ten pounds,
for which they are to be accountable to the magistrates and
council, they having always allowance of the third part thereof
for their under officers and nightly guard. Captains names are
John Donaldson, captain; Alexander Young, captain; Walter
Jamieson, captain; James Low, captain." Such were the preparations of the bishop, the town council, and community, probably made by the different parties in different spirits. All
were hostile to the Roman Catholics, and some possibly to King
James; but the bishop was a determined opponent of, and no
doubt authorised these preparations in the hopes that they would
be effectual against, the Prince of Orange. The bishop of this
period was James Drummond—a near relation of the Earl of
Perth, who was a Papist; but the bishop is reported to have
been a man of strict Protestant principles, and a decided opponent of King James's interference with the Church, although he,
like most of his brethren, was a keen supporter of hereditary
monarchy, and took a decided part with King James when most
of his other courtiers deserted him. Bishop Drummond, therefore,
no doubt, meant this arming to be for protection of James and
the support of his throne and power; but others, if we may
judge from their conduct on the accession of King William,
intended it for a very different purpose. With this minute
terminates the appearance of the bishop in council, and with
this minute may be said to terminate the reign of Episcopacy in
Brechin. William and Mary were, in April 1689, declared
monarchs of Scotland, and with their accession closed the
supremacy of Episcopacy in Scotland. The rental of the see at
this time was 293 bolls 3 firlots victual, (wheat, bere, meal,
and malt,) and £941, 13s. 4d. Scots money, besides 500 merks,

payable by Scott of Ancrum, and some small feus from tenements in Brechin.

Bishop Drummond preached in Brechin for the last time on
Sunday, 14th April 1689; his text was taken from the 12th
chapter, 1st verse, of Paul's Epistle to the Romans, a text which
does not imply Drummond thought this sermon was the last
which would be delivered by a bishop in the cathedral church
of Brechin, but a text which seems to have been a favourite one
with him, as he is recorded as preaching from it on a previous
occasion. Whatever may have been the feelings of the bishop
and his clergy in regard to the person of King James VII., they
do not appear to have approved of his policy; for, on 16th May
1689, they hold a solemn " thanksgiving for deliverance from
Popery "—Mr Lawrence Skinner preaching from an appropriate
text. Again, in the October of the following year, a " sermon
of thanksgiving" is preached "for the King's arrival from
Ireland," and the texts adopted forenoon and afternoon by the
Messrs Skinner are evidently meant to be applicable to James's
then presumed condition, although the statement of his arrival
from Ireland proved to be a mistake.

It may not be out of place to remark that the Episcopacy of
this era was of a very moderate cast. Dr Russell, in his edition
of Keith's History of the Scotch Bishops, tells us that " all the
moderate Presbyterians attended the Episcopal worship and
communion in the parish churches; and in fact, at the period
in question, there was scarcely any outward distinction between
the two parties in faith, in worship, or in discipline."—" With
regard to discipline, the Established Church of that day had their
kirk-sessions as the Presbyterians have at present; they had
their presbyteries too, where some experienced minister of the
bishop's nomination acted as their moderator." Such was the
Church which King William put down, much it is believed
against his own inclination; but the bishops refusing to recognise him as their sovereign, policy called for the establishment
of Presbyterianism as the national religion. The officiating
clergymen of Brechin at this date were Mr Lawrence Skinner,
and Mr John Skinner his son; and in continuing to officiate as
clergymen after the removal of the bishop, they laid themselves

open to no charge of change of doctrine. Mr Lawrence Skinner was originally doctor of the grammar-school, afterwards minister at Navar, and was, as we have already seen, nominated minister of Brechin in 1650, in which office he continued to labour till his death in 1691. Looking at the texts which are recorded in the session minutes as those from which he preached on the 29th May, the birthday and anniversary of the restoration of Charles II., we should say he was a determined loyalist. And this is made still further evident, when on 5th September 1689, after the Convention of Estates in Scotland had declared James VII. to have forfeited the throne, he preaches from the text of the 14th chapter of Jeremiah and the 17th verse, which we leave our readers to consult for themselves. Mr John Skinner, again refusing to sign the test required when Presbyterianism became completely predominant, was deposed in 1695, but he remained about Brechin, and appears to have had no little influence amongst his flock notwithstanding of his deposition, as we shall afterwards see.

As already noticed, there appears to have been a violent storm of wind in November 1683, for the kirk-session records of the 5th of that month bear that " By order from the session there was ane hundredth merks lifted, which was in the Cordiners' hands, (the shoemaker trade,) for the repairing the head of the litl speeple, blown ower on the 5th day of this month, and for other works about the kirk, in regard the kirk-master was superexpended, as his last accompts will show." The same minute directs payment " to James Kinnear 1s. 4d. for mending a holl in the porch door." The session therefore at this time had defrayed the expense of all repairs on the church.

The board in the session-house, previously referred to, records that in " 1690 Master John Glendei, Dean of Cashels, and prebend of Sant Michaels of Dublin in Ireland, gifted £40." We have been unable to learn what connexion Mr Glendei had with Brechin, but likely he had been a native of the city, for the name, now written Glendey, is still common in the town. Besides this donation to the session, Mr Glendei in 1697 mortified £120 sterling in the hands of the United College of St Andrews, to found a bursary for young men belonging to Brechin ; and the bursary, which now yields £7, 16s. 8d. annually, was to be held for nine years, and often was of importance to students proceeding to St Andrews from Brechin. However, the royal commission which visited all the colleges some years since ordained that it should be lawful for the patron of the Glendey bursary " to present thereto any person, without restriction as to kindred or place of birth ; " so that Brechin has ceased to have any particular interest in the matter.

In the spring of 1689, Graham of Claverhouse, Viscount Dundee, attempted a rising in favour of King James, which was closed by the battle of Killiecrankie, at which this famous champion of national conformity in religion terminated his career—a career held by some to have been glorious, and by others inglorious, but admitted by all to have been bloody, if not cruel. On the 22d August 1689, there is an entry in the session records stating that there was " no sermon on the Sabbath day by reason of the Highlanders who are roving the country ; " and in the June of that year the council enact that, as the inhabitants are extraordinarily oppressed for baggage horses to transmit English forces to the north and back again, " this place being the public road," a month's cess should be raised to remunerate such of the citizens as were compelled to this service. A reason assigned for this taxation is that the public purse was low, or, as the phrase is, that " the common good of the burgh is far at under," in consequence of the expense of rebuilding the common mill. The meal mill of Meikle Mill, therefore, had been rebuilt at this time, and as it stood till 1808, when a new mill house was erected, this building had existed for a hundred and twenty years. Eheu ! this last erected mill house is now degraded into a store for rags for the use of the paper mill.

On the accession of William and Mary, the town councils in Scotland were restored by poll elections ; but in the burgh of Brechin, where the bishop had acted as provost, and also named one of the bailies, while Lord Panmure chose another bailie, and the council only elected the third ; and where there was now no bishop, and consequently no bishop's bailie, (James Alan, by the by, the bishop's bailie having disappeared from the council along with Bishop Drummond,) a poll election could scarce restore the magistracy. This, at least, was the statement made to the

Privy Council by the gentlemen who remained in office, and the Privy Council in consequence gave the remaining councillors power to choose a new council, and to dispense with the election of a bishop's bailie. Perhaps there was a lurking suspicion in the minds of the councillors that a poll election might have terminated unfavourably to them, for no doubt the bishop had left a party in Brechin friendly to his side of politics. This idea is confirmed by finding that in October 1689, the council made preparations for the maintenance of two troops of horse sent to quarter in Brechin that winter, likely to keep the friends of the bishop in order; and the military seem to have been continued in the burgh for some time, for in 1695 the commissioner to the Convention of Burghs is directed " to make moyan to get off the thrie companys of foott sojers presently quartered at this place." On 21st August 1690, we have recorded by the session that there was " no sermon on the Lord's-day, by reason of the armies coming into the town ; " and the burgh registers show that in the following September Lord Cardross, Lord Belhaven, and a number of gentlemen, officers in General M'Kay's troops, were entered burgesses—a compliment likely intended to propitiate the Government of King William, and bestowed on these persons when in Brechin. Soon afterwards other officers are admitted to the same honour, amongst whom is a Dutchman named Gerardus van Catenburgh. Possibly, as James Earl Panmure was a high cavalier, the quartering of troops in Brechin was the more necessary. At any rate it would appear that Lord Panmure and the council were then not of one mind, for his lordship appointed James Cowie not only to be bailie and his justiciar and constable within the burgh, but he gave him power to sit and affix courts and choose all necessary members of court, and to uplift and receive the fines and bluidwits, thus claiming for Bailie Cowie a power superior to, and independent of, the other magistrates ; and that too contrary to the arrangement made between the town and the family of Panmure in 1635, and agreement following thereupon in 1637. The council resisted and appealed to his Lordship, who issued another deputation " in the old and ordinary form," and matters then went on as smoothly as usual. Mr Francis Molison, who suc-

ceeded Bailie Cowie as justiciar, was the first member of council
who took the oaths to the new Government ; and having brought
a letter certifying this fact from Mr James Muddie, member of
Parliament for Montrose, and bailie of that burgh, Molison then
administered these oaths to the other members of council.

In 1691, David Falconer, Esquire of Newton, attempted to
establish a fair at the North Water Bridge, in opposition to the
great fairs held by the burgh in Trinity Muir. This was an
encroachment on the rights of the city not to be tolerated ; and
accordingly the burgesses dispersed the laird of Newton's friends
by main force. For this some twenty or thirty of the inhabitants were cited before the privy council as guilty of riot ; but
the case was taken up by the town council, manfully resisted for
years, and finally carried in favour of the good town. In commemoration of this victory, the burgesses, when they were wont
to "take in the market," or open the fair, used to ride to the
North Water Bridge, cut a besom of birch there, and bring it to
the cross of Brechin with them, in evidence that they had boldly
swept the road of all encumbrances. A good deal of fun and
humour prevailed on these occasions. It was deemed an honour
to carry the besom, but an honour which must be bought; and
all the burgesses present at the North Water Bridge were expected to bid for the honour, commencing with the oldest and
going down to the youngest, and to the youngest generally the
honour was consigned, as a second *bode* was not expected from
any person. The last time when the market was thus opened
was in 1823. On this, perhaps the last occasion of the kind, the
besom was bought and borne by Mr William Sharpe, then
surgeon in Brechin, afterwards a bailie of the burgh. We remember with no small pleasure the delight which we took in our
boyhood in witnessing the horsemen surrounding the ring at the
cross, the riders and animals decorated with birks ; and we have
a little pride in recollecting that in maturer years, we were called
on to prepare and superintend the programme of this mighty
affair—more profitable matters have not given us more pleasure.
Might not the marches be yet ridden, or the market " taken in "
occasionally, for the amusement of such burgess bairns as ourselves ?

Most of our readers will be acquainted, "practically," with the Little Mill stairs, a lane leading from the High Street down a precipitous bank, and by an alley overshadowed with trees, to the river Esk—altogether a romantic walk, affording a beautiful view of the church of Brechin, with a peep of Brechin Castle; and, although lying in the middle of the town, having all the stillness and rural scenery of a remote country situation. On the south side of the point where the lane leaves the High Street is a rising, which was formerly called the Mealhill; and at the foot of this rising was a mill for grinding meal, driven by water taken from the Den Burn, into a reservoir at the place still called the Dam Acre, and then brought by a runlet through the town and precipitated down the steep bank to drive the Little Mill. This Little Mill, like minor states, was finally swallowed up by its larger neighbour the Meikle Mill ; and in September 1693 the council, finding the Little Mill then useless, directed it to be converted into a waulk-mill, which also was ultimately abolished and the site reduced into garden ground. On the occasion of the conversion of the Little Mill into a waulk-mill, the lane passing down the ravine was causewayed, or pitched, as our "ancient enemies of England" term it ; and agreeably to the orders of the magistrates, "two or three steps of" broad quarry stones were laid immediately beneath where the Little Mill stood, where George Matthie has now a dwelling-house and weaving-shop, "in respect of the straightness of the passage there." Recently the steps have been enlarged, the causeway removed, and a comfortable road formed, leading down to the river.

Mr Harry Maule of Kellie, of whom we have before spoken, was at this time the parliamentary commissioner for Brechin ; and in April 1693, Bailie Francis Molison is appointed to go to Edinburgh to meet Mr Maule and to endeavour to procure a ratification of the grant made to the burgh at the time of the abolition of Episcopacy in 1640 of the feu-duties belonging to the bishop ; to resist any attempt made by Mr Falconer of Newton to procure a right of holding a market at the North Water Bridge; and to endeavour to get all Saturday and Monday markets abolished—the last being an object with the religious part of the community to prevent encroachments on the Sabbath, and to which object the attention of the town council of Brechin was repeatedly directed. Mr Molison was successful in all his commissions. In virtue of an Act of Parliament obtained in 1695, the town council have now right to all the feu-duties previously belonging to the bishop ; and the greatest part of the burgh owns the town council as their superiors or over-lords, either in virtue of this grant or of other titles belonging to the community. On 17th July 1695 also " our Soveraign Lord, with advice and consent of the Estates of Parliament, statutes and ordains that in all time coming there be a free fair settled and established yearly upon the Mure of Brechine called Trinity Mure, to begin the first Wednesday of August and continue eight days." Under this authority the present Lammas fair is held, which, however, is now limited to the second Thursday of August yearly.

In the year 1693 also, which seems to have been one of no little business, an Act of council was passed, prohibiting any of the councillors from revealing what passed at the council table, under the penalty of loss of their office of councillors, and of being found incapable of holding any public office within the burgh, besides being fined in a sum of £20 Scots. The year 1833 saw the affairs of the council board made patent to the public.

The marches of the burgh property continued to be a source of trouble in the seventeenth century, and they are still some trouble in the nineteenth. After several minutes in regard to giving off to Mr John Carnegy of Cookston part of the Loan (uncultivated land) near that property, we find this gentleman and his son differing with some members of council on the subject, and almost taking masterful possession of the burgh. A minute dated 27th January 1694, (Saturday,) appoints Bailie Alexander Young and Mr George Spence, town-clerk, to " take journey for Edinburgh on Monday next by *five o'clock in the morning* " to attend to a complaint preferred to the Privy Council by Cookston against the town council of Brechin and a number of the inhabitants. The next entry in the council books is dated 29th January 1694, which we find was a Monday, " 5 *hours forenoon,*" that is, five o'clock morning—an hour at which we fear few of our modern councillors would choose to be called from their couches to attend to council matters ; but an hour, early as it is, at which we find most of the councillors present. A formidable minute is then made, and Bailie Molison, who appears to have been absent from the former sederunt, is conjoined with Bailie Young and Mr Spence in the Edinburgh commission. The record narrates minutely that young Carnegy had, four years previously, struck Alexander Low, a burgess, in his own house " betwixt ten and twelve hours at night," and had broke Bailie Cowie's cart, and therewith forced open his outer gate, then his hall door and the windows of his dwelling-house, and, finally, fired a gun at the worthy bailie when standing at his own window ; and that Carnegy, being imprisoned for this riot, had broke the jail and come out of it with a cocked pistol and drawn sword ; for all which he is directed to be prosecuted. But the minute holds out the olive wreath, provided the bailies and town-clerk can agree with Cookston regarding the Loan ; and we rather infer that such agreement had been made, for next day " James Carnegy, younger of Cookston," is created an honorary burgess along with some officers and other gentlemen, and we hear no more of the matter. Subsequently, however, we notice that this gentleman was as contumacious towards the kirk courts as towards the civil authorities ; and the session finding it impossible to procure any one bold enough to cite him before them for an alleged breach of discipline, were in 1707 obliged to apply to the presbytery to take up the case and to send officers from Montrose to execute the warrants.

The African Company planned by William Paterson, a Scotchman, for the colonisation of the isthmus of Darien, met with many supporters in Brechin. This Paterson was the person who first suggested the idea of the Bank of England, and afterwards of the Bank of Scotland, but he was excluded from any share in these wealthy concerns by men of greater influence. Paterson then turned his attention to the colonisation of the neck of land connecting the two great continents of North and South America, and after beating about for supporters, was finally, by the assistance of Fletcher of Saltoun, enabled to procure an Act of Parliament incorporating a company by the name of " The Company of Scotland trading to Africa and the West Indies," with power to plant colonies, build forts, and govern the country to be colonised. There is little doubt the scheme would have proved successful, if King William had not, with that cool-blooded policy which disgraced his other qualities, thrown every obstacle in the way of the settlers of Darien, and ultimately left them to perish of hunger, lest the colony should prove a rival to the English East India Company. But at the outset the Scottish nation saw no difficulties. A mania prevailed for sub-scribing into the stock of the company, and the people of Brechin were infected by it. The council gave £100 from the common good; and because no less sum was received by the company than £100, the books of the town council were laid open that the burgesses and the incorporations might subscribe such sums as they pleased, for which stock was to be bought in name of the magistrates for behoof of the subscribers. Accordingly very many availed themselves of this privilege; the guildry incorporation sub-scribed £50, 13 ladies gave £95, and 28 gentlemen £455, and no less than £700 went from Brechin to this unfortunate con-cern. To propitiate the people of Scotland towards the Union, a fund was set aside from the public purse to make good the stock of the company when England and Scotland were made one kingdom, by Act of Parliament, so that ultimately the share-holders lost nothing.

Previous to this period, any very special Act of the town council was subscribed by all the members of council, and queer sub-scriptions occasionally they made, but ordinary Acts were not subscribed at all, the mere engrossing in the council record being deemed sufficient proof that they were the resolutions of the council. In 1696, an Act was made and subscribed by all the members of council, declaring that in future the subscription of the preses of the meeting should be sufficient to authenticate the minutes, and in 1698 the resolution was renewed; but notwith-standing of this, the old practice was persevered in till 1700, when Mr John Doig became provost. A similar practice pre-vailed amongst the different incorporations, and even the records of the kirk-session are not better authenticated.

The town's privileges being ratified in Parliament in 1695, the council of 1696, on the motion of Bailie Alexander Young, re-solved that a provost should in future be elected, agreeable to

the charters in favour of the burgh, and the resolution was subsequently followed up by the election of Mr Young to that office,
since which time a provost has been annually chosen. This
measure was succeeded by an attempt to gain precedence for the
town's bailie over the bailie nominated by Lord Panmure, but
after some sparring with his lordship, the council wisely enacted
that in future the bailie selected by Lord Panmure should, in virtue
of the resolution then adopted by the council, have the precedency.

In 1697 the tolbooth was repaired, and a resolution adopted to
repair the schoolhouse and cross, and to apply to the Convention
of Burghs for money to assist in these measures. What cash, if
any, was given, does not appear, but next year the council borrowed 1000 merks to assist the public purse in executing the
repairs on the jail.

The Common Den, which now, under the superintendence of
Messrs Henderson, nurserymen, forms so beautiful a prospect
from Southesk Street, formed in our young eyes no less pleasing an object when covered with the turf nature had bestowed
upon it, and decked with the daisies and buttercups of nature's
planting. The braes are beautiful, covered with dahlias, roses,
and other equally lovely plants, but the *Bonnie-brae* was truly
bonnie with the gowans glinting out amongst the short thick
grass, before Messrs Henderson put spade into the soil to convert
it into a nursery. We repine not. The Den is improved. It
is a source of revenue to the town, and affords healthy employment for many of its inhabitants, and were it restored to its
wonted wild state, we could not bicker up and down the braes
as formerly, or leap, one after another, as in days gone by, the
many wimples which were then in the burn, now covered over,
nor toss our dyed and hard-boiled eggs with the same zest we
did of yore. But we wander from our point. What we meant
to say was, that in April 1698, an Act of council was made appointing 40s. Scots to be paid yearly for each animal grazed on
the Common Den, which appears to have been always appropriated for the pasturage of cattle belonging to the burgesses,
and that out of the sums thus raised, £32 Scots were first to be
paid to the town, then a proper salary to the herd, and the balance, if any, to be handed over to the town-treasurer for the

public use. The town's herd was a man of no little consequence. Each morning, at an appointed hour, he went through the town blowing his horn, a cow's horn, when every burgess who had a right of pasture, sent out his horse or cow; and away stalked the animals from the one port to the other, gathering their fellows as they went, and followed by their noisy herdsman, who turned them all in at the foot of the Common Den, pastured them up to and out at the top, and returned them to their respective masters and mistresses at mid-day, to be again gathered out for afternoon pasture, and sent home by sound of horn in the evening. The volume of the records of the Hammermen Incorporation, previously alluded to, contains an entry, under date 11th April 1580, bearing that the bailies and council had elected Walter Erskine to be common herd till All-hallow day next, and therefore requesting all concerned to deliver their nolt into his custody, "as use is." In 1580 there is an Act of council ordaining the Common Den to be "hained" from 11th May to Midsummer day, from the Gallowgate at the north to the road leading to Montrose at the south, and no cattle to be allowed to be pastured thereon, evidently with the view of improving the grass. This practice of common pasture, with slight variation, continued till 1805, when the exclusive right of pasture was let by public roup to the highest bidder, by way of a tentative measure to wean the public from the practice of common pasturage; and after two or three such lettings, the Common Den was let in 1813 to the late Mr John Henderson, senior, and by him converted into a nursery. For some years previous to the Den being let for exclusive pasturage, the money collected from those who used the ground for common pasturage scarce paid the wages of the herd employed to take charge of the cattle; and some burgesses even kept cattle without *lawfully* providing any other food for them than what was picked up by the animals from this common pasturage. The letting of the Den for a term of years was one of the first measures which improved the revenue of the town; the letting of the bleachfield and mills for a series of years, in place of giving them off, as had long been the custom, on triennial leases, was the next great step which increased the income of the burgh.

H

CHAPTER VI.

PRESBYTERIANISM was fully established in Scotland in 1700, and, with a very partial interruption, the Presbyterian clergy have exercised all the powers and enjoyed all the privileges of Established clergymen in Brechin since that time. The records of the Presbyterian kirk of Brechin are commenced with a sketch of the state of Church affairs in 1700, a sketch which we give at full length in preference to any abridgment, as it appears to have been the joint production of the committee of the presbytery of Brechin appointed to attend to the settlement of all matters connected with the parish of Brechin. This sketch is in these terms: — " The church of Brechin being a collegiate charge, supplied by two ministers, the bishop in time of Episcopacy did supply the vice and room of one of them two, either by himself or his chaplain preaching a diet in the Sabbath's forenoon ; and he that was called the second minister ordinarily preached the afternoon's diet. Episcopacy being abolished in Scotland in the year 1689, Mr James Drummond (who was then Bishop of Brechin) was laid aside, and his charge became vacant. But Presbyterian government not being then fully constitute, and judicatories presently erected in Angus, Mr Lawrence Skinner, the Episcopal incumbent, who supplied the afternoon's diet, took occasion to possess the forenoon's diet also, having assumed his son, Mr John Skinner, to be his helper ; and thus the whole charge was possessed and supplied for some years thereafter, till the death of the said Mr Lawrence Skinner, which happened in August 1691, whereupon the said Mr John Skinner, his son, took possession of the whole charge alone, and continued preaching the whole day till the month of (*blank*) in the year 1695 ;

at which time Mr (*blank*) Abercrombie, minister at Lauder, by virtue of a commission from the Presbytery of Dundee, took possession of the forenoon's diet of preaching in the church of Brechin, and declared vacant that charge formerly supplied by the bishop; and thereafter the said diet was supplied by several Presbyterian ministers, the said Mr John Skinner still preaching in the afternoon, until the first day of August 1697 years, on which day Mr Ninian Lumie, minister at Preston, by commission from the presbytery of Dundee, did declare vacant the charge possessed by the said Mr John Skinner, and supplied the afternoon's diet of preaching also; after which time both diets of preaching, forenoon and afternoon, were constantly supplied by Presbyterian ministers and probationers, until the month of March 1703, at which time Mr John Skinner foresaid, at his own hand, invaded the pulpit, and took possession of the afternoon's diet of preaching, and dispossessed the presbytery thereof. Thereafter, the united presbyteries of Brechin and Arbroath, in conjunction with a committee of the synod, did, in the church of Brechin, upon the third day of December 1703 years, by prayer and imposition of hands, solemnly set apart, consecrate, and ordain Mr John Willison, first minister of the Gospel there. There being no session constitute at the time of the said Mr John Willison his settlement, the foresaid united presbyteries did appoint a committee of their number to meet at Brechin from time to time, and take care of the concerns of said town and parish of Brechin instead of a session, and till such time as they should procure the legal establishment of a session there, as an extract under the hand of the presbytery clerk at more length bears, the tenor whereof is as follows: ' At Brechin, December 29, 1703, the united presbyteries of Brechin and Arbroath, taking under their consideration the many scandals abounding in the parish of Brechin, and understanding by Mr John Willison, now minister there, that there is a necessity of setting about the establishment of an eldership in the place, for management of the poor's money, who are now at a great loss, Mr Skinner having deserted the landward session, with whom formerly he had met, as also for exercise of discipline against scandalous persons, and strengthening his hands in the work of the ministry;

therefore, for carrying on the foresaids ends, they do nominate
and appoint their following members, viz., Mr George Wemyss,
Mr James Forsyth, Mr John Glassford, Mr James Robertson,
Mr John Willison, together with Mr James Kerr, clerk, to meet
as a committee of the said united presbyteries:—and do hereby
fully empower and authorise you to call before you all scandalous
persons in Brechin, and order them to satisfy the discipline of
the Church when required thereto, to take under their inspection the case and necessities of the poor of the place, and to set
about the constituting an eldership, either by ordination or admission of such persons in the place as have been formerly elders,
or been named to be elders, in Brechin, as they shall see cause,
and to do every other thing they shall find necessary and expedient for the exercise of discipline, for suppressing of vice
and immorality, removing of disorders and irregularities, and
strengthening Mr Willison's hands in the place :—and it is
hereby also appointed that the said committee (of whose number
three are to be a quorum) shall be answerable and accountable
to the said united presbyteries in all their actings and proceedings, and shall produce their minutes to them when called for ;
and the said committee are appointed to have their first meeting
to-morrow, at Brechin, against ten o'clock in the forenoon, with
power to them to choose their own moderator and clerk, and to
appoint the diets of their meetings afterwards as they shall see
cause.   Extracted furth of the records of the Presbytery by (sic
subscribitur) James Kerr, clk. presb.'"   This entry is succeeded by the records of the committee of presbytery, acting as
a session till February 1704, when a session is constituted from
the members of the congregation.

The Presbyterian Church government, thus re-established,
does not seem to have commanded unanimous approbation—at
least the town council talk very unceremoniously of " Mr John
Willison and his *pretended* session ;" and from various entries
in the public records, it is evident the gentry in the neighbourhood were still favourable to Mr John Skinner, the deposed
Episcopal clergyman.

Mr Skinner seems to have put the presbytery to no little
trouble before they got quit of him.   In 1704 he was called

before that church court, but he gives the members plainly to understand that he will continue to exercise the office of minister in the church of Brechin as he had formerly done, upon which the presbytery " declared the said Mr Skinner an intruder, and therefore to have no relation to the parish or congregation of Brechin." When this was intimated to Mr Skinner, he, as the records of the presbytery inform us, very abruptly threw down a paper, neither signed nor indorsed, and thereupon took instruments in the hands of the clerk, and "also at the same time delivered a double of the said paper to one John Spence, fiscal in Brechin, and took instruments in the hands of the said Spence," a contumelious way of speaking which does not show that the members of presbytery were then themselves in the mildest of moods. Various attempts at adjustment seem to have been made, recommended even by the Lord Advocate, but all apparently failed; and Mr Willison, the Presbyterian clergyman, reported to the presbytery in 1705 that Mr Skinner had repossessed himself of the afternoon diet, and that he, Mr Willison, had been informed, that if he should adventure to retake the pulpit from Mr Skinner, he would be actually rabbled by a violent mob, who were resolved to support the Episcopalian clergyman, "to which they were not a little encouraged by the magistrates, who refused all concurrence or assistance to him, Mr Willison, on this matter." Energetic measures were resolved upon by the presbytery, and proceedings seem to have been commenced in different courts of law, but still the matter hung up, and the affair is again and again adverted to in the records of presbytery, till finally, in 1708, a libel is raised against Mr Skinner, charging him as an intruder, and a preacher of unsound doctrine. Mr Skinner declines the jurisdiction of the presbytery upon various grounds, all of which are repelled, and a number of witnesses being examined, the libel is found to be proven; and, finally, on 14th September 1709, Mr Skinner is deposed, a sentence which is subsequently enforced by warrant of the Court of Justiciary. In one of his papers, Mr Skinner states that he was "legally settled minister at the church of Brechin in the year 1687, as appears by my presentation, collation, and instrument of institution," so that it would appear he had been twenty-two years a clergyman in Brechin. Mr Skinner resumed the pulpit of Brechin in 1715, during the brief rebellion raised by the Earl of Mar, and in 1722, as the presbytery records informs us, he attempted to open a "meeting-house" in Brechin, but we find no mention of Mr Skinner in any public records after this period, and we have understood that he left Brechin and went to Edinburgh, where he died about 1725. There can be no doubt that Mr Skinner was an intruder, and acting contrary to the laws of the land, but there scarce appears to be any ground for the other charges brought against him, and of this the presbytery themselves seem to have been aware, for, in 1709, they "shew Mr Trail (then clerk) that it is not the mind of the presbytery that the minutes of the process should be produced in open court" in the General Assembly.

Mr Skinner being got rid of, the next step was to fill up the vacancy in the church of Brechin, for which purpose the presbytery named two of their number "to speak to the magistrates and desire them to call some fit person in time, and appointed also letters to be written to the landward heritors about the same business." The magistrates, however, did not pull with the church courts, and in March 1710, the presbytery find that the right to fill up the vacancy had fallen into their hands, and they therefore choose Mr William Trail, probationer, and appoint a call to be drawn up to him; but Mr Trail "because he had heard the people in Brechin were dissatisfied with him upon the account of his voice," declined the office; and therefore the presbytery "resolved to give a call to Mr John Johnston as soon as possible, seeing the people of Brechin are so desirous of him." Mr Johnston was in consequence ordained minister of Brechin, upon the 18th of May 1710, since which time the church of Brechin has had two clergymen.

We have formerly noticed that there were two sessions in Brechin, a landward session and a burghal session; but by the exertions of Mr Willison, an Act of the General Assembly was obtained in 1708, uniting the two into one session, and since then there has been but one session in the parish of Brechin.

Mr Willison was a very popular preacher in the Kirk of Scotland, a leading member in the local church courts, and a firm supporter of the kirk. His name still stands deservedly high as the author of the " Afflicted Man's Companion," written, as he himself says, " that the afflicted may have a book in their houses, and at their bedsides, as a monitor to preach to them in private, when they are restrained from hearing sermons in public." He is also the author of " The Mother's Catechism," a little work still in use, besides which he wrote two treatises on the Lord's Supper, and a variety of other religious works. Mr Willison was likewise the principal composer of the " Impartial Testimony," a work held to contain a true statement of what were then deemed the principles of the Kirk of Scotland. Mr Willison's Presbyterian principles were not in accordance with the feelings of the people in Brechin ; and we are informed that he was persecuted in every way by the inhabitants, especially by those of the higher ranks, most of whom were violent Jacobites and Episcopalians. Mr Willison was translated from Brechin to Dundee, where he died on 3d May 1750, in the seventieth year of his age, and forty-seventh of his ministry. When he removed to Dundee he found it impossible to command the services of a Brechin carter to convey his furniture to his new charge, so violent was the prejudice against him. In his difficulty he applied to Mr John Guthrie, tenant of Kincraig, great-grand-father of Mr Alexander Guthrie, present provost of Brechin ; and Mr Willison received from Mr John Guthrie the assistance of which he stood so much in need. In 1746, the horses of Mr John Guthrie were seized by the Hanoverian party, to convey their baggage to the North, when the farmer of Kincraig posted to Dundee, and obtained from his friend Mr Willison a letter to the Duke of Cumberland, who, the moment he read the letter, caused the horses to be returned to Mr Guthrie.

It is curious enough to find the Presbyterian Church drawing a revenue from a Popish ceremony. In 1704, the session considering that it is ordinary for people to cause toll the bells at the interment of their relations, fix the rates which are to be paid for doubling of the three bells, knelling of them, or knelling any of the bells. This practice, commenced in Popish times, and then intended to give warning to those within hearing of the bells to pray for the souls of the departed, whose bodies were about to be committed to the earth, continued down as late as 1807 ; when, in consequence of the bells having been frequently broken by this mode of tolling, the town council, at whose expense the small bells then cracked were recast, prohibited the practice.

Men's minds were still unsettled in regard to political matters, as well as in regard to church government, and a good deal of manœuvring seems to have taken place in the burgh about the commencement of the century to gain the political ascendancy ; amongst which manœuvres we may notice the resolution not to elect a provost, whereby the bailie nominated by Lord Panmure would have taken the chief direction as senior magistrate. But these plots were met by counterplots, and it is hard to say which party was right, when Queen Ann herself was hesitating between the Whigs who had called her to the throne, and the Tories who supported her exiled brother. Still the town council, although plotting with a view to the affairs of the State, found time for minor matters. Thus, in 1703, they strictly prohibit any one from casting feal in the Den, unless for the repair of the bow butts, that is, for repair of the butts erected in the time of James I., for the practice of archery, and retained as butts for ball shooting, till the late Mr John Henderson superseded them by shooting espaliers on the same place. Next year the council make an ordinance, scarcely so legitimate ; for they ratify the whole former Acts of council, discharging the inhabitants from pursuing their neighbour inhabitants before any judicatory without the burgh. An Act more self-denying occurs in March 1705, when the council, " in respect that the town's common good is greatly emburdened," appoint that at all meetings " ordinary ale " shall only be drunk, " and no strong drink to be called for or paid on the public account." We have formerly adverted to the expense the burgh incurred in supporting their member of Parliament. In May 1700, it is enacted that " there be allowed to the present session of Parliament, and in all time coming, for the commissioner's expenses, thirty shillings Scots money for each day he is absent, and this besides the ordinary horse hire, back and fore, and no more to be allowed, and that for each day the commissioner is detained at the Par-

liament allenarly." The right to elect a member to Parliament
was then considered a burden, instead of a privilege, as at the
present day; and the member, we see, was allowed his expenses,
in place of being put to great cost in obtaining his seat, and
maintaining himself in it, as is the present not very creditable
practice.

On 1st May 1707, England and Scotland were legally united
into one kingdom, under the title of Great Britain, and the Parliament of Scotland was abolished. This measure created no
little sensation throughout the two kingdoms. The town
council of Brechin instructed their commissioner, Francis Molison, to vote in the Scotch Parliament for the " union betwixt
Scotland and England, and for all necessary supplies by this
kingdom," thus showing that the court party was then predominant in the burgh; but we have understood that the commissioner disobeyed these instructions and voted against the
union. The mode of electing the first member from this town
to the British Parliament, is not made plain in the burgh
records. It is stated, on 24th September 1707, that Provost
Young is appointed "commissioner to meet with the burghs of
Aberdeen, Montrose, Aberbrothick, and Bervie; and that at
Montrose the 26th day of September instant, anent giving instructions to (*blank*) Scott of Logy, younger, *who is to represent*
in the British Parliament, the 14th October next, the burghs of
Aberdeen, Brechin, Montrose, Arbroath, and Bervie;" and this
is all which we learn from the record on the subject. In May
1708, the council, in obedience to a precept from the Earl of
Northesk, then sheriff of Forfar, nominated Provost Young their
commissioner, to go to Aberdeen on 26th May, and meet with
the other commissioners from this district of burghs, and elect
a member to the Parliament of Great Britain, summoned to
meet at Westminster on the 8th July ensuing. Who was then
elected member is not recorded. This mode of election continued,
each of the five burghs presiding alternately, till the Act of 2 and
3 William IV., c. 65, in 1832, put the election directly into the
hands of the people, and conjoined Brechin with the other three
Angus burghs, Forfar, Arbroath, and Montrose, and with the
burgh of Bervie in Kincardineshire, in the right to return a

member of Parliament. It may be noticed in passing, that the order of precedence adopted in convening the burghs for the first election of a member to the Parliament of Great Britain was " Aberdeen, Montrose, Brechin, Aberbrothock, Inverbervie; " so that the designation of the " Montrose District of Burghs" in the Reform Act, when Aberdeen had a member assigned to itself, is only carrying out the old designation of this district of burghs, notwithstanding that Arbroath certainly now is the largest of the whole. According to the order in which the shires were called in the Scottish Parliaments, Edinburgh of course stood first, Ross was the thirty-third and last, while Forfar stood the twenty-fifth.

In 1709 all the burghs of Scotland were called upon to make returns of their *setts* to the Convention of Royal Burghs, and the following is engrossed in the council book of Brechin, as the then recognised constitution of the burgh, and as a copy of what had been sent to the Convention :—" That the town council of the royal burgh of Brechin consists of thirteen members, where- of eleven merchants and free brethren of the guild of the said burgh, and two tradesmen, all residenters and inhabitants of the said burgh, they do out of the aforesaid number of eleven, elect and choose a provost and two bailies, a dean of guild, town- treasurer, and master of the hospital. There is no fixed day for the annual election of this burgh of Brechin, but either the town council of the said burgh, some time before Michaelmas, yearly, do appoint and fix a day for the same peremptorily, or otherwise, the provost or preses of the town council for the time do call a council to meet at any time they think fit, some few days more or less as they please, not exceeding five or six days, and most frequently fewer days before Michaelmas, in order to choose a new council and leet the magistrates ; and then the old council elects the new council, and both old and new councillors leet two persons of the new council, in order to choose one of them provost ; and a leet also of four persons of the new council to the end two bailies may be chosen out of the same ; and cause public intimation thereof to be made by tuck of drum through the whole burgh ; and upon the day appointed for the election, the new council meets, and in conjunction with the six deacons of crafts of the said burgh, out of the foresaid leet of two persons for the provostry, do elect a provost for the ensuing year, and then, by virtue of a contract betwixt the Bishop of Brechin, Patrick Maule of Panmure, and the magistrates and town council of Brechin in anno 1637, the Earl of Panmure, or any having right from him, being called, name a bailie out of the said leet of four persons so elected and chosen by the said town council of Brechin, and to which bailie he is obliged to give and grant deputation of the offices of justiciar and constabulary within the said burgh of Brechin; and then the council and deacons of crafts, out of the remaining three persons, choose another bailie, and thereafter the council choose a dean of guild, treasurer, and master of the hospital for the ensuing year." Subsequently, in 1729, an Act of council was passed, declaring that in case of equality of votes, the provost had both a deliberative and a casting vote, and that the neglect to state this was an omission when transmitting the sett to the Convention. This sett was slightly altered at different times. The family of Panmure being forfeited in 1715, the council thereafter elected both bailies. In 1726, by an agreement with the trades, the deacon convener was received as one of the tradesmen who were necessarily members of council; and in 1820, by a like agreement, the incorporated trades were allowed to name both the trades' councillors; and the guildry incorporation were authorised to elect their own dean, who was granted a seat in council. Of the thirteen members of council, ten continued to be self-elected, while one was elected by the guildry, and two by the incorporated trades, till the Act of Parliament, passed in 1833, generally known as the Burgh Reform Act, placed the election of the whole councillors upon a new footing, and gave to the proprietors and tenants of houses rented at £10 the right and privilege of electing the town council.

Mr John Doig, an elder of the Presbyterian Church, and a decided enemy of the Jacobites and of Episcopacy, had, in 1709, obtained the ascendancy in the councils of the burgh, and then held the office of provost. He is not much indebted to popular tradition, nor does he seem to have owed much to popularity during his life. No doubt he was a zealous and able man, and did many things for the *weil* of the burgh, as well as for his own benefit. In 1709 he had an Act passed appointing the council to meet " each Monday by ten hours in the forenoon ; " but if such weekly meetings took place, the transactions then discussed have not been minuted. In April 1712, a serious riot is recorded as having occurred in the burgh, in which James Millar, deacon of the shoemakers, led on a party to " beat, blood, and wound in the head and other parts of the body, the said John Doig," and the offenders are recommended by the council to the attention of the Lords of Justiciary. What was the result we are not informed.

We have formerly mentioned that the cathedral church was not originally supplied with fixed seats, but that desks, as they are termed, gradually crept in after the Reformation. So late as 1715, we find applications made for liberty to fix seats in empty places in the church, and in 1710, the session appointed " intimation to be made to the people who take their chairs out of the church, that they who do so shall lose their ground right." In the subsequent year, 1711, the session, with the view of increasing the poor's funds, granted liberty to the parishioners to erect *headstones* in the churchyard ; but there is a strange distinction drawn between the burgh and landward part of the parish, for, while the burgesses are allowed to erect headstones on payment of 20s. Scots, the landward parishioners are ordained " to pay half-a-crown for the said privilege."

The linen trade had by this time taken root in Brechin, and on 6th October 1712, Robert White and David Windrim were appointed by the council " to be stamp-masters of this burgh for stamping all linen cloth." Under various Acts of Parliament this office of stamp-master was continued, and by the increase of the linen trade the situation came to be one of considerable emolument within the burgh ; but, in 1824, Parliament saw cause to abolish the practice of stamping linens, and it is believed that, since then, the linen cloth made has been fully as good as it was during the period when each web was measured, examined, and stamped by a public officer. When the council named the first linen inspectors, they also ordained " two stamps, bearing the town's arms, to be made and delivered to them for stamping of the cloth." The stamp which was used when the office was abolished, was a large Scotch thistle, with the name of the stamp-master and the word " Brechin" below the thistle. This same thistle, with the stamper's name and residence effaced, was long used in the office of the first printers in Brechin, as a decoration to the ballads which they occasionally issued from their press. These same printers, we may add, were, under the firm of Black & Co., the printers of the first edition of this work.

In 1713, Brechin was the returning burgh for this district of burghs, and Provost Doig was then named commissioner ; but Bailie James Spence was named the commissioner to choose a member to the first Parliament of George I. in 1715, when Arbroath was the presiding burgh. In this same year, 1715, Mr Andrew Doig was sent commissioner to Arbroath to meet with commissioners from some other burghs, appointed, agreeable to Act of Convention, " to endeavour to adjust a plan for the common interest of the said burgh of Arbroath, so that the magistrates thereof may proceed to elect a dean of guild and council." This was with a view to the establishment of a guildry in Arbroath, but we presume the troubles which arose in Scotland at this time had prevented the carrying out of this municipal improvement then ; for it was not till 1725 that the magistrates and town council granted a seal of cause to the incorporation of guildrymen, a legal recognition which they claimed in virtue of a charter of Novodamus by James VI. in 1599. The guildry then constituted in Arbroath was framed after the model of the Brechin guildry ; and the Brechin guildry would now do well to follow the example of the Arbroath guildry, which in 1856 was formed into a friendly society by the authority of the Court of Session, in virtue of the Act of Parliament for abolishing the right of exclusive trading within burghs.

But we approach to " Mar's year," the attempt to restore the exiled Stewarts in 1715, for which so many plots and counterplots had been carried on in the State, in every burgh, and in this our small city. Queen Ann died suddenly in 1714 ; George I. ascended the throne ; he was austere with the Earl of Mar ; that nobleman hastened to Scotland ; raised the standard of revolt in Braemar ; proclaimed James VIII. of Scotland

and III. of England as king of Great Britian, and involved
himself and many a noble family in ruin by a hasty and ill-
timed rebellion. Earl Panmure proclaimed King James at the
cross of Brechin, and joined the standard raised by Mar. Earl
Southesk also joined this unfortunate attempt. Both forfeited
their estates in consequence. Many of smaller name, connected
with the burgh, also acceded to this rebellion ; and for years
afterwards we find the kirk-session refusing church benefit to
great numbers till they had satisfied the discipline of the kirk for
joining this " unnatural rebellion." The session-clerk chronicles
the rising very briefly and distinctly. After an entry, dated 31st
August 1715, he says :—" In the month of September following
broke out the late Earl of Mar's rebellion, against our most
gracious sovereign, King George, and the Protestant succession
in his family, and in favour of a Popish Pretender whom they
called King James the Eighth ; the which rebellion continued
till the month of February thereafter ; and this is the reason
why there was no meeting of the session from the foresaid thirty-
first of August to the twenty-ninth of February thereafter."

The records of the session of Menmuir show the distracted
state of the times in a very interesting minute, of which this is
a copy:—"4th September 1715. After prayer, sederunt, ministers
and elders met in session. This session taking to their serious
consideration the troublesomeness of the times, and the distracted
state of this land, and considering also, that they have in their
hands the most part of the poor's stock in specie, and being very
solicitous and concerned that it should be safe in this critical
juncture ; therefore earnestly recommend to, and appoint the
minister to secure and hide the poor's money the best way he
can—viz., the money received from Grandtullie's factor, and a
hundred pounds Scots received from Bailie Spence, in name of
the Laird of Balzeordie. Sederunt closed with prayer. Whereupon the minister went to Brechin, and the Reverend Mr John
Willison, one of the ministers of Brechin, did direct him to a
retired and safe place for securing the said money ; upon which
the minister returned home, and did communicate the matter to
two of the elders, and with one of them did carry the money
received from Grandtullie's factor to the said place, and secured

the other hundred pounds got from Bailie Spence, in name of
Balzeordie, another way." This retired and safe hiding-place
had most likely been somewhere about the church, not impro-
bably in the bottom of the round tower.

Mr Gideon Guthrie, an Episcopal clergyman, or nonjurant
minister, as those of his persuasion were then generally termed,
gave great offence to the Presbyterian clergymen at this time,
and in August 1715, Mr Johnston, one of the Established clergymen of Brechin, reports to the Presbytery "that the affair anent
Mr Gideon Guthrie is come to this issue, that he is discharged
to preach or exercise any part of the ministry within the parish
of Brechin, under the pain of 500 merks, *toties quoties*, and
further declared incapable, for seven years, of any post or benefice within Scotland, as also fined in 100 merks and ordered to
go to prison till payment thereof, as the sentence in itself more
fully bears;" but in place of going to prison, Mr Guthrie went
to the pulpit of Brechin, which he and Mr Skinner jointly
assumed possession of, for the brief period when their party was
predominant during Mar's rebellion. For this proceeding,
Guthrie was called to strict account by the presbytery when the
rebellion was suppressed, but he seems to have fled from the
effects of his rashness, and we hear no more of him after that.
No proceedings apparently were adopted against Mr Skinner,
whose age probably had mollified the feelings of his opponents
in reference to him.

Provost Doig was superseded during this rising—Bailie Spence,
whom we have alluded to as the commissioner for electing a
member of Parliament to the first House of Commons assembled
by King George, having apparently assumed the sway of the
town. On 29th September 1715, eight of the members of
council meet, the whole council, as the minute bears, having
been lawfully summoned "except John Doig, who could not
be found at home," and these eight re-elect six of themselves
with seven others of true Jacobite principles, and this Jacobite
council then choose office-bearers, carefully, however, avoiding
to elect a provost, an office which they probably held belonged
to the bishop, whom doubtless they expected to see restored.
Spence is named by Panmure to be his bailie, "justiciar, and

constable," and thus Spence in fact acquired all the powers of chief magistrate. The minutes of this council are few, and only such as appear to have been forced upon them in ordinary routine. This council had more important matters to attend to than make minutes. On 11th May 1716, however, a poll election takes place in the church of Brechin, under the superintendence of John Scott of Heatherwick, Esq. ; Alexander Duncan of Lundie, Esq. ; and Colonel Robert Reid, commissioners appointed by Government; when all our Jacobite friends are superseded by Provost Doig and his party. The whole thirteen members of council are *unanimously* elected on this occasion, from which circumstance we may fairly infer that, in 1716, none dared vote but in such way as Mr Doig chose, without the risk of being reckoned Jacobites and enemies to the Government of King George. Previous to the poll election the town seems to have been ruled by *Governors*, likely appointed by the Government of George I. Thus the mills, weighhouse, and flesh booths are exposed to let on 4th May 1716, in presence of " Mr Andrew Doig, one of the governours of Brechine," and they are finally let on 7th May, in presence of " John Doig, Mr Andrew Doig, and Robert Whyte, governours." We presume *Mr* Andrew Doig had been a literary man ; for while he always receives this title in the council minutes, the other members are designated by their simple names. The Doigs were a powerful family about Brechin at this time ; and the board in the session-house records that Bailie David Doig of Cookston gave the church a new folio Bible in 1728, which we believe was in use till another was got when the church was repaired in 1807. Bailie Doig's Bible superseded that given to the church in 1655 by the Rev. Mr Lawrence Skinner, as recorded on the session-house board ; and we have it from tradition that Bailie Doig's book was given to supply the place of Mr Skinner's, because the latter was of a prelatic, if not of a Popish tendency !

But the session record gives the most graphic account of the state of matters, and we quote it at length, leaving our readers to apply such saving clauses as their own feelings may suggest:— " Brechin, March 4, 1716. The session being constitute, sederunt, ministers, elders, and session clerk *ut supra*. This day the session taking to consideration that during the late unnatural rebellion the ministers were forced to retire for their safety, and the church was intruded upon by Mr John Skinner, late Episcopal incumbent here, now deposed by the church and banished out of the bounds of this presbytery by a sentence of the Lords of Justiciary, and Mr Gideon Guthrie, late Episcopal preacher in the meeting-house here, and turned out by a sentence of the said Lords, and that John Doig of Unthank, the present provost, was imprisoned by the rebels, and Bailie Spence usurped a most tyrannical power over men's bodies and consciences, and threatened and forced people to hear the foresaid rebellious intruders drink disloyal healths, and otherwise to countenance the said rebellion, and particularly did wickedly impose a base and traitorous oath upon the people, called the Test, in which, beside other absurdities and contradictions, they did swear to the Popish Pretender as king, and renounce our only lawful sovereign King George as a foreign prince, with which wicked impositions and base oath a great number of the people, and *even several of the elders*, have complied, either out of ignorance or slavish fear, or desire to shun suffering. And the ministers having laid this affair before the presbytery for advice, it was the presbytery's judgment that all the elders who had so complied and taken the foresaid oath, should be discharged from the exercise of their function of elders, and for removing of the scandal that they and all others, guilty of the foresaid compliances, should not only confess their sin in so doing before the session, but appear publicly and acknowledge the same before the congregation, and that they and every one of them should do this before they be admitted to partake of sealing ordinances or church benefits. And the ministers having represented this day to the session that they had accordingly been dealing with the elders and a great many others, privately, who had made defection and sinfully complied as aforesaid, in order to bring them to a sense of their sin, and they being willing to compear and confess in manner above written, and for that end were attending this meeting of the session, in order to appear this day before the congregation, whereupon compeared (certain individuals who are named,) all which persons above mentioned

I

professed their sorrow to the session for their said defection, and their willingness to acknowledge the same before the congregation and be rebuked therefor." But no "rebuke" was given, the session contenting themselves with the admission of their power to rebuke. With more contumacious spirits, some years afterwards, the session was more severe.

The church records of the neighbouring parish of Stracathro are much of the same stamp. They state, under date 2d November 1715, that " Mr John Davie, factor to the Earl of Southesque, intruded on the minister's charge by taking the keys of the church, ordering the kirk-officer to ring the bells at the ordinary time of day, the people being warned the day before to wait on, and join in, the worship of a pretended fast or humiliation-day for success to the Pretender's arms, and that under the pain of taking each man, master and servant, to the camp at Perth ; which warning so prevailed that it brought the whole parish together at the time appointed to the church, where and when Mr Davie himself came in the head of near eighty men under arms, with beating drums and flying colours, and *preached a little* in the church, and after that kind of worship was over, he mustered up his men again at the kirk gate, and on their front went to Kinnaird." Truly Mr Davie had been a *factor*, and not a mere rent collector. The same minutes mention that during this intrusion, which continued to February 1716, the minister preached in the manse, and the collections made being inconsiderable, he applied them " to the relief of some poor indigent people in the parish of Brechin "—true Hanoverians, no doubt. Order being restored, the minister, in April 1716, laid before the session an appointment on him by the presbytery of Brechin to inquire at them the reasons why they joined Mr Davie, " and the minister finding their reasons no way satisfactory, he solemnly rebuked them," and also for their pecuniary intromissions with the collections, of which they were unable to give any account, further than it was spent on the poor. The minister, Mr Glassfurd, seems to have been in a minority in his own parish.

James, " the Pretender," as it is known to the historical reader, landed at Peterhead on 22d December 1715 ; came to

Brechin on Monday 2d January 1716; remained there till Wednesday; then went to Perth and met his army, the members of which were as little pleased with him as he was with them. After playing the king at Perth for a brief space, James returned to Montrose, and from thence quitted *for ever* " his ancient kingdom of Scotland," having embarked with the Earl of Mar on the evening of 4th February 1716, on board a French vessel lying off Montrose to receive them.

Tradition tells us that the northern lights were extremely brilliant during the winter of 1714–15, and we have ourselves received it from a person who was told by her mother, that, during this winter, armies of men and horses were seen fighting in the sky ! Our narrator believed this as much as she believed the holy writ, and said that all Mar's fortunes and misfortunes were distinctly portrayed in the sky ere he himself had raised the standard of revolt. Truly might the fate of this nobleman be compared, in the words of Burns, to

> " the Borealis race,
> That flit ere you can point their place."

So far as appears, Brechin became perfectly quiet after this insurrection was quelled. A company of soldiers was stationed in Brechin for some time, but these soldiers were more an annoyance than a protection to the civil and *ecclesiastical* authorities. Provost Doig remained in office till his death in 1726. Bailie Spence died some time previous to 1722, for we find in that year his daughter, Miss Katherine Spence, designed as daughter of the *deceased* Bailie James Spence, elected to the office of schoolmistress, for instructing little ladies " in the arts of sewing and working of lace." Miss Spence is the first schoolmistress of the burgh, and it is pleasing to observe Provost Doig, her father's opponent, voting her a salary of £30 Scots for her services. In this same year 1722, the meal-market was erected, in the street now called Swan Street, on the site of an old tenement purchased for the purpose. This erection, demolished in 1788, led to the opening up of the street alluded to, which still occasionally receives, jointly with its new title, its old name of the Meal-Market Wynd, although the meal-market was removed about 1787 to the same place as the butcher-market, in a building a little below the Bishop's Close. The meal-market has been long non-existent, the trade being carried on by grocers and bakers in their private shops, and the place formerly used as the public meal-market being let for a warehouse. The butcher-market also is now non-existent, all the modern fleshers resorting to separate shops, and the court and covered sheds formerly occupied by them being now used on Tuesdays as a market for poultry, butter, and eggs, brought into town by the country people; and the front part of the house, where carcasses were formerly hung in warm weather, being now wholly occupied as a public weigh-house, for which it was originally intended, and always partially used.

In 1723 the six incorporated trades established a general fund for the relief of their poor. It was agreed that this fund should be maintained by small contributions levied on each entrant freeman or apprentice, by fines imposed for offences against the rules of the corporation, and by a fine imposed in these words: "And if any prentice, journeyman, freeman, either young men or widowers, shall (as God forbid) fall in the sin of fornication, then, and in that case, each person so transgressing shall pay into this fund the sum of two pounds Scots," to be doubled in case of aggravation. The fund has been long in abeyance, but we humbly think the six trades might do worse than apply their funds for the maintenance of such a charity. In 1726, as already noticed, an arrangement was made between the town council and the trades, whereby the council agreed to receive the deacon convener, *ex officio*, as a member of council yearly. This arrangement was effected by a bond subscribed by seven members of council only, and seems to have arisen out of a wish to give the superiority to the then dominant party in council ; but the agreement, although frequently questioned, was regularly acted upon, and so became part of the set of the burgh after its date, the convener, when changed by the trades, being as a matter of course changed by the council.

The affairs of the guildry appear to have excited very little interest about this period. Year after year passes without any meeting, and even when a meeting does occur, a brief minute is entered as an apology for the neglect; but in 1748, the members resolved to meet on the third Thursday of October yearly, a practice which has been pretty regularly followed ever since. The dean of this time was Mr John Lyon, a connexion of the Strathmore family, through that branch to which the estate of Aldbar for some time belonged.

The north side and north aisle of the church having fallen into decay, the session, after much difficulty, prevailed on the heritors to repair the building in 1718, "the factors appointed by the Government on the forfeited estates of Panmure and Southesk promising to pay what lies to their share when called for." But this repair does not seem to have been complete, for next year the session demand a further repair on the steeples and aisles, an expense to which the heritors again demurred, but which they were ultimately compelled by "horning" to pay. Some of the items of the expenses of the repairs are curious as showing the price of building materials in 1722; they are thus stated in the Act of Presbytery on which the law proceedings followed : Thirty-two bolls of lime with the sand cost 1s. 6d. per boll of lime, and 2s. Scots for the load of sand to each boll, inde £32 Scots; forty deals are 12s. Scots each; three hundred nails are £2, 8s. Scots; twenty garron nails, 10s. Scots; "item for a big teakil, being double the hight of the small steeple, £40 Scots;" but this "big teakil," whatever that word may mean, and certainly it had been big, when it was double the height of the small steeple—this teakil, after being used, is to be sold, along with some other materials for scaffolding, at £33, 6s. 4d. Scots. The slating is estimated to cost ten merks Scots per rood, and there being three roods and twenty-four ells of slater-work required, the expense of the roof is £24, 10s. Scots. The whole repairs, after deducting for scaffolding, &c., to be sold, are decreed to cost the heritors £380 Scots.

In consequence of the disturbed state of the kingdom after 1714, the sacrament of the Lord's Supper was not celebrated in the church of Brechin for several years, but in 1720 the session "resolved to set about that work," and in the March of that year the ordinance was dispensed. The discipline of the church gradually grew stricter after this period; and persons were now censured for faults which had for some time previously been looked over, the session having resolved "to revive their old laudable custom of sending some of their number through the several corners of the town every Lord's day." Marriages, up to this date, were usually celebrated in the cathedral, and we have various acts of the session censuring individuals whose mirth had overcome their prudence, and led them to behave indecorously at such ceremonials. In 1717, however, marriages in private houses are recognised by the session, for there is a minute in that year imposing a small fine on parties who prefer to have the ceremony performed elsewhere than in church. A public marriage, in a Presbyterian kirk, before the congregation, would at the present day draw general attention—no such thing having occurred with the parents of any of the oldest persons alive.

Although Mr Skinner had now retired from the field, the Presbyterian kirk was annoyed by Episcopalian clergymen still visiting the burgh, and in 1726 the ministers of Brechin laid before the presbytery "a presentation against Masters John Grub and Francis Rait, who keep an illegal meeting-house in the town and parish of Brechin, and baptize and marry, to the great disturbance of the said town;" a presentation which was subsequently enforced before the Lords of Justiciary to the effect of shutting up this meeting-house.

George I. died in 1727, and with the close of his reign we shall close our chapter.

Amongst the poets of the period to which this chapter relates, we can notice, as connected with Brechin, David Watson and James Carnegy. Mr Watson was born at Brechin in 1710, was educated at Saint Andrews, and afterwards became Professor of Moral Philosophy in Saint Leonard's College of that city, but retired from the Professor's chair when his college was united with Saint Salvador's in 1747. He then became author by trade, went to London, and fell a prey in 1750 to the dissipation which was the ruling vice amongst the wits of that time. He published a translation of Horace of no mean merit, and a "History of the Heathen Gods," which, in our day, was a standard school-book. Mr Carnegy was the son of the laird of Balnamoon, where he was born in 1715. He came of a good stock —in the moral acceptation of the word—and was himself a man of genuine worth and warmth of heart. In early life he composed the beautiful and still popular ballad of " Low Down in the Broom," adapted to a chorus of great antiquity, noticed in the " Complaynt of Scotland," written about 1540. Mr Carnegy was a staunch Jacobite, and was out in 1745, after which he was obliged to consult his safety by living as a servant with one of his own tenants, till the Act of grace in 1748 restored him to his family and the world.

William Guthrie, an eminent miscellaneous writer, was the son of Mr Gideon Guthrie, the Episcopal clergyman spoken of above, and was born at Brechin in 1708. In early life he commenced author by profession, and removed to London in 1730· For many years he collected and arranged the parliamentary debates for the *Gentleman's Magazine* and other periodicals, and lived in habits of intimacy with Dr Johnson. About 1745, he managed to let it be known to Government that he was a person who could write well, and that it might depend on circumstances whether he should use his pen as the medium of attack or of defence. The matter was placed on its proper footing, and Mr Guthrie received from the Pelham administration a pension of £200 a year. On a change of the ministry, nearly twenty years afterwards, we find him making efforts for the continuance of his allowance. " The following letter, addressed to a minister," says Mr Robert Chambers, in his " Biographical Dictionary," " is one of the coolest specimens of literary commerce on record. June 3, 1762,—My Lord, In the year 1745-6, Mr Pelham, then first lord of the treasury, acquainted me that it was his Majesty's pleasure I should receive, till better provided for, which never has happened, £200 a year, to be paid by him and his successors in the treasury. I was satisfied with the august name made use of, and the appointment has been regularly and quarterly paid me ever since. I have been punctual in doing the Government all the services that fell within my abilities or sphere of life, especially in those critical situations which call for unanimity in the service of the Crown. Your lordship will possibly now suspect that I am an author by profession—you are not deceived,

and you will be less so, if you believe that I am disposed to serve
his Majesty under your lordship's future patronage and protection,
with greater zeal, if possible, than ever.   I have the honour to
be, my Lord, &c., WILLIAM GUTHRIE." As a reward for his sub-
mission to the powers that were, Mr Guthrie's pension was continued to the day of his death, which took place on the 9th
March 1770, in the sixty-second year of his age.   His body was
interred in the churchyard of Mary-le-bon, London, where a
neat monument, which we have seen, erected to his memory,
states him to have been " the representative of the antient family
of Guthrie of Halkerton, in the county of *Angus*, North Britain,"
a statement erroneous at least in one respect, as to the locality
of Halkerton, which is in Kincardineshire.   Mr Guthrie's name
is best known by his " Historical and Geographical Grammar,"
which had reached its twenty-fourth edition in 1818.   In 1765,
he published, jointly with Gray and other literary men, " A
History of the World," and in 1767 appeared his " History of
Scotland," in ten volumes, in which, with true national fervour,
he maintains the high antiquity of everything connected with
Scotland.

GROUND PLAN OF BRECHIN CATHEDRAL.

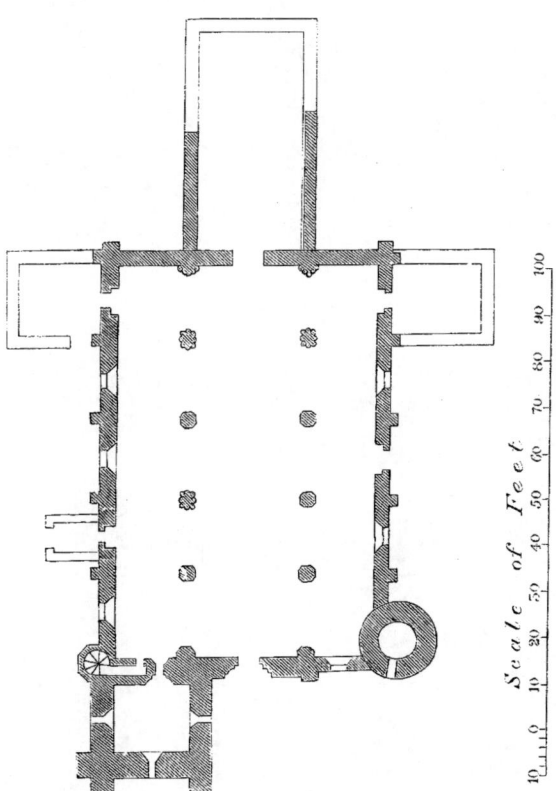

The shaded parts only, now remain, 1867.   *Page* 230.

BRECHIN CATHEDRAL.

VIEW FROM THE WEST.

Page 234.

CHAPTER VII.

THE early part of the reign of George II. is not marked by any-thing peculiar. People had now begun to look on the exiled Stewarts as a family whose fate was no longer connected with that of Scotland, and the arts of peace engrossed the attention of most burgesses. In May 1728, the council of Brechin re-sumed the practice, forborne for some time previous, of riding the marches, and in the same year the Little Mill was utterly demolished, and the stones of it taken to repair the *gainshott*, or ginshot, as it is sometimes called—the wall which defends the north-west side of the Inch, or public bleaching-green, from the ravages of the river South Esk. Next year the council took a more decided step; they feued off a piece of muir to John Ogilvy, under the name of "*Little Brechin*," and this grant was soon followed by other feus. The numerous houses which have recently arisen there, promise fairly to realise the ideas enter-tained by the inhabitants of *Muckle* Brechin a hundred years ago. This village lies upwards of two miles north of the town of Brechin, about the centre of that tract of ground denominated " Trinity Muir," of which the town council of Brechin are the superiors. But the other feus which followed close on the heels of the one to Ogilvy, alarmed the incorporations that all the " common guid" was to be sold off. To quiet them, the council in 1729 voted a sum in name of a grant to the poor's box of the six trades, and as a consideration for their trouble in riding the marches ! A new clock was, the same year, procured for the burgh from Alexander Gordon, silversmith in Dundee, at a cost, including *extras*, of £23 sterling; but the workmanship does not appear to have been fine; for in 1736 £42 Scots are paid to " William Lawson of Ballewny," for repairs on this piece of machinery.

The practice of granting indiscriminate burgess tickets continued till this time; so much so, that in 1732 the town-clerk is ordained to keep the provost always possessed of twelve blank tickets " to be disposed of at the discretion of the provost, or any of the magistrates."

The ports of the burgh, which had been repaired in 1709, were in a ruinous and dangerous condition in 1733; but they were then repaired by " pinning and harling," under directions of the magistracy; and in the subsequent year " the council taking into their consideration the ruinous state and condition of the cross and public market-place of this burgh," directed the same to be rebuilt for " the good, utility, and profit of the inhabitants," and " for the accommodation of the country people, merchants, and traffickers." Thirty years saw cross and ports all removed as useless encumbrances in the way of the citizens. The contract for rebuilding the cross shows the price of labour in 1734. George Miller and John Hunter, masons, received for their fees seven hundred merks, besides a crown of earnest, and this exclusive of the expense of casting of the " pit for the vault to be built below the cross." Robert Walker in East Drums, for furnishing the stones, got £126 Scots, including the price of the " stang or standing-stone for the top of the cross," with one shilling of earnest. George Davidson, " deacon convener," and Alexander Low, carter, were allowed 6s. Scots, for each load of stones driven, " they being obliged to lead *three* stones at each draught, excepting where the stones are extraordinary bigg."

The council had, no doubt, exercised the privilege of sending an elder to the General Assembly of the Kirk of Scotland, from the period their right to do so was recognised by that august assembly; but we see no notice taken of the exercise of such privilege till 1734, when Bailie Edward Leslie was named commissioner. The council yearly elected a ruling elder after that time till after the Disruption, when the Free Kirk was established in 1843, since which the election has been pretermitted. The certificate of the " uprightness of the walk" of the person elected to this office in 1843 was exactly in the same words as the certificate granted Bailie Leslie more than a century ago.

James Watson, tailor, applies to the council in 1735, to have feued to him the Gallowshill; and the burghal rulers finding that it is of small value, " and, as it now stands, of no use to the common good," dispose of it to the man of needles. This formidable spot is now occupied with a square of houses, belonging to that enterprising body the North Port Distillery Company.

It is not a little interesting to observe the accommodation which was at this period deemed ample and sufficient for a gentleman. A committee of the town council report, that, in their opinion, a new house should be built for Mr Shanks, the minister of the second charge in Brechin, " 49½ feet, within the walls, in length, 14 in breadth, and 15 in height from the sole of the door, which will admit of two rooms on the first story, each 14 feet square; a stair with two flights or turnings, 7 feet broad, and a cellar 10 feet; in the second story there will be two rooms, each 14 feet square, a closet above the cellar, with a chimney upon the side wall, and above them garrets; and that a house of no less dimensions can serve the minister and family." It is also said that in each room " there cannot be less than two windows;" and the other comforts of the family are provided for by "a brew-house of 12 feet of length, a stable and byre of 14 feet, and a barn of 15 feet of length." Mr Shanks, we notice, gave £66, 13s. 4d. to the session in 1744. The building erected, in consequence of this recommendation, in favour of Mr Shanks, was pulled down in 1803, when the house at present occupied by the Rev. Alexander Gardner was erected, to which manse, however, considerable additions have been made at various times since 1803.

But we must not imagine that because the nation was now quiet, the pugnacious people of Brechin were at peace. A fierce political contest arose in 1728, when Provost Robert Whyte was unseated, and John Knox was called to fill the chair. A law plea ensued, which only terminated with the death of Mr Whyte and his brother magistrate and adherent, Bailie Windram, and for which law plea the council paid a pretty round sum of sterling moneys in 1730. In 1733, Mr Knox was him-

self unseated, and succeeded in his office of provost by David
Doig of Cookston, son of Mr Doig who was provost in 1715, and
who was then imprisoned by the army of the Earl of Mar for his
adherence to the House of Hanover. Provost David Doig was,
like his father, a man of considerable energy, and, like him, he
is not under any obligation to tradition. A legend, still preserved, notices his death in no very courtly phrase, and the
popular voice asserts that " large screids " were acquired for the
estate of Cookston from the public property, at small prices.
The legend, playing upon the provost's name, vulgarly pronounced Dog, runs thus :—

> "Provost Doig's dead—God be thankit ;
> Mony a better dog's dead, since he was whelpit."

The demon of discord, however, again invaded the council in
1740, and Mr Doig was turned off, Provost Knox being recalled
to the chair.

Mr John Johnston, who had been a minister in Brechin, mortified in 1732, as the board in the session-house, so often referred
to, tells us, " for a school in the west side of the parish, and other
pious uses, upwards of £1000." This school was long known as
the school of Pitpullox, pronounced Pitbuiks, on the farm of
Broomfield, but is now removed to a place farther north, a short
way from Little Brechin.

In September 1741, the six incorporated trades fixed the
second Wednesday of September for the yearly election of deacons
and deacon-convener, and appointed that the latter official might
be elected thrice in succession, but that no deacon should be
continued in office for more than two years. This act yet regulates the mode and time of electing the convener and deacons
of crafts.

About this time the first tea-kettle seen in Brechin made its
appearance, specially commissioned from Aberdeen by the lady
of one of the principal merchants, Mr John Smith. The carrier
who delivered the kettle, declared it was the greatest curse ever
brought to Brechin by him or any other person. The practice
of tea-drinking, however, spread quickly, and superseded the
pottage and milk, the former breakfast meal, as well as the ale

and bread which previously formed the afternoon's repast of all classes.

The records of the burgh are miserably deficient during that interesting period of Scottish romance, the insurrection of 1745-6. All that we gather from these records is, that the elections were pretermitted for two years, and that a new council was chosen by poll of the burgesses in July 1747. A majority of the old council was re-elected at the poll election, but the dynasty was changed; and the family of Molison, aided by the Panmure interest, turned out Provost Knox and his friends, although the latter were supported by the Presbyterian clergy of the day, and eiked out their canvass by distributing to the populace rum punch, made in washing-tubs in the porch on the north aisle of the church, in which distribution one of the clergymen, an enemy to all Jacobites, is reported to have taken an active hand. Mr John Molison and his party continued predominant after this, during all the period which we mean to embrace within this chapter. Mr Molison took an active superintendence of municipal affairs, and deserves no little credit for the labour he bestowed in adjusting the rentals of the town and of the hospital, previously allowed to go into great confusion. The reason assigned for the poll election alluded to is, "that those in whom the right of election was, at Michaelmas 1745, were interrupted from completing their election at that time by the rebels who were then in possession of this place." During this interregnum, the municipal affairs were conducted by two gentlemen within the burgh, acting as sheriffs-depute. An unhappy wight, James Warden, a town-officer, was then debarred from his office, for his attachment to *Charlie*, but, in 1748, the council records tell us that this worthy was reinstated in his situation, because, poor man, he was "actually forced by the rebels" to join them. The town council records of Montrose are equally defective at this period; on 23d September 1745, there is a minute of council about the ordinary affairs of the burgh, and the next entry is on 10th July 1746, when the old officials meet, by virtue of a warrant from the Privy Council, and elect, after a stormy debate, a new set of municipal rulers for the burgh, of whom David Doig of Cookston, formerly provost of Brechin, is chosen chief magistrate, he having by this time become a merchant in Montrose. But although the authentic records are thus scanty, tradition has given us many circumstances connected with this period.

It will be recollected that Prince Charles Edward Lewis Cassimer Stewart, son of James, who claimed the throne of Great Britain, as Eighth of Scotland and Third of England, landed in the Western Isles in July 1745, with only seven friends, and that, with little or no assistance from foreign aid, he took possession of the principal places in Scotland, and even bade fair to restore his father to the British throne, having advanced as far as Derby ; when, on the 6th December, he saw fit to pause, and to commence a retreat to the North of Scotland. " Bonnie Prince Charlie" never was in Brechin, but he had many admirers in the burgh, and most of the gentry in the neighbourhood joined his standard. William Duke of Cumberland, the second son of George II., was sent by his father to cope with Charles ; and on the field of Culloden, near Inverness, was witnessed, on 16th April 1746, the spectacle of two princes, the sons of kings, contending at the head of their respective armies for the right of their respective fathers to rule these realms. The result is well known — Charles was defeated — William was successful ; the family of Stewart was for ever superseded, and the family of Guelph has since swayed the sceptre. We ourselves have received it from an individual, long since gathered to her sires, but who, as she described herself, was "a wee bit callant o' a lassie," in 1746, that Lord George Murray passed through Brechin with part of Charles's army early in the year, and was followed in a few weeks afterwards by Cumberland and his troops. She pictured Charles's army as containing a most uncultivated set of beings, who excited terror amongst the inhabitants, even amongst those most friendly to the Stewart cause, and who were no ways scrupulous in helping themselves to anything which struck their fancy, and was of a palatable description, but who were chiefly noted for their predilection for *ginger-bread*. These Highlanders were several days about Brechin, at least the advanced-guard, main-body, and rear-guard was each one, if not two days in the town. Murray's men took possession of the Town-hall for their guard-room, broke up the benches, tore open the presses, and burned such records as fell into their hands to supply them with fuel. But notwithstanding of all these peccadilloes, the hearts of the ladies went with the Highlanders, and our little friend herself even found a sweetheart amongst them, whom she stated to have been a " protty lad." The troops of Cumberland were better disciplined, and the little lass alluded to described them as affording a beautiful sight when they marched along the Bridge of Brechin, having come from Forfar by Angus Hill, and what is now denominated the old road, the present turnpike not having existed till fifty years afterwards. A brewer who then lived at the end of the bridge, either from fear or loyalty, perhaps partly from both, spread tables in front of his house, and covered them with bickers full of beer, and small loaves of bread, to which he invited the soldiers of Cumberland; but Prince William, suspecting this over-hospitality, would not allow his men to taste a thing offered to them, not even a glass of water; and he caused his soldiers to seat themselves by the side of the Esk, eat what provisions they brought with them, and lap out of the river like dogs, or like the army of Gideon. When the troops were thus refreshed, and had enjoyed a few hours' rest, Cumberland marched them up by the East Mill road, round by Pitforthie, and away by the King's Ford, in the direction of Stonehaven and Aberdeen; so that King George's army passed the south end of the town of Brechin, but was never in the city. The duke himself and his staff, however, rode through the town, and joined the army at Cairnbank. Mr David Mather, one of the bailies of Brechin and a favourer of the fortunes of the family of Hanover, met Cumberland as he entered the limits of the burgh at the Muckle Mill, and, with a bottle of wine and a glass in his hand, pledged the duke, and requested of him and his officers to partake of a refreshment then prepared for them by some members of the town council and other gentlemen of influence in the burgh. Cumberland took the glass out of the bailie's hands, and put the wine towards his mouth, expressing good wishes for Mather and his colleagues, but he did not even venture to let his lips taste the beverage, and pointedly refused to allow his officers to partake of the *dejeuné* provided for them. Perhaps the duke's suspicions were more strongly excited at this time, in consequence of the folks of Forfar, the neighbouring town, having, a day or two before, contrived to cut the girths of his horses when he lay at Glammis, so as to retard his march northwards. Be this as it máy, it is reported that neither the duke nor any of his army would taste a morsel that was *offered* to them ; and that they drew their supplies wholly from their own commissaries, who were harsh enough in *exacting* what suited them from the country people, at such nominal price as the commissaries chose to put upon the articles. When the duke was slowly parading up the long main street of Brechin, anxiously gazed on by the inhabitants, he observed a singularly pretty girl standing on a *stairhead* opposite the cross ; and, struck by the girl's beauty, he bowed towards her ; but the little minx, to the no small mortification of her admirer, and the great delight of the spectators, replied to this courtesy by the most contemptuous gesture she could adopt—a gesture fully as expressive as delicate.

Cumberland, it would appear from the records of the presbytery of Brechin, was at Montrose on the 22d and 24th February. On the first of these days that presbytery met at Brechin in the forenoon, and adjourned to Montrose in the afternoon to address the duke, but " his Royal Highness having called together his general officers to consult about matters of importance, could not be at leisure this night, but would very willingly receive them on Monday next in the forenoon ;" and accordingly, on the 24th February 1746, that reverend body having desired access to his Royal Highness, they were graciously received and had the honour to kiss the duke's hand ; and after a short address by their moderator, testifying their loyalty and steady adherence to his Majesty's person and government, " and expressing their just abhorrence of the present unnatural rebellion, and wishing safety and success to his Royal Highness," they had a most favourable answer by his Royal Highness himself. Whether it was before or after this that Cumberland was in Brechin we have no certain information ; but we should rather suppose the duke had come to Brechin to meet a detachment of his troops, after he had left Montrose, where apparently he had kept his head-quarters for a few days.

Before marching into England, in October 1745, Prince Charles named David Ferrier, tenant of Unthank and merchant in Brechin, to be commandant of a party of troops left at Montrose. Mr Ferrier was a captain in Lord Ogilvie's regiment, and had raised two companies of militia, with whom he did much service to the Pretender's cause, and was in consequence appointed deputy-governor of Brechin by James Carnegy Arbuthnott of Balnamoon and Findowry, who acted as deputy-lieutenant of the county of Angus for the Stewart party. During the winter of 1745-46 the *Hazard*, sloop-of-war, anchored in the river South Esk, off Montrose, preventing all intercourse by sea, and annoying Ferrier's troops when they made their appearance on land within range of the guns. Captain Ferrier planned, and with no little boldness executed, a scheme for getting rid of the annoyance. He first mounted some old guns found about the harbour, and placed them at a narrow part of the river, to prevent the vessel running out to sea, and he next availed himself of a thick fog to surround the ship with boats manned by his own soldiers, and steered by sailors favourable to his cause. The crew of the sloop, taken by surprise, surrendered at discretion ; some were killed in the action, and the rest were marched into prison. This vessel was afterwards despatched into France as a *Snow*, under the name of *The Prince Charles*, and returning to Scotland with a valuable cargo, was chased by the *Sheerness*, man-of-war, to avoid which the crew ran the vessel ashore on Lord Reay's country, where it was plundered by the Hanoverian party. In the library of Carmichael, Lanarkshire, there is a book entitled, " List of Persons concerned in the Rebellion, with Evidences to prove the same, transmitted to the Commissioners of Excise by the several Supervisors in Scotland ;" and in this volume Mr Ferrier is thus noticed:—
" David Ferrier, merchant in Brechin, acted as deputy-governor of the town of Brechin, practised the highest tyranny over the loyal subjects of the Government in every shape, and particularly extorted men, money, and horses and arms throughout the whole country, levied his Majesty's Excise, and gave his own

K

receipts for the same; was the principal person who promoted
and carried on the affair of taking the *Hazard* sloop-of-war, in
which some of the crew were killed and wounded, and the rest
made prisoners, and treated by him in so barbarous a manner
that they must in all probability have perished had it not been
for the assistance they received from the Government in Montrose, Brechin, and elsewhere.   He also bore arms in Lord
Ogilvie's regiment, and recruited and forced out no less than
two companies of rebel militia; was present at the skirmish of
Inverury as captain of one of said companies; burnt the custom-
house at Aberdeen; received and conveyed the French arms and
ammunition to the rebel army, for which purpose he harassed
and oppressed the whole country, in pressing their horses and
carts.   He joined the main body of the rebels at Stirling with
his companies, accompanied them to Inverness, from whence he
returned to Glenesk, raised a great many of the inhabitants there
with a design to force back rebel runaways, and make well-
affected people prisoners, and marched with the said Glenesks
to Cortachie, in order to force a garrison of the king's troops
there.   These facts are well known to every person in these
places of the country.   Supposed to be lurking among the neighbouring hills."   Mr Ferrier succeeded in getting abroad, and,
not being included in the Act of Amnesty, he subsequently resided in Spain, where he died.   He must have been a bold, clever
fellow, and well deserving of a better fortune.

Many of the natives of Brechin were present at the battle of
Culloden, but only a few returned to give an account of that
awful day; and these few, for obvious reasons, were not very
anxious to speak of what they had seen.   One gentleman, who
had served in the army abroad, but whose predilections led him
to join the prince, (he was careful in avoiding to say which
prince,) used to tell that he surveyed the Highland line immediately before it charged the regular troops, and that the eyes
of each Highlander then gleamed like coals, while each countenance was marked with an expression of determination fearful
to look upon.

Amongst those who did return from "following Prince
Charlie," was Peter Logie, the cripple tailor of the Tiggerton of

Balnamoon. Mr Carnegy, the laird of Balnamoon, already alluded to, was a zealous Jacobite, collected the cess of the county of Forfar in name of James VIII., and followed to the "battle-field" with all his train, for which he was subsequently taken to the Tower, and only escaped in consequence of a "misnomer," when brought to trial for his connexion with the rising. Mr Carnegy, although he made as much haste home as was possible after the battle of Culloden, found that Logie, with his club-foot, had preceded him by a day. The tailor was subsequently apprehended, and questioned about his connexion with the rebellion, by the Elector of Hanover's magistrates, as he termed them. When asked if he was present at the battle of Preston, the battle of Falkirk, and the battle of Culloden, he answered affirmatively, and with much seeming candour, to each question; and when asked what station he held in the rebel army, he replied, with a glance at his club-foot, "I had the honour to be his royal highness's dancing-master." Peter, it is needless to add, was immediately liberated. Balnamoon used to tell this story with considerable glee. Though there was no doubt that Logie was in attendance upon Balnamoon at Preston and Falkirk, those in the secret doubted whether the "sly tailor loon" had ever got the length of Culloden Muir.

Another retainer of Balnamoon's, in the same rank of life as Logie, and who was generally believed to have seen the flight at Culloden, retained all his keenness for the cause till the close of a very old age. When he heard his neighbours complaining of the taxes, his usual answer was, "Deil hae't cares, ye widna hae a guid king when we gae you the offer o' him."

Many of the prisoners taken to England at this time were confined in Tilbury Fort, a low dull-looking place, upon the side of the Thames; and so wearisome was the detention of these active spirits in this *inanimate* place, that none of them could ever afterwards bear to hear even the name of their prison. One person belonging to Brechin was seated by his fire on a winter evening, when his wife, honest woman, was reeling the yarn which she had that day spun. Our friend was musing on his past fortunes, and, dreaming that the click-cluck-clack, click-cluck-clack noise made by the reel in its evolu-

tions resembled the word Til-bury-fort, Til-bury-fort, he started
up in a passion, seized the poker, and, with one ruthless stroke,
demolished the emblem of industry, exclaiming, " I 'se Tilbury-
fort ye." The person who thus allowed his imagination to get
so much the better of his reason, was a James Allardice, who
resided in the Nether Tenements, now called River Street.
During his imprisonment, he displayed no little heroism and
firmness. Being strongly tempted to give evidence against his
associates, he replied, " My life is in your hands, and you may
take it, as you have taken the lives of better men ; but my
honour is in my own hands, and I will keep it—*that* you shall
not take from me."

The Swan Inn, the principal inn of the town, was kept by a
Mr Low, who was a member of the town council in 1746, and,
as was alleged, one of those who prevented an election of magistrates and a renewal of the oaths to Government at that time.
After the rebellion was quashed, Mr Low was taken to London,
upon the information, as was supposed, of an over-zealous Presbyterian clergyman, Mr Blair. Nothing particular could be
brought against Low, but it was thought he might be cajoled
or frightened into being a witness against some of the leading
men of the county, for whose conviction evidence was rather
scanty. Accordingly, Mr Low was confined under the charge
of one of the king's messengers, who gave him every indulgence,
and took him round London to see all the sights. One day
Low was suddenly sent for and examined by one of the secre-
taries of State. After some preliminary questions, to all of
which Mr Low gave very distinct answers, the querist said,
" You will recollect, Mr Low, on such a day, of seeing Lord
Airlie and other gentlemen of the county (whom he named) in
your house, wearing white rosettes (the Stewart livery) in their
bonnets ? " " It 's not the practice, my lord," responded Low,
" for gentlemen in my country to wear their bonnets in the
house." " Take him to jail," was the rejoinder, an order which
was instantly obeyed, and Low was for nearly twelve months in
confinement ; but he ultimately returned to Brechin, to be the
choice host of all the Jacobites of Forfarshire, and the general
favourite of his townsmen. Being in a friend's house with the

suspected clergyman, years afterwards, the conversation turned upon London, when Low and the minister, who had also been in London, detailed, for the amusement of the company, what they had seen there. One of the gentlemen present, without reflecting, remarked it was strange. Mr Low and Mr Blair appeared to have been in London at the same time, and yet had never met. " Sir," said Low—with a Johnsonian dignity which he could easily assume—" sir, I was sick and in prison, and he visited me not." The minister soon found an excuse for leaving the company, and, it was said, ever after shunned talking of London when Mr Low was present.

The Duke of Cumberland was much exasperated at the Scottish Episcopalians, most of whom were Jacobites, and he was especially exasperated with the Episcopalians of Forfarshire, who raised no few men to assist Prince Charles. After the battle of Culloden, therefore, Cumberland adopted very harsh measures against the Episcopalians, causing their chapels to be burned, and all their property to be destroyed. His soldiers, under the superintendence of the Christian pastor alluded to, tore up the benches of the Episcopal chapel of Brechin, and burned all the wood-work of the interior, together with the prayer-books found in the chapel. The soldiery were also about to destroy the building, when the presbyter spoken of requested it might be spared, as it could be used for the Wednesday sermon—the sermon then usually delivered in the cathedral each Wednesday, and for which purpose the kirk was rather too large and cold. This was spoliation and appropriation in the true sense of the terms. The house was spared, but never used for the purpose intended. It is now occupied by a congregation in connexion with the United Presbyterians.

It would appear, however, the Duke of Cumberland had some cause to be alarmed at the Brechin Jacobites, if the representations made to the Presbytery by the ministers of Brechin are correct. The Presbytery records of 2d March 1748, contain the following curious entry:—" Then Mr Blair and Mr Fordyce, ministers at Brechin, being called upon, gave in the following representation. That they were sorry to say that a spirit of disaffection did greatly prevail in their town and parish, and

that, for the present, there was little appearance or probability of
its decrease—nay, that it was more than before the late unnatural
rebellion, which will be evident when it is considered;—1st
That of thirteen members of which the town council of Brechin
consists, six were the constant attendants of a non-jurant meeting-house, during the time of the foresaid rebellion, and it deserves a remark, that the provost or first magistrate, and one of
the bailies, are of that number; 2d, That all the members of
the said town council, except three, were some way or other
concerned in the late execrable attempt, some of them by keeping guard on the *Hazard* sloop prisoners, others of them by
harbouring the goods of rebels, others of them by drinking the
Pretender's health publicly at the cross; 3d, That in the month
of August last, his Majesty and the royal family were made the
objects of scurrilous language and songs upon the public streets.
That Mr Blair, one of the ministers of Brechin, took notice of
these wicked and treasonable practices from the pulpit on a
Lord's day, and warned the people against them, as things extremely evil in themselves, and which, if continued, behoved to
draw down the just displeasure of the Government upon the
place. That though he did this on a Lord's day in presence of the
gentlemen who had lately been put upon the magistracy, yet this
warning was so far from having its proper effect, that a daughter of Mr Allardice, one of the present bailies of the town, sung
a song in contempt of his royal highness, the duke, by way of
insult upon Mr Blair, on the Monday immediately after the said
warning was emitted; 4th, That sometime in the month of
August last, John Strachan, who had been committed to Tilbury Fort on *suspicion* of treasonable practices, and had returned again to this place, said, in a public company, that the
Pretender, whom he impudently called King James the Eighth,
was the only rightful sovereign of those realms, for whom he
had suffered, and wished to God there were not a living man in
Bergenopzoom, which was then besieged by the French; 5th,
That so little care has been taken to put persons well affected
to his Majesty's person and Government in the place upon the
administration, that one Alexander Low, (*our merry host of the
Swan,*) reputed a Jacobite by all that know him, and was taken

into custody for treasonable practices during the time of the rebellion, and detained prisoner for several months, undertook to be evidence for the crown, and afterwards declined it, was, notwithstanding all this, by the influence, no doubt, of his brother-in-law, Mr Molison, the chief magistrate of this place, made one of the town councillors at Michaelmas last, since which time, as a proof that he is still under the influence of the old spirit of rebellion, he had a child baptized by the non-jurant minister who resides in this town ; 6th, That there are no less than two non-jurant ministers, one who has his constant residence in the town, and another who comes from the country, viz., Mr James Lyall at Carcary, in the parish of Farnwell, who make it their business to go from house to house, and to instil bad principles into the minds of their deluded votaries, and baptize their children, and it's apprehended with too great success, for numbers of those frequented the meetings of the Established Church immediately after the rebellion, yet they have now, almost to a man, withdrawn from them, those three or four excepted, who being upon the public management, still continue to attend them in order to save appearances. Nay, to this purpose, it's observable that on the seventeenth of February last, being the day of public humiliation appointed by his Majesty, there was not above three or four who had been the attendants of non-jurant meeting-houses before, and during the time of the late unnatural rebellion, who attended worship in the Presbyterian Church, or paid the least regard to that solemn day ; 7th, That, so far as the ministers foresaid know, the magistrates of the place bestow no care to discourage the spirit of disaffection which rages here, or to give check to the non-jurant ministers, or so much as to inquire into their conduct and seditious practices. It is a strong presumption of this that though (as said is) they attend public worship in the Established Church themselves, yet none of them have ever brought their wives or any of their children, who are come to majority, along with them. Nay, that it is well known that their wives and daughters are among the most zealous friends of the non-jurant preachers ; 8th, That his Majesty's most zealous friends who have persisted in attending worship where King George was prayed for, when both ministers and people were in the greatest danger from armed rebels in the church, have been insulted and beat upon the public streets by disaffected persons, and such as bore arms in the rebellion, without receiving the smallest redress from the magistrates of the place, who ought to protect the king's lieges by the execution of the laws." A report grounded upon this representation was laid before Government, but no proceedings followed in consequence against the contumacious magistrates.

Mr James Fordyce, who concurs with Mr Blair in the report of the Jacobitical spirit in Brechin, was the eloquent writer of " Sermons to Young Women," and " Addresses to Young Men," besides other theological works. He was ordained to the second charge of this parish in 1745, and continued a clergyman in Brechin for eight years, when he removed to Alloa, and soon after to London. Mr Fordyce was the first Presbyterian clergyman settled in Brechin in consequence of a presentation from the Crown ; and it was only after his case had gone through all the church courts that the settlement took place, a number of his brethren contending that a leet by the Presbytery, followed by a call from the people, ought to have preceded the presentation.

Mr Blair, who held the first charge of the parish, died at Brechin in 1769, aged 69, in the thirty-sixth year of his incumbency, as recorded in a marble tablet placed inside the church, which also states, that about 1760 he established in Brechin the first Sabbath evening school in Scotland.

In 1748, the church of Brechin was repaired at an expense of £753 Scots, a sum which appears to have been entirely expended on the roof and windows.

Mr William Maitland, the laborious historian of London and Edinburgh, died at Montrose on 16th July 1757. He is generally supposed to have been born in Brechin about the year 1690, and the newspapers which report his death, mention that he died at an advanced age, and possessed of £10,000 sterling, realised by trade. In the prosecution of his business, he travelled through many foreign places ; but, in 1730, he settled in London, and applied himself to the study of English and Scottish antiquities ; and, in 1733, he was elected a Fellow of the Royal

Antiquarian Society. In 1739 appeared his "History of London," which was well received. The same year he removed to Scotland, and in 1740 published his "History of Edinburgh," a valuable and useful work.

The unfortunate close of Charles's romantic attempt destroyed all the hopes which the Scottish Jacobites had hitherto nourished, and although, for a few years, some zealous song-singing ladies, and equally zealous three-bottle, health-pledging gentlemen, might entertain hopes that the "king should enjoy his nain again," every cool thinking Jacobite saw that the sun of their hopes had set on the field of Culloden. Hereditary jurisdictions and military tenures, which had been as vexatious to the subject as they were annoying to Government, were now abolished. The nation became united, and free from faction; it grew less warlike, but it became more attached to agriculture and manufactures. The advantages of the Union with England then began gradually to be perceived. The town council of Brechin, anxious to display their new-found loyalty, were active in offering bounties and raising men for the Royal Navy. Yea, they published proclamations against smuggling, and petitioned to have the alehouses in Scotland regulated like those of England; and, still more strange assimilation, they applied to Parliament to raise a militia in Scotland upon the same footing as in England. With the aid of a grant from the trustees for improving manufactures, the Inch was levelled, and let to a person regularly bred to the bleaching of linen, the son-in-law of Mr Low, so often mentioned. Nuisances were removed from the streets; the waste lands of the burgh were turned to account; the regular maintenance of the poor was thought of; and for the thirty years succeeding this civil war, the attention of the town council of Brechin was occupied with matters of a peaceable and profitable nature. One act only, prohibiting the letting of houses within the burgh to strangers, shows that the civil rights of the citizens were not yet fully recognised. Finally, the town council, in 1759, pulled down the ports of the burgh and sold the materials, thus showing that for their part they feared no further invasion.

CHAPTER VIII.

THE long reign of George III. affords many circumstances of heart-stirring interest to the general historian, but few circumstances which can be rendered of much excitement by the chronicler of local events. The internal affairs of burghs in the eighteenth century may be of vast importance to the inhabitants of these burghs, but they have little connexion with general history, and hence have little interest for the general reader. Our subsequent details, therefore, we suspect, will command the attention of few persons not directly connected with Brechin, if indeed what we have already written shall command attention from any not so connected, or even from persons interested in the ancient burgh. But in the hopes that we may find some readers of some description, we shall hold on the even tenor of our way.

Situated inland, the expense of sea-borne coal has always been severely felt by the inhabitants of Brechin. Originally, feal and peats were the fuel generally used, and rarely is an excavation yet made in the streets but the site of some ashes' pit, or peat stack, is discovered. Besides peats, pob, the refuse of lint, was very generally burned by the poorer part of the community ; and so many accidents had occurred from the use of this fuel, that, in 1761, the town council passed an act prohibiting the burning of pob in time to come. For the same reason, and at the same time, the council discharged flax-dressers from having their shops under the same roofs with dwelling-houses. Still further to prevent accidents by fire within the burgh, the council, next year, prohibited the repairing of any house with thatched roofs or wooden vents, and ordained that all new houses should be covered with slate or tiles, and have the vents carried up with stones. These acts, like many others of the same stamp, were only observed by those whom it suited to observe them. The evils then attempted to be remedied by municipal enactments have been all removed by the progress of improvement. The last thatched tenement within the burgh was a house in the Lower Wynd, now called Church Street, next to the site of the present schools, and long inhabited by a primitive personage, named Tibbie Patter, whose only companions were a cat and a brace of ducks. Upon Tibbie's death, in 1810, the house, which was composed of stone and clay, and thatched, was pulled down, and replaced by a substantial erection of stone and lime. A humorous friend of ours was wont to style this last of the thatched biggings "Patter Hall," the house and inhabitants being unique of their kind. Recent improvements in machinery have rendered the employment of flax-dressers so dependent on spinning-mills, that the trade, as a separate profession, is almost entirely abandoned, the flax being heckled at premises adjoining the mills, or more generally by machinery within the mills, and thus hecklers' shops are now unknown in the town, while the pob which served for fuel in 1760, is now wrought up into coarse yarns for the manufacture of bagging and like purposes.

A contest rather amusing, but not without interest in a political view, occurred amongst the incorporated trades in 1731. The tailors had resolved to augment their wages to sixpence per day, and had made a regular act of their craft to that effect. This was viewed as a serious matter by the other five trades, and the convener assembled the incorporations to debate the point, upon which the deacon of the tailors lodged a protest, bearing that the deacons of the other crafts were not competent to judge what wages were sufficient for tailors, and ought not to interfere in the matter. There appears much reason in the protest, but the convener and his court did, notwithstanding, interfere ; found that the tailors had been " guilty of a *highnous* trangression " in making of their act, ordered it to be rescinded, and fined them in 20 merks for their conduct. The tailors gave in, pleaded they had made the offensive act " inadvertently," and the convenery court reduced the fine to 4s. 6d. sterling.

The convenery court went still further at this time. They ordained that no matter relating to trades' affairs should be taken before any other court than the convenery court. Possibly it was in consequence of this enactment that, in March 1766, a solemn complaint was laid before the convenery court against a tailor for "mismaking of a great or big coat." On this complaint the court, after due inquiry by three tailors, found that the fault of the coat lay in the tightness of the sleeves only, and that this tightness arose from the shrinking of the cloth in consequence of exposure to rain, and not from the cabbaging of the tailor, who was honourably acquitted, but, rather inconsistently, appointed to "widen the sleeves upon his own proper expenses."

In 1763, a garden, situated at the mouth of the Bishop's Close, was purchased for the purpose of building a flesh-market upon. This market was used both for the killing of animals and retailing of their flesh till 1797, when a slaughter-house was erected at the Den-side; and now that has been superseded, and premises for the slaughtering of cattle erected in 1865, on part of the Trinity Muir market stance. The flesh-market, which, in 1763, was doubtless a very great improvement, has now become of no use for the purpose intended, all the butchers occupying separate shops in different parts of the town, a distribution of the craft which is much more convenient for the inhabitants than when the whole fleshers were collected in one public market, even although in the most centrical part of the town. The number of butchers too has so much increased that the flesh-market would not accommodate above half of those of the present day, and this increase we look upon as no uncertain sign of the increased comforts of the people of Brechin since the time when the flesh-market was erected. The market, as we formerly noticed, is now however used for the sale of dairy produce, poultry, &c., on Tuesdays.

A serious riot occurred amongst the trades at the "intaking" of the Trinity Fair in July 1765, in consequence of which the council published a formal order regulating the precedency of the incorporated trades upon all subsequent similar occasions. This enactment, we believe, has been strictly observed ever since.

The order of precedency is this: The free members of the hammermen, glovers, and bakers go first, abreast; the free members of the shoemakers, weavers, and tailors follow next; then the wrights and butchers; and, lastly, the apprentices and servants of the different crafts, keeping the same order as that assigned for their masters. The butchers and wrights never had any voice in the municipal elections, although they enjoyed corporate privileges. About the end of the eighteenth century the butchers and wrights formed themselves into two friendly societies; and in 1827, when the rage came for breaking up such societies, the funds of these two bodies were divided, and the butchers and wrights then ceased to exist either as societies or corporate bodies. The glovers at present are in abeyance, having neglected, in 1836, to elect office-bearers, and we presume they will be content so to remain in time to come, the more especially as there has been no actual glover in the burgh for many years. The other five trades still exist—the hammermen, bakers, shoemakers, weavers, and tailors: the last four composed chiefly of persons, handicraftsmen of the trades to which their names point; the first including smiths, watchmakers, and saddlers—the saddlers having originally been claimed by this craft, from the quantity of iron work about the ancient trappings for horses. In 1766, the guildry incorporation renewed an existing ordinance of that body, by which any individual claiming admission as a guild brother was obliged to renounce all right to vote in the elections of the trades; and the trades as strictly prohibited those who became guildrymen from any title to interfere in their elections; so that within the town there were two public bodies jealously watching over the aristocracy and democracy of the burgh, and both looking with Argus eyes at the magistracy and close council of the town, till the Reform Act of 1832 threw the incorporations comparatively into the shade, and brought forward the £10 voters as a body commixing and superseding both guildry and trades.

Upon the petition of the doctor of the grammar-school, or second teacher in that establishment, the council, in July 1765, in respect that "the expense of living and other necessaries was, of late years, much increased," augmented the quarterly fee payable to the doctor from 1s. to 1s. 6d., but ordained him " to teach each scholar who shall apply for the same, writing and arithmetic for the said quarterly payment, as well as Latin." This office of doctor was abolished in 1783, when Mr William Dovertie was appointed " teacher of English, writing, and arithmetic within the burgh," and allowed the salary formerly paid to the doctor, with authority to uplift from his scholars, " from those he teaches English only, 1s. 6d.; from those who he teaches English and writing, 2s.; and from those who he teaches English, writing, and arithmetic, 2s. 6d.," quarterly. Mr Dovertie, however, taught the foreign languages, because Mr Linton, the rector, taught English and figures, and thus, in each of the schools, all the branches of education were taught till a formal division was made in 1834. The fees exacted about 1780–90 did not exceed 3s. 6d. per quarter for every branch of education except book-keeping, which was charged at a guinea the course. The fees were not augmented till 1801.

In July 1766, the Dove Wells of Cookston were purchased from the proprietor of that estate, and water was introduced into the town by means of lead pipes. It was then agreed, at a head court called for the purpose of considering the matter, that the expense should be defrayed by an assessment of 1s. per £ on the rent, laid on for fifteen years. The person employed to lay the pipes was a Robert Selby, plumber in Edinburgh, and his con-tract amounted to £287, 4s. for pipes of one-and-a-half inch diameter, weighing 20 lbs. per yard, all carriages being defrayed by the burgh. By means of these pipes the town till recently was well supplied with pure spring water of an excellent quality. The increase of population, however, has led to the introduction of water from Burghill by means of cast-iron pipes, these being cheaper and equally effective as lead. To enable the community to pay the original expense, a credit was applied for and obtained from the Dundee Banking Company for £500; but, in 1769, an arrangement was entered into with Earl Panmure, whereby he acquired a right to a pipe of half-an-inch diameter, for conduct-ing water from the town's fountains to Brechin Castle, and the earl paid the bond to the bank. In consequence, the proposed tax of 1s. per £ was never levied, and the inhabitants were formally relieved of it by an act of council, dated 1st November 1770. A tax, however, was raised for *maintaining* the wells, which was collected by a treasurer named by the inhabitants. Many of the proprietors bought up this tax, by which means about £100 were raised. Unfortunately, however, the fund came into bad hands, and most of the cash was lost, while the whole expense of maintaining the public wells was thrown on the burgh funds. The maintenance of fountains, wells, and pipes has cost, first and last, no little money; but this expense, together with the other municipal expenses, have hitherto been paid from the burgh funds. The cross, the capital, as it may be termed, of the burgh, was pulled down in 1767, by order of the council, and the stones were employed in " building the six wells proposed for discharging the water in the town;" the reasons given for this demolition being the saving of expense to the community, and the increased accommodation afforded at the market-place by the removal of the cross. The site of this ancient erection was pointed out by a circle intersected by a cross, marked by stones placed in the causeway, opposite the town hall, till, in 1837, this memorial of bygone magnificence was entirely effaced by the devoted followers of Macadam.

The proposal for a canal between Glasgow and Carron in 1767, seems to have alarmed the magistrates of Edinburgh, and the council of Brechin were weak enough, in consequence of a communication addressed to them from a committee of the convention of royal burghs, to write their then representative in Parliament, urging him to use his endeavours to have the measure delayed, " that an affair of such importance to the country in general may be more deliberately gone about." The canal has since been made, and carried on to Edinburgh, but is now all but superseded by a railway between these two extensive towns.

In 1768, some of the country gentlemen in the neighbourhood had a regular battle with the magistrates in the Trinity Muir market, arising out of a dispute about enclosures erected by the council in the Common Muir. The magistrates were supported by the council and incorporations in going to law, and after a long discussion before the Court of Session, it was found that the right to enclose lay with the council, but that they had enforced their title in an improper manner. Thus both parties were, to a certain extent, found wrong, and both were mulcted in no small sums to the Edinburgh gentlemen who condescend to wear wigs and gowns, and to pocket the money and laugh at the simplicity of those who employ them.

In 1770, and the years immediately succeeding, large portions of the Common Muir were feued off to the Earl of Panmure, Mr Carnegy of Balnamoon, and other gentlemen, to the advantage equally of the burgh and of the feuars. From the feuing of this muir a great part of the revenue of the town now arises, and as this muir continues to be subdivided and improved, so will the revenue of the burgh continue to increase. A plan of all these feus will be found in the charter room, framed by Mr George Henderson, land-surveyor and nurseryman, in 1829, and will afford to any one inclined to examine it a distinct view of the great extent of the Trinity Muir, originally belonging to the town, and described as extending from the Gallows of Keithock to the Gallows of Fearn. We had many a pleasant early morning walk and ride with Mr Henderson in ascertaining boundaries to be inscribed on this map, for it well deserves that name, and is of great value to the corporation.

A melancholy account is given of the state of the public school-house in 1772. It is said to be " ruinous, and in great danger by the back wall thereof being in daily hazard of falling," in consequence of which the council directed it to be repaired—not too soon, certainly.

The river Esk overflowed its banks in 1774. The whole bleachfield was then covered, and the inhabitants of the Lower Tenements were driven to the higher apartments of their houses, the under stories being quite under water.

It was in 1776, that the famous act was made, which we have so often heard referred to at public meetings, as an instance of how the best of measures may be misapprehended by public bodies. In June that year, the council directed the magistrates to oppose the bill then intended to be brought into Parliament for making toll roads in the county, because, as the minute of council bears, " the establishing a toll would be highly prejudicial to the trade and manufactures of this burgh in particular, and to the country adjacent in general." The toll roads were, however, made, and in the year 1793 the council subscribed thirty guineas towards the erection of a bridge at Finhaven upon the line of the toll-road, which has ever since continued the direct route be- tween Brechin and Forfar, although travellers now generally go by the *round about* railway between these places; a *circum- bendibus* which will surely soon be superseded by a direct line between the two towns. Roads must always continue for the convenience of the internal intercourse of the country, but modern economists have begun, like the Brechin council of 1776, to doubt whether the public highways of a nation might not be more fairly maintained than by a tax on the passengers travelling over them, so that the act, which almost since its date has been matter of mirth to the political philosophers of the burgh, may yet come to be held up as proof of the wisdom of our ancestors.

The *muckle* bell was recast in 1780. The expense was de- frayed chiefly by public subscriptions. How this recasting came to be necessary is not on record; but tradition tells that some limbs of the law, and other young bucks, having become too jovial, climbed up into the steeple one Saturday night by means of the timber then kept in the *fore* churchyard by the carpen- ters of the town, and having thus gained admission to the belfrey, rung the bell till they broke it. Doubtless, these gentlemen, though keeping in the shade, would be liberal in their subscrip- tions towards the recasting of the bell. A few friends of ours, now all in their graves, were in their heydays seized with a similar fit of frolic and mischief. Amongst other tricks, they pulled down the sign of a worthy burgess, more noted for *jaw* than judgment. We shall never forget the queer appearance of the gentleman of the brush, who was employed next day to re- place the demolished sign, and who had the utmost difficulty in answering, with becoming gravity, the numerous questions put by passers-by regarding the cause of his labour. The painting, which might have been finished by the clever, good-humoured artist in half-an-hour under ordinary circumstances, occupied him for four or five hours, but the account of cost we believe was never rendered. Many guessed at the offenders, but the

L

fiscal, if he sought it seriously, got no clue for a prosecution, and the lads, who had been foolish enough for once, gave up all such tricks for the future.

A very formal act of the town council, dated 3d October 1781, regulates the mode of sitting in the loft of the church belonging to the municipal authorities. By this act it is appointed that the office-bearers shall sit in the front pew, the provost in the chief seat with the first bailie and dean of guild on his right hand, and the youngest bailie, clerk, treasurer, and master of the hospital on his left, and that the other members shall sit in the pew behind. The cause of this formal minute is said, by tradition, to have been, that the deacon convener for the time usurped a seat in the front pew, and we have heard that the " bold bad man " persevered in his claim notwithstanding of this act of council. The magistrates, therefore, wishing to shame the convener out of his presumption, put the town-officers into the front pew alongside of him, and retired themselves to the back seat. The audacious tradesman, however, at the end of the sermon, rose, and, with great *nonchalance*, made his bow first to the clergyman, and then turning to the right, bowed most profoundly to the one town-officer, and turning to the left, bowed as profoundly to the other town-officer, agreeable to the mode then practised by the provost " himsel', worthy man." When called to account before the council for infringing the act alluded to, the deacon replied that it was not he but the magistrates who had infringed the act, by sending the town-officers to the front seat, and retiring themselves to the back one. The contest, like most others of the same kind, was dropped by the magistrates, and the convener, meeting with no opposition, quietly seated himself where he found most room. But the act has ever since been referred to as regulating the *right* and precedence on the subject. So many of the members of council, of modern times, have been dissenters from the Kirk of Scotland, that, generally, " ample room and verge enough " is to be found for any councillor fond of a front seat.

John Duncan, Esq., a native of Brechin, and sometime proprietor of Rosemount, who realised a handsome fortune in the exercise of the medical profession in India, presented the town council with a China bowl still in existence, and which bears on its base this inscription:—" Canton, 1785—from John Duncan per favor of Captain Stewart, Belmont." A ship, the crest of the family of Duncan, appears on two sides of this bowl, while the remaining two sides carry copies of the city arms ; and the centre of the bowl is graced with a similar ornament, surrounded with the words, " Success to the City of Brechin." The bowl is a splendid specimen of china, and capable of containing twenty Scotch pints, or a gallon of whisky made into punch. When it arrived in Brechin, the topers of the day considered it necessary to try if it would hold in. Accordingly a feast was proclaimed and a company assembled, one of whom, on returning to his family circle, and expatiating upon the beauty of the bowl, declared, amongst other wonders which it possessed, (speaking with a lisp,) that " there were mith in the bowl ; " the jolly citizen having mistaken the lemons put in to season the punch for Chinese mice swimming amongst the potent liquid.

On Saturday, the 19th March 1785, Andrew Low, a native of Brechin, was hanged on the west end of the hill of Forfar, between the hours of twelve midday and four in the afternoon, having on the 28th January previously been found guilty by the unanimous voice of a jury, of two separate acts of housebreaking and theft. Low is said to have been the last person in Scotland upon whom the sentence of death was passed by a sheriff. The judge presiding was Patrick Chalmers, Esq., of Aldbar, who, it may be interesting to know, acted at the time as sheriff-depute of the whole of Forfarshire for the salary of £150 yearly. The office of sheriff principal was then in Scotland, as now in England, an honorary office, and the sheriff-depute was really the highest legal authority in the county, having a substitute or substitutes under him, officiating in the ordinary courts as at present. The place where Low was executed is still pointed out upon Balmashanner hill; and at no distant date the name and age of the unfortunate lad were cut out upon the turf, on the old site of the gallows. Fortunately the laws now are not so bloody, and crimes like those of Low would only be visited by transportation for life, or a term of years. Low's fate was long a matter of conversation and regret in Brechin, but it was darkly insinuated that he had been led by cunning men to be participant in a deeper crime than mere housebreaking and theft.

The Bridge of Brechin stood very much in need of repair in 1786, and a Mr Stevens, mason, estimated that £350 were required to put it in a proper condition. The council, who by this time began to see that the county had as much interest in this bridge as the burgh, subscribed £21 to assist. The remainder of the cash was raised partly by voluntary subscription in the town and neighbourhood, and partly by a county assessment.

In the same year, 1786, a collection was made at the church door for the benefit of the Infirmary of Aberdeen, to which the kirk-session minutes state this parish had been much indebted; and in the following year, 1787, a similar collection was made for the benefit of the lunatic asylum of Montrose, upon the assurance, as the minutes of session bear, that in consequence " our insane poor, after this, would be admitted to the said hospital on easier terms." The session minutes of the same year record, that his majesty's proclamation for the suppression of vice and immorality, and for the more religious observation of the Lord's Day, had been read from the pulpit, " and the congregation suitably exhorted."

The council, in January 1788, "considering that the meal-market of this burgh has not for many years been used for the purpose of selling meal, and that the wynd wherein it is situated is a very public entry to the town," ordained the market to be pulled down. This market was situated in Swan Street, which was then called the Meal Market Wynd, and this market was directly opposite where the Union Bank now is.

This was rather a stirring year this 1788. The town-hall and prisons were pulled down, and the present erections built by public subscription. The town council commenced the subscription with £300, and resolved to begin the work when £500 were subscribed. Sir David Carnegie of Southesk, then Member of Parliament for this district of burghs, came forward with fifty guineas, and the rest of the sum having been readily contributed, the work was commenced early in the spring of 1789. The total amount subscribed, including the £300 given by the town, was £529, 11s. But the extra work went beyond the subscriptions, and another £100 were voted from the town's funds to finish the work, and to procure a new clock, which was furnished by Mr John Drummond, watch and clockmaker of Brechin. More extras yet arose, and finally, a *carte-blanche* was given to the treasurer to pay all accounts still remaining due. The guildry incorporation gave £50 to the rebuilding of the town-house, in consequence of which the council, on 9th September 1790, passed an act, declaring that the large east room or hall immediately above the ground story, " shall, in all time coming, have the name of, and be termed the guild hall of Brechin, with liberty and privilege to the guildry of Brechin to hold therein their annual head court, and any other meetings called or summoned by the dean of guild of Brechin for the time." The right thus granted still continues to be exercised. The hall when finished was ornamented with two very handsome crystal chandeliers, which tumbled down, first one then another, within the year, leaving the suspicion that the suspending rod had been cut through with a file by some miscreant. The debris lay in the garret till some twenty years ago, when it, with other lumber, was disposed of. Then it was discovered that a ring on each suspending rod had caused a current of electricity to circulate round each rod, and cut it neatly through, as if done by a workman.

" Application having been made from the magistrates and town council of Montrose to the magistrates and town council here, asking aid for making an intended road from the Bridge of Tayock to Montrose ; " the Brechin council, by a minute in February 1789, authorised twenty guineas to be subscribed for this purpose.

One of the little bells having been cracked, was recast at London in 1789, at an expense of £6, 18s. 5½d., which sum, with £2, 5s. 5½d. of incidental expenses attendant on the rehanging of the bell, was chiefly defrayed by a contribution at the kirk door.

Disputes arose in 1790, about the rights of publicans to pitch tents in the Trinity Muir markets, when the council very properly passed an act ordaining that all the then possessors of sites should be allowed to occupy them themselves, but not to give them over to any other person; and that upon the death of these possessors, or upon their absenting themselves from the principal market, the sites should revert to the magistrates, to be by them disposed of to new comers. The same rule yet continues, and some rule certainly is required when these canvas houses amount in number, occasionally, to nearly fifty.

Lady Saltoun, happening to be in Brechin in 1780, walked with another lady from the inn, then the Swan Inn, where the Union Bank now stands, down to see the church and steeple; and in returning it came on a shower, when Lady Saltoun put up her umbrella, a large green silk one. This caused a general turn out in the street, with " Lord preserve us, what is that she has got above her head?" And " God guide us, only see what is above her head!" Our informant, a very aged gentleman, says he was then only a boy at the school, but the thing was so new and so very remarkable that he never forgot it. Lady Saltoun's was a visit and away, but a few years afterwards an umbrella was again brought to Brechin by a lady from Montrose on a visit to her friends in this quarter, and such attention did it command that the lady was never permitted to walk the streets, with the instrument displayed, without attracting a host of spectators, male and female, who, despising the rain, followed her wherever she went. Previous to the introduction of umbrellas, the ladies, in rainy weather, wore cloaks with immense hoods spread out by splits of bamboo, and which covered caps, bonnets and all. Females in the lower ranks of life wore plaids over their heads, closely pinned under their chins. A few of such plaids were till lately to be seen, worn by the old ladies, who, from poverty and deafness, occupied the seats alongside the pulpit of the cathedral church, but they have all now disappeared.

Gin was the peculiar drink of the people at the period we write of, and it was customary to give a dram in a cup. A lady, to whom we owe our existence, being by the death of her parents left early in charge of the household, had, according to the practice common then, and not uncommon now, to give a dram to a washerwoman, and, thinking to be genteel, presented it to her friend in a glass; the woman of soap-suds repudiated the offer with scorn, and desired to have no one watching, and ordered a *sŭp*

in a cŭp in the *guid auld folks' way*, and was quite contented
when the same measure was served up to her in a china cup.
Gin and water was too common a beverage amongst bibbers, and
a *meridian* was frequent at this time with men considered otherwise sober. Whisky, however, gradually superseded gin; and
whisky toddy, tumblers and glasses, put cups and pint stoups
out of fashion.

The same household to which we refer had at the beginning
of the century, when we were young, the kitchen dresser and
plate-rack *handsomely* decorated with well scoured, bright shin-
ing plates, ashets, &c., of pewter; but Wedgewood, with his
cheap stoneware, so easily kept clean, has put pewter out of
fashion. We have when a boy ate off pewter flat plates, meat
cut from flesh served on pewter salvers or ashets, the handles
of the knives used being also of pewter. At this time we were
dressed in corduroy clothes, the breeches buttoned *over* the
jacket, a most unbecoming dress; we had leather thongs for
shoe-ties, each shoe being equally well suited for either foot, and
being duly changed each morning so as to wear fair; while our
head was covered with a leather cap, flat to our caput and with
a glazed front; the cap being a most handy thing for carrying
either water or dust as play might require. Some of the charity
boys in England still wear the same dress which was usual in
Brechin for years after 1800.

A statistical account of the parish, written in 1790, states
that " there are neither Jews, negroes, nor Roman Catholics in
the parish, but some of those sturdy beggars called gypsies occasionally visit it." The gypsies still continue their visits, and
a few negroes and Roman Catholics may now be found amongst
us, but the Jews consider us " too far north" for them as yet.

In the following year, 1791, the council of Brechin and county
gentlemen were up in arms against the community of Montrose,
because the Montrosians purposed erecting a bridge across the
Esk, opposite what was then called the Fort Hill, without leaving any passage for vessels to go farther up the river. The
agitation was renewed in 1800, when the town council of Brechin
" considering that the open and free navigation of the river
South Esk is of the utmost importance to the interest of the

town of Brechin," agreed to sist themselves as parties in an
action at the instance of Sir David Carnegie of Southesk, and
John Erskine, Esquire of Dun, against the commissioners then
appointed for erecting a wooden bridge at Montrose. These
differences were all happily settled, and part of the wooden bridge
was made to rise and fall so as to allow vessels to pass; and this
wooden bridge having subsequently, in 1826, been superseded
by an iron suspension bridge, accommodation for the passage of
vessels has been found by converting the stone bridge farther
on, over another narrower and deeper branch of the Esk, into a
swivel bridge.

The Dundee Banking Company established an agency in
Brechin about 1792, being the first bank which did business
regularly in Brechin. The Bank of Scotland opened an office
in August 1792, but the agency having been unfortunate, was
withdrawn in 1803. The Dundee Banking Company was succeeded by the Dundee New Bank about 1804, and this branch
of the Dundee New Bank remained till 1818. The Dundee
Union Bank in 1809 opened an agency in what was then termed
the Upper West Wynd, now called Saint David Street, and
when the Dundee Union Bank was amalgamated with the
Western Bank in 1844, the agency was continued in the same
place as a branch of the Western Bank; but when that bank
failed in 1857 the same agents procured a branch of the Royal
Bank, which is still continued, now in Swan Street, by Mr James
Guthrie, a member of the family under the original firm of
Messrs David Guthrie & Sons. A Provincial Bank was established in Montrose in 1814, which sent agencies to Arbroath
and Brechin. The agency in Brechin was under the management of different gentlemen at different times, but was never
fortunate. The agency was withdrawn in 1828, and the bank
was dissolved in 1829, when it was ascertained that there had
been a great loss incurred, chiefly arising from misfortunes in
the Arbroath and Brechin agencies. The British Linen Company sent a branch here in 1836, under charge of Messrs Speid
and Black, and the agency still continues in the same house in
Clerk Street, under the management of one of the original
agents, Mr D. D. Black. The City of Glasgow Bank established

an agency in 1854, which is conducted by Mr John Don, in St David Street. The Union Bank has an agency in Brechin, which was opened in 1855, under the charge of Messrs Gordon and Lamb, and their office is also in Swan Street. Recently the Clydesdale Bank has appointed Mr George Scott to be their agent in Brechin, and his office is in Panmure Street. There are thus five bank agencies in Brechin, besides the Post-Office Savings-Bank, a Tenements Savings-Bank, and a Parochial Savings-Bank conducted in the parochial school-room each Tuesday evening, by Mr David Prain, parochial schoolmaster, which began first in 1847 as a branch of the Montrose Savings-Bank, but was in 1852 constituted a principal bank, under authority of the acts of Parliament made for the benefit of Savings-Banks.

Two acts of the town council of 1792 display no little liberality; the one is directing a petition to government for the removal of the penal statutes against Episcopalians, from which act the two members belonging to the trades alone dissent; and the other is authorising a petition against the slave trade.

In the same year Adam Gillies, esquire, then advocate in Edinburgh, afterwards one of the senators of the college of justice, by the title of Lord Gillies, was appointed ruling elder, an office which he continued to fill for forty years, when he resigned the situation. Lord Gillies, who was youngest son of Mr Robert Gillies, merchant in Brechin, died in December 1842.

In this year also the council subscribed £10 towards the erection of the new University of Edinburgh, and the guildry bought for the public use a set of standard weights and measures; so that this year 1792 may truly be marked in the annals of Brechin with a white stone, unless indeed we reckon as of a less liberal and tolerant spirit, the resolution then adopted by the council " to address his Majesty, expressing their gratitude for his royal goodness" in publishing a " proclamation relative to suppressing seditious and inflammatory publications which tend to dissatisfy the people with the present happy constitution."

At this time the public streets were much in need of repair, but although the guildry contributed twenty guineas, the council found their means would go no farther than to pave the street from the South Port to the Path Head, and a contract was accordingly formed in 1793 with Charles Jack, mason, for the completion of the work. Jack adopted the then rather novel, but since frequently practised mode of *ploughing* up the old road to make room for the new causewaying. It is somewhat remarkable that this street, while it was the first which was causewayed, remained the last in that state, the others having been all previously Macadamised, as all the streets are now.

On the 21st January 1794, we have this minute of council:— " Which day the council having taken into their consideration, the present critical situation of the country, are unanimously of opinion that it is necessary to declare their affection to their sovereign and their firm attachment to the present happy constitution, and that they will use their utmost exertions to suppress all seditious principles, tumults, and disorders that may arise, tending to subvert the same ; and they do hereby express their detestation and abhorrence of all levelling and equalising principles. The council further appoint a meeting of the principal inhabitants, to be held in the guild-hall of Brechin, upon Monday next, the sixth current, at 11 o'clock forenoon, to concur with them in their loyalty and attachment to the king and constitution. And the provost having laid before the council a subscription paper he had received from Sir David Carnegie of Southesk, baronet, deputy-lord-lieutenant of the county, in consequence of the county resolutions of the 28th July last, published in the different newspapers, and recommended to the members of council to subscribe the same, and which paper met with the approbation of the members of council, and was accordingly subscribed. Lastly, the council recommend to the provost to publish those, their resolutions, in the different Edinburgh newspapers." The six incorporated trades passed similar resolutions, even more decided, and certainly better expressed. These loyal addresses were followed up by as loyal actions. In 1796, four men were raised from the burgh to serve in his Majesty's navy, the expense being defrayed by an assessment on the burgesses, amounting to upwards of £100, and in 1798 the town gave £105 as a subscription to the loyalty fund, and for the prosecution of the war then pending with France.

The incorporations and burgesses began in 1770 to stir " in

the matter of reform," as it is generally called in their books, and to demand inspection of the town and hospital accounts, that is, to control the ways and means; but the council of that period were noways inclined to be so controlled, and although they agreed to give access to these accounts to a limited committee named by themselves, they refused to lay the accounts before the incorporations as a body. The struggle was subsequently renewed at different periods, and partial concessions were, from time to time, made by the council. In 1799, the council, for the first time, appointed the accounts of the burgh to be laid open for public inspection. This practice continued till the act of 1822, which ordained the accounts to be yearly exhibited for a given period. An abstract of the whole accounts is now printed and published each year for the information of the burgesses, agreeable to act of Parliament. In 1790 the agitation of reform was renewed. It was then moved in the guildry, that the dean, appointed by the town council, was a mere police magistrate, and had no right to interfere in the management of the funds of that incorporation; and although this motion was not persisted in, the fact of such a proposal being seriously entertained, shows the feelings of the period, and that the knowledge of the rights of the people had made considerable advances.

The "dear years," as they were termed, produced considerable distress in Brechin; meal, then the staple of the labouring classes, being scarce and high priced; the consecutive bad harvests about the close of the century having created almost a famine in the land. In 1796 the town council voted £20 from the town's funds, and £20 from the funds of the hospital, for the aid of the poor. In 1799, a similar subscription was made. The other corporations in the burgh came forward as readily, and private charity was very active. The oldest recollection which the writer of this work has, is of seeing the people crowding about the door of the flesh-market, part of which had been converted into a meal market, and struggling hard with each other for liberty to purchase, at a ransom, a small quantity of meal, every man holding his *pock* or little bag at arm's length above his head, while he attempted to force his body through the mass of suffering humanity around the door of the market.

We have already mentioned that what was then the flesh-market
is now used as a market for the sale of dairy produce, and is
situated on the High Street, immediately below the Bishop's
Close. It was a trying time then—war abroad, and famine at
home. To alleviate these distresses in part, a soup-kitchen was
opened in Brechin in 1800, a species of charity which has often
since been resorted to with much benefit to the poor members
of the community.

The ministers of the crown were seriously alarmed at the
threats of invasion held out in 1798 by the French directory
and Bonaparte, then general of the French armies, afterwards
emperor of that great nation, and, finally, an exile in the Island
of St Helena. We have in our possession some of the circulars issued to the magistrates of this district, giving directions
for the protection of the country in the event of invasion. One
schedule requires a return of all the male inhabitants between
fifteen and sixty, distinguishing those capable of service from
those serving in the volunteer corps, and from aliens and quakers,
and it requires also a return of the persons, who, from age, in-
fancy, or infirmity, might be incapable of removing themselves
in case of such a necessity. Another schedule demands a return
of the number of bestial of different kinds in the district; of
carts and waggons; of corn-mills, with the quantities of corn
they could grind in a week; of the ovens, and quantity of bread
they could supply in twenty-four hours, and of the dead stock
in the round. A third schedule applies to the arming of those
willing to serve as soldiers on foot or horseback, with swords,
pistols, firelocks, and pikes, and of those willing to act as pioneers.
More private instructions directed the blowing up of bridges,
felling trees across roads, and picking up the highways, removing the inhabitants to the Highlands, and burning the provender
left behind. How thankful ought we to be that it was not necessary to resort to any of the extremities contemplated in case of
invasion, and that no such precautions as those then adopted are
requisite in our days. But we may remark that the tactics recommended in 1798 were exactly those pursued nearly five
hundred years before by King Robert the Bruce, when Scotland
was invaded by Edward II. of England, and which mode of

defeating an invading enemy is so strongly enforced in " Good King Robert's Testament," or in the instructions which Bruce left for his nobles at the time of his death in 1329.

Our gentlemen burgesses were not behind others in determination to stand up for their homes and their hearths, and to maintain the constitution. A regular paper was drawn up and subscribed by forty-eight individuals, on 6th July 1795, by which they " agreed to enter into a voluntary company for supporting the present constitution of this country, and for suppressing of riots and quelling disturbances in the city; the corps to be under the directions of the magistrates for the time being, and not to be marched more than two miles beyond the liberties of the city during our pleasure; we are to have the election of our own office-bearers, are to furnish our own clothing, are to serve without pay, and being all, or most of us, engaged in trade, are not to be bound to attend the exercise but when convenient." The magistrates certify these heroes " to be respectable inhabitants of the place and loyal subjects, and that arms may be safely put into their hands." Of these forty-eight gentlemen, when this work was published in 1839, five still resided in the town, one in the immediate vicinity, and two at a distance, but the remaining forty, and the three magistrates who approved of their conduct, were then gathered to their fathers. Since then all have succumbed to the fate of humanity. The terms of service thus proposed were not such as Government required, and the gentlemen, after studying the act of Parliament then passed for the embodying of volunteers, were obliged to write to Sir David Carnegie, baronet, of Southesk, the acting deputy-lieutenant in this quarter, " that, considering their close engagements in business, it will be impossible for them to come under the provisions of that act;" and so terminated this display of loyalty. But a regular corps of volunteers, embracing men of all classes in the burgh, capable of bearing arms, was subsequently raised under the provisions of the act. This regiment was under the command of Major Colin Gillies, whose sword and symbol of authority is in our custody. The corps was disembodied at the peace of Amiens in 1802, and was succeeded by another which ultimately merged into the local militia—a set of troops which

came to be not a burgh but a county force, the different companies raised in different towns having been amalgamated and
formed into one regiment. " *Fuit Ilium*; the days of burgh
soldiering are over,"—we said in 1839 ; not so, we have at present
two companies of gallant defenders, which, united with the companies in the neighbouring towns, make a very handsome regiment of light infantry.

James Hutton, one of the town-officers of Brechin, appointed
in January 1788, and who survived till 1825, and William
M'Arthur, another officer of this period, who lived till 1837,
occasionally trespassed so far on the good nature of the magistrates as to dictate the sentences to be pronounced both in civil
and criminal matters. When any of the bailies ventured to
differ in opinion from Hutton, he would say, " Well, bailie, you
may do as you like, but what *I* state is the law." M'Arthur,
again, when gently reprimanded by the provost for some mis-
demeanour, pulled off his coat and tossed it in the magistrate's
face, desiring him to wear the livery and be his own officer.
M'Arthur existed for many years on public charity. Hutton
was the pensioner of the burgh at his death. So difficult was
it found to procure proper officers in the eighteenth century, and
so demoralising was the situation presumed to be, that one of the
chief magistrates declared, he verily believed, if the senior bailie
were made a town-officer, he would become a blackguard in a
month. Happily, steady men are now found to fill these situations with credit to themselves and advantage to the community,
without exposing the virtue of any of the magistracy to a trial.

The statute labour road act came into force about 1790, and we
have in our custody a valuation made up with reference to the
act, from which it appears, that at this time, the dwelling-houses
within the burgh, exclusive of shops, manufactories, &c., were
estimated as being rented yearly at £899, 5s., and that 97 burgh
acres of land were valued at £250, 11s. ; that the number of
saddle-horses within the burgh was 24, carriage horses 34, and
horses for hire for working land 2, while there was ostensibly
only one riding horse for hire in the town.

Dr H. W. Tytler, who was a practising physician in Brechin
during the greater part of the period embraced in this chapter,

and who died in 1808, was a man of eccentric habits, but an
excellent scholar. He was the son of the minister of the parish
of Fearn, a learned, zealous, and popular clergyman. Dr Tytler
was first known as an author by a translation of "the works of
Callimachus" from Greek into English verse, published in 1793;
and in 1798 he laid before the public, "Pædotrophia, or the
Art of Nursing Children; a poem in three books, translated from
the Latin of Scavola de St Marthe, with medical and historical
notes," a work which has been much commended by critics. Dr
Tytler also translated the poetical works of Silias Italicus, which
remain unpublished, with the exception of a very few beautiful
specimens which appeared in the *Scots Magazine* for 1808.

Mr James Tytler, the author of the once popular songs of
"The Bonnie Bruikit Lassie," "Loch Errochside," and "I've
laid a Herrin' in Saut," was a brother of the doctor's, and spent
a good deal of his time about Brechin. Mr James Tytler, who
was also bred to the medical profession, was the principal editor
of the first edition of the "Encyclopædia Britannica," and was
engaged in many other literary works, but although a man of
great abilities, was a person of very unsteady habits. He was
the first person in Scotland who adventured in a balloon. The
attempt was made from a garden within the sanctuary of Holyrood, where poor Tytler was then from necessity residing, and
was made in a balloon constructed by Tytler himself, upon the
plan of Montgolfier. The attempt was unsuccessful, and en-
tailed upon the aeronaut the sobriquet of "Balloon Tytler."
Of course, such an attempt excited no little interest in Brechin,
where the man was so well known. A strolling company of
players had their then residence in Brechin, and in the evening,
when the news of the failure of the balloon came to the burgh,
this party were performing a piece in which a gentleman is supposed to despatch his servant to procure some intelligence. The
person who acted the part of the servant had either got too
much liquor, or been too deeply imbued with the success of the
balloon scheme, or perhaps partly both, for when he returned
on the stage, and was asked, according to the trick, "What
news?" he rejoined, "News, news, why Tytler and his balloon
have gone to the devil," an answer which enraged one part of

the audience as much as it amused another. Balloon Tytler died in America in 1803, having been obliged to emigrate there in consequence of some of his writings having given offence to the British Government of the time.

Burness, the author of the romantic and popular legend of " Thrummy Cap," as well as of some other poems of less note, was a baker in Brechin. While in Brechin he wrote a play, and prevailed on his acquaintances to enact it. The poet baker not only wrote the stage directions, but he instructed his " corps dramatique " to repeat them. Accordingly, the first words uttered by the hero of the piece were, " Enter Lord Buchan, bowing," the actor, of course, suiting the action to the words. The mirth of the audience was unbounded, and the play was received with raptures of applause—but not repeated. Burness's habits were erratic. He left the baker trade, and served for many years as a soldier in the Forfarshire militia. When that regiment was disembodied, he became a traveller for a periodical publishing company in Aberdeen, and while thus employed, lost his life amongst the snow, near Portlethen, in February 1826.

About the close of this century, there lived in Brechin, the proprietor of a small Highland estate in the vicinity, of whom many facetious stories are told. An Englishman was boasting mightily in the company of the laird, of the wonders of his native land. " Hoũts," says Ogil, " come awa' to the Den and I'll show you a greater wonnar." Accordingly he led the southron to what was called the Sandhole Brae, and stationing the gentleman in the recess made in the brae by the removal of the sand, Mr Simpson went himself to the foot of the bank, some thirty yards off, and gesticulated violently as if screaming loudly, but took care not to utter a sound. The Englishman, of course, heard nothing, and when questioned by Ogil, declared, that although from the motions made by the laird, he was sensible that gentleman was speaking loud, yet he had not been able to gather a syllable. " A' owin' to the wonnarfu' nature o' the grund," said Mr Simpson; " but try 't yoursel'!" The situation of parties was then changed, the English gentleman going to the foot of the brae and bawling as loud as he could, while our friend gazed upon him with lack-lustre eyes as if hearing nothing. The southron was satisfied that if there were astonishing things in England, and amazing echoes in Ireland, there were as wonderful braes in Scotland which interrupted all sound. On another occasion the laird called on Mr Colin Gillies, corn merchant of Brechin, with a sample of barley which he wished to sell. Mr Gillies, our Volunteer Major, expressed himself highly pleased with the quality of the grain, but said he did not think Mr Simpson's estate could have produced such fine barley:—"Was it not a picked sample?"—"I' faith is't, Colin," rejoined Ogil, "I pick't it out o' Sanny Mitchell's bere-stack, as I cam' by this mornin'." Mr Mitchell rented a piece of the best land in the neighbourhood; but Ogil's humour secured a purchaser for the barley, whether the stock should or should not be equal to the sample shown. When people were inclined to boast of their birth or connexion with nobility, Ogil would remark, "Ou, ye'll be like the laird of Skene's bastard dochter, wha said she was not only Noble but she was Nignoble." The laird of Ogil's *facetiæ* would make no *nignoble* volume.

Dr David Doig, though not a native of Brechin, was born in its immediate neighbourhood, and received his early education at our schools. His father rented the small farm of Mill of Melgund in the adjoining parish of Aberlemno, where David was born in 1719. In his sixteenth year he was the successful candidate for a bursary in the University of St Andrews. Having finished the usual course of classical education he commenced the study of divinity, but was prevented from completing his studies by some conscientious scruples regarding certain of the articles in the Confession of Faith. Thus diverted from his intention of entering the Church, he taught for several years in the parochial schools of Monifieth in this county, and of Kennoway and Falkland in Fife. In 1740, his reputation as a teacher obtained for him the situation of rector of the grammar-school of Stirling, where he remained till his death in 1800. Though Dr Doig never published any separate work of his own, his contributions in prose and verse to the *Encyclopædia Britannica*, the *Scots Magazine*, the *Bee* of Dr Anderson, and other respectable periodicals, would have filled many volumes. The doctor

M

lived in terms of the closest intimacy with most of the literary
men of his time, particularly Lord Kames, Dr Robertson, Dr
Anderson, and Hector Macneil, Esq., the latter of whom dedicated to him his justly popular poem of " Scotland's Scaith, or
the History of Will and Jean."

George Rose, a late eminent political character, was born at
Woodside of Dunlappy, a parish adjoining to Brechin, on 17th
January 1744. His father, who was a clergyman of the Scottish
Episcopal communion, had a brother who kept an academy at
Hampstead, near London, where young Rose received his education. Having the good fortune to attract the notice of the
Earl of Sandwich, then at the head of the Admiralty, Rose was
appointed Keeper of the Records by this nobleman. After occupying several subordinate situations in the public offices, Mr Rose
was, in 1803, made Vice-President, and soon after President of
the Board of Trade, with a salary of £4000 a-year, in which
situation he continued till his death in January 1818. Mr Rose
was the author of " Observations on the Historical Work of Mr
Fox," and of several political pamphlets.

Mr Norman Sievwright was the *English* Episcopal clergyman
of Brechin of this period. He died on 21st March 1790, in the
forty-first year of his ministry. He was settled in Brechin, we
believe, about 1750. Mr Sievwright was a learned man, fully
impressed with the dignity of the English Episcopal order, in
contradistinction to the claims of the Scottish bishops. " He
was," says his son, Mr John Sievwright, " the champion of the
Church of England, and of the constitution settled at the Revolution in 1688, which brought on him the hatred of the disaffected party in the country." Mr Norman Sievwright published several works on divinity and controversy, and left behind
him five manuscripts, one on the Hebrew language, a subject
upon which he had previously published; one entitled " A Sup-
plement to the Ecclesiastical History of Scotland;" another entitled " The Church of England Defended;" and two musical
pieces, none of which has ever been printed.

Dr John Gillies, the author of the " History of Greece," and
of many other works of learning, and long historiographer for
Scotland to his Majesty, was born at Brechin on 18th January

1746, and died in 1836, at the age of ninety. He was the brother of Mr Colin Gillies, whom we have just mentioned as a corn merchant in Brechin, and major of the Brechin Volunteers ; and of Mr Adam Gillies, one of the senators of the College of Justice, under the title of Lord Gillies. Another brother, William, was an eminent corn factor in London.

In 1770, great improvements were made in the burgh by the removal of outside stairs, projecting gables, and other obstructions. In 1790, similar improvements were effected, and about 1800 the remaining obstructions of this description were almost all swept away. These alterations cost the town council heavy sums of money. By these improvements the Timber Market, now called Market Street, formerly so obstructed with *foreshots*, covered with thatch, that the fraternity of freemasons were prohibited from walking in it by torchlight, became a regular, if not an elegant street. The High Street, which previously consisted of as many terraces as there were separate houses, was then brought to one inclined plane, while, by the removal of the steps at the end of each separate pavement, the footway was thrown upon one gradual slope. The Upper Wynd, now called St David Street, formerly little else than a sink, was made a respectable thoroughfare ; and St Mary's Street, previously scarce wide enough for one cart, and disfigured by an unseemly ditch on the north side, was made a decent passable street. All the other streets met with similar improvements. Credit, therefore, belongs to the magistracy and town council of this period, and although their successors have done much for which they deserve praise, yet we must not forget, that in the period succeeding the rebellion of 1745, improvements first began to be seriously thought of in Brechin. Any one who has seen the ancient and decayed burghs of Fife, and will contrast the streets of these burghs with those of Brechin, may form some idea of the herculean tasks which the town council of Brechin encountered in bringing the city to its present state, defective as that may be in the regularity and uniformity of the buildings.

CHAPTER IX.

We are now come to our own days, to a period when it would be indecorous to animadvert upon public men or the acts of any public body. The sequel of our history, therefore, must be confined to a narration of facts strung together, with little remark, in the order in which the events occurred.

In 1800, the customs of the burgh brought £71, 5s., and the dues of the weigh-house, &c., £31, 15s.—total, £103 sterling. They were let in 1837—the common customs for £111, and the weigh-house dues for £31,—total, £142. It was the practice at this period to sell the right of collecting the street dung, and this right, in 1800, brought £3, 0s. 6d. In this transaction the comfort of the inhabitants was but little consulted. The purchaser of the right claimed the privilege of allowing the inhabitants to puddle through as much mud as he chose to permit to accumulate, till it suited his convenience to collect it and cart it away. The Wash Mills for cleaning yarn were improved in 1800, and a new Wash Mill built; and the Bleachfield, with all the mills belonging to it, were then offered by public roup in set for seven years, and brought £95. The same premises further improved, together with the Meal Mills, which usually let for £26 or £28, were offered, in 1807, for a lease of twenty-five years, and then brought £181. The same subjects, with some further additions, partly made by the town, partly by the late tenants, were, in 1832, again offered by public roup for a nineteen years' lease, and brought £331 per annum. This shows the propriety of giving a tenant such length of lease as may induce him to make improvements for his own profit, the benefit of which the landlord receives at the expiry of the tack. Prior to 1807, large sums had been expended at the end of every triennial or septennial lease on the improvement of the mills; and the frequent change of tenants led to so many repairs that it was often questioned if the town realised any profit from the mills and bleachfield.

Poverty pressed hard on the inhabitants at the commencement of the century; provisions were still very expensive, and the town council found it requisite to subscribe £50 to aid the most indigent. The guildry gave £20 for the same purpose, and the other incorporations assisted in the good work.

The Trinity Muir spring market was established by an act of council, dated 25th March 1801, passed in consequence of a representation made by the farmers and cattle-dealers in the neighbourhood, of the advantage that would arise from a cattle-market being held on the third Wednesday of April, yearly; and the market was accordingly held on the 15th April 1801, for the first time. This market has continued regularly ever since, and has proved of infinite advantage to all parties interested in the cattle trade.

In 1801, the school fees, on the representation of the school-masters, were increased, and fixed thus:—for teaching of *all* branches of education, 5s. per quarter; for writing and arithmetic, 3s. 6d., and for writing and teaching of English, or for teaching of English alone, 3s. per quarter. The charge of 3s. 6d. for "writing and arithmetic," was construed, practically, to include "teaching of English." *Books* were always used at these public schools; but we were taught our letters, at a private school, from a *broad*, a board the size of an octavo page, having the alphabet pasted on it; the broad had a handle, and was similar to what is still used in England with the letters engraved on it, and is called a "Horn Book." Our teacher wore a cocked hat, a three-storey-high wig, a waistcoat with large pockets, a coat with tails sweeping the ground, and buttons the size of a two shillings piece; knee breeches with buckles, and shoes with broad buckles on them, and carried a long cane. He was a strict disciplinarian; read a roll-call of the scholars at the hours of assembly each forenoon and afternoon; punished

absentees when they did appear, and kept great decorum in his
school, closing it each Saturday with a long prayer.

Volunteering was now the rage. In 1803, the " Brechin
Volunteers," which afterwards became the "Local Militia,'
were embodied. The town council subscribed £21 towards the
expense of their clothing, and because the bleachfield was used
as a drill-ground, the tacksman of it was allowed £10 from the
town for permission to *soldier* over it. The youths also imitated
their seniors, and " playing soldiers " was quite the order of the
day; and really some of these juvenile troops, with their drums
and their fifes, their majors and their captains, were wonderful
near approximations to the regular Volunteers. Dr Russel records the same thing as having occurred in America during the
recent unfortunate civil war there.

The state of the cathedral kirk again claimed attention; the
old fabric was found to be decayed; meetings were called, resolutions entered into, and, by general agreement, the aisles of
the kirk were pulled down, leaving, however, the nave, to which
new aisles and a new roof were added; and the whole, at considerable expense to the heritors, the town, the different incorporations, and the private seat-holders, was converted, in the
years 1805-7, into a more modern but still inconvenient church.
Gothic cathedrals never make good Presbyterian kirks; and the
Brechin church is no exception to the rule. Previous to the
rebuilding of the church it was customary for *deaf* people
to sit in the baptismal seat adjoining the *letterin* or precentor's desk; and all the females who sat there then wore the
Scotch plaid pinned under the chin, and gathered in a fold
over their caps, secured with a pin or ornament on the forehead,
—a becoming dress, very like the Spanish mantilla. Similar
dresses were to be seen in different parts of the church. After
the repairs on the church very few of the old ladies returned to
the baptismal seat; and these few gradually died out; but a
solitary plaid might have been seen in 1820. Red nightcaps
were then occasionally worn by tradesmen at their work; we
know now of only one solitary individual thus attired, and who
made himself very conspicuous at the procession on the occasion
of the Prince of Wales's marriage, mounted on his charger and

attired in his bonnet rouge, in the end of last century the miscalled emblem of liberty during the revolution in France.
The broad blue bonnet was also a pretty common wear, and
went out of fashion in like manner as the ladies' plaids. Substantial farmers wore the bonnet, as did respectable tradesmen; but merchant burgesses used that uncomfortable head-
dress the hat, ever since we recollect. The person who
then officiated as precentor in the old church was a David
Simpson, who, having held the office of deacon of the
shoemakers, was generally known as Deacon Simpson. The
line was then generally read, that is, the precentor or "letter
gae," read a line of the psalm, and sung this line in conjunction
with the congregation, then read and sung a second line, and so
on till the psalm to be sung was completed. Simpson had a
stentorian voice, and when making a proclamation of banns
caused the church to ring with the words, "There is a purpose
of marriage between A and B; if any person has any objections
let them give it in, in proper time, or *for ever after hold their
peace.*" The deacon also disappeared with the auld kirk. In the
old church, as now, each incorporation had a loft of its own, then
however decorated in front with the arms of the trade and suitable pious inscriptions. The scholars also had a loft assigned to
them; a small erection perched above that belonging to the
town council, and where, as may be believed, when a number of
young men were assembled together in a dingy place, anything
but religious studies went on, even although the masters were
present.

The Common Den, to which we have adverted in a previous
part of this work, was let, in 1805, for a rent of £19, 10s. upon a
lease of three years, as a tentative measure of the right of the
council to do so, but after some wrangling with the trades, the
title of the council was acquiesced in. Upon the expiry of the
first lease, the subjects were again let for another three years, at
a rent of £21 per annum, to November 1811.

New office-houses were built jointly by the heritors and town
council, for the accommodation of the second minister in 1807.

The ringing of the *muckle* bell was to us, as we doubt not it
was to many of our readers, a source of considerable amusement

in our boyish days. So much had the tolling of the bell become the province of the boys, that it was almost neglected by the beadles of the kirk; and the council, in 1809, authorised the magistrates " to engage a person for ringing the great bell in the steeple, regularly every day and night, at the following hours, viz., at seven in the morning and eight at night in winter; and, during the spring, summer, and autumn at six o'clock in the morning and eight in the evening; and upon the Saturday of each week, also, at ten o'clock at night—being thrice that day; and to continue ringing said bell at the fore-said hours for the space of one quarter of an hour." The person then engaged, James Craig, continued to ring the bell regularly as pointed out in this minute, till his death, about 1840, and the young folks still continued to get a swing in the tow at the last toll. We were very much struck, when going to satisfy ourselves in regard to the dates of the bells, in reference to the first edition of this little work, to observe that the younkers who crowded round the ringer, were the sons of those with whom we ourselves had been so often similarly engaged, and many of the fathers of whom lay in the graves around. The steeples are the same, the bells are the same, the ringers are changed; one generation having succeeded another, as one crop follows another in succession. We find now, however, that the present official, *Barney O'Neill,* does the whole work himself, and that there is no more tugging at the bell tows for the little lads.

The table of petty customs was regulated, of new, in 1809, printed and published, and has been since acted upon, although abstruse enough in some points.

In the same year, 1809, on the death of Mr William Dovertie, who had supplanted the *doctor* of the Grammar School, Mr George Alexander was elected parochial schoolmaster, from which office he was worthily promoted to that of rector of the Grammar School in December 1833. He has now retired from scholastic duties, and enjoys from the council a well-merited pension, while an elegant portrait of the worthy gentleman, by Mr Colvin Smith, adorns the Mechanics' Hall, and records the gratitude of his numerous pupils, at whose expense it was painted. In the same year, 1809, the house near the West

Port, called Carcary's House, was bought of Mr Lyall of Carcary, with the view of accommodating the schoolmasters and
schoolmistresses with schools and dwelling-houses : but, although
partially occupied by some of the teachers, as tenants, under the
town council, it has never been found expedient to apply the
property to the purpose for which it was ostensibly purchased.
In 1811, it was proposed to erect new schools ; and the year
following a piece of ground, formerly occupied as a corn-yard
and tannage, was purchased and converted into public schools.
The expense was defrayed by subscriptions from the heritors,
town council, and private individuals. The whole expense, as
recorded in a minute of council of 28th May 1814, was £1216,
17s. 4d. For this sum a building containing three school-rooms
was erected, plain, but neat, ornamented with a belfry on the
top, containing a *wooden* bell, and embellished with a rather
handsome clock-*face* below the belfry, the funds for purchasing
a genuine bell and clock not having been procured; but the
great improvement effected by this erection, was the removal of
a nasty barn, a quantity of ill-built stacks, and a filthy tan-yard,
at the principal entry to the town from the west, at the point
where the Lower Wynd, now called Church Street, and St
Mary's Street meet, being the exact site which Lord Panmure
chose for the handsome structure erected by him in 1838, to
replace the schools and afford accommodation for a library and a
mechanics' institution.

   Mr Dovertie, whose death we have just mentioned, dressed
till the last of his days in knee-breeches with buckles, long coat
with broad tails, and ties in his shoes, while he carried a cane
about six feet long, grasped by his hand towards the top. A
gentleman, a baker in town, and a member of the town council
of this period, dressed in the same style, with the addition of a
pigtail tie of his hair behind. Another party wore broad buckles
in his shoes for twenty years after this. These signs of old
fashions gradually died out, as did the custom amongst gentlemen of wearing hair-powder, which was practised by a few down
to 1820.

   The habits of the people of this period were still very hospitable—too hospitable. A laird in the vicinity, recommending

a gentleman for a public office, described him as " an honest
man and a fair drinker." But the " full flowing bowl" gradually
gave place to the tumbler and glass; in place of every man
being obliged to empty his glass in due course, and send it
in to have it refilled with the rest at the bowl—the weak with
the strong—each man brewed his own tumbler and filled his own
glass, and drank according to his ability for potations. The
drinking habits of the present day are bad enough, but they are
nothing to what they were within our recollection and our own
experience; and, indeed, they appear to have gradually gone
down from one class to another, till now the custom of drinking
to excess seems to be limited to the very lowest class of society.

A juvenile society was instituted in 1811 amongst the young
men of literary pursuits, and existed for several years, the members devoting an hour very early each morning, during summer,
for discussing literary subjects. The ages of the members of this
juvenile assemblage ranged from twelve to fourteen. This club
merged into a debating society when the members attained a few
more years and a little more experience. Similar debating
societies have since, from time to time, been called into existence in the burgh; ceased, and been again renewed.

In 1812, the council passed an act regulating the mode of
warning out tenants within the burgh, by which, at an expense
of 1s. 9d., this necessary form is put through. In place of a
penny above a pound Scots, the same process costs nearly a pound
sterling without the burgh. In the same year, the town purchased an acre of land from Mr John Gray, part of which has
since been added to the Den at the north end, having indeed
been bought at the time for this purpose, with the view of the
Den being converted into nursery ground. Accordingly, on 11th
May 1812, the Common Den was let by public roup to Mr John
Henderson, for the purpose of being converted into a nursery,
the rent being £21 per annum for the first ten years; £25 for
the next seven years; and £30 for other seven years, the tack
running for twenty-four years. At the expiry of his lease Mr
Henderson retook the property, jointly with his sons, for twenty-
seven years, at a yearly rent of £61. Hence the town now derives a large revenue from a piece of ground which was previously

all but useless. This year, 1812, was a hard season upon the poor in the burgh, and the council united with the heritors in raising a subscription for the aid of the poor in the parish. It was in this same year that Provost Thomas Molison, piqued by the inattention of the then member of Parliament for this district of burghs, who considered the whole as pocket burghs which he could twist as he pleased, and who therefore did not deem it necessary even to call on the council, far less on the community of the burgh,— it was in this year that Provost Molison, when called on as a delegate from Brechin for his vote, declared that he voted for himself, and thus gave rise to an opposition, and to the introduction of a Liberal instead of a Conservative member of Parliament.

The landed proprietors and farmers in the eastern district of Angus formed themselves into an agricultural association in 1814. The society still continues, and has done much to improve the breed of cattle and the implements of husbandry in the district. It has two meetings annually, and reckons Brechin as its head-quarters, although cattle shows are held in different parts of the county for the accommodation of the farmers.

In 1816, the council agreed to allow the master of the parish school £13 to assist in paying an assistant. This vote was renewed from year to year till 1821, when £500 were raised by subscription, and vested in the hands of the town council to pay an assistant or third teacher; and when the schools were divided in 1834, this annuity of £25 was assigned to the burgh schoolmaster. Of the money thus raised, by far the largest part was contributed by the town council.

There is a long entry in the council book of April 1816, approving of the table of customs then fixed for the Montrose harbour; and in November of the same year the council added to their own *customs* by rouping, for the first time, the use of a weighing machine then erected, and which brought, as rent for one year, £4, 4s. The same machine brought in 1837 the rent of £6, 6s.

The year 1817 commences, in the records of council, with a minute characteristic of the then state of the times. An address is voted to the Prince Regent, afterwards George IV., "upon his escape from the late daring attempt upon his person in returning

from the House of Peers;" and a committee of council is named
to meet with a committee of the inhabitants, petitioning for re-
trenchment and reform in the administration of public affairs.

In 1816 and 1817, the weavers were very much distressed for
want of work in Brechin; to alleviate which, in part, the town
council employed a number of people to trench the ground, formerly under wood, now known as the town's parks, and lying
immediately south of Murlingden. From the same generous
motive, Lord Panmure caused the ground at the Haughmuir,
then known as the Haughmuir Wood, to be trenched, and gave
a preference in his employment to the inhabitants of Brechin;
and the ground thus trenched is now occupied as a farm by Mr
George Henderson.

In 1816 meal was dear, and a Meg Inglis, a fishwife in Montrose, gathering her sisterhood from Ferryden, took possession of
that town and mobbed the farmers, crying for a reduction in the
price of the staff of life. A Rob Ruxton, a tailor in Montrose,
came to Brechin and paraded the streets, blowing a horn, and
summoning the Brechiners to the aid of the Montrosians; and
although we believe no Brechin man or woman responded to the
summons, the poor silly man was tried for this overt act of treason and banished for seven years.

In May 1817, the right of pasturage of the grass on the Trinity Muir market-stance was let for the first time, and brought
a rent of 15s. The same right was let in 1838 for £5. This
year, 1817, the council were again obliged to extend their aid to
the poor of the town, and to import and sell, at a reduced price,
a quantity of barley for the use of the inhabitants of the burgh.
Almost every two or three years since, some public subscription
or other has been raised for the poor, at times wholly by the laity,
and unconnected with the *Kirk* or *State*, at other times by the
heritors and council in aid of the kirk-session funds.

Burgh and Parliamentary *reform* began now to be seriously
discussed. The guildry, in October 1817, petitioned to have the
right of electing their dean, who should be received, *ex officio*, as
a member of council; and, in December, the trades, in like
manner, applied to the council to have the liberty of electing the
second trades' councillor, they having the right at that time to

choose the convener, who, by the sett of the burgh, formed one of the 13 members of council, consisting of 11 guildrymen and 2 tradesmen. The council pronounced a legal-like decision on these petitions, declaring that they had no power to alter the existing sett of the burgh. This did not give satisfaction. At the booking of the dean, named by the council in 1817, the guildry went into open rebellion; and, at the next election of magistrates in September 1818, protests were entered against the selection of councillors and office-bearers. A process of reduction followed in the Court of Session. The deacons of the trades, the prosecutors, lost heart, and proposed to withdraw the action upon each party paying their own costs. The town council refused this offer; the war was renewed; a new election came round in 1819; new protests were entered; new proposals of compromise were made; parties became more moderate; the action was withdrawn; and the council, guildry, and trades, all applied to the Convention of Royal Burghs in 1820 so far to modify the sett of this burgh as to allow the dean, chosen by the guildry incorporation, to be received by the council as dean of guild and member of council, and to give to the trades the right of electing the convener and trades' councillor, who were to be received in council as the trades' members accordingly. The Convention agreed to the request; and the sett, as thus altered, remained the constitution of the burgh till 1832, when the Burgh Reform Act put all incorporations on their beam-ends, and vested the right of electing councillors in the householders possessing property of the value of £10 per annum.

In 1818, the trades made a long act, ordaining that the deacons who had a vote in the election of magistrates, although in no other act of the council, and the deacon convener, who was *ex officio* a member of council, should consult the trades before voting on the *leets* of magistrates proposed by the council for their consideration, and that signed lists should be tendered by the deacons to their constituents. In 1819, says the trades' record, " it having been resolved that the deacon convener and deacons should not vote in the election of magistrates this year, no signed lists were made out." In 1820, " they dispensed with the signed lists for this year only," and no more is heard of the matter.

When the right to elect a trades' councillor was obtained by the six incorporations, however, they adopted a set of very judicious regulations or by-laws for the regulation of the election.

The agitation of these questions led one of the unincorporated trades, the wrights, to endeavour to shake off the burden imposed upon them of furnishing a quota of men to attend the chartered markets as a guard to the magistrates; but, after a process on the subject, the wrights were found to be liable with the other trades in this service.

A new market, or " Tryst," as it is called, was established by the council in August 1819, and appointed to be held on the Trinity Muir market-stance upon the Tuesday preceding the last Wednesday of September yearly. This market was appointed at the request of the farmers in the neighbourhood, and has, we believe, been found fully to answer the expectations of those who petitioned for its establishment, and for whose encouragement the market was exempted from all custom for three years.

The road up the Path was widened and the steepness greatly removed in 1818 and 1822, at no little expense, but certainly much to the advantage of those having to carry heavy weights by that road. A railway, too, was planned between Brechin and Montrose in 1818; but, after much canvassing, was dropped, as not likely to yield proper returns, because a short line of that description is nearly as expensive in working as one of thrice the length.

The town-officers had been long in the practice, on the first Monday of the year, agreeable to the old style, or Handsel Monday, as it was called, of waiting upon all the inhabitants of any means and wishing them a good new year, expecting a douceur in return. The practice was found to lead to partialities by these officials in the discharge of their duties, and was abolished in 1819, when each of the officers was allowed 30s. in lieu of those " handsel fees."

The two small bells belonging to the kirk were so damaged by tolling, the one on the occasion of the death of Queen Charlotte, consort of George III., and the other on the occasion of the interment of an old lady belonging to the town, that the council were obliged to have them both recast in 1820, and since then the practice of tolling the bells at private funerals has been discontinued, although, when royalty is laid in the dust, the bells are yet tolled under the direction of the regular bell-ringer.

In February 1821 the council appointed sworn valuators, to appraise the properties held in feu of them, when these subjects should be in non-entry, upon which occasion the council stated it as their unanimous opinion, "that a composition of two third parts of the rents, payable to the vassals, should be demanded and paid to the superiors, that is, of the yearly rent where the houses or tenements are new and in good repair, but a smaller proportion if the houses are old and in bad repair; but, in all cases, a full year's rent of the vassal's land, which is cropped, ought to be demanded." This rule has been acted upon ever since, but the council are not rigid over-lords.

George IV. visited Scotland in 1822, when the council of Brechin, following the example of other burghs, voted him a loyal address; and further voted £10, 10s. of a subscription towards the bronze statue of that king which now stands in George's Street, Edinburgh.

Mr John Wood, engineer, from Edinburgh, was, at this time, travelling Scotland, making plans of each burgh, and the town council of Brechin subscribed for ten copies of his plan of the town of Brechin. Mr Wood was successful in procuring other subscriptions, and the plan was accordingly completed and published in 1823.

On 6th March 1823 the heckle-houses at the Muckle Mill took fire, in consequence of an escape of gas, as was understood, from one of the pipes of the private gas work belonging to the mill. The whole range of these buildings, with the materials in them, were destroyed, although water was in abundance in the neighbourhood, and every exertion was made to save the premises. Luckily for the parties interested, an insurance had been effected, a few days before, with the Sun Fire Office, to almost the value of the buildings and flax thus destroyed.

A public Dispensary, for affording medicines to the poor of the place, was established in 1823, and was then so endowed from subscriptions and donations, that it was enabled to supply all demands upon it, with very few occasional calls on the richer

members of the community. Somehow the Dispensary gradually fell into abeyance, but now there is a prospect of its resusci-
tation in connexion with an Infirmary.

A bridge at the Stannochy Ford, over the river South Esk, was
begun in 1823, and towards the erection the council gave £42
from the corporation funds. The other expenses were defrayed
by the heritors in the immediate neighbourhood. A grand procession of the magistrates, town council, and incorporations,
along with the masonic bodies, was formed; and the foundation-
stone was laid in great style, dinners of course following, and the
health of the worthy builder, Mr William Smith of Montrose,
being duly pledged

About this time died Cruizin, a well-known blind beggar, who
had frequented Brechin and the surrounding country for fifty
years, and amused old and young with his songs.

> " His name was Jamie; but the rest, alas!
> Has vanished from my memory.——
> ' We 'll gang nae mair a Cruizin',' was one song,
> But he had many, though from that there came
> The sound which most amused the listening throng,
> And hence the title CRUIZIN grew a name."

So sung Mr James Bowick, editor of the *Montrose Review*, when
announcing in that paper the death of Cruizin. The poet himself, alas! is since numbered with the dead,—a worthy, simple-
minded, good man he was.

A railway along Strathmore was projected in 1825, and the
council of Brechin subscribed £10, 10s. towards the expense of
the survey from Brechin to Forfar. The project went no further
than a plan, but has been again and again renewed, and must be
perfected at some future period from Laurencekirk by Brechin
to Forfar, as the scheme is easily practicable and certain to pay.

An unfortunate fire happened this year in a stable belonging
to a publican, who had converted part of the old Maisondieu
Chapel into a receptacle for carriers' horses. It was supposed
that one of the carriers had carelessly snuffed a candle, and
thrown the snuff unextinguished amongst the wet straw; so it
was that the straw was consumed, and, though no flame was observed, such a smoke arose that all the horses were destroyed.

The misfortune was discovered by the stamping of the horses, and when the stable-door was opened one of the animals burst from its stall, rushed to the door, turned suddenly round, leaped a paling of some eight feet high, and fell dead. Others expired in their stalls. Two or three lingered for days unable to eat or drink. Eight or ten very valuable horses were thus destroyed. Two gray horses, of great size and strength, and of very considerable sagacity, survived longest. It was really melancholy to see the sufferings of these poor brutes, and no less melancholy to observe the distress of their driver, who spoke of them as friends, and bestowed as much attention upon them as he could have done upon his own family. The poor horses seemed really sensible of, and grateful for, their driver's kindness.

The East Back Vennel was widened and its steepness lessened in 1827, and it was then dignified with the title of " City Road." The Latch Road, formerly a mere swamp, was made out the same season, and has since given an opportunity for building a number of neat villas in that part of the town. An arrangement was also this year made with David Blair, Esq. of Cookston, in regard to the Dove Wells, by which the rights of the town and of Mr Blair were distinctly defined in a decree-arbitral, pronounced by Andrew Robertson, Esq., Sheriff-substitute of Forfarshire; and in consequence of which arrangement, and the improvements made in virtue of it, the town was well supplied with water, till the increasing population lately demanded an addition. In the December of this year also the council renewed an old act, by which any party proposing to build within the burgh is obliged to call the dean of guild, with one of the bailies, to the spot, and to satisfy them and his neighbours regarding his plans. This mode of proceeding has been found highly advantageous for the public, and greatly destructive of litigation; for where disputes do exist, as they will exist, regarding petty marches, the parties interested being confronted before judges, anxious to bring them to an agreement, do almost always make arrangements, frequently for the advantage of both, and which arrangements would not have been thought of had each stood on his *right*, and gone to law to ascertain who was wrong. The proceedings are conducted by printed formal papers, which ter-

N

minate in what is called a building warrant, and the whole expense varies from 2s. 6d. to 5s. It is but bare justice to the legal gentlemen to say that they have done everything in their power to make this summary court, so prejudicial to their interests, work to advantage, and it does accordingly work well for the public.

The lands called the Crofts of Brechin, were bought by the council in 1828. These lands had belonged to a Mr M'Gregor, servant to the Duchess of Perth, who went abroad with his mistress in 1747, after the fall of Prince Charles's party, to which she was devoted; and, in the absence of the proprietor, the titles had got into confusion in consequence of heritable securities granted by him, very likely with the view of avoiding a forfeiture of the ground, to which he had rendered himself liable by his connexion with the Stuarts. All matters were, however, cleared up, and the council became absolute proprietors of a piece of ground upon which they had long exercised the right of holding a market. Being vested with the absolute right, the council enclosed the ground and changed the site of the weekly cattle-market, held each Tuesday during winter, from the Crofts to the Timber Market, alike to the advantage of the proprietors of the Timber Market, now Market Street, as to the comfort of the farmers, who, in the Croft Market, were often wading ankle-deep among mud. Since then Clerk Street has been widened, Panmure Street made, and the long street called Southesk Street has been formed mainly from the Crofts lands, as noticed afterwards.

Another change, by a different body, but one no less an improvement, was made this year. On 25th September 1828, the six trades entered this act in their minute-book : " Which day, the deacon convener, deacons and trades' councillor, and whole trades having met, and deliberately considered the serious inconveniences resulting to the trades from the practice of meeting in the churchyard for the purpose of their annual elections, both from the inclemency of the weather and the disturbance and annoyance of the multitude, as well as considering the impropriety, if not indecency, of assembling multitudes and transacting their business over the graves of their ancestors and of their friends and families, have unanimously resolved, enacted, statuted, and

ordained, that, in future, the whole trades shall assemble in their
ordinary place of meeting for the purpose of electing the deacon
convener, trades' councillor, their respective deacons, and other
office-bearers; and appoint this regulation and minute to be engrossed in the record of the respective incorporations." In consequence of this enactment, the subsequent elections of the trades
have been held in the Mason Lodge, which they selected as
" their ordinary place of meeting." We recollect enjoying a very
hearty laugh at the last election which took place in the burying-
ground, although certainly the place forbade such demonstrations.
On the occasion alluded to, we had wandered into the kirkyard
to notice the excitement created by the elections; and, observing
three individuals seated demurely on a burial-stone, we approached
them just as the clock struck eleven, and just as the three individuals started up into active life. One produced a paper, and
read, " The T. trade have leeted A. and B. for deacons—any
objections to that leet?" said the reader, Deacon C. " None,"
replied A.; " None," replied B.—" For whom do you vote, Deacon A.?" said C. "For myself," rejoined A.—"For whom do you
vote, Deacon B.?" " For A.," replied he.—" And I vote for A.,"
added C., " and that settles that election." He read again from
his paper, " The T. trade have leeted C. and B. for treasurer—
any objections to the leet?" None were offered. " For whom
do you vote, Deacon A.?" " For B.," was the answer.—" For
whom do you vote, Deacon B.?" " For myself," was the reply.
—" And I vote for B.," said Deacon C., " and that closes the
election." These three worthies were the whole members of the
trade who had a right to vote, or, at least, who chose to exercise
the right of voting at elections; and accordingly they handed
the two offices about amongst themselves quite in an agreeable
manner.

This year died Alexander Malcolm, one of the public characters of Brechin. For more than half a century Sandy had picked
up a living by " gatherin' bawbees for himsel," as he phrased it;
and on each public occasion, be it sorrowing or rejoicing, wedding
or burial, Sandy bore an active part, although the king's birth-
day, kept as it was in the days of George III. by a general satur-
nalia on 4th June, was the principal occasion through the year

on which Sandy chose to disport. Mr Bowick, in his sketches of characters, describes " Sandy Maukim" as

> " Ane curious wight, of stature low,
> Withouten trews to clothe his naked knee,
> But clad in petticoat, that down did flow,
> With fringes tattered to ane great degree.
> No leathern shoon upon his feet had he,
> But worsted huggars, which contrived to hide
> His legs and feet. "

Malcolm was a great wag, and fond of a glass, partly rogue, partly simpleton. He had the misfortune to break his leg one winter, being, as was alleged, much inebriated at the time. A pious clergyman in town called to pray with Sandy, and rated him soundly for his inebriety, to which the minister ascribed the misfortune of the broken leg. Sandy denied the charge, but the clergyman persisted in it ; and Malcolm, hard pressed, burst out in a sly manner with, " How 's Mrs Burns's leg ? " The pastor's most worthy lady had met with a similar accident, certainly not from the same cause, although Sandy insinuated as much, to get rid of the good man's further reproofs. Malcolm might be styled the King of the Beggars. Before the legal assessment for the poor was commenced in 1841, the administration of the funds provided for the purpose was in the hands of the kirk-session ; but the regular recognised poor of the town paraded the burgh each Thursday forenoon, and stopped at every door where they expected an " aumous," when the charity was dealt out to them generally in the shape of a halfpenny to each. If the giver was not provided with coppers, then Sandy Maukim took charge of the coin given, and ruled and distributed, it was said, in a very imperious manner. This practice of public begging gave rise to the children's cry, now all but forgotten, " Fuirsdae 's the puir's dae ; Fridae 's the bride's day ; and Saturdae we get a' the play." The same practice prevailed in other towns. Public begging was put down by the town council in February 1839, at the request of the aggregate committee of the heritors, kirk-session, and town council, then in management of the funds raised, partly by voluntary subscription, for the maintenance of the poor of the parish.

A printing-office was, for the first time, established in Brechin in 1829. Our first edition issued from the Brechin press, and displayed a fair specimen of typography. The principal employment of the Brechin printers was the printing of handbills, circulars, and the like. The press was found to be a great convenience to the inhabitants, who were formerly obliged to go to Montrose or Forfar for anything which they required in the printing line. Now there are two printing establishments in Brechin, at one of which *The Brechin Advertiser*, a weekly journal published each Tuesday, is printed.

Most of the rivers in Scotland were greatly flooded in August 1829. The South Esk rose far above its banks, covered the greater part of the Inch, and put the inhabitants of the Lower Tenements, now termed, appropriately enough, River Street, in a state of blockade, the whole road from the Ford-mouth down to the bridge being under water, in some places to the depth of two or three feet; but no serious damage was done, and indeed the people on the banks of the South Esk had to congratulate themselves that few who lived near rivers escaped so easily.

The death of George IV. and accession of William IV. led to a new election of Parliament in 1830, and an entry in the council books of the time is strongly characteristic of the excitement then prevailing. This entry bears that letters were laid on the table from Mr Joseph Hume, the then late member for this district of burghs, soliciting to be re-elected; "also a letter of 3d July, on the same subject, from the Honourable J. E. Kennedy Erskine of Dun; and a similar letter from Mr Lindsay of Edinburgh on behalf of Captain Ross of Rossie; and it was also stated that Sir James Carnegie, Bart. of Southesk, and Mr Smith, of the house of Messrs Smith, Payne, & Smiths of London, had applied verbally to the council." Mr Hume was returned to serve in that Parliament for Middlesex, and Sir James Carnegie was elected for this district after a keen and *outrageous* contest. Mr Ross succeeded Sir James in the next Parliament, and he again was succeeded by Mr Chalmers of Aldbar. On the occasion of the contest in 1830, the Brechin press, then recently established, was called into active duty, and there being no local newspaper till years afterwards, the candidates for Parliamentary and civic honours generally applied to the printing-office for spreading, in the shape of placards or circular letters, either their own merits or the demerits of their rivals, and occasionally both. King William was proclaimed at the cross of Brechin by Andrew Robertson, Esq., then Sheriff-substitute of Forfarshire, on 3d July 1830, in presence of the magistrates, council, and community.

The butcher trade purchased up, in 1830, an immunity from the service of attending the magistrates to the fairs ; and the craft having sold all their property, and divided their funds amongst the members, the butchers ceased to exist either as a corporation or society. Unfortunately almost all the other societies in the town, and indeed in Scotland, followed a similar course, and thus a source of support for the aged and sick was at once withdrawn, the effect of which has since been severely felt. Doubtless these friendly societies were founded upon erroneous data, but the regulations of most of them might have been altered, and the scales of contribution and disbursement adjusted so as to meet each other. The Government had passed acts for the *improvement* of these societies ; the contributors became apprehensive that Government meant to take hold of their funds, and hence the almost universal breaking up which followed the act of Parliament. To add to the evil in Brechin, a Savings Bank, which had existed for many years, also began to fall into disrepute, and was finally dissolved about this time. However, under acts of Parliament for the encouragement of Savings Banks, a new agency was opened in 1847, as a branch of the Montrose Savings Bank, and was converted into a principal bank in 1852, and, as a principal bank, is in a very thriving condition. It is open every Tuesday evening in the parochial school-room, under charge of Mr David Prain, the parochial schoolmaster, and a committee of gentlemen as managers.

The council, in this year, 1830, for the first time, organised a set of special constables, a body which proved of considerable advantage in preserving the peace of the burgh, but which is now superseded by the regular police. About forty gentlemen were annually sworn in, who elected from among themselves a captain for the whole, with a lieutenant and ensign for each of the three districts into which the town was divided ; the first, or north division, comprehending all to the north of the Upper West Wynd, (St David Street;) the third, or south division, comprehending all to the south of the South Port; and the second, or centre division, comprehending all that lay between the other two.

Cholera visited Brechin in 1831–32, and a board of health was formed in consequence, under sanction of a proclamation by his Majesty in council. The cases of actual cholera which occurred were few, not exceeding a dozen, but bowel complaints were very common at the time. It is, however, worthy of remark, that the general health of the community was not bad, and that there were fewer deaths this winter than usual. It may be questionable how far a board, such as that alluded to, can prevent contagion; but certainly this board did much in removing nuisances, and we must say that the burgh has been more cleanly since the alarm of cholera. In aid of the funds of the board of health a concert was given by a number of amateurs, followed by a ball, and the affair was a very successful one, although some severely censured piping and dancing at such a time. These concerts and balls for charitable purposes were pretty frequent for some seasons about these years, when amongst the gentlemen of the town there were many of good musical abilities. Subscription balls or assemblies amongst the ladies and gentlemen occurred every winter in those days, and were always well attended. May they soon be renewed!

Amongst the victims to the cholera were the wife and daughter of one of the Brechin characters, a poor but honest man, David Walker. This person, generally styled " Davidie Walker," was the regular, and for long the only *carrier* between Brechin and Arbroath. Davidie generally rode his cart, driving horses that seemed to have escaped from the tan-yard, purposely to keep him company, but animals which he was wont to describe as " fine norse, fine norse, fit for a caravan." The distance travelled was about twelve miles; and David, steady in all his movements, seldom occupied *more* than six or seven hours in travelling the road. Well, one fine frosty evening, David left Arbroath in the pale moonshine, about his usual hour, six o'clock, and progressed his way to Brechin with his load, drawn tandem fashion ; and to beguile the way David had one outside passenger, a sprig of womankind, seated on the top of his vehicle, while his faithful cur walked by the side of the cart. Matters went on swingingly, certainly not *smoothly*, till about mid-way, when poor David's cart stuck fast in the mud. The cattle were whipped, the shoulder was applied to the vehicle, but all in vain, move it would not. David, however, was fertile in devices ; he loosed the tracer, leaped on its back, left the cart and wheel-horse in charge of his dog, and desiring the woman to sit still went off, giving her this assurance, " There's help at hand, help at hand." The poor woman sat till benumbed by cold, when she thought of leaving the top of the cart to take a little exercise. Then she, for the first time, discovered that truly *Help* was at hand ; for David's dog, faithful to its charge, would allow nothing to leave the cart, and the poor female was compelled by Help (the dog) to keep her seat on the top of the cart for six hours, starving of hunger, and almost frozen to an icicle, till David arrived from Brechin with a third horse to pull her out of the mire.

The mode of conveyance between Brechin and Forfar at this time was not much more expeditious. It consisted of an omnibus drawn by a pair of horses, which poor animals, with the exchange with a third horse at Finhaven, did the journey of twenty-six miles, out and in, each working day. The expedition with which the vehicle travelled may be illustrated by the fact, that two young Edinburgh boys left our house one morning, under charge of the driver, to proceed to Forfar ; but when the driver opened the door in the end of the omnibus at Forfar to let out his passengers, no boys were to be found there,—the truth being that the youngsters, noticing the slow mode of conveyance, had, without the driver's knowledge, repeatedly left the coach, and played their ball along the road, resuming their seats when tired with walking ; but the driver, as he neared Forfar, having gone off at a more rapid rate, the young men were left behind, and unable to overtake the omnibus till it reached Forfar.

The alarm of the cholera, it was thought by some, presented an opportunity for establishing a temperance society, an institution which, notwithstanding the many good effects it was calculated to promote, scarce outlived the year 1832, in which it had its rise. A similar society has since been renewed, and now reckons a respectable number of members.

A new road, direct between Dundee and Brechin by the Stannachy Bridge, through the parish of Aberlemno, and by the village of Letham to the old road at Luckyslap, was planned in 1832, and partly executed in that and the following year. The town council of Brechin subscribed £200 to assist the undertaking, but it has been of little, if any, advantage to the burgh.

On 21st August 1832, the first list of persons claiming right to choose a member of Parliament, as proprietors or occupants of subjects of the value of £10, was made up under the act then recently passed. The total number of persons who so claimed was 237, of whom 9 were found disqualified, either from errors in their claims or other causes, thus leaving a constituency of 228, in place of the 13 members of council who formerly possessed this right. Of these parties only 38 now survive.

The Honourable William Maule of Panmure, then member of Parliament for the county, was, in 1832, called to the house of peers by the title of Lord Panmure, and in honour of the event a dinner was given in the Town Hall, on Tuesday 20th September, " to drink (as a handbill in our possession states) farewell to the Hon. William Maule, and many happy days to Baron Panmure of Brechin and Navar." The provost presided, the bailies were croupiers, the town-clerk was treasurer ; and the affair, a truly corporate one, passed off in great style,—for Mr Maule was loved by rich and poor.

The death of the rector of the grammar school, Mr Linton, who had been teacher in Brechin for half a century, gave an opportunity, in 1832-33, of new modelling the schools; and after a great deal of consultation, and no little bickering, it was arranged that there should be three teachers, a rector to teach the languages and higher branches of education, a parochial schoolmaster to teach English reading, writing, and arithmetic, the branches naturally expected to be taught in a parish school ; and a burgh schoolmaster who should teach the same branches ; as the population of the town and parish seemed to afford ample field for two teachers of these, the really necessary branches of

education. The schools have been thus regulated mostly ever
since, changes attempted in the arrangement not having been
found to work well; but a new arrangement has recently been
made, by constituting the burgh school into a junior school. In
a place the size of Brechin, there is not room for minute sub-
divisions of the labour of teaching, nor is there wealth sufficient
for the increase of fees to which sub-division necessarily leads.
The patrons were lucky in selecting teachers for the schools of
Brechin, which, no doubt, contributed considerably to the well
working of the system of teaching adopted. The rector, by an
arrangement with the town council, had a salary of fifty guineas
in lieu of the rents, casualties, &c., arising from the præceptory
of Maisondieu and the rectory. The burgh schoolmaster had
£30 from the town. The parochial schoolmaster again was
allowed £34 by the heritors, and £10 by the town, raising his
salary to £44, which has since, very properly, been increased to
the maximum salary of £70 from the heritors, besides the £10
from the town council. The fees as then fixed were very
moderate. In the rector's department, the quarterly payments
were—French, 3s.; Latin, 4s.; Latin and French, 4s. 6d.; Greek,
5s.; Latin and Greek, 5s.; geography, 2s. 6d.; French and geography, 4s.; Latin and geography, 5s.; Euclid, 5s.; Euclid and Latin,
5s.; other branches, including combinations of the above, 6s. 6d.
During winter, each pupil in the rector's class paid the master
1s. for coal-money, but no other fees or gratuities were payable.
In the other two schools the fees were—reading, 2s. 6d.; writing,
2s. 6d.; reading and writing, 3s. 6d.; arithmetic, with or without reading and writing, 4s. 6d.; book-keeping and practical
mathematics, 5s. But there was another class of scholars belonging to the burgh and parish school who were taught for
even less fees. These were the partial or half-day scholars,
those who were pupils at other schools, for whom there was
provided this scale of fees—reading, 1s. 6d.; writing, 1s. 6d.;
arithmetic, 2s.; reading and writing, 2s.; practical mathematics,
2s.; reading, writing, and arithmetic, 2s. 6d. This class of
scholars, however, was soon found not to answer, and the regulation regarding them fell early into abeyance. English grammar, recitation, and history, imposed an additional 6d. per

quarter on all classes of pupils. During winter, the half-day scholars paid 6d. each, and the whole-day scholars 1s. each, to provide fuel for the burgh and parish schools. No other fees or gratuities of any description were payable in these departments.

In 1833 the council bought the ground adjoining the Crofts formerly belonging to Mr Robertson of Bangaton. In consequence of this and of the previous purchase of the Crofts, the council were, in 1837, enabled to open two new streets, Panmure Street, running west from Swan Street and Clerk Street; and Southesk Street, communicating with Panmure Street, and running south from Clerk Street, at the top of the Den, down by a beautiful sweep to the Montrose road at the Cadgerhillock. By means of these new streets, a road of easy ascent to the top of the town, long a desideratum, was secured. The ground along the north side of Panmure Street, the west side of Southesk Street, from Panmure Street upwards, and on the east side of Clerk Street, was sold off by the council for building stances, at such a rate as fully to indemnify the community for all the money they had disbursed in the purchase of the property. Panmure Street and Southesk Street were so styled out of respect to the two principal proprietors in the parish. Scales Lane, which leads out of Panmure Street, was so named in commemoration of a person to whom the Crofts had at one time belonged, and by whose surname they were distinguished in the title-deeds of the adjoining properties as " Scales' Acre." Macgregor Street, *meant* to connect Clerk Street with Southesk Street, and yet to be made, is to commemorate the last proprietors of the Crofts. Clerk Street obtained its name in 1829, when the town-clerk built the first house, erected expressly for a dwelling-house in that part of the town.

A new washing-house, fitted up with fixed tubs, and supplied with hot and cold water, was erected at the Inch in 1833, and put under such regulations as to afford ample accommodation, at a very moderate rate, for the inhabitants. At first, the regular washerwomen were in arms against this innovation, but experience has convinced them that it adds much to their comfort and convenience, and now they are highly delighted with the ample accommodation which they enjoy for washing and drying clothes.

The resort of customers, too, has been such that the washing-house, although expensive in the erection, has, from the rent drawn, afforded a fair return to the town for the capital expended. In October 1837 it was let for £23, 5s. for the year following; in 1863 it brought £40. Attached to the washing-house are a couple of very nice bath-rooms, with hot and cold plunge-baths and a shower-bath in each, which may be had at a very cheap rate, but they are very little used by the public. Besides the Inch bleaching-green, which consists of about an acre of ground, there is a small bleaching-green at the North Port, well supplied with running water, and the use of which the inhabitants enjoy gratuitously.

In 1833 the council gave £50 to aid in repairing the road between Arbroath and Brechin. This road is still far from excellent, but it is passable, since improved at the expense of the adjoining heritors and of the burghs of Brechin and Arbroath, and it is good compared to what it was when our late friend " Davidie Walker" travelled it; but it is little used by general travellers since the railway was opened.

It was in 1833 that the council first ventured to abridge any of their markets. Lammas Muir, as the market held in August is called, had, from the change in the mode of farming, dwindled to a petty fair; and, on 14th August 1833, a proclamation was published, recommending to dealers to bring forward their stock of sheep, horses, and black cattle (as the bovine race, whether white, yellow, or brown, are denominated) on the Thursday, in place of bringing the sheep on Wednesday, cows and oxen on Thursday, and horses on Friday, as formerly. The market has since been held on the second Thursday of August, yearly, and, although not a great fair, is now a respectable market.

On 5th November of this year, 1833, the first election took place under the Burgh Reform Act, which vested the election of the council in the holders or occupiers of property of the yearly value of £10, and annulled the law which allowed the old council to elect the new. The council, when completed, stood thus : James Speid, provost; David Dakers and William Sharpe, bailies ; Thomas Ogilvy, dean of guild ; James Millar, treasurer ; Robert Mackenzie, hospital master ; Messrs David Guthrie,

James Laing, William Shiress, David Lamb, Alexander Guthrie, David Craig, and Alexander Mather, councillors. Provost Speid and Messrs Sharpe, Ogilvy, Shiress, Lamb, Craig, and Alexander Guthrie still survive, the last being the present provost of the burgh, while Mr Craig holds the position of senior bailie.

It was on 11th September 1834 that the Right Honourable Henry Lord Brougham and Vaux visited Brechin, upon which occasion the greater part of the council, incorporations, and burgesses turned out in their best array to greet the Lord High Chancellor of England, and the freedom of the burgh was presented to that nobleman on a platform erected in the cathedral church, the ancient pile being crowded with the inhabitants of Brechin, and the multitudes assembled from the neighbouring towns and neighbouring country. On the early part of the same day a public meeting had been held, at which it was resolved to establish a joint-stock company for lighting up the town with gas. The gas-work has since proceeded successfully, and the streets, shops, public buildings, and most of the private houses are now lighted with gas. It may therefore be said that the two great lights of the age were made denizens of Brechin on the same day! As a gentleman, whose wit was not very brilliant, used to say when he murdered a bon mot, " That 's a pun."

A Mechanics' Institution was established in Brechin on 25th July 1835, and, under the patronage which Lord Panmure extended to it, by erecting a hall and library for the accommodation of the members, and giving and leaving endowments for it, surely it will flourish.

The proposal for a railway between Brechin and Montrose was revived in 1835, but, after a plan and report, it was again found that the concern would not pay. The town council voted £50 for the plans obtained, and it is but proper to say that the engineers employed, Messrs Grainger and Miller, did every justice to the measure. The accommodation since afforded between the two towns by the Aberdeen Railway Company is not of the best ; but we suspect the community of Brechin must just put up with this railway, tortuous as it is.

In 1836–37, an infant school was erected on a piece of ground lying between the Path Wynd and the Cadger Wynd, now called

Bridge Street and Union Street, a very suitable situation for such an establishment. The house, grounds, and premises are commodious, and the directors having been fortunate in their selection of teachers, may safely congratulate themselves on doing much for the moral and religious habits of the rising generation, and for the promotion of a taste for cleanliness and order amongst the poorer ranks, still a great desideratum in Scotland. The funds of the institution are not adequate to the demands upon it, but hitherto the school has been supported by annual subscriptions from the wealthier classes in the burgh and surrounding country, liberal to a wish in most cases, although it is much to be wished that a permanent endowment could be got for the school.

In 1836, the Lower Wynd, or Church Street, was levelled and macadamised, and the High Street, from the Bishop's Close to the South Port, was improved in the same manner, a very considerable hollow being filled up opposite the Mill Stairs, which reduced the sudden steepness of the street by many feet. But Brechin is built on a hill, and notwithstanding all the improvements on the streets—and they have been many of late years—it is, and must be always, a heavy pull from the lower to the higher part of the town.

A long contemplated sale of a piece of ground at the Trinity Muir market-stance, and skirting the toll road, was carried into effect in 1836. The purchasers have since named the place Trinity Village, and built several neat houses there. The council had previously cut the wood growing on an isolated portion of muir. at Little Brechin, and they disposed of the ground, by public roup, on the day of the sale of the lots at Trinity Village. Both sales brought good prices, and left the council and community no room to regret that they had made a number of new lairds and voters in the county.

The jail had been constantly receiving improvements. In 1836-37 it was thoroughly repaired, cleaned and altered, having then, in our opinion, received as many improvements as its situation rendered it susceptible of, but remaining a very secondary jail, which is now converted into a very secondary police office. The town-hall, too, was repainted, lighted up with gas, and otherwise improved this season. In short, improvement, in its march, had reached Brechin, and its inhabitants progressed with the tide and the times.

In 1837, a bill was brought into Parliament to enable the sheriffs to hold courts in each town in their shires for the disposal of small-debt cases. The bill proposed to give only four courts yearly to Brechin ; but, on the application of the council, backed by their indefatigable representative, Mr Chalmers, six courts were appointed to be held annually at Brechin. On Tuesday, 16th January 1838, the sheriff opened his first small-debt court in Brechin, when, out of the nine parishes attached to the Brechin district, only *four* cases were brought before the judge. Since then the importance of the court has been fully recognised by the country, and now the cases which are disposed of bimonthly are pretty numerous.

The official intimation of the demise of William IV. reached Brechin about two o'clock of 24th June 1837 ; the town council were immediately assembled ; and, in two hours afterwards, Victoria was proclaimed Queen of Great Britain and Ireland at the Market Cross of Brechin.

In the course of making some excavation at the East Mill brae, in 1837, several graves containing beads of a round black substance were discovered. The bodies were found interred after the manner of the ancient Britons, doubled up in kistaveens or cists, composed of undressed stones placed upright on their edges, and covered with thin slabs. The spot where the bodies were found had a southern exposure, and lay close upon the banks of the Esk, within a mile of the Cross of Brechin, at the place called the Middle Den of Leuchland. Similar cists have since been found in different places in and around Brechin, all having a similar exposure.

An act was obtained on 3d July 1837 for improving the harbour of Montrose, in virtue of which the town council of Brechin was authorised to appoint four trustees to attend, jointly with others named by the county and the burgh of Montrose, to the interests of that port. Under this authority the town council of Brechin, on 7th August 1837, named Messrs David Guthrie, David Lamb, James Hood, and Thomas Ogilvy, merchants in

Brechin, as trustees from Brechin; and since then an annual election of Montrose harbour trustees has always been made.

The town council, shortly after the passing of the Municipal Reform Act, agreed to meet statedly on the first Monday of each month; but this having been found a rather inconvenient day, it was agreed, on 1st January 1838, that in future the council should meet on the *second* Monday of each month at six o'clock evening. Besides these stated meetings, the town council meet, on other occasions, when business requires them, upon getting twenty-four hours' notice.

The High Street, from the Prentice-Neuk to the Lower West Wynd (Church Street), was levelled and macadamised during the spring of this year, and the Timber Market (Market Street) was similarly improved during the summer; so that the only street which remained within the burgh, paved with "whin bullets," was the Path Wynd (Bridge Street), and it was soon after subjected to the same process which the other streets had undergone; so that pitched or causewayed streets are now wholly unknown in Brechin, and there is no room at this time for the ancient boast of being able to keep the crown of the *causey.*

But the great event connected with Brechin during the year 1838, was the rebuilding of the public schools. The want of a proper lecture-room and library for the Mechanics' Institution, and the demand for accommodation for the increasing number of pupils at the grammar school, parish school, and burgh school, had struck Lord Panmure, and his lordship most nobly proposed to erect at his own expense, on the site of the old schools, a handsome new building of two storeys, surmounted by a tower, and containing apartments to accommodate all these institutions. After no little consultation as to the plan of the building, and the individuals in whom the property ought to be vested, everything was finally arranged in the month of February 1838. The *constitution* is most liberal. The property is feudally vested in the town council of Brechin, to be held by them as trustees, under the direction of four managers, one to be named triennially by each of the patrons of the parish school, the patrons of the burgh school, the patrons of the grammar school, and the patrons of the Mechanics' Institution. These patrons are again respectively declared to be, of the grammar-school, the magistrates and town council of Brechin ; of the parish school, the heritors holding land rated at £100 Scots of valued rent, the minister of the parish, and the magistrates of Brechin ; of the burgh school, the town council of Brechin ; and of the Mechanics' Institution, the life members, the provost and two bailies of Brechin, the dean and treasurer of the guildry incorporation, the deacon convener of the incorporated trades, the heritors who are patrons of the parish school, and the preses, treasurer, and secretary of the Mechanics' Institution. It will be observed that Lord Panmure reserved no control over the erection ; nay, when it was urged upon him, he positively refused to have a voice more than any other heritor. The coronation of Queen Victoria having been fixed for the 28th June 1838, it was resolved to make that day a gala day in Brechin, and then to lay the foundation stone of the public schools. This proposal, in parliamentary phrase, was carried *nemine contradicente.* Every one set himself to work more anxiously than another to make a day of it. A Fantoccini theatre, and having Marionettes or wooden figures, then in the Mason Lodge, was laid open at the expense of Lord Panmure, from nine o'clock morning to six o'clock afternoon, for the amusement of all the children attending all the schools, public and private, within the burgh. The amusement which was then seen in Brechin for the first time, was under the management of a Mr Stephen, whose sons still travel the country in the same line ; but the theatre is better known by the name of " Shuffle Katie," from a popular dancing figure belonging to it. The Marionette figures gave great delight to the Brechin children on this happy day. Lord Panmure entertained all the trades-men connected with the building of the schools, in Bruce's Crown Hotel. The incorporated trades had a dinner at their own cost in Walker's Cross Guns' Tavern. A subscription dinner took place in M'Bain's Swan Inn. Several other similar convivial parties met in different parts of the town. Each burgess was furnished, from the burgh funds, with a ticket of the value of 1s. 6d. The guildry made a like provision for their members. The widows and orphans of the different incorpora-

o

tions had a similar gift, while private charity provided a something for most of the poor who had no corporate claims. Lord Panmure and Mr Cruikshank of Stracathro were at the expense of a grand display of fireworks for the amusement of the public after nightfall. And, finally, a subscription ball took place in the Town Hall, and was kept up with great harmony to an early hour next morning. The procession, however, was the main point of the day. At eleven o'clock forenoon, exactly, the procession marched off in this order:—Three constables; Odd Fellows' Society; Messrs Hebenton, Wilson, and Laing, private teachers, with their pupils, four abreast; three constables; trades-officer; six incorporated trades, three abreast; Brechin band of music; three constables; town-officers; pupils of the public schools, four abreast; town council, clergy, masters of public schools, and directors of Mechanics' Institution, four and four; St James's Lodge of Masons; Stephens's band of music; guildry incorporation, burgesses, and handicraftsmen, all three abreast. The procession thus marshalled, proceeded from the Town Hall down the High Street, but scarce had they started when flashes of lightning were succeeded by violent peals of thunder and torrents of rain. Still, " On " was the word, and although some anxious mothers took away their children, the great majority proceeded, along with the other members of the procession, down the Cadger Wynd, (Union Street,) up Southesk Street, and through Panmure Street, arches of flowers being raised over these new streets in honour of their being thus publicly opened; up Clerk Street went the procession, round the Distillery Lane, down the Timber Market, (Market Street,) round by Upper West Wynd, (St David Street,) and St Mary Street, to the schools. The rain, though violent, did not continue any length of time, and when the multitude reached the new building the day was fine. The bands of music, pupils of the public schools, town council, clergy, teachers of the public schools, directors of Mechanics' Institution and St James's Lodge of masons, entered the square of the schools, where they were joined by Lady Panmure and a party from Brechin Castle. The masonic ceremony of laying the foundation stone was then gone through in capital style, the late Mr

James Laing, surgeon, acting as master of St James's Lodge, and the Rev. Robert Inglis, then of Lochlee, now of the Free Church in Edzell, officiating as chaplain. In a stone in the middle set of the base course of the front of the building, and between the north-west abutment and north-west octagon turret of the tower, the stone being that adjoining the turret, was deposited a glass vase, containing the coins of the realm, an *Angus Register*, the newspapers of the day, a copy of the tables on weights and measures published by Mr William Shiress, writer in Brechin, a printed copy of the contract of the gas company, a list of the special constables of the burgh, the regulations and fees of the public schools, and a variety of other local publications, including a programme of the procession. The vase also contained the following inscription :—

This Building was Erected
For the accommodation of the Teachers of the Youth of
Brechin, and their Pupils,
By the Noble Munificence of
The Right Honourable
William,
Baron Panmure of Brechin and Navar.
1838.

John Henderson, Architect :
Robert Millar, Mason :
Robert Memes, Carpenter :
Robert Welsh, Plasterer :
David Shiress, Slater :
John Wilson, Plumber.

The vase likewise contained another inscription, written in Latin, of which the following is a copy :—

Gulielmi
Panmurij Baronis, Brechinensis et Navarensis,
Liberalitate Munificentissima,
Hoc Ædificium,
In Usum Juventutis Brechinensis, Qui Literarum
Studijs Dent Operam, Necnon et Præceptorum,
Conditum Est,
Anno Domini, MDCCCXXXVIII.

Joanne Henderson, Architecto :
Roberto Millar, Fabro Murario :

Roberto Memes, Fabro Lignario :
Roberto Welsh, Cæmentario :
Davide Shiress, Scandulario :
Joanne Wilson, Plumbario.

The masonic ceremony was very imposing, and when the sweet infant voices of the pupils, aided by the deeper tones of some professional gentlemen, raised the Queen's Anthem, while the thunder rolled over the heads of the assembled multitude, the effect was really sublime. Many was the deep-drawn sigh which we heard, and not a few faces were bedewed with tears ; the best feelings of the heart were awakened and thus found utterance. The ceremony being completed, three cheers were given in grateful acknowledgment of the obligation which the inhabitants of Brechin lay under to Lord Panmure for erecting the new seminaries. The procession afterwards moved by the Lower Wynd (Church Street) to the High Street, where the Queen's Anthem, and other pieces of music, vocal and instrumental, were performed in honour of her Majesty Queen Victoria, and the whole assemblage then broke up, after giving three hearty huzzas for the then youthful queen.

Thus, from sunrise to *sunrise*, Thursday 28th June 1838, was one continued round of amusement to the old and the young, the rich and the poor of Brechin ; and we are truly happy to record that all these festivities went off without the slightest accident, and, as we believe, to the satisfaction of every person. This description may be tedious to the general reader, but we flatter ourselves that the account of this affair may be agreeable to many a gray head which joined in the procession when a youth.

With the account of the proceedings on this auspicious day we closed the continuous history of the *important* burgh of Brechin in our first edition.

DOORWAY FROM THE WEST. *Page* 249.

CARVED STONE

IN CHURCHYARD OF BRECHIN. *Page* 254.

CHAPTER X.

WE continue our *brief* chronicle from the day on which we originally closed our little work down to the time when. we ceased to hold the position of clerk of the ancient city of Brechin, leaving it for a future town-clerk to revise more particularly the events of this century, and to continue the work to such date as he may find convenient—if, indeed, it shall ever be thought worth while to do so.

Church matters occupied much of the public attention during 1838. The heritors of the parish and the managers of the East Church had a litigation about the collections at the doors of that kirk, the heritors claiming, and ultimately obtaining, the right to a half as belonging to the poor's funds. The first charge of the parish church being. vacant, the crown, to the disappointment of some Brechin expectants, presented a Mr Norval to the charge. The gentleman certainly was an eloquent preacher, and delivered, for his trial discourses, three very excellent sermons, and hence was generally popular. But it was discovered that the presentee's sermons were *all* from the printed discourses of the Rev. Henry Melville, an English divine ; proceedings against Mr Norval in the Church courts were the consequence ; and Mr Norval, having been found wrong, left the Kirk of Scotland altogether and joined the English Episcopal Church. The Rev. James M'Cosh was then appointed to the charge, and this gentleman, now a doctor of divinity, at present fills the office of Professor of Logic in the College of Belfast, and is the author of many learned theological works. These disputes in the Churches were the cause of much acrimony in Brechin; and, indeed, Church affairs were at this period the cause of much contention throughout Scotland, which culminated in the disruption of 1843, and the establishment of that body of Christians which rejoices in the name of the Free Church of Scotland. A severe hurricane occurred on 11th October 1838, which did a great deal of damage in town and country; and, as the stormy Thursday, was contrasted by the old inhabitants with the windy Wednesday of some sixty years previously. Amongst other damage done, the top of the spire of the East Church, with its vane, was blown down. A similar accident from a similar cause, but not to so great an extent, occurred to the same steeple during a storm of wind in October 1840.

In February 1839 very important regulations were framed by the council authorising the introduction of the water from the public fountains into private dwelling-houses and working establishments, and appointing a master of the water works. The privilege thus given was largely taken advantage of, and the rates of charge then fixed still remain the rule of payment. Improvements on the streets were still carried on with energy at this time. A July fair was, at the instigation of the farmers and cattle-dealers, established in the Trinity Muir for nolt, horses, and sheep, and was opened in 1840 with games and rejoicings, but never seemed to take the public, and, after lingering on for some years, was extinguished by a small fair opened in Edzell which, too, barely exists. The celebrated Dr Chalmers, having visited Brechin in the June of this year, was entertained to a public dinner, at which clergy of various church politics assisted; and the council, on the motion of a gentleman, now a keen Voluntary, resolved unanimously to walk " in procession to the parish church to hear the address of Dr Chalmers on church extension." A railway between Montrose and Brechin, and another between Brechin and Froickheim, in connexion with the Arbroath and Forfar Railway, and a junction of both schemes, were projected and surveyed at this time, but were all ultimately abandoned; the prospect of the Aberdeen Railway being made having thrown the other schemes into the shade. A horticultural society, which has since existed under various fortunes, was established for the first time in Brechin in July 1839. The new schools were opened on Monday 9th September 1839.

The parish church was repaired internally, air stoves for heating the building were introduced, and the fabric was lighted up with gas during this year and the two following, the expense being defrayed by voluntary contributions from heritors and others interested in the church. The minister of the first charge having moved for a manse and glebe, considerable discussion arose amongst those interested, which led to the discovery that the manse, which it was understood had belonged to the Exchequer, and was leased from them, in reality belonged to the church in virtue of a Crown grant ratified in Parliament in 1641. A new manse and a glebe for the minister of the first charge have since been obtained, but not till considerable sums had been spent in litigation. Thus each of the two ministers of the parish church has now a manse and also a glebe. Agitation for the abolition of the Corn Laws and Radical Reform was prevalent at this time, and in March 1839 a handbill, headed "Female Radical Association," was published "at the request of upwards of fifty females" calling a public meeting of ladies "to consider the propriety of forming themselves into an Association to assist their male brethren in forwarding the cause of universal liberty!" Another handbill of that period, published by the Working Men's Radical Reform Association, calls for "Universal Suffrage, Annual Parliaments, Vote by Ballot, Equal Representation, No Property Qualification." In aid of this Association a concert, combined with speeches, was held on 30th December 1839.

The jail was finally closed, so far as the jurisdiction of the magistrates was concerned, and given over to the county board in 1840, when the jail assessment, a new tax on property, was imposed and levied; but tramps and vagabond wanderers continued to be an annoyance in town and country, which demanded additional police force. A melancholy accident happened in November of this year to Charles Hendry, weaver in St Mary Street, and his daughter. It was supposed the girl had incautiously left the water department of the gas meter open, and that the gas escaping through the water when additional pressure came on after the most of the lights in the town were extinguished, and after the parties had gone to bed, had gradually filled the house from the roof, till it came to the level of the sleepers and overpowered them. Neither Hendry nor his daughter having made their appearance at their usual time in the morning, the house was forced, when they were found lying insensible in their several beds. The bodies were immediately removed to the open air, and medical aid obtained, but the girl died within a couple of hours, and Hendry only existed in an unconscious state till next morning. The Bible from which the parties had been reading before they went to bed was found open on the table of their room. Willie Gun, a public character, a hawker of almanacs, last speeches, and dying words, died this year, and has left no successor. Willie was endowed with the organ of acquisitiveness, for although constantly pleading poverty, and displaying it in his person, he was found to have had coats, vests, trousers, &c., without number, and a little hoard of cash. The Justice Hall in Trinity Muir, with a barn and byre erected thereon, and the right of pasture of the muir, when not required for markets, was first let to a tenant in 1840, and has always since brought a respectable rent to the town. The Queen was married on 10th February 1840, and the usual demonstrations of loyalty took place, graced in Brechin by a new appropriate anthem from the pen of a local poet and worthy man, the late Mr James Crabb, painter.

The road between Arbroath and Brechin had long been in a bad state, but it was improved in 1841, and made a pretty good road, under a guarantee fund subscribed by various parties interested. The town of Brechin subscribed for £300 under a sub-guarantee from various public spirited individuals to the amount of £253. The tolls on the road defrayed the expenses, and the subscribers were never called on to pay. The Aberdeen Railway, the roundabout railway, as it is generally called, is now, however, the general mode of communication between these two burghs. A census of the population was made up this year by Mr David Prain, parochial schoolmaster, under the Act 3 and 4 Victoria, c. 99, and we give a copy of the return made in an appendix. The *legal* assessment for the poor was also first paid in February 1841, all modes of raising means by voluntary assessments having failed. The birth of a Prince of Wales gave the town council an opportunity to congratulate the Queen " on the auspicious event, which (on 9th November 1841) has given to your Majesty a son, and to the kingdom a Prince," and loyally to pray that " when it shall please the Almighty Disposer of all events to call the Prince, your son, to the throne of his ancestors, he may prove, like your Majesty, a sovereign noted for virtue and ability." The same event gave an opportunity for *heating* the Mechanics' Hall with a ball opened by Lady Panmure. Soon after this Lord Panmure invested the members of the Mechanics' Institution with the hall, along with the handsome donation of £1000 in money ; and on Wednesday, 16th February 1842, Dr Dick of Broughty-Ferry opened the hall as a scientific institution with a lecture " On the Diffusion of Knowledge, and the Means by which it may be Promoted," a very excellent and very appropriate lecture. The only other notable events of the year 1841 were the hanging of an excellent bell in the East Church steeple, and the establishment of a ladies' clothing society for the benefit of the poor.

The year 1842 was one of dull trade, and to relieve the want of employment in Brechin, Lord Panmure, Sir James Carnegie of Kinnaird, and Mr Chalmers of Aldbar, trenched and improved large pieces of ground, at which work all who chose to apply were employed, and paid wages fully equal to their labours. The interest of money being very low at this time, the town council availed themselves of the favourable opportunity of disposing of various pieces of ground around Trinity Muir market stance, on which since then several neat houses have been erected, the place being known as Trinity Village.

The *Montrose Review* newspaper, of 2d June 1843, contains this paragraph : " Sabbath last will be long remembered in Brechin, the doors of the old church having been locked. A portion of the congregation, adhering to their out-going ministers, remained at home, and improved the solemn occasion in private, others of them repaired to the Secession Churches, while the non-adhering portion helped to fill Bishop Moir's chapel, thus showing in plain characters the direction in which the two antagonist

principles are working." Thus began the Free Church in
Brechin. A building, commenced immediately after the disruption in the Lower Wynd, now called Church Street, was opened
for service on Sunday, 26th November, by the Reverend A. L.
R. Foote as the West Free Church, and in which the worthy
gentleman still continues to officiate. The same Montrose newspaper in August has this paragraph—" It is a somewhat curious
coincidence that there is at present in Brechin an equal number
of the several learned professions, nine ministers of the gospel,
nine lawyers, and nine professors of the healing art." An efficient fire-engine was procured for the town in July of this year,
in addition to the old little one, which, little as it is, however,
is well calculated for use in confined places. These two still
constitute the fire establishment in Brechin.

Unfortunately, on Monday 29th April 1844, the necessity for
a fire-engine was too well proved. On that morning the manufacturing premises at the end of Southesk Street, next to Montrose Street, and then belonging to Messrs Guthrie and Hood,
manufacturers, were burned, and property to the value of £2000
destroyed. A man of the name of James Gibson, weaver, was
tried before the High Court of Justiciary on 22d December for
the crime, found guilty, and condemned to fourteen years transportation, but died in the Lunatic Asylum for prisoners, near
London, in a year or so afterwards, having turned out to be a
madman, as was believed by many at the time the crime was
committed. Another fire, arising from accident, occurred in
November, when a quantity of damaged flax, in the course of
being dried in a drying-house near the gaswork was totally
consumed, and the house itself destroyed. The old jail was
bought by the council from the county board for £85, and
finally closed in July, and the new prison in Southesk Street
opened, and that now too is closed, but whether finally remains
to be seen. Railways occupied much attention this year. The
Aberdeen people originally proposed to go direct from Laurencekirk by Brechin to Forfar, but were induced to abandon this
line, and adopt the present tortuous course, from the influence
of interested parties holding position in the county. The Mid-
land Junction Company took up the line favourable for Brechin,

but unfortunately were too late in going to Parliament, and lost their Bill, as that railway was then held to be a competing one with the Aberdeen line. But some day, not distant, the line originally planned *must* be made. Exactly at half-past four o'clock, afternoon of Tuesday 19th October 1847, the *first* railway train left the Brechin station, and reached the Dubton station on a trial trip in twelve minutes. The great event of 1844, however, was the landing of the Queen at Dundee, on Wednesday 11th September, when the council voted an address to her Majesty, which was presented to her by a deputation from the council, when she came ashore that morning, hanging on the arm of her husband, Prince Albert, who led the Princess Royal, then a child, by the hand. Many of the inhabitants were present, and the sight was a very pretty one. The Queen was then *en route* to her Highland home.

Little of local note occurred during 1845 ; Church matters, railways, and Corn Law abolition, continued to occupy the attention of the inhabitants, who had still reason to complain of dull trade ; but the Corn Laws being repealed in 1846, a grand demonstration in honour of the event took place in June of that year. The principal affair in the council in 1845 was the perambulation of the muirs, a full report of which was engrossed in the council book in 1846. In this last-named year, the town council bestirred themselves to get the Church steeples, the choir, and the round tower repaired, and in 1847, Lord Morpeth, at the request of Mr Hume, M.P., procured a grant of money from the treasury, which, with contributions from the town council, heritors, and gentlemen in Brechin, was judiciously applied to this work. A writer, in advocating these repairs in the local newspaper of the day, strongly contended for the repairs of the choir, where, he says—

> " Orisons at rising day,
> Were chanted sad, in solemn lay ;
> Vesper anthems swelling high,
> Echoed through the twilight sky."

The interior of the Round Tower was at this time refitted with new platforms and ladders, the old ones having been for many years dangerous and useless, while externally the Tower was all carefully pointed with cement. The apex of the tower was taken down, and the top rebuilt. This apex was of a very peculiar shape ; the top of the tower is octagonal, but it would appear the sides had not been carried up correctly—not one of the eight sides was equal, and they varied from one inch to four inches in size. An exact drawing of the size of the top of the apex is bound up with the *Montrose Review* for this year in the Mechanics' Institution Library. We presume this apex had been one of " the great stones of the steeple-head " when it was re-paired in 1683 ; it is now in our garden in Clerk Street.

A keen contest took place in 1847 between Mr Hume and Mr David Greenhill of Fearn, when Mr Hume was again returned to Parliament by a large majority, very few in Brechin voting for Mr Greenhill. In July a fancy fair, the first in Brechin, was held in the hall of the Mechanics' Institution, under the patronage of Lady Carnegie of Southesk, when as much money was raised as paid off the debt on the Infant School—a laudable purpose ; but whether fancy fairs are laudable things we say not. Lady Carnegie, who took a great interest in the Infant School, died in 1848, and her worthy husband, Sir James Carnegie, died in 1849. The Right Reverend David Moir, D.D., Bishop of Brechin, died on 21st August 1847. On the 7th October of this year there were great floods in all the rivers of Scotland, and the Southesk laid the Inch and River Street under water, and did considerable damage to property otherways. This was an unhealthy season, and the crowded state of the churchyard attracted much notice ; a joint stock company for a cemetery had been attempted, but failed, and it was not till 1857 that the burying-ground in Southesk Street was opened by the parochial board, after much battling with opposing individuals.

The Currency Laws were much discussed in 1848 ; and the Brechin council, like other communities, passed resolutions on the subject,—not more wise than most other resolutions of a like kind. Postal arrangements and school arrangements also engrossed attention during this and former years ; but these arrangements have been arranged and re-arranged often since then, and would yet " thole amends." Church affairs, too, continued to agitate the community, and a Sabbath Alliance Society was formed in the city. A new educational institution in connexion with the Free Church was opened in Bank Street in the September of this year, and still flourishes. The local newspaper records a fact perhaps worthy of remembrance, that at this time there were daily carried through Brechin blocks of stone, from Aldbar Quarry, for shipment at Arbroath on their way to Prussia, to aid in the completion of the celebrated cathedral of Cologne, which had been in the course of erection for 130 years. Louis Philippe having *absconded* from France, we notice that a respectable company of players, who were in Brechin in March, avail themselves of the fact, and advertise that "a new and interesting drama," written expressly for their establishment, will be produced, entitled, "The Revolution in Paris in 1848." For Brechin, how- ever, a greater abdication occurred; the Defiance coach, the sprightly, dashing conveyance, with its careful drivers and civil guards, their red coats and white hats, and the noble four horses, to whom their work seemed a pleasure, all drove through Brechin for the last time on Monday 31st January 1848, superseded by the railway. We may truly sing with Sir Mark Chase, the old country gentleman, "We shall never see the like again." But the great affair of the year was the establishment of the *Brechin Advertiser* newspaper, its spirited proprietor, Mr David Burns, bookseller, having published the first number on Monday 10th October 1848.

Cholera visited Brechin and the neighbouring towns in August 1849 ; but in Brechin the victims were not numerous, while the general health of the burgh was good. A cheerful exercise in a cricket club, which still continues and flourishes, was established at this time, the players having got liberty from the council to use the Trinity Muir market stance ; various juvenile clubs are now also in existence. Sir Robert Peel and his lady and his daughter spent the evening of 12th October in the Commercial Hotel, and left early next morning by railway ; but as their visit was unknown till after they had left, of course no public notice was taken of the celebrated statesman. We believe the party were on a tour of pleasure in Scotland. An attempt was made this year to adopt the Police Act in the burgh, but was defeated, which compelled the council, from want of funds, to give up lighting the public lamps, and to adopt various other plans more economical than popular. This defeat or disappointment was, however, in a measure compensated by the successful establishment of a wool fair in July. This market, which continues to be regularly held, is mainly indebted for its existence to the exertions of Mr David Craig, writer, one of the bailies of Brechin.

The *Montrose Review* of 20th September 1850 records that "a gentleman walked dry-shod across the river a considerable distance below the bridge last week; the river has for some weeks been lower than in 1826." Water for the use of the inhabitants was, as can easily be supposed, very scarce, and loud calls for an additional supply were made, the Cookston fountains being found deficient, and a law plea having arisen with the proprietor of the estate as to the town's right to search for more water. Application was therefore made to Lord Panmure, who, with his usual liberality, in September 1851 granted the town a tack of the Burghill fountains, which has been a great boon to the town, although from the increasing population there is still a desire for more water.

The lease of the mills and bleachfield having expired, the premises were relet, in March 1851, to Messrs Oswald, Guthrie, and Craig, for twenty-five years, at a rent of £360. These gentlemen converted the spinning-mill into a paper work, and the old corn-mill into warehouses, and subset the bleachfield to the Inch Bleaching Company. A Ragged School, under the name of the Educational Society, was commenced in February 1851, and has done much good since its establishment. It was in May of this year that we witnessed the curious sight of the carts belonging to the Kinnaird tenantry passing through Brechin loaded with snow, in which were placed sprigs of whin and broom in full blow. The winter having furnished no ice, these carts were sent to Glendye for snow, with which to fill the ice-house at Kinnaird Castle. It was a pretty sight; and when the lads, the drivers, began to pelt their female friends with snowballs, it was curious to witness a snowball battle on the streets of Brechin in May. The necessity for the adoption of the Police Act in the burgh became more and more obvious, and a public meeting was held in October on the subject, at which, however, the natural hostility to taxation prevailed, and a motion against the adoption of the Act was carried. The decennial census, taken up this year, we subjoin in an appendix.

On Tuesday 13th April 1852, died at Brechin Castle, aged eighty-one, William, Baron Panmure of Brechin and Navar,— the best friend Brechin ever had. His remains were interred in the churchyard of Brechin on Tuesday 20th April, in the north-west corner of the churchyard. Almost all the public bodies in Brechin desired to form a part of the funeral procession, but the magistrates and town council of Brechin, with their officers, and the directors of the Mechanics' Institution, were the only parties whose offer of attendance was accepted by the family. The funeral, notwithstanding, was a very large one, for besides the deceased nobleman's family and friends, and the tenantry on the Panmure estates, and professional men and tradesmen connected with the property, almost all the landed proprietors in the county, with the magistrates of Dundee, Arbroath, Montrose, and Forfar were present, making in all about 700 persons. The shops were shut from twelve to three o'clock, and the bells tolled at intervals during the day, while the assembled thousands of spectators showed, in their respectful demeanour, how highly the deceased gentleman was esteemed. The Honourable William Ramsay was born (the second son of the Earl of Dalhousie) on 27th October 1771, and succeeded to the Panmure estates, on the death of his father in 1787, as heir under the entail executed by his maternal grand-uncle, William, Earl Panmure, on which occasion Mr Ramsay adopted the name of Maule. Mr William Ramsay Maule entered the army as a cornet in the 11th dragoons in 1789, and afterwards raised an independent company which was disbanded in 1791. On 28th April 1796, Mr Maule was returned as member of Parliament for the county of Forfar, and represented that county in Parliament, always voting on the Liberal side, till he was called to the House of Peers on 9th September 1831 ; having been in the House of Commons from his twenty-fifth till beyond his sixtieth year. He was a consistent Whig, and a great intimate with Charles James Fox, after whom he named his eldest son, now

Earl Dalhousie. Mr Maule, for we delight to call him by a name which was so long popular throughout Scotland, indeed we might say throughout the three kingdoms,—Mr Maule came to his estates when *extra* hospitality was the order of the day amongst Angus lords; and " admirably (says the *Edinburgh Courant*) was he fitted to excel on such a stage, by his handsome figure, his iron frame, his ready wit, his enjoyment of humour, and his boundless flow of spirits." The town council, in their minutes, noticed the death of Lord Panmure in very handsome and just terms. During Lord Panmure's life a bust of him was placed, by public subscription, in the hall of the Mechanics' Institution, and for many years preceding Lord Panmure's death his birth-day was annually celebrated in Brechin in great style. His remains lie in a spot in the churchyard of Brechin, selected by himself, amongst the community of Brechin he loved so well and benefited so much; but no public monument marks his grave.—Shame ! * On 17th September of the same year the Duke of Wellington died, and on the day of his interment the bells were tolled as a mark of respect for the deceased general. The Burghill water was fairly introduced into the town, and the city was again lighted with gas at the expense of the town council in the end of this year, which was marked by great floods in the Esk, inundating the Inch and filling the houses on the side of the river.

The Right Honourable Fox, Baron Panmure of Brechin and Navar, (now Earl Dalhousie,) was created an honorary burgess of Brechin in April 1853, and a similar compliment was paid him by the other Angus burghs soon after. The refreshment rooms in Union Street, and the reading rooms in Montrose Street and River Street, and the parochial lodging-house in City Road, were all established in 1853.

David Guthrie, Esq., who had long been a most efficient member of the town council, died in May 1854, while holding the office of provost, an office which he had filled for many years. The council recorded the death in proper terms in their

---

* Since these lines were penned, a movement has commenced for a monument over Lord Panmure's grave, and we have no doubt a suitable one will *now* be erected.

minutes, and attended the funeral officially, every respect being paid to the deceased, by tolling the church bells, shutting the places of business, &c., during the funeral. Mr Guthrie took a great interest in, and gave much aid to, the first edition of this little work. The same year Patrick Chalmers, Esq., of Aldbar, died on 23d July at Rome, where he had gone for the benefit of his health. Mr Chalmers took an active interest in the affairs of the town of Brechin, and represented the Angus burghs in three successive parliaments. Latterly he devoted himself entirely to literary studies, especially in archæology, and we have availed ourselves of his labours by using freely his " Registrum Episcopatus Brechinensis," two quarto volumes published by him, containing the charters of the burgh found in the charter room, and gathered from other sources. The Honourable Colonel Lauderdale Maule, second son of the late Lord Panmure, fell a victim to cholera at Varna on the 1st of August of this same year ; being in the position of adjutant-general of the army in the Crimea. The colonel, who was a great favourite in Brechin, was the primary cause of the establishment of reading-rooms for the tradesmen of the town. A Russian gun in Brechin Cemetery, mounted on a block of freestone, is inscribed with a suitable legend recording the death of Colonel Maule, and of the other soldiers from Brechin who fell in Turkey during the Crimean war. Colonel Maule was member of Parliament for the county when he died. The Patriotic Fund established for the benefit of the widows and children of parties who had fallen in the Crimea was largely contributed to in Brechin at this time. In 1854 the Old Flesh Market was converted into a place for the sale of butter, eggs, &c. ; and Mr James Smith, clothier, introduced into his works a sewing machine, the first used in the tailor trade in Brechin. Another attempt to introduce the Police Act failed.

On Friday 26th January 1855, the Right Reverend David Low, bishop of Argyle and the Isles, died at the priory of Pittenweem, of which he was the clergyman. Bishop Low was a native of Brechin, where he was born in November 1768, and was educated at the schools of Brechin. He inherited from his father some houses in the town, and the ground occupied by

P

Messrs Dickson & Turnbull as the City Nursery. The bishop was a man of considerable literary abilities, and had a great store of tales connected with the royal family of Stuart. Never having been married, he left the bulk of his property to the Episcopal Church in Scotland. The feuing of the Caldhame lands adjoining the railway, where there is now a *little* town, was begun in 1855 by Lord Dalhousie, then Lord Panmure. Baths at the washing-house on the Inch were opened in the beginning of the year. Curling, which had been in abeyance for many years, was recommenced in Brechin this winter, and still continues a favourite game. A thunderstorm of unusual severity passed over Brechin in June of 1855, but without doing any damage. The annual holiday on the last Friday of July was established this year, and about the same time the masons gained the liberty of ceasing work each Saturday afternoon at two o'clock, while the writers cut an hour off each night's labour, by agreeing to close their offices at seven o'clock, in place of eight, as formerly ; and they, too, have since adopted the Saturday half-holiday.

The court-room was enlarged to its present dimensions by taking in a shop which previously fronted the street, and other alterations were made on the Town Hall buildings in 1856. The question of sending a ruling elder to the General Assembly of the Kirk of Scotland was again mooted in council this year, but rejected by the casting vote of the provost. The Parochial Board having acquired ground on the Caldhame lands for a cemetery, obtained from the council liberty to erect the existing bridge, to give access to the burial ground. The East Free Church was built in 1856, and the large sum of £743 was raised by a fancy bazaar to aid the building.

The mode of assessment for the poor had been the invidious one of means and substance ; but in 1857, after much keen discussion, the mode was changed to rental, modified according to the nature of the subjects leased. The Tenements Schools were erected and chiefly endowed this year by John Smith, Esq., of Andover, Massachusetts, America, a native of Brechin, who has since made several most handsome additional grants to the Institution. The Police Act was at last adopted on 23d Sept.

1857 ; without this law it would have been impossible longer to manage the burgh. The water from Burghill fountains was increased by the laying of new and larger pipes this season. On 14th October 1857, died Alexander Laing, a local poet of considerable eminence, and a worthy man. The new cemetery in Caldhame lands, after no little litigation, was licensed by the sheriff as a burying-ground, and on Monday 26th October 1857 the corpse of William Gray, gardener at Brechin Castle, was interred therein. The consecration of the cemetery, at the request of the Episcopal part of the community, caused a great deal of contention, but the majority of all creeds being in favour of the ceremony, which, if it pleased the Episcopalians, they justly deemed could do them no harm, the Right Reverend Alexander Penrose Forbes, LL.D., bishop of Brechin, assisted by the clergy of his diocese, consecrated a portion of the grounds, on 12th November 1857, in presence of an immense assemblage, who all behaved with becoming respect. The bankruptcy of the Western Bank created a great sensation in Brechin, as elsewhere over the country, in November of this year, but, as usual with Scotch banks, the creditors lost nothing from the misfortune.

Many events, no doubt important to the parties concerned, occurred in Brechin during 1858, but we only record the death of a townsman, an eminent literary man, Dr John Smyth Memes, who died in May of this year at Hamilton, of which parish he was one of the ministers. Dr Memes was an excellent linguist, a good painter, and a beautiful swimmer, as we can vouch. He is perhaps best known by his first book, " The Life of Canova, the Italian Sculptor ; " but he wrote, translated, and edited several other works.

In 1859 occurred the centenary of the birthday of Robert Burns, and on 25th January the festival of the poet was duly celebrated in Brechin, as in most towns in Scotland, and, indeed, in every quarter of the world where Scotsmen were to be found. In May, the foundation-stone of the Tenements Schools was laid in grand style. In June a rifle corps was commenced in Brechin. The United Presbyterian Church in City Road being rebuilt, was opened for worship in September. And in November the Rev. George Alexander, A.M., rector of the Grammar School, having completed his fiftieth year as a teacher in the city, a festival was held by his old pupils and friends on the occasion.

The Den Nursery was let in February 1860 to Mr George Henderson, on a lease of twenty-one years, after Martinmas 1862, at a rent of £70. In April the streets were renamed by the police commissioners, and the old and new names engrossed in the council book, and the extent of each street defined. In June of this year died General Sir David Leighton, K.C.B., a Brechin man, who by great courage and perseverance raised himself to the highest eminence in the Indian army. We may be permitted to add, that on 30th Nov. 1860 died Mr Alexander Strachan, writer and depute town-clerk, a man universally beloved. The census taken up this season we give in an appendix.

The Ladies Coal Fund, for supplying poor families with coals was established in 1861, and an excellent charity it has proved. No less than £550 was raised from a bazaar held in June, to defray the expenses of our gallant defenders—the Brechin Rifle Corps. The Marches of the Trinity Muir lands were perambulated by the council in September 1861, and the result recorded in a long report engrossed in the council minute-book in 1862. His Royal Highness, Albert, Prince Consort, having died on 14th December, a loyal and dutiful address of condolence was sent by the council to the Queen—the unexpected visitation being one which excited general sympathy.

In 1862 the Brechin Bowling Club was established, and still flourishes, but cricket seems to be more the favourite of the juvenile classes. The Duke of Cambridge passed through Brechin in August, on a visit to the Earl of Dalhousie, and the jolly, worthy gentleman was welcomed with hearty good-will by the citizens; very different from the reception given to his royal predecessor of Cumberland in 1746. On 11th November the prison, which had been erected at considerable expense in Southesk Street, was closed by the County Board.

The marriage of the Prince of Wales, on 10th March 1863, was the occasion of great rejoicings in Brechin. A petition from several ladies who patronised the washing-house on the Inch, complaining of the access by the mill stairs, led to the great improvement which has been made on that pathway. The parish church was repaired outside and inside this year, and not before renovation was needed. Swan Street was also widened and greatly improved by the erection of new buildings in it, begun at this time.

Our brief chronicle has brought us to our concluding year 1864, during which handsome power-looms were begun to be erected in Southesk Street, by Messrs Lamb and Scott, and Messrs D. & R. Duke, which will change altogether the mode of manufacture in linen in Brechin. On 24th August, Mr James Loudon Gordon was elected town-clerk of Brechin, when *we* finally ceased to be an official character—and so ends our little history.

CHAPTER XI.

THE cathedral is supposed to have been originally erected by
David I. in the twelfth century, and to have been then dedicated
to the Holy Trinity, but there is no distinct account of the date of
the erection of the cathedral or adjoining steeple and tower; the
only document we have seen bearing on the subject being that
already mentioned, (p. 24,) by which it is proved that between 1354
and 1384 the belfry of Brechin was built. In the dike at present
surrounding the churchyard, and immediately above the western
iron gate, there is a stone said to have been in the wall above the
porch door, which was in the north aisle of the old cathedral about
the centre, and this stone bears a crosier proper above a shield
carrying in the first and fourth compartments three bears' heads,
or, as others read them, three leopards' faces or panthers' faces, and
a lion rampant in the second and third compartments. These,
most likely, are the arms of the bishop who built the porch door;
for, it is well known, cathedral churches were never all built at
once, but at different times, as the different bishops had taste for
building or means at their disposal. We have not been able to
ascertain positively to whom these armorial bearings belong,
although we believe they are those of George Sherwood, who
was bishop of Brechin in 1455–61. The cathedral, as used by
the Presbyterian congregation, was a handsome Gothic building,
consisting, till 1806, of a nave with two side aisles, and a transept formed by the extension of these aisles at the east end. In
the north transept there was a small door on the west side on a
level with the ground, and used, along with the porch door and

west door, at the " scailin' of the kirk," the dismissal of the congregation—the assembling of the congregation being mainly by the porch door, and occasionally by the west door. About the centre of the south aisle was another small door with an arched head. This door, in 1806, was considerably below the level of the churchyard, to which there were steps up from the inside of the church. The door spoken of was only occasionally used by the church officials at the time we knew it. We give a ground plan of the cathedral made from measurements, and revised by parties who were well acquainted with the church before the alterations in 1806. So far as we can learn, the cathedral was never finally completed. The great western door, at which extremity, generally, cathedrals were commenced, seems to have been fully finished, and the nave appears to have been also completed, but there was no appearance that there had ever been any pillars or arches in the transepts, which are now wholly swept away, and which, as already said, seem to have been merely extensions of the side aisles. Notwithstanding of the beautiful ruins of the chancel, of which we give a woodcut, we question if the high altar had ever been properly finished, and if there had been anything more than a " Lady Chapel," of which the foundations are occasionally met with to the east of the ruins alluded to. In 1806, the north and south transepts were removed, new aisles were built on each side of the nave, and one immense, abominably ugly, roof made to cover the whole, thus totally eclipsing the four beautiful windows in the nave, and covering up the handsome carved cornice of the nail head quatre-foil description, which ran under the eaves of the nave. This building, as modernised, is used for the parish church. It is supported by 12 pillars, measures 84 feet in length, 30 feet in breadth, or 58 feet including the aisles, each of which measures 14 feet. The western door, of which we give a woodcut, has been beautifully carved, and the large Gothic window above it is still much admired for the elegance of its mullions and tracery. It is described by architects as slightly flamboyant, and is supposed to be of an age much later than the square steeple adjoining. Part of the side walls of the choir and chancel, measuring on the north wall 23 feet, and on the south wall 26 feet, in

length, 24 feet in height, and 23 feet in width, are still standing, the windows of which, as seen in the woodcut, are tall and
narrow, graced with chaste small columns supporting beautiful
lancet-shaped arches. At the north angle of the nave, and close
on the west door, is the steeple, a noble-looking square tower,
70 feet high, supported by buttresses on the west side, measuring 25 feet 2 inches on each side, and having handsome
belfry windows, adorned with that species of opening called the
quatrefoil. The walls are 5 feet thick at the base, and in the
bell-house, which is immediately above the session-house, they
are the same. The top of the steeple is battlemented and surrounded with a bartizan, out of which rises an elegant octagon
spire 58 feet high. The ascent to the bartizan is by a spiral
stair of 111 steps, contained in a handsome octagonal tower,
at the north-east corner of the steeple, as may be seen in a
view which we give of the church from the north. From the
bartizan there is a beautiful prospect of the surrounding country,
bounded on the west and north by the Grampian Mountains, on
the south by Burkle Hill, and on the east, extending as far as
the eye can see, into the German Ocean, over Montrose. A
very beautiful moulding of floral ornaments runs round the projecting base of the west side of the bartizan; and on the top of
one of the battlements on the east side of the bartizan, being
that to the north of the clock-face, is carved an antique head,
while on the corresponding battlement on the south side of the
clock-face is the date 1642 in *alto relievo* letters. We find from
the accompts of John Liddell, kirk treasurer in 1642 and 1643,
that various repairs had been made on the church in these years,
and we presume this date refers to them. The accompts are
very minute, from 2s. 8d. given to Alexander Talbert for " lad-
dering the church;" 3s. 4d. to " James Stirling for carrying in
the *burn;*" 1s. 4d. " given for mending the lyme ridll;" to
" Sept. 1643 given out in general for expenses disbursed upon
the glass windows, £145, 2s. 2d." At this time there appears
to have been a clock belonging to the church, which, if it
had then stood where the clock removed in 1806 stood, would
have been immediately above the east window of the square
tower, the works being placed on a flooring opposite inside

the steeple. This clock, like those of modern days, seems to have required much attention, for Mr Liddell has various entries in his accounts regarding the *knock;* as, for example, in November 1642 there are 4s. " given Hendrie Valentine for making *changies* to the knock," and in January 1643 Mr Valentine has 2s. 8d. " for mending some things the knock had need of." Notwithstanding the age of these buildings, not a decayed stone can be seen in the cathedral, steeple, or spire. The base of the steeple, which is now occupied as the session-house, has a handsome groined roof, springing from four corbels, three of them ornamented with a leaf beautifully cut in high relief, and the fourth with a dog picking a bone, which may lead some antiquary to the exact date of the building, as the dog possibly has some allusion to the name of the builder. The arch or groin terminates in an open circle of about four feet in diameter, and about seventeen feet from the floor. The session-house measures 15 feet 3 inches on each side. In the east wall of the steeple, and about the middle of the second floor above the session-house, is a square opening like a door, but with *teeth* or stones projecting from each side, so as to be easily filled up to accord with the original building. This door leads by a zigzag course through the centre of the wall into the roof of the church, the exit from the door being on a level with the side walls of the nave. For what purpose this opening had been left, can only now be matter of conjecture. Possibly it might have been intended for a person, stationed in it, to communicate with the bell-ringers how to toll the bells at different parts of the ceremonials of the Romish Church. This seems the more likely, as within this passage through the wall there is in a recess a stone seat and a small window commanding the exterior view of the north side of the church. At present no person can see from this passage into the body of the church, in consequence of the flat plastered roof of the church; but when the original Gothic roof of the cathedral existed, similar to that of the Parliament House of Edinburgh, or Westminster Hall of London, there was no difficulty in seeing, from this point, what occurred in the cathedral. In the spire of the steeple are now placed two bells which were formerly in the round tower, and in the steeple, itself, is hung a large bell. A clock, placed on the bartizan when the church was repaired in 1806, strikes the quarters on the small bells, and the full hour on the large bell. Of course, these bells are all used for giving notice of divine service on Sundays, and the large bell is rung on the evenings of each of the six working days during the week, at eight o'clock, and is also *tolled* or *jowed*, that is, made to strike solemnly on one side, consecutively, each Saturday night at ten o'clock; and it is rung each work-day morning, during the summer, at six o'clock, and during the winter at seven o'clock. It is a deep full-toned bell, and the tolling, or ringing on one side, on the Saturday nights, has a peculiarly solemn effect. A musical friend informs us that the first or great bell sounds A exactly, concert pitch; the second, or one of the smallest bells, A sharp, or B flat, an octave above, and the third or smallest bell, C. in alt.; and that, had the second bell been A exactly, the chime would have been perfect, A, A 8va. and C the 15th. Although not a complete chime, he tells us the Brechin bells may be stated as very nearly so. The same friend informs us that the bell of the old Episcopal chapel in High Street sounds E in alt., and the town-house bell a note or two lower, say, perhaps, C in alt.

At the south-west angle, but entirely separated from the nave of the church, stands the celebrated round tower, one of those singular buildings which have so long baffled the researches of antiquaries.* The tower of Brechin is quite a distinct erection from any of the buildings of the church, although the south aisle now embraces nearly one-fourth of its circumference. From this aisle there is an entrance of comparatively modern date, at least evi-

---

* We give a woodcut of the cathedral of Brechin from the west, carefully prepared from a photograph, in which the lower part of the round tower is exactly depicted. We also give an enlarged view of the doorway of the round tower, engraved from a photograph. Farther, we give a woodcut of a peculiarly carved stone, which, for the purpose of photographing, is placed against the base of the east side of the round tower. In all of these woodcuts the mason work of the round tower is represented exactly as it exists, each stone being carefully engraved as shown in the building. From these engravings, therefore, the reader may obtain a correct notion of the different styles of building of the tower, the cathedral, and the square steeple.

dently struck out of the wall after the tower had been built, supposed to have been made for the convenience of the ringers when
there were bells in the tower.* However, when the church was
last repaired, these bells, as already noticed, were transferred to
the steeple. There is no stair in the tower, and the only access
to the top is by means of six ladders. One ladder rests on the
earthen† floor within the tower; and the other five ladders are
placed on wooden semicircular floors, each floor being supported
by a circular projection or abutment, or corbel, as architects
term it, within the tower.‡ These corbels form part of the wall
of the tower, and, of course, are parts of the original structure of
the tower. Each of the third and fourth floors is lighted by a
small window or opening; the fifth and sixth, by the windows
in the top; and the first, by the door; but the second has no
window or light. The window in the third floor is on the east
side; the window in the fourth floor on the south side. The
height of the tower from the ground to the roof is 85 feet; the
inner diameter at the bottom, 8 feet; the thickness of the wall,
at that part, about 4 feet; so that the whole diameter is nearly
16 feet, and the external circumference very near 50 feet; the
inner diameter, at top, is 6 feet 7 inches, the thickness of the
walls 2 feet 10 inches, the circumference 38 feet 6 inches. These
proportions give the building an inexpressible elegance.§ The
top is roofed with an *octagonal* spire, 18 feet high, which makes
the whole height of the building 103 feet.|| Near the top of the
tower there are four windows, facing the four cardinal points, of
oblong shape, with flat plain stones for sills, rybats, and lintels.
In the octagonal roof there are also four windows, having their
sills on the top of the tower, alternating with the windows in the
tower. The windows in the roof are brought to a point at the
top, by means of two stones resting on each other, like an in-

---

* Now again built up.

† Now flag-stone floor.

‡ Rather a string course, but variously termed, by different writers, bracket,
plinth, projection, offset, &c.

§ Our woodcut of the cathedral from the east, with the ruins of the chancel,
gives a good general representation of the round tower from top to bottom.

|| These measurements, as afterwards noticed in the text, were made under
difficulties before 1839. We give the exact dimensions in a subsequent foot note.

verted ⋀, and springing from the square sides of each window. Near the bottom, on the west side, there is a handsome small arch or doorway, composed of four large stones, employed, one as a door-sill, two as rybats, and one as a curved lintel.* The width of the door at the sill is 1 foot 11½ inches, and at the spring of the arch or circle 1 foot 9 inches, the height of the rybats to the arch, 5 feet 9½ inches, and the height of the arch 10 inches, making the total height 6 feet 7½ inches. Each stone is the depth of the wall, and presents an external face of about 11 inches. The sides of the door and the arch stand out in relief from the tower, and on the top of the arch is a crucifixion, also in relief. Between the mouldings on the sides, and about half the height of the sides below the arch, are two figures, apparently monks, leaning on staves, and wrapped in close cloaks with hoods. The introduction of two monks into the crucifixion is an anachronism similar to what may be found in the paintings of some of the old masters. On each corner of the sill of the door, which also stands out in relief from the tower, is the figure of a beast, and in the middle between them is a lozenge, on which apparently some arms have been engraved. Probably these animals may have represented the supporters of the shield of the pious lady whose arms had been contained in the lozenge, and who may have been at the expense of making the door-way. But, except the crucifixion, the whole figures, which have been all sculptured in *alto relievo*, are so much decayed as to leave considerable scope for imagination. The door-way is filled up in a slovenly manner with coarse rubble work.† One side of the door, within the tower, presents the appearance of a staple having been made to go into a hasp, neatly formed in the stone-work, while the other side of the door shows where bands had

---

* Since this doorway was opened, in 1842, the curved lintel of the top is found to be composed of two stones, neatly joined and jointed. We give the exact dimensions of the tower, as now ascertained, in a subsequent foot note; but here we may, in addition to what is given above, state that the door-way, at the sill, measuring across the whole stone, is 4 feet 5 inches, and at the spring of the arch, or circle, 4 feet 2 inches ; and that the wooden door now put on measures to the soffit of the circle 5 feet 6 inches with 8½ inches for the circle,—in whole, 6 feet 2½ inches.

† Now re-opened, as seen in our woodcuts.

been fastened for hanging the door, which thus must have opened upon the interior side of the door-way. The figures, on the exterior of this door-way, bespeak it to be of Christian architecture ; and after repeated and minute examination, in presence of architects and master masons, we are satisfied that the doorway must have been built when the tower was erected, be that era when it may.* The wholé tower is built of large stones, not one of which is yet blasted, cut to the circle, but not squared at top or bottom, nor laid in regular courses, but running round the building in sloping courses, which rise above each other somewhat like a screw, forming one spiral course from top to bottom ; although Mr Grose asserts, we think without sufficient examination, that it is composed of sixty regular courses of mason work. This mode of building seems ruder and more ancient than the regular coursed ashlar work of the steeple ; and the roof of the tower, corresponding in the style of building to the steeple, would lead to the belief that this tower, like most others

* We have had the door-way again and again inspected by people of skill since 1839, when this was published, and they have all agreed with the statement in our text. Mr R. W. Billings, the eminent English architect, in the first volume of his beautiful work, " The Baronial and Ecclesiastical Antiquities of Scotland," published in 1852, in which he gives two views and a description of the cathedral and round tower of Brechin, says, " Everything connected with the round tower but the conical roof has the appearance of being part of one original design, and where it is but barely possible that, with great exertion, a part of the lower range could have been removed for the incrustation of these Christian symbols, at a cost which might have been sufficient to erect a separate tower." We omitted in our first edition to state, that on each side of the door-way, immediately opposite the crucifixion, and on the same stone with it, which forms the arch of the door-way, is a projecting stone of 1 foot 10½ inches by six inches, left as if intended for figures being sculptured thereupon, but never finished. We omitted also to state that part of the south side of the door-way at the foot is of a red sandstone, as may be noticed in the enlarged view of the door-way, as if a piece had accidentally been broken off and renewed at a later period. This has the same ornament as surrounds the door-way, but of inferior workmanship. This ornament is sometimes called the tellet and button-shaped, but we style it a bead-like ornament. The smaller of the two saints, that on the right side of the doorway, measures 1 foot 4 inches, and with the plinth 1 foot 9 inches; the larger figure on the left measures 1 foot 5½ inches, and with the plinth on which it stands 1 foot 10¼ inches. The breadth of each stone on which the figure is cut is 5 inches. The crucifixion again measures, height of figure, 1 foot 3½ inches ; figure with pedestal, 1 foot 8 inches ; breadth of stone on which figure cut, 4 inches ; width across the arms, 1 foot 3¼ inches ; width of that part of stone, 1 foot 6 inches. The stones on which the animals at the foot of the door are sculptured measure each 11 by 8 inches.

of the same description, had been originally open at top, and had received its present roof at the time the steeple was built, or by architects who imitated that style of building. The handsome door-way, however, rather contradicts the supposition of the want of skill in the original architects. Certain it is, that during high winds this tower has often been observed to vibrate ; and we, ourselves, can vouch for having witnessed this fact on different occasions. It is by a high wind from the southeast that the tower is most generally shaken. While it stands perpendicular on the east, it *appears* to be about three feet off the plumb on the west side, likely an original error in the architecture, as no *sit* in the building can be detected, and apparently arising from a difference in the thickness of the walls on the east and west side.* We intended to have given the internal dimensions more particularly, but, in consequence of two of the ladders of the tower being altogether gone, and the others being in a rotten and decayed state, and the impossibility of introducing any additional ladder through the very small entry now left from the church to the tower, we found it unsafe, if not impracticable, to ascend to the top ; and we are, therefore, obliged to rely on measurements, not so particular as we could have wished, made some years ago when the ladders and floors of the Brechin tower were in a better state than they are at present. †

* We now think this is a mistake and an optical *de*-lusion, although many of our friends still contend for the truth of the statement in the text. Mr Billings, however, in his " Baronial and Ecclesiastical Antiquities," says, " The round tower slightly tapers upwards, but it has a decided inclination in one direction, so that while the side towards the church is perpendicular the other forms an obtuse angle with the horizontal line."

† This was written and published in 1839. The steeples and towers were repaired mainly at the expense of Government in 1847, and new ladders and flooring introduced into the tower by the west door, then re-opened, as mentioned at page 219. We are therefore now enabled to give the exact dimensions of the tower. We adopt those made in October 1855 for Albert Way, Esq., M.A., of Wonham Manor, secretary to the Archæological Institute of Great Britain, by Mr William Ormiston of Edinburgh, and given in plate III. of vol. iii. of the " Proceedings of the Society of Antiquaries in Scotland," along with remarks on the round tower of Brechin, then communicated to the Society by Andrew Jervise, Esq. of Brechin. We have verified these measurements with the aid of Mr John Baxter, builder in Brechin, and have found them correct, and, with Mr Baxter's assistance, we have made some additional measurements, which we give. Again, the total height and total thickness of the tower have been kindly ascertained for us by Mr George

Towers of this description are said to occur frequently in Ireland. Mr Richard Gough, in his " Observations on the Round Towers of Ireland," published in 1779, tells us that " these round towers are spread through divers parts of Ireland; they differ from each other in degrees of height, some thirty-seven feet, others fifty and more; that of Kildare is 132 feet high; and that at Kilkenny is little less. Their outward circuit at the base rarely exceeds forty-two feet; walls three feet thick; diameter within, seldom more than eight feet; they gradually

Henderson of the Den Nursery, Brechin, by trigonometrical survey, and have been found to tally with the reports of Messrs Ormiston and Baxter. The dimensions, then, are these—From level of ground outside to first corbel inside, 3 feet 5½ inches; from first to second corbel inside, 12 feet 8½ inches, the width here 7 feet 11 inches; from second to third corbel, 12 feet of height, width, 7 feet 9 inches; from third to fourth corbel, height, 13 feet 10 inches, width, 7 feet 3 inches; in this storey there is a window on the east side of the tower, measuring 1 foot 8 inches by 11 inches at the bottom and 10 inches at the top; from fourth to fifth corbel, 10 feet 7 inches in height and 7 feet of width, in which storey there is a window, on the south side, of similar dimensions with the one below; from the fifth to the sixth corbel measures 18 feet 8 inches of height, width, 7 feet; from sixth corbal to a shelf on the wall, 7 feet 2 inches. As the walls are considerably thinner here, the width inside the tower is 7 feet 8½ inches. Within this division are the four windows looking to the cardinal points of the compass, measuring 3 feet 8 inches by 1 foot 9 inches each. All the windows mentioned are plain and unornamented. From the head of the shelf on the wall to the top of the wall is 3 feet 10 inches, the width being 8 feet 2 inches, as the wall is again considerably thinner. In the tower there are six corbels, averaging 9 inches each, giving in whole 4 feet 9 inches. Thus from the ground to the top of the *round* tower the height is 86 feet 9 inches. The octagon top measures 15 feet 9 inches from the head of the wall to the inside of the roof, and the ridge of the roof is understood to be 3 feet thick, which gives in all for the octagon top 18 feet 9 inches. The stone ball on the apex of the roof measures 12½ inches. Consequently the whole mason-work measures 106 feet 6½ inches in height, tallying exactly with Mr Henderson's trigonometrical survey. If to this are added 3 feet 5½ inches for the iron rod and vane on the top of the steeple, we have a total height of 110 feet for this obelisk. The base course or ground plinth measures 12 inches in height, and projects 2 inches from the wall, and from the top of this plinth to the door-sill is 5 feet 8 inches, so that the door-sill is 6 feet 8 inches from the ground. At the base the walls are 3 feet 8 inches thick, and the internal diameter or width being 7 feet 11 inches; the whole diameter is 15 feet 3 inches, which gives a circumference of 47 feet 10¾ inches at the bottom. At the top again, the walls are 2 feet 5 inches and 2 feet 6 inches thick; the internal circumference 8 feet 1 inch, making in all 13 feet of diameter and 40 feet 10 inches of circumference. Thus the taper, or entasis, or batter, as it is more familiarly termed, from bottom to top is only 7 feet 6-8ths of an inch in whole, or 3 feet 6⅜ inches on each wall, which gives the tower an inexpressible elegance.

diminish from the bottom to the top, which is covered with a stone roof. Withinside are abutments on which to rest the timbers for the several floors or stages, to which they ascended by ladders; every storey has a little window; the four upper windows looking different ways; the door for entrance from eight to twelve, and to fifteen feet from the ground, without steps or stairs."

In Scotland there are but two such towers, one at Brechin, and another at Abernethy, in Perthshire. We made a pilgrimage to the Abernethy tower in 1838. Thomas Simpson, the then beadle of Abernethy, informed us, readily, that it was built by the Picts 1300 years ago, and that a gentleman had read the whole account of it out of a book to his daughter. Thomas was, otherwise, very communicative and obliging, and under his superintendence we made a survey of this tower. We found that the height was under eighty feet. The door-way, which is on the *north* side, and attained by three steps, evidently of modern architecture, is about seven feet in height, and three in width. The diameter of the tower, inside, level with the door-sill, is seven feet ten inches. The thickness of the wall, at the door-way, is three feet six inches, but as the rybat of the door projects two inches, the true thickness of the wall here is three feet four inches; consequently the external diameter of the building is fourteen feet six inches; but as this door-way, from the fall of the ground, is six feet nine inches above the foundation on the west side, the external diameter at the base will, most likely, be about fifteen feet. From the base on the west side, to the top of the door-way, a height of about fourteen feet, there are twelve courses of regular masonry of a dark-coloured stone, not unlike the Brechin stone. Above this the courses are of a yellow stone like the Cullalo stone, and the sills, rybats, and arch of the door-way are of this yellow stone. The door-way is of a very rude architecture, composed externally of six stones, one used for the door-sill, four for the side rybats, and one cut into a curve or arch for the lintel. The sill and rybats go through the wall; the lintel is *backed* by some small stones built in arch-ways. The top of the tower is attained by means of four ladders, resting upon wooden floors supported by internal

rings or corbels, exactly similar to those of the Brechin tower.
The first of these floors is level with the door-sill, and below
this floor, there is a vacuity of three or four feet. By the help
of the four ladders, the aspiring antiquarian may reach the floor
where the bell is hung, but those who wish to attain the *leads*
of the tower must apply to Thomas Simpson, or his successor,
to keep the bell stationary, and then, by mounting upon the top of
it, they will gain the highest floor, which is about three feet
from the extreme top. This floor is covered with lead, in which
there is a small hatchway, and the individual whose curiosity
may induce him to mount so high, will be gratified by a beautiful view of the Tay and Earn, the Castle Law Hill above Abernethy, and the undulating grounds of Fife and Perth shires in
the distance. Measured at this height, the internal diameter of
the tower is found to be 6 feet 8½ inches, and the walls 2 feet
7 inches thick; but as the top is covered with stones which
project with a moulding of about seven inches beyond the wall,
the real thickness of the wall, at the top, is two feet, and, consequently, the external diameter nearly 10 feet 9 inches. The
projecting moulding, we are informed, was added about the
middle of last century. Previous to this addition, the tower
must have have had a very unfinished-like appearance. The
internal stone circles, or corbels, are six in number, supporting
as many floors; and these projections all evidently form part
of the original building of the tower. There is no stone
roof, and so far this tower is defective in beauty compared with
that of Brechin. Thomas Simpson said the Picts built it
all in a night, and were about to put on the roof of a morning, when an old woman, looking from her window, frightened them away, and hence the building was left unfinished.
At the top, and immediately below the highest internal ring or
corbel which supports the leads of the building, there are four
windows, but these do not look to the cardinal points, and we
should suppose they are some three or four degrees of variation
off the cardinal points. Each window measures, inside, about
six feet in height and two feet in width. They are all arched,
and, externally, there is a higher circle some foot or so above
that which gives light, and small carved pilasters, of which one

Q

or two yet remain, have supported or ornamented the external arch. In this respect they differ from the windows in the Brechin tower. The tower of Abernethy differs also from the Brechin tower in being composed of regularly squared and coursed ashlar of moderate sizes. Internally, there is the distinct appearance of the tower having been built to a circular mould or frame, the cement projecting beyond the stones, being run together to the circle, and smoothed on, not squared to, the joints of the stones. The cement upon the inner side of the circle has much the appearance of Roman cement; at the windows the lime appears in the centre of the wall, as if poured into the walls in a liquid state. Externally, the stones of the tower are pretty entire, except on the north-west side, near the top, and the joints having been pointed up about 1835, the courses of the building in 1838 were very distinct. In the interior many of the stones are very much decayed and eaten into, like water-worn stones, the softer parts being removed, and the harder standing out similar to ribs or joints. The tower is one-half within, and one-half without, the churchyard, the dike of which embraces the north-east half of the tower. Upon the south side of the tower, without the dike of the churchyard, and opposite to the *Cross* House in which the councillors make their elections and hold their magisterial feasts, and affixed to the wall of the tower, is to be found that ancient instrument of punishment, the "jugs," an iron collar, namely, of three pieces, attached together by two joints, and which, opening in front to receive the culprit's neck, was then secured by a padlock, while, behind, it was fastened by a chain to the building, and thus the offender remained in durance till it pleased the men in power, and the keeper of the key of the padlock, to relieve him. Our friend Thomas Simpson assured us that the magistrates *dared* not now use this instrument of punishment, and as Thomas is town-officer as well as beadle and sexton, and as the day of our visit was the day of the election of magistrates and head court of the burgh of Abernethy, we deem ourselves as having derived our information from the highest, most direct, and purest source! !

Above Abernethy, a little to the south-west, is a hill, called the Castle-Law Hill, upon the top of which are the remains of a vitrified fort, which we visited; and amongst the names of places in the neighbourhood, we find Pittenbreigh, Pittendrioch, &c., and below the hill, on the south side, we saw, if we mistake not, the remains of what is generally termed a Druid temple. Similar names of places, and similar druidical remains are to be found in the immediate vicinity of Brechin. The hill of Finhaven, on which are the remains of a vitrified fort, is at the distance of some five or six miles south-west from Brechin, and Catterthun is some four miles north-west of Brechin. We leave it, therefore, to abler antiquarians to ascertain if there is any connexion between these circumstances and the round towers of Brechin and Abernethy.

The Rev. Dr Small of Edenshead, Abernethy, who has written a book on Roman Antiquities, states the tradition regarding the tower of Abernethy to be, that it was erected as a burying-place for "the kings of the Picts," and to the doctor "it is as clear as a sunbeam, that the Pictish race of Kings lie ALL buried within it." In confirmation of this hypothesis, the reverend doctor writes, that on 10th May 1821 the interior of the tower was dug into, when, at about four feet from the surface, the sexton found, in presence of the gentlemen assembled, "plenty of human bones, and the fragments of a light green urn, with a row of carving round the bottom of the neck," and that, digging still farther, they "came to three broad flags, which either served as the bottom of the first coffin or the cover of another, and by removing one which seemed the largest, found that there were plenty of bones below; *and thus, after gaining our end in ascertaining the original design of building it, as a cemetery for the Royal Family, we desisted,*" says the doctor. We introduced ourselves to Dr Small, from whom we purchased a copy of his work. We are quite satisfied he is a gentleman on whose veracity implicit reliance may be placed; but we rather fear he jumps at conclusions, and is not a little credulous—and, still worse, we doubt his antiquarian skill. Shade of Huddleston, how wouldst thou shudder, if shades can shudder, to learn that Dr Small derives Pittendreich, your burial-place of the Druids, from two common Scotch words—ascribing the origin of the term to the circumstance of the Romans having "got a more *dreich* piece of road *pitten* to them," when forming their famous way through North Britain! The doctor, in describing his researches in the tower, adds that the sexton of Abernethy afterwards found " seven other human skulls all lying together, all of them full-grown male skulls," buried in the tower, one of which, the most entire, was carried away by Sir Walter Scott. Our friend, Thomas Simpson, the successor of the sexton alluded to by the doctor, hints very broadly, that situated so close to the kirkyard as the tower is, there would be no great difficulty in finding skulls in the latter, when it was once seen there was a demand for them. Thomas applies to this case the famous axiom in political economy, that the demand regulates the supply.

Regarding such erections, Mr Pennant in his tour through Scotland has given the following observations:—" The learned among the antiquaries," he remarks, " are greatly divided concerning the use of these buildings, as well as the founders. Some think them Pictish, probably because there is one at Abernethy, the ancient seat of that nation ; and others call them Danish, because it was the custom of the Danes to give an alarm in time of danger, from high places. But the manner and simplicity of building, in early times, of both those nations, was such as to supersede that notion : besides, there are so many specimens left of their architecture, as tend at once to disprove any conjecture of that kind : the Hebrides, Caithness and Ross-shire, exhibit relics of their buildings totally different. They could not be designed as belfrys, as they are placed near the steeples of churches, infinitely more commodious for that end ; nor places of alarm, as they are often erected in situations unfit for that purpose. I must therefore fall into the opinion of the late worthy Peter Collinson, that they were *inclusoria, et arcti inclusorii ergastula,* the prisons of narrow enclosures ; that they were used for the confinement of the penitents ; some perhaps constrained, others voluntary, Dunchad o Braoin being said to have retired to such a prison, where he died, A.D. 987. The penitents were placed in the upper storey ; after undergoing their term of probation, they were suffered to descend to the next, (in all I have seen, there are inner abutments for such floors :) after that, they took a second step, till at length the time of purification being fulfilled, they were released and received again into the bosom of the Church. Mr Collinson says that they were built in the tenth or eleventh century. The religious were, in those early times, the best architects ; and religious architecture the best kind. The pious builders either improved themselves in the art by their pilgrimages, or were foreign monks brought over for the purpose. Ireland being the land of sanctity, *Patria sanctorum*, the people of that country might be the original inventors of these towers of mortification. They abound there, and, in all probability, might be brought into Scotland by some of those holy men who dispersed themselves to all parts of Christendom to reform mankind." Mr Gough, the antiquarian, to whom we have already alluded, offers a pretty similar solution. He tells us, that " about the year 1750, Mr Charles Smith, author of an account of the counties of Down, Waterford, Kerry, and Cork, who, with great industry, was searching ancient records for materials for these works, met with some ancient MSS. which clear up this long-disputed subject. From these, it appears that these towers were built in the 10th or 11th centuries, and were used for imprisoning penitents." In the churchyard of Drumlahan, county of Cavan, Ireland, there is one of these towers, on the top of which, tradition asserts, an anchorite lived. Mr Harris, the gentleman, who, in a work on the antiquities of Ireland, reports this tradition, states, that the earliest mention which he found of anchorites in Ireland was in the year 732. These anchorites were called *Stelites*, from their living on pillars ; and Mr Harris adds, he was informed by a skilful critic in the Irish language, that a tower of the description in question is called, in that language, *cloch ancoire*, or the stone of the anchorite, and not *cloghad*, or the steeple. The Styletic system began in the East in the year 460, and some anchorites are mentioned as late as the year 1200. Evagrius, an author, who writes on this subject, describes the mansion of the founder of the sect as *on* a pillar 40 cubits or 60 feet high, but he also describes that of Simeon and that of Daniel as *in* a pillar.

Notwithstanding of all this, the theory of Dr Small, though fanciful in many respects, is not unworthy of notice. The towers in question may have originally been intended for mausoleums, and the fact of only two being found in Scotland, one at Abernethy and another at Brechin, both of which places are reputed to have been seats of the Pictish kings, supports the notion that the towers were connected with that peculiar people, and might have been designed as mausoleums for their princes. The fact also that the door-way in the tower of Brechin is 5 feet 10 inches from the ground, and of Abernethy, about seven feet from the foundation of the building, gives room for supposing that the space between the ground and the doors may have been set aside for containing dead bodies. At Abernethy, there is an inner abutment, level with the door-sill, for supporting a floor, below which the bodies might have been deposited; at Brechin, there is a similar projection or abutment, about nine inches below the door-sill. We own we should like to see the interior of the Brechin tower dug into,[*] although, even if as many skulls were found as the sexton of Abernethy produced to Dr Small, we would not then conclude that the building had been erected expressly for a mausoleum, or that it was the vault of the Pictish kings, but we might then hazard a conjecture that some of the race had been interred at Brechin. The round tower of Brechin is much more perfect than the tower of Abernethy, and the materials are decidedly better; but the style of architecture at Abernethy, by squaring the stones and laying them in regular courses, is superior to the style of building at Brechin, where none of the stones are squared, and no regular courses are kept, and where, near the foundation especially, there are a number of broken joints, that is the joining of two stones being placed immediately above the joining of other two stones; but then the architecture of the doorway of the round tower of Brechin is decidedly superior to any part of the building of the tower of Abernethy; and although we long flattered ourselves that this difficulty was got over by supposing the Brechin door-way to have been introduced into the building at an after period, we are now as much convinced, as strict personal examination and the opinions of eminent practical masons can convince us, that this door-way and all its carving must have been put into the building at the time

* Our wish was gratified in 1842, as is particularly noticed afterwards.

of the original erection. It may be conjectured that the tower was built in a hurry, of which, indeed, there are many proofs in the mason work, and that it was so hurried on to receive a royal corpse; but that, while the rest of the materials were being prepared in the most expeditious way possible, time, attention, and labour, were bestowed on the comparatively small matter of the door-way. Tradition, in Brechin, as well as at Abernethy, ascribes the erection to the *Peghts;* and although tradition has not reported at Brechin that they were interrupted by any old woman, it has stated that they were only allowed a trifle for their work, and were cheated out of part of this trifle; and, possibly, both traditions may import that the buildings were erected in comparatively short time. The existence of similar buildings in Ireland would not controvert the theory that they were originally intended as the burying-places of princes, for, in Ireland, where there were, till a comparatively late period, so many independent kings, there may have been as many distinct burying-places. To be sure, the lozenge on the door-way of the tower of Brechin, throws a doubt upon the theory, that these buildings were erected as the burying-places of the Pictish kings, for it may be questioned if the Picts or *Peghts* used armorial bearings, or if the Pictish ladies carried their quarterings on a lozenge; but then there is another question, whether this lozenge, may not have been cut into its present shape from something else, at a recent period; and there is yet the more primary question, whether, what we have described as a lozenge, is a lozenge after all, although we are pretty well convinced it is really a lozenge or diamond.

We own Dr Small's speculation does not coincide with our opinions, and we are inclined to fall into Mr Collinson's theory, approved of by Mr Pennant and Mr Gough, that the round towers in question were built by the *religieuse* of the tenth century, as places of mortification, and perhaps of sepulture, and we think the fact of the emblems of Christianity being found cut on stones, which are evidently part of the original structure of the Brechin tower, goes far to prove the correctness of this hypothesis.

Our readers will recollect the proof we adduced, (page 24,)

that Henry de Lichton, vicar of Lethnot, gave to Patrick, bishop of Brechin (1354-84) a cart, made by Elisha Wright, to lead stones to the building of the belfry of the church of Brechin. Now, if the supposition we have made is correct, the stones which were thus driven could not have been driven for the erection of the round tower, which we suppose to have been erected nearly 400 years before. The belfry alluded to in the proceedings with the vicar of Lethnot, may have been the square tower, or steeple, in which the largest bell was hung, and which, since 1806, has been exclusively used as the belfry of the church, but we own we can scarce think the vicar of Lethnot would have been allowed to get off with so trifling a contribution as a cart, to assist in driving stones for so immense a building; and, besides, the square tower is universally called the *steeple* in all writings which have come under our notice. The round tower itself can scarce be meant, because, towards such an erection, the whole members of the chapter must have contributed more largely than Lichton did in the instance alluded to. The octagon top of the round tower is clearly of a different and superior style of architecture from the rest of the tower, and we cannot help thinking that, as the tower of Abernethy is without a top, the Brechin tower had originally been also without any top, and that the tower of Brechin had received its top for the purpose of being used as a belfry, sometime about the year 1360; and that the top, then erected, was built by Patrick,* bishop of Brechin, in the same style as the square tower, bartizan, and steeple, then existing; for it is a legitimate conclusion, that the cathedral itself was erected when the bishopric was created by David I., and that the large steeple was built at the same time, or about 200 years before the belfry was built on the top of the round tower. Here, however, we are again met with the difficulty of the arms borne on the lozenge, for, as the practice of carrying armorial bearings was little known till the tenth century, and was not brought to perfection till nearly 200 years afterwards, we can scarce imagine that, if this tower was built in the ninth or tenth century, the arms of the founder could appear upon it. Granting that the lozenge is an armorial bearing, then the tower

* See an account of this active bishop in Appendix No. II.

must date somewhere about the year 1200, and, after all, the vicar of Lethnot's cart may have assisted at the erection of it. We are almost satisfied that the figure, so often alluded to, is a lozenge, but we are by no means satisfied that it is an armorial lozenge, and rather conceive it to be one of those fancy figures which an architect would use to relieve the appearance of a heavy door sill, and that the lozenge and the two figures of animals at the corners were introduced for this purpose. This supposition, however, we hazard with very great diffidence, and we own our theory is not much less free from attack than that of our Pictish friends.

We find ourselves, however, bound to come to some conclusion, and we, therefore, offer it as our humble opinion that the shaft of the pillar, or round tower of Brechin, was erected somewhere about the year 1000, the cathedral and steeple about 1150, and the belfry, or top of the round tower, about 1360.

All this in the text we wrote and published in 1839, and as it has been often quoted, and not unfrequently misquoted and misrepresented by different authors since, in place of rewriting we prefer to allow it to remain as then printed, but with the explanations given in the foot-notes. We have now, however, to state that in the month of April 1842, the round tower was explored at the expense of the late Patrick Chalmers, Esq., of Aldbar, by the late Mr James Jolly, mason in Brechin, acting under our directions. The door facing the west, which was previously filled up with coarse stones, was opened; rubbish, which had accumulated to the first corbel, was removed to the depth of five feet; the natural soil was dug into for upwards of other five feet and under the foundation of the building; but nothing deemed of the least consequence having been found, a printed inscription, stating how the tower had been explored, was placed in a glass jar, enclosed in a leaden case, which was again surrounded by a thick oak box, well covered with coal-tar, the space between the lead and the oak being filled up with fine sand; and this box was then placed below the foundation-stones of the tower on the west side, and the natural soil dug out was replaced in the tower, and a stone pavement laid above it. We give in an appendix a detailed list, made up from day to day during the excavation, enumerating everything discovered in the bottom of the tower, which, according to our ideas, had served as a general receptacle for all the odds and ends of the several beadles of the church, and the refuse of the nests of the owls and of the jackdaws, called kaes in Scotland, which, from time immemorial, had built on the top of the tower. But some antiquarians may view the list in a different light. What we have said is no new idea on our part, as may be seen from the letter which we wrote at the time to William Hackett, Esq., of Middleton, in county Cork, Ireland, brother-in-law of the famous Father Matthew, and which we also give in our appendix. At the date of this exploration, the foundation of the tower on the south-east side was found to be 12 feet 2 inches below the door-sill ; 10 feet 2 inches below the corbel or projecting course, where the digging was begun ; and 5 feet 7 inches below the ground level outside ; and the foundation on the west side proved to be 10 inches below the bottom of the foundation on the south-east side. The stones used in building the inside wall of the tower below the external ground level are all, with the exception of one freestone, rough whinstones, kept as near as possible to the circle, and the tower is shaken in three places below the external surface, apparently from the extreme pressure upon a coarse foundation. Mr Jolly was clearly of opinion that the slight vibrations of the tower, which occasionally occur in high winds from the south-east, may be ascribed to the fact of the tower being built on a circle or corbel of firm freestone masonry, placed on the rough foundation of whinstones, with projecting points brought to a level for the corbel with small stones. We know that the allegation of the occasional vibration of the tower is questioned by many ; but we can vouch for having witnessed the motion of the tower on two several occasions, and several beadles have assured us of having seen the same thing repeatedly, while the late Mr William Shiress, slater, who had a house and garden adjoining the churchyard, proved the fact by erecting a perpendicular plank of wood, and watching the top of the tower appear and disappear beyond it on one stormy day, and calling on others to witness the same thing. We have noticed, at page 96, and in our appendix, the

fact of the top of the steeple having been blown down in 1683.*
We have also noticed, at page 219, the repairs made on the tower
in 1847.

On 29th September 1845, the famous Irish archæologist, Dr
George Petrie, visited Brechin, accompanied by some friends,
and we had the pleasure of a long meeting with the worthy, mild,
simple-minded gentleman, who is but recently removed from this
earthly scene. Dr Petrie's views exactly acquiesced with what
we had published in regard to the round tower of Brechin ; and
in his " Ecclesiastical Architecture of Ireland," a second edition
of which was published shortly before his death in 1865, he re-
iterates his statements of the Irish and Scotch towers being of
Christian architecture, and combats at great length all the different theories as to their pagan origin. We beg to refer to that
beautiful volume. From pages 91 to 96 he discusses the round
tower of Brechin, and, quoting the opinion given by us in our
first edition, that the tower was erected somewhere about the
year 1000, he says, " An opinion which I shall hereafter show is
not far from the truth ;" but a purpose which he did not live to
fulfil, although towards the end of his volume, at page 410, he
again says, " The round tower of Brechin, in Scotland, as I shall
show in the third part of this work, there is every reason to believe was erected about the year 1020, and by *Irish* ecclesiastics."
Indeed this is so far confirmed by drawings, which we have in
our possession, of parts of the round tower of Cloyne in Ireland,

* While this work is passing through the press, we find the following in the
Athenæum newspaper of 16th February 1867 :—" One of the most interesting of the
ancient monuments of Ireland suffered damage in the hurricane of Wednesday week.
The pointed stone forming the apex of the round tower at Ardmore, county Waterford, (weighing about 12 stones, and being 2 feet 6 inches in height,) was blown
down, and, in falling, deeply imbedded itself in the ground. This conical cap of
the very ancient pillar stood a little out of the perpendicular, having once been
struck by lightning. The tower remains a venerable object of great interest. At
the base of the tower a discovery was once made of two skeletons buried there, a
circumstance which led to Mr Windell's assertion that the towers were used as
burying-places, an assertion in which Mr Petrie could not agree. The old bell of
the tower could be heard eight miles off, and its situation near the church, like
that of other towers, may lead us naturally to infer that it was a *campanile*, de-
tached from the church, as was once the case with ecclesiastical bell towers." The
tower of Ardmore, we have understood, is very like, in point of appearance and in
height and dimensions, to the round tower of Brechin.

the style of building of which is identical with the Brechin tower, while the storeys, the circumference, the thickness of walls, and the total height, 102 feet, correspond as near as may be with the Brechin tower. Dr Daniel Wilson, in his " Prehistoric Annals of Scotland," published in 1851, discusses the subject from pages 587 to 599, and comes to the same conclusion, that the Irish towers, the towers of Brechin and Abernethy, and the small church and tower of St Magnus, on the island of Egleshay in Orkney, were all built by Christian architects about the close of the tenth century. There is a fact worth mentioning connected with this Orkney church and tower. They are built of the un-hewn clay slate of the district, and the tower, unsymmetrical, and bulging considerably at one side, much resembles the burgs so common in Orkney and Shetland. The tower on the island of Mousa in Shetland, of which a fac-simile is in the Antiquarian Museum of Edinburgh, is just a rude dry stone round tower, with the stair in the centre of the wall rising to the top in a spiral form. Can the round towers of Ireland and Scotland be the successors of the burgs of Orkney and Shetland, which they so much resemble in outward appearance ? We think not; but the more ancient burgs in figure have certainly the style of the more modern towers.

In the " Le Revoir " at the end of our first edition we said, " On various parts of the church, steeple, and towers are to be found initials and dates, affording evidences of the *longings after immortality* which possessed the persons who cut these inscrip-tions, but affording no evidence of the date of the erections; at least the inscriptions yet discovered all subsequent to 1600 afford no clue to the date of the buildings." We have nothing to add to this, but that the mason marks, which are also to be found on various places inside and out of these buildings, appear to us to be of very various dates and far from ancient.

We remain of our original opinion, that the shaft or pillar of the round tower of Brechin is of Christian architecture, and was erected about the year 1000,—most likely soon after 990, when, as noticed at the beginning of this work, (pages 3, 4,) Kenneth

Macalpine endowed a church at Brechin, as recorded in the ancient Pictish chronicles of that time; and that the belfry or octagonal top of the round tower was built about 1360. The cathedral and square steeple, we still think, dates about 1150.

We give in this work woodcuts of the church from three different points of view, and we also give an enlarged view of the door-way in the round tower. By comparing all these woodcuts, which, as already said, have been very carefully prepared from photographs, and especially by examining the woodcut of the door-way of the round tower, which gives, on an enlarged scale, each stone of the building identically as it exists at the present day; by such examination, the reader can satisfy himself of the correctness of our statements.

The cathedral is bounded on the south and east by a steep ravine, which is, by some, supposed to have also bounded the site of the church on the north, leaving the only access by the west. This theory is countenanced by the fact, that *travelled* or artificial earth has repeatedly been found, at a great depth, a little to the north of the church within the confines of the supposed ravine, and it is farther supported by the fact, that peatmoss, leaves, and deers' horns have been found in digging graves of some depth, within six yards of the foundation of the steeple, while no appearance of original soil was to be seen.

To the east of the church is a lane, leading to the High Street, termed the Bishop's Close. Over the mouth of this close, next the High Street, is a pend or arch, the sides of which display part of the ancient walls which enclosed the bishop's palace, and part of the abutments, from which sprung the original arch over this entry, which, as we believe, was erected by Bishop Carnock between 1429 and 1450. On the north side of this lane stood the bishop's palace, but no vestige of it now remains, the foundation having been dug out when the house, formerly occupied by the senior clergyman, was erected in 1771. This house itself was demolished in 1850, and a new manse built in the grounds on the south side of the Bishop's Close, while office houses were erected on the site where the bishop's palace had stood. When digging the foundations for the new manse in

April 1850, there were found the remains of a strong wall, under
ground, running east in a line with the south wall of the nave
of the cathedral, supposed to have been erected to support the
flat on which the new manse stands, all which is of *travelled*
earth.

Near the round tower there lies an oblong stone which was
dug out of the churchyard some years ago. The stone is covered
with figures, and its general aspect very much resembles the
outer case of an Egyptian mummy. We had the stone placed
upright against the east side of the round tower, and a photograph of it taken in this position, from which we give a woodcut.
The stone has at one time been used as a burial stone, for on
the flat, or lower side, there is an inscription, in *alto relievo*
letters, wholly illegible, as if worn out by feet passing over it, at
the centre and foot, but bearing along the top and sides that
" Heir rests in the hope " of a blessed resurrection, we presume,
some now nameless wight, who, as the legend farther reads,
" feared God and eschewed ill, and departed" this world, we suppose, some 200 years ago, as little known now as the party for
whom the stone was originally made. There are the remains
of three stone coffins lying in the churchyard, but it is hard
to say if this carved stone had been the cover of any of
them. Most probably two of these stone coffins, which lie
at the east end of the church, had formed receptacles for the
bodies of some of the bishops of the see, who had, according
to the practice of the Popish Church, been buried under the
high altar; but this is mere speculation, as we have no history
on the subject, only these two coffins were found near the place
where the high altar must have stood. The third coffin, which
is of larger dimensions, was found near where it lies, on the south
side of the church. The two stone coffins first mentioned, and
which were found more than fifty years before the third one, are
placed alongside a *vault* or enclosed burying-place, belonging to
the family of Speid of Ardovie, a family that has been long connected with this part of the country. On 6th May 1519, the
Archbishop of St Andrews granted a charter of confirmation and
novodamus in favour of Thomas Speid, of the lands of Cuikston,
lying in the regality of St Andrews and barony of Rescobie, on

the narrative, that Mr Speid and his ancestors had possessed these lands beyond the memory of man, without any interruption. On 9th September 1549, George Speid exchanged the lands of Cuikston for the lands of Auchdovey, now called Ardovie, in the parish of Brechin, by contract of excambion with Robert Carnegy of Kinnaird, and the lands of Ardovie have been in possession of the family of Speid ever since—for ten generations. Immediately opposite the Ardovie vault, and affixed to the ruins of the choir, is a monument, erected in 1806, by Alexander Ferrier, Esq. of Kintrocket, to the memory of his brother, Captain David Ferrier, who made a voyage round the world in the *Dolphin*, and who died in his native parish of Brechin in 1804, at the age of sixty. The *fore* churchyard has a monument to the memory of Mr Alexander Ferrier himself, who died in 1809, also aged sixty, and to whom might justly be applied the celebrated line of Horace, inscribed on the monument of Captain Ferrier:—

" Multis Ille Bonis flebilis occidit."

A modest stone, a little to the north of the Ardovie vault, records the death of Alexander Mitchell, " who departed this life the 28th March 1800, aged one hundred and one years and two months ;" and who, consequently, saw the year 1699, a century more, and the year 1800, and thus may be said to have lived for parts of three different centuries. The Rev. William Linton, A.M., rector of the Grammar School for fifty-five years, died in 1832, at the age of eighty years, and'a very handsome granite monument, built into the north wall of the churchyard, immediately adjoining the large gate, records in classic Latin the acquirements of the learned gentleman. We have already noticed the inscription, built into the north-west wall, relating to the visitation of the plague in 1647.

William de Brechin, as we previously mentioned, founded the chapel of Maisondieu about 1256, and part of the walls of the chapel still remain. They are situated in the Maisondieu Vennel, or Lane, a little west of the Timber Market. We give two views of the chapel, an exterior and an interior view, carefully engraved from photographs, and exhibiting each stone as it now actually exists. These views prove that the chapel had been, originally, an elegant little building of the pointed, or early English architecture. Within the building, there is still the remains of an aumrie, or ambrey and piscine, with an iron pipe for leading to the earth the water used in washing the holy utensils. The aumrie is seen in the woodcut. The house itself, and the property about it, with the superiority of some other lands, and a small revenue, payable from the farms of Maisondieu and Dalgetty, in the immediate vicinity, are generally gifted by the crown to the rector of the grammar-school during his incumbency, who hence takes the title of præceptor of Maisondieu, and in signing charters or other writings relating to his office, puts " Præceptor Domus Dei" after his name. Alexander Hog, who held a chaplainry in the cathedral church in 1485, is the first person recorded as assuming the title of rector, which, however, is as old a title as many of higher pretensions. There have been instances, however, of these revenues being granted for other purposes than education. James Duke of Ross claimed the patronage of Maisondieu in 1488, for in January of that year there is a dispute before the Lords of Council between his nominee and another party, who pretended to have got a grant from the Pope, and this dispute is only settled on 26th February 1489 ; and the Panmure family seem at one period, previous to the year 1716, to have been in the receipt of the revenues. The annual income of the præceptory at present is about £42, 19s., besides occasional entries from vassals, and the property is estimated as being worth £960.

Within the burgh, at the junction of what was the Upper West Wynd with the Timber Market, now respectively called St David Street and Market Street, there is a house said to have been a *hospitiüm* of the Knights Templars, and which holds feu of the Earl of Torphicen as their successor in the superiority, lately and appropriately enough used as the Crown Inn, now belonging to, and occupied by, Messrs Dickson and Turnbull, nurserymen, and on which, till a recent repair of the roof, there was a small iron cross on the highest chimney. These knights had also some lands in the neighbourhood, as there are pieces of ground, one on the estate of Southesk at Dalgetty, called the Templehill, and another on the estate of Cairnbank, close by Brechin, bearing the title of Templehill of Bothers.

A house at the foot of Chanonry Wynd, attached to which is an excellent garden, now belonging to Mr Mitchell, tenant of Nether Careston, was formerly the manse of the rector of Kilmoir, " de antiquo manses rectoris de Kilmoir," says a charter of 1605 amongst the title-deeds.

CHAPTER XII.

HAVING finished the historical part of our work, we propose to devote this chapter to a statistical account of Brechin, town and parish, and to a notice of the non-ecclesiastical buildings and other particulars worthy of observation in the burgh—in brief, having looked on Brechin, hitherto, mainly as it was, we mean now to look to it as it is.

The PARISH OF BRECHIN extends in length, from east to west, about seven miles; and in breadth, from north to south, about six miles. It contains about 24¾ square miles. The river South Esk runs through the parish in a south-easterly direction, and is the only river in it: Esk is simply the English pronounciation of the Gaelic word *uisge*, water. The parish of Brechin is bounded by the parishes of Menmuir and Stracathro on the north, by Farnell on the south, by Careston on the west, and by Dun on the east; while, on the south-west, it marches with Aberlemno. The only hill of any considerable eminence in the parish is the hill of Burkell, to the south-west of the town, sometimes spelled Burghill and Buttergill Hill; but the sloping ground on which the town is built is no mean hill, and the high lands of Maisondieu, Pittendriech and Barrelwell, on the north-west of the town, are rising grounds of some consequence. The greater part of the parish, however, is composed of level or gently sloping ground. The soil is, in general, light but good. The total number of imperial acres in the parish is estimated at about 14,423, of which 14,056 are capable of tillage; while there are actually cultivated annually about 8300 in corn, turnips, and potatoes, and 3300 in grass; about 450 acres are in wood; 239 in roads; 18 in railways, and 110 in water. The area of the royalty of the burgh is 224 acres nearly; of which about 18 are in roads and streets, and four in water; while within the Parliamentary boundaries the area is about 417½ acres, thus leaving for the landward parish 13,781½ acres. Large quantities of corn, the produce of the parish, are annually exported. The cumulo valued rent of the parish is £8772 Scots. The rental of the landward part of the parish is £16,017; of the burgh, £15,082; while the railway is assessed, within burgh, on a rental of £15,820, and, without burgh, on £17,625; the total rental of the parish thus being for land and houses, £31,100; for railway, £2345. The average rent of arable land is supposed to be about thirty shillings the imperial acre; and of grass, for the season, forty shillings. The mode of husbandry followed is, for the most part, agreeable to the modern improvements. The principal green crops raised in the parish are turnips and potatoes for domestic purposes and for the feeding of cattle. Potatoes were pretty largely exported for some years, but that trade is now again much restricted. Wheat is generally sown after the potato crop. From the fourth to the sixth part of each farm is usually sown with turnips, or planted with potatoes each year, unless on farms adapted for wheat, in which case a proportion is fallowed. No beet, and few cabbages, are cultivated. No meadow hay is raised in the parish. Of flax there are only a few acres annually sown. Few sheep are reared in the parish, and these are generally of the kind called blackfaced. The horses are now of the common size usual throughout the southern parts of Scotland. The other cattle are mostly of that breed, known as peculiar to Angusshire, middle-sized, and well formed; although a good many short-horned are now fed off in the parish, and a few Teeswater and Ayrshire cows may be seen on the pasture lands. The management of cattle is well understood and attended to. The length of leases is generally nineteen years; leases of this duration being considered more favourable than those for a shorter period; but lands, in the close vicinity of the town, are often let on leases to endure from five to fourteen years. The state of farm-buildings and enclosures is good, the buildings being usually of stone and lime,

and slated, and the fences principally dry-stone walls, although
hedge-rows are becoming more prevalent. For temporary enclosures flakes are generally used, consisting of four longitudinal
spars of nine feet each, morticed into a spar of about four feet
of height at each end, the flakes being bolted together by pins,
and supported at each joining by lateral posts, sloping to the
ground, at an angle of fifty degrees or so. Improvements have
been general throughout the parish during the last sixty years.
Some seventy years ago a medical practitioner in the town took
a good deal of land in the vicinity of the burgh, and set to work
seriously to improve it. For this purpose he bought great quantities of dung, and raised the price from ninepence or tenpence
to one shilling the cart-load, when a worthy magistrate of the
city, also a farmer in a small way, gave up purchasing manure,
declaring " he would drive no one shilling dung." Manure now
fetches, in the burgh, from five to ten shillings each load, according to the quality.

The following has been hazarded as the average gross amount
of raw produce yearly raised in the parish, which some friends,
with whom we have consulted, consider to be rather under than
above the mark:—Oats, 8000 quarters; barley, 6000 quarters;
wheat, 1200 quarters; turnips, 2000 acres; potatoes, 1000 acres;
hay, 500 acres; flax, 20 acres. Agricultural male labourers receive about fifteen shillings per week; females, so employed,
six shillings per week, or rather one shilling per day; but the
latter class is mostly employed during the summer only, while
the former may command work in draining, &c., all the year
round. The wages in harvest are something more, being, males
twenty, and females eighteen shillings per week. The number
of agricultural workers in the parish is supposed to be, males,
200; females, 100, as field workers, generally called "out
workers." Including allowance of meal, milk, and potatoes, a
ploughman's wages may be estimated at £36 per annum. The
usual food of the peasantry is milk, meal, and potatoes, with a
little butcher meat and fish. The fuel is principally coals and
wood.

The inhabitants, according to the census of 1831, were found
to be, males, 3048; females, 3460; together, 6508; consisting

of 1673 families lodged in 900 houses, of which number of families 306 were ascertained to be engaged in agriculture. This, of course, included the urban district. The rural district contained, males, 699; females, 749; together, 1448; families, 286; employed in agriculture, 186; in trade, 68; other families, 32; inhabited houses, 285; uninhabited, 20; males upwards of twenty years of age, 361; female servants, 145; male labourers, 186. In 1755, the population of the parish was supposed to amount to 3181; and in 1790, it was guessed at 5000; the census of 1811 returned 5559, and that of 1821 gave 5906. As seen in our appendices, the population in 1841 was reported to be 7555; in 1851 it was found to be 6638; and in 1861 it was 7180. The number of burials in the parish, during the year 1836, was 193; and during the year 1837, it was 191, both being unhealthy seasons; in 1838, the number was 129, which was supposed to be about an average of ordinary years. There is an ancient burial-place at the eastern extremity of the parish, called Magdalene Chapel, although no traces of the chapel now remain. Very few bodies are interred in this cemetery, and those so buried are not included in the register kept by the sextons of the Brechin churchyard, who were our authorities for the details we have given. In 1864 the deaths were, landward part of parish, males, 6; females, 13; total, 19; in the town, males, 72; females, 86; total, 158; together, 177; the greatest age being that of an old shoemaker in town, who had attained to ninety-three years. Births the same year were, in the landward, 47; town, 254; together, 301; of which, in the town, 43 were illegitimate, and in the country 6. The marriages in the country part of the parish in 1864 were 6; in the town, 44; together, 50. These statistics we have from the registrar, Mr Macintosh, who also adds, that of the 301 births registered in 1864, there were 266 successfully vaccinated; 24 died before vaccination; 2 were insusceptible of vaccination; and 9 were born before the Vaccination Act came into operation.

The climate of Brechin is considered temperate and salubrious. Low intermittent fever is the most general complaint, but agues, formerly prevalent, are now rarely heard of, this disease having disappeared when wet lands were drained.

The northern part of the parish is composed of the old red sandstone, the strata of which range from east to west. The dip of this rock is to the north, with an inclination of about thirty-five degrees. It encloses within it two strata of limestone of various dimensions. The first stratum is from eighteen inches to two feet in thickness. The second stratum is composed of loose boulders, mixed with thin layers of argillaceous sandstone, having the same dip as the rock. No animal or vegetable remains are found in the lime or sandstone strata. Veins of calcareous spar, however, are occasionally met with amongst the lime, which sometimes enclose crystals of sulphate of barytes. In the southern part of the parish several stone quarries are wrought, each of which exhibits a fine section of the gray sandstone. This rock is well adapted for building, being of great durability and susceptible of a high polish. The position of the sandstone is nearly horizontal. No metals have been discovered in any part of the parish. There are no plants or animals peculiar to the parish. The *linnea borealis*, a very rare plant, is often found in the woods of Kinnaird, which are partly in this parish and partly in the neighbouring parish of Farnell. The kinds of trees generally planted on moors are Scotch firs, with sometimes a mixture of larch and spruce, sometimes larch alone ; of late years a proportion of hardwood has been planted with the firs, &c. In belts of planting and in gentlemen's policies, and where there is depth of soil, hard wood is generally planted, no more soft wood being put in than is necessary for shelter to the hard wood, and the soft wood being cut out after a few years, when the other trees have attained sufficient strength and age.

The chief heritors of land in the parish are, the Earl of Southesk ; the Earl of Dalhousie ; the Earl of Fife ; John Inglis Chalmers, Esq., of Aldbar ; Henry Speid, Esq. of Ardovie ; T. M. Grant, Esq., of Pitforthie ; Francis Aberdein, Esq., of Keithock ; Mrs Elizabeth Smith of Cairnbank ; George Robertson Chaplin, Esq., of Cookston, and Alexander Collie, Esq., of Murlingden.

In the parish there are 3 miles 880 yards of turnpike road to the west, leading to Forfar, and 2 miles 594 yards to the north in the direction of Aberdeen. and 3 miles 880 yards to the south.

proceeding in the direction of Dundee by the Stannachy Bridge across the Esk, a neat bridge of one arch, built in 1823. South, towards Arbroath, there are 1 mile 220 yards of turnpike; and east, towards Montrose, 3 miles 880 yards are also in the parish. Thus, there are altogether 15 miles 454 yards of turnpike road in the parish of Brechin. All the other roads are maintained by an assessment raised under an act of Parliament, and laid partly upon houses and land, and partly upon the number of horses, carts, and carriages kept. There are 22 roads of this description in the parish, the total mileage of which is 31 miles; so that, irrespective of streets in the town, there are 46 miles of roads in the parish.

The CITY OF BRECHIN is the centre of the parish of that name in the county of Angus, commonly called Forfarshire, because Forfar is the county town. Brechin is situated in 2° 18′ west longitude, and 56° 40′ north latitude, is 8½ miles from the sea-port of Montrose, 13 from the county town of Forfar, and 42 miles distant from each of Aberdeen and Perth. The town lies upon the face of a hill, on the left bank of the river Southesk, and consists of one main street running north and south, and breaking off towards the south into two branches. The street formerly called Timber Market, now named Market Street, com-mences at the North Port, and continues till the place where it is intersected by Swan Street and the Upper West Wynd, now called St David Street, and below that the street bears the name of the High Street, till it branches off into two divisions. The eastern branch, which formerly was termed the Cadger Wynd, while within the boundaries of the burgh, is now designated Union Street, and beyond these boundaries this branch formerly bore the names of the Cadger-hillock and Upper Tenements, now changed into Montrose Street. The western branch, again, had the titles of the Path Wynd and Muckle Mill, now Bridge Street; and when it stretches beyond the confines of the burgh, it was termed the Nether Tenements, but is now River Street. The road to Arbroath is by River Street, across a bridge over the Southesk, an ancient fabric of two arches. The road to Montrose, an ex-cellent road, passing through a most beautiful piece of country, is by Montrose Street, formerly called the Upper Tenements of

Caldhame. These two suburbs of Upper and Nether Tenements, according to their old names, now Montrose Street and
River Street, are connected together by means of *paths*, as they
are termed. Running west from the north end or head of the
High Street, is the Upper Wynd, now called St David Street,
and running west from the centre of the High Street is the
Old Nether Wynd, now Church Street, both of which streets are
connected by St Mary Street at the west end, from which proceeds the road to Forfar, by the street now called Castle Street.
Running west from St David Street, where St Mary Street commences, is a street formerly called Gold's Yards, now Airlie
Street, with Pearse Street branching off from it, and connecting
it with the Latch Road, all of which form egresses to the country
on the west side of the town. Running east from the High
Street, and in a line with St David Street, is Swan Street, which
leads into Clerk Street, and thence northward across a mound
over the Den Nursery to the Gallowhill, from which the road to
Aberdeen, a capital toll-road, proceeds. Clerk Street, at the
north, is connected with Market Street by Distillery Road, and
these run on by another road, the Latch Road, at the junction of
which the Cookston Road turns off, forming an outlet to the
north, being the road used by the inhabitants of the parishes of
Lethnot and Navar, and also by most of the inhabitants of the
parishes of Menmuir, Dunlappie, &c. From the top of Clerk
Street, down the west side of the Den to Montrose Street, a new
road has been opened, termed Southesk Street, from which
branches off Panmure Street in a straight line with Swan Street,
cutting across the bottom of Clerk Street. From the point where
Panmure Street, running past James's Place, intersects Clerk
Street, the City Road runs south, down to the South Port, so
that Clerk Street and City Road pursue the same line on the
east which Market Street and High Street do on the west.
Besides the streets enumerated, there are wynds and closes " too
tedious to mention." The river Esk runs upon the south-west
side of the town. Parallel to it runs a burn, designated the
Michael Den Burn, where it runs through Michael Den, part of
the policies of Brechin Castle ; the Kirkyard Burn, where it
runs below the churchyard brae ; and the Skinners' Burn from

the churchyard to the river Esk, because the skinners or tanners formerly had pits upon the side of the burn at this place for tanning leather. This burn is of pure water till it leaves Michael Den, but there it begins to collect the impurities of the town, and at the foot of the Mill Stairs the principal common sewer of the city has long joined this burn, which, therefore, has little to boast of in point of beauty or cleanliness. Down the Den again runs another burn which formerly was pure, but is now loaded, during its course through the burgh, with the refuse of the North Port brewery and North Port distillery, and afterwards with that of the gas work and other works ; and having become more a nuisance than an ornament, is now put under cover for almost its entire course through the confines of the city. Another burn, the Caldhame Burn, joins this one, near the south end of the Den Nursery, and as it only brings with it the refuse of Glencadam distillery, it is comparatively pure; but neither of the two tallies with our juvenile recollections of the bonnie wee wimplin' burnie of the Den, here hid with grass and daisies, there expanded into a broad pool, and anon converted into a miniature waterfall.

The properties within the burgh are generally held by burgage tenure, but many are held of the town council in feu from the town, or under that body as patrons of the hospital, some of the præceptory, and a few of the kirk-session. The properties in River Street are all held in feu from the family of Southesk, and those in Montrose Street again are held in feu from the family of Panmure. In all cases the feu-duties are small, and the casualties of superiority are not rigorously exacted. All these properties are situated within the parliamentary boundaries, and the inhabitants and proprietors, possessing sufficient qualification, are entitled to vote for a member of Parliament. The parliamentary boundaries, or the boundaries within which property of £10 of annual value must be situated, to give the proprietor or tenant a right to vote in the election of a member of Parliament, are thus described in the Act 2 and 3 William IV., cap. 65, " From the point, on the south of the town, at which the Skinners' Burn joins the South Esk River, down the South Esk River to the West Den of Leuchland, thence up the hollow of the West Den of Leuchland, and up Barrie's Burn, to the point, near the source of Barrie's Burn, at which the several boundaries of the properties of Caldhame, Pitforthie, and Unthank meet; thence in a straight line, in a westerly direction, to the point at which the several boundaries of the properties of Maisondieu and Cookston, and Mr Mitchell's land meet; thence, in a south-west direction, along the boundary of the Maisondieu property, to the point at which the same meets the Menmuir road; thence, in a straight line to the westermost point at which the Skinners' Burn crosses the Forfar road; thence, down the Skinners' Burn to the point first described." The registered electors in the parliamentary boundaries of Brechin join with those in Montrose, Arbroath, Forfar, and Inverbervie, in the election of a member to Parliament. The number of persons registered as entitled to vote for a member of Parliament, at the Brechin polling station, in September 1864, was 273.

In 1831, the population within the royalty was estimated at, males, 1615; females, 1902; together, 3517; and in the Upper and Nether Tenements; males, 734; females, 809; together, 1543; giving for the parliamentary boundaries 2349 males and 2711 females, making a total of 5060. The number of inhabited dwelling-houses in the royalty was, at this time, found to be 425, without the royalty 190, making within the parliamentary boundaries 615 houses, inhabited by 1387 families, of whom 944 resided within the royalty, and 443 in the suburbs, the latter employing 18, the former 190 female servants, giving a total of 208 female servants. The male servants in the royalty were then 26, of whom 17 were above 20 years of age, and 9 under that age—none in the suburbs. The uninhabited houses were, royalty 8, suburbs 4. The number of families residing within these boundaries engaged in agriculture was then reckoned at 120, being 72 within the royalty, and 48 without the royalty; and of the members of these families, 68 were labourers residing within the royalty and 35 in the suburbs, together 103. The families engaged in trade, residing within the royalty, were, in 1831, ascertained to be 645, suburbs 317, total 962. Other families within the royalty were estimated at 227, suburbs 78, together 305. The number of unmarried men upwards of 50 years of age was supposed to be

144, and of unmarried females upwards of 45 years of age 469 ; these classes of course including, respectively, widows and widowers. The number of males upwards of 20 years of age was then ascertained to amount, in the royalty, to 878, in the suburbs, to 389, total 1267. The average number of births was supposed, in 1831, to be about 150; of deaths, about 100; and of marriages 55. The number of *Objects* was then found to be 37, consisting of 24 fatuous persons, 10 blind persons, and 3 deaf and dumb. We give in our appendix the census tables for the three succeeding decennial periods. In 1861, the total population in the parliamentary boundaries is estimated at 7180, whereas, as above stated, it was only 5060 in 1831, having in these thirty years increased by 2120.

The habits of the people are, in general, orderly. They are, like most Scotch people, cautious and observant. Many of them are fond of reading, especially works on history, practical theology, and politics. Indeed, the people of Brechin, in general, take a very keen interest in political movements; an interest which they have occasionally displayed in rather a *forcible* manner. The usual food of the labouring people in the burgh, is meal, milk, and potatoes, with wheaten bread and fish, or a bit of butcher meat once a day. Almost every individual has a garden attached to his house, which adds not a little to his comforts and to his amusement. The modern built houses are dry ; but those of ancient structure, used by the working classes, are too frequently damp, and not always so cleanly as could be wished. The rents paid by tradesmen for their houses yearly, are generally about 50s. In their own persons, the inhabitants, especially the females, are neat and tidy. Wages in Brechin, as elsewhere, vary according to the nature of the employment. There are two tobacco works in Brechin, manufacturing above 60,000 lbs. of dry leaf tobacco annually ; paying to Government nearly £10,000 of duties; and employing five journeymen at above 20s. of weekly wages, four apprentices at 4s. 6d., and thirty-three little boys at 2s. 4d. weekly each. Again, at the Brechin Gas Works, common labourers earn 17s. per week, ordinary workmen, 19s. ; superior workmen, 21s. ; but the work is not pleasant. In 1864 the gas company manufactured

9,332,100 feet of gas, and had 8,523,721 feet accounted for, the balance being waste. This gas was consumed by seven public works, eight churches, and 181 street lamps, and a host of other consumers, not easily numbered, but it may be stated that 2000 gas meters were employed. The coals used were 875 tons of parrot, and 119 tons of small coal. There are four quarries in the parish of Brechin, namely, Bridgend, Reisk, Hillhead, and West Drums, which employ about fifty men, who work ten hours daily, gaining, labourers, 15s. per week, and quarrymen, 16s.; but of course bad weather often lessens the week's wages. There are six master masons in Brechin, employing about fifty journeymen and fifteen apprentices; the apprentices are allowed 5s. weekly, and journeymen earn 24s. per week, working ten hours per day, interrupted of necessity by broken weather. Roadmen have 2s. 3d. per day, but are affected also by the seasons. There may be about 100 common labourers in Brechin, who, for ten hours' work daily, gain from 14s. to 15s. per week. Carpenters' wages are 19s. weekly, but then they have constant employment, the weather not affecting their work; apprentices are allowed 4s. weekly; there are six master carpenters in Brechin, keeping about forty journeymen; besides all which there are eight or ten jobbing wrights. It should be mentioned that all tradesmen now have the Saturday afternoon to themselves, and thus, for the wages mentioned, only work fifty-seven hours per week. The licensed houses and shops for the sale of exciseable liquors within the burgh, number thirty-four, of which nine are inns or hotels; the pawnbrokers, almost a new trade in Brechin, are six in number. The other trades within the parliamentary boundaries may be thus enumerated :—Auctioneers, 2; bakers, 7; blacksmiths, 7; booksellers, 4; boot and shoemakers, 21; druggists, 3; earthenware dealers, 5; coal merchants, 4; confectioners, 3; coopers, 3; corn merchants, 2; fleshers, 10; grocers, 19, of whom 9 are also spirit dealers; hair dressers, 2; small-ware dealers, 3; ironmongers, 3; joiners or carpenters, 15; drapers, 9; linen manufacturers, 5; milliners and dressmakers, 17; painters, 4; plasterers, 2; plumbers, 4; saddlers, 3; *shopkeepers* or dealers in provisions, &c., besides the grocers enumerated above, 14; slaters, 5; stone

masons and builders, 4; tailors, 14, including 4 clothiers; vete-
rinary surgeons, 3; besides a variety of small trades, scarcely
admitting of enumeration, and no less than thirty-two agents
for fire and life insurance companies, many of the companies
having more than one agent, and several of the agents acting for
more than one company, but absurd in number in any view.

Coals are the chief feul used by all classes, and are brought
by land carriage from Montrose, generally by railway, although
three or four coal-carters still linger on the road. A barrel of
English coals, which contains 163¼ lbs., costs, on an average, about
1s. 4½d.; Scotch coal, 16s. per ton, and chews, 15s., delivered
into private dwelling-houses. A small quantity of wood is used as
fuel, but peats have gone entirely out of use. The town is well
supplied with butcher meat, which is generally sold at from 7d.
to 10d. per pound imperial. Fish are also plentiful, brought
in carts from the coast, and varying in price with the change of
weather and abundance of supply, but, generally, only about a
fourth dearer than at the sea-side. Butter, cheese, and eggs are
abundantly supplied by the neighbouring country district; the
first selling from 1s. to 1s. 2d. per imperial pound; the second
from 6d. to 8d., according to quality; and the last at from 10d.
to 1s. per dozen, according to the season of the year. Chickens
bring from 2s. 6d. to 2s. 10d. per pair; hens, each, from 1s. 4d.
to 1s. 6d.; ducklings, 8d.; pigs, of which a number are now
brought to the market every Tuesday, bring from 14s. to 15s.
each; large pork is sold at from 34s. to 36s. per cwt.; small, at
from 44s. to 46s. The quartern loaf, in August 1864, was sold
at 5d., the second quality at 4½d.; flour, 2s. per stone; barley
flour, 1s. 4d.; oatmeal, 1s. 5d. per stone, and potatoes 10½d. The
professional gentlemen in the town are, 9 clergymen, 4 physicians,
4 surgeons, or 8 doctors, as they are generally termed, and 8
writers, total, 25, besides the different schoolmasters. In 1790,
there were 1 physician, 2 surgeons, and 3 writers in Brechin. The
British Linen Company Bank has an office in Clerk Street; the
Royal Bank and Union Bank have offices in Swan Street, and the
City of Glasgow has an office in St David Street. The Brechin
National Security Savings Bank is held in the burgh schoolroom
every Tuesday evening; the Upper and Nether Tenements Sav-

ings Bank is held in Bank Street schoolroom every Saturday evening; and the Post Office Savings Bank is open daily at the Post
Office in Church Street. The office of the superintendent of
the parochial cemetery, and of the collector of the police-rates,
and also of the collector of the poors-rates, and inspector of
poor, and registrar of births, deaths, and marriages, are in the
same house in Church Street. The office of the local newspaper,
the *Brechin Advertiser*, published every Tuesday, is in Swan
Street, and the town clerk's office is also in Swan Street. The
stamps and taxes office is in High Street.

The chief manufacture in Brechin is the different branches of
the linen trade. The fabrics made in Brechin, at present, are of
considerable variety, but may be all ranked under the head of
coarse linens. These, again, may be divided into two classes,
the one for the home and the other for the foreign market. The
linens made for the foreign market generally range from a reed
of 24 to 32 porter ; but, in some cases, higher numbers are used
such as reeds of 32, 34, 36, 38, and 40 porter of 25 inches.
These linens are made from flax yarns of from 2½ to 3lb. per
spindle before being bleached, and are called Spanish goods ; but
these are neither so regularly in demand nor so easily made here
as the kinds sent to the New York and West India Markets.
For these markets, 24, 26, and 28 porter dowlas are made from
flax warps of 3 lb. per spindle, wefted with tow of from 3½ to 6
lb. per spindle ; also 28, 30, and 32 porter dowlas of 25 to 27
inches in breadth, from 3 lb. flax yarns, warp and weft. Previous to being woven, the yarns are all bleached, in which process
they undergo a waste of from 20 to 25 per cent. The same sizes
of yarns, also bleached, are made into sheetings of 35, 38, and 40,
inches in width for the same markets. Osnaburghs and diapers
are occasionally made here for the New York market, but they
are not to be considered as regular staple manufacture. Those
fabrics made for the New York market are considered light
labour, and are, therefore, much sought after by the weavers.
The goods manufactured in Brechin for the home market are
chiefly dowlas and sheetings, made from flax yarns varying in
size according to the fineness of the cloth. Those most commonly made are 34 to 36 porter dowlas, of from 27 to 30 inches,

and sheetings of same reed, varying in breadth from 36 to 42 inches, all made from flax yarn, both warp and weft, the size of which is 3 lb. per spindle before being bleached. Of late there has been a gradual inclination to finer fabrics than the above, and now, 38, 40, and 45 porters of from 30 to 40 inches, form a part of the regular manufacture. They are made of smaller sized yarns of a finer texture, all bleached before being wrought. Goods similar to those used in our own country were at one time freely sent to France, but that trade has not been pushed of late. A few webs are occasionally made by some of our manufacturers from brown or self-coloured yarns, which undergo a simple process of steeping, plashing or knocking, wringing and drying. The greater part of such webs are considered to be for the home market, and are chiefly made from flax yarns. It may be proper to say, for the sake of the general reader, that the reed is that part of the apparatus used in weaving which more immediately divides the warp and drives up the weft. Reeds in this part of the country are made on a scale of 37 inches, varying in thickness according to the fineness or coarseness of the fabrics to be made ; for instance, a thirty porter, or 600 reed is divided into 600 openings in the breadth of 37 inches ; 20 of these openings are called a porter ; into each opening there are put two threads making 1200 threads of warp and as many of weft in a square yard of linen, through a 30 porter reed. The weaving trade in Brechin is meantime in a transition state from hand-loom weaving to power-loom weaving. Messrs Lamb & Scott, and Messrs D. & R. Duke are in the course of erecting large power-loom factories for 300 looms each, in Southesk Street, on the ground formerly called the Lower Den ; and Messrs J. & J. Smart are largely increasing their works in River Street. These looms when in full employ will turn out weekly as much cloth as could be wrought by 3000 hand-loom weavers.

There is a bleachfield on the Inch of Brechin, conducted on chemical principles, which employs on an average, during the year, 70 males and 30 females, at wages varying from 14s to 20s per week for men, and from 7s to 9s for women ; but this bleach-field is also being enlarged, and will soon do one-half more business than at present. At the Inch there is also a paper work which manufactures annually from 400 to 500 tons of cartridge paper, and paper for newspapers, employing 33 males and 40 females, and paying weekly £35 in wages.

The spinning of lint by machinery into yarn was begun in Brechin, about 1796, at a small mill then erected on the Den burn within the piece of ground known as the Witch Den, now occupied by the gas company, and part of the original buildings is still used by that company as a warehouse. Thomas Jamieson, a millwright in town, was the originator of the scheme, and was aided in his endeavours by three gentlemen of some capital in Brechin. Jamieson made the machinery himself, and so much was thought of the affair, that within the mill-house, where the machinery was made, no stranger was allowed to enter, and the door of the building was duly sealed with the words " No Admittance," on it. Jamieson made four frames, so that each partner had a spinning frame for his interest in the matter. It is said the partners met regularly in a small house occupied by Jamieson at the gate of the premises, and each Saturday night duly *liquidated* the profits of the week. Jamieson, who was a clever workman, but unsteady man, soon left the Witchden Mill, and started other similar works in different parts of the country, always, however, struggling with the world. The Witchden Mill was continued under different managements till 1826, when it was finally disannulled. In 1837 a mill for sawing wood was erected within the old spinning-mill house. The mill was wrought by *two wheels*, the one above the other, both driven at the same rate of speed by the water of the Den burn, but that, too, was no success.

The East Mill Spinning Company was started in 1799, and the machinery being driven by the Southesk, the concern was originally much larger than Thomas Jamieson's work. These premises are without the burgh, but within the parliamentary boundaries. A cotton-mill was carried on at Eastmills for a year or so, but that was soon abandoned, and a lint spinning-mill of 24 frames was started. On 20th April 1799, their pay-book states that £3, 12s. 5d. were disbursed in wages, and 60 spindles of yarn spun for the first week, but these are soon increased to £6 of wages, and 220 spindles. In 1810 four power-looms were opened at Eastmills. The highest wages paid was, 10s. 6d. to the foreman, and the lowest 1s. to girls, while 3s. seems to have been the average wages of ordinary hands. The Eastmills of the present day are thus described in an account kindly furnished us by Mr James Ireland, the manager:—" There is a flax spinning-mill and bleachfield on the banks of the river Southesk, which is driven both by water and steam-power. The indicated horse-power for the spinning-mill is equal to about 450 horses, which requires about 2250 tons of coals annually. They import the flax principally from Russia, which is spun into yarns of various sizes and then bleached, and the yarns are sold to manufacturers in Brechin, Forfar, Kirriemuir, Dundee, and Fifeshire, to be manufactured into cloth, and a considerable part is exported to Spain, Germany, and other parts of the Continent. In 1864 they consumed 1450 tons of flax and tow; this was spun into yarns of various sizes by 78 spinning frames, containing 5084 spindles, which produced 844,000 spindles of yarn, the value of which would be about £125,000 sterling. The people employed was, 153 males; 266 females; the wages paid amounted to £8300; the hours of labour, 60 per week. The bleachfield has two water-wheels of 30 horses power. In 1864 they bleached 1820 tons of yarn, and employed 104 males and 50 females, and paid in wages £4000; hours of labour 60 per week, and consumed about 500 tons of coals for drying the yarns." Mr Ireland adds—" I was led into making a calculation of how many miles of yarn we spin in the course of the year, and I find it amounts to 6,905,454 miles in length; and assuming the circumference of the globe to be 25,000 miles, it would go round it 276 times. The length spun per week is 132,793 miles; this would go round the world fully more than 5 times."

Formerly the neighbourhood of Brechin was much infested with bands of smugglers, carrying whisky from the Grampian Highlands to the low country; and Brechin itself depended on these *merchants* for its supply of *mountain dew.* Now the matter is reversed. There is one extensive distillery in the town, called the North Port Distillery, which consumes upwards of 4000 quarters of barley annually, sending out yearly above 70,000 gallons of whisky, and employing constantly 25 men at

S

14s. weekly and upwards, besides gentlemen of the Excise, *not* employed by the distillery company. There is another neat distillery, called the Glencadam Distillery, in the immediate vicinity. These distilleries supply a far purer spirit than was formerly drunk, under the name of smuggled whisky. There is only one brewery in the town, a long established concern, at the North Port. Whisky, however, is the chief potation of all classes, raw, in grog, or in *punch*.

Messrs Dickson and Turnbull of Perth have long had a nursery in the lower part of the town of Brechin. Mr Charles Young had a similar establishment on the west side of the city, which, some years ago, merged into that of Messrs Dickson and Turnbull, and is now considerably extended, and known as the " City Nursery." On the east side of the town, Messrs Henderson and Sons occupy the Den, besides a large field of their own, and some other ground in the neighbourhood, for a nursery. Messrs Mitchell and Young have also a field in the lower part of the town, and another in the east side of the burgh, occupied as nursery grounds. Altogether upwards of thirty-five imperial acres are occupied as nursery grounds, affording healthy employment to a number of men and women, and paying yearly about £1000 in wages. These nurseries raise forest and fruit trees of all kinds, ornamental shrubs and bushes, seeds, &c. ; and have hothouses and green-houses attached to each establishment.

A regular market is held in Brechin every Tuesday, at which very considerable quantities of grain are bought and sold. The grain merchants meet the farmers in town ; a bargain is made by sample ; the grain is delivered at some of the neighbouring sea-ports during the week ; a printed receipt is then granted for the quantity delivered, and on the following Tuesday the farmer presents his receipt to the merchant and receives his cash. It is astonishing, out of the great number of bargains thus made, how few disputes arise, and the fact is equally creditable to farmer and merchant. During the autumn and winter months there are also weekly markets, each Tuesday, for cattle, and during the months of February and March, commencing on the last Tuesday of February, and ending on the last Tuesday of March, markets for the sale of horses are held. The first Tuesday after

Whitsunday, old style, is a great market day, chiefly for the hiring of country servants; and so is the first Tuesday after Martinmas, old style. If any of these term-days happens on a Tuesday, then the market is held that day. Formerly these term markets were attended by chapmen, who formed a society amongst themselves, termed " The Chapmen of Angus," and on market days they had a double row of booths on the High Street, forming a street of itself, each booth being open to the front, and well supplied with all manner of haberdashery and soft goods. The chapmen met at the cross at a certain hour the day previous, and drew lots for the situation of their stands or booths, which were framed of wood, and neatly covered with blanketing to keep out the wet. A cooper in Brechin made a trade of hiring out the wooden framework of these booths. These chapmen travelled in the country regularly, carrying their goods some in spring-carts, some on horseback, the bales being slung on each side of the horse, and some on foot; an inferior class, called packmen, travelled always on foot, and some of them carried immense packs on their backs. Then the farmers' wives were supplied with most of their braws by the chapmen and packmen, and the farmer himself got his best suit from a like source. As the chapman waxed old and wealthy, he settled down as a merchant in some borough town. The race is now all but wholly extinct. On a piece of ground of nearly 33 acres in extent, belonging to the burgh, and about a mile north of it, called Trinity, or more generally *Tarnty* Muir, a great fair is annually held for three days, commencing on the second Wednesday of June, to which cattle-dealers and horse-dealers resort from all parts of Scotland and some parts of England. Wednesday is the sheep-market day, most of the business being done in the morning; Thursday, all day, is given to the sale of *nowt*, (cows and oxen;) and horses are exposed for sale on the Friday. There are other markets held on this ground in April, August, and September, but the June market is *par excellence* termed " the Trinity Fair." The April market, called the Spring Tryst, generally a large market, is held on the third Wednesday of that month. The August market takes place on the second Thursday, and is called Lammas Muir. The last market, held in September, and which takes place on the last Tuesday of the month, is styled the Autumn Trinity Tryst, and sometimes the " Convener's Market," in commemoration of Mr David Mitchell, repeatedly convener of the trades of Brechin, who took an active interest in the establishment of this market, but it is now a market of no note.

The town is governed by a provost, two bailies, and dean of guild, with nine other councillors, chosen by the municipal electors, the registered number of whom, in September 1864, was 235. The property of the burgh, at Sept. 1864, was valued at £23,856, 6s. 1d., the debts at £11,505, 10s. 10d., leaving a surplus of £12,350, 15s. 3d. The income of the burgh arises chiefly from feu duties and rents of properties let on long leases; but there are certain subjects let annually by public roup, and in 1864, the common customs of the burgh brought £140; the dues of the shambles and weigh-house, £51; and the public washing-house, £20. The last item varies considerably: in 1861, the rent was £52, 10s.; in 1862, £31; and in 1863, £40. The other two subjects generally remain at about £190. The expense of lighting, watching, cleaning, maintaining streets, &c., are all defrayed from the police assessments, which are equal to 1s. 1d. per pound, being for watching, 5½d.; lighting, 2d.; cleaning, 1d.; paving, 4½d. The expense of water is, in the meantime, defrayed from the burgh funds, but evidently a water rate must soon be imposed. The stipends of the Established clergymen are paid from the teinds of the parish. The entry money, for a stranger, to the corporation of Brechin, including stamp-duty, is only 17s.; the sons and sons-in law of freemen pay no more than 14s. 6d. A guildry incorporation exists within the burgh, ruled by the " dean of the guildry," the fees of admission to which incorporation are, for strangers, £10, 10s.; freemens' sons, 13s. 4d.; and freemens' sons-in-law, £1, 6s. 8d., while *free* apprentices are also entitled to be entered at a reduced rate, although few or none avail themselves of the privilege intended for free apprentices. The guildry give their decayed members £4, and their poor widows £2, annually; but these allowances are given as a favour and not as a right. The hammermen, bakers, shoemakers, weavers, and tailors, are also *existing*—barely existing—incorporations, charging from £8 to £10 for the admission of stranger members, and nominal fees for the admission of the sons and sons-in-law of freemen. All these incorporations contribute to the support of widows, orphans, and decayed members.

The magistrates hold a burgh or bailie court each Wednesday, except during short recesses in spring, autumn, and winter, and a police court each Wednesday, and oftener if required. The dean of guild holds courts as occasion requires. The town-clerk is clerk and assessor of all these courts, and the procurator-fiscal the public prosecutor in each. A justice of peace court is held the first Wednesday of each month, and the sheriff holds a court, for the disposal of cases under the Small Debt Act, on the third Tuesday of each alternate month. The police of the burgh is maintained by one superintendent, one sergeant, and four constables, besides the town-officer. The livery worn by the town-officer consists of a scarlet coat trimmed with lace, scarlet vest, dark corduroy or plush breeches, white stockings, and black gaiters—rather a showy livery.

The town is supplied with water from the high grounds of Cookston, on the north, collected there in two reservoirs, having small houses built above them, and in a third large reservoir under ground ; and from the high grounds of Burghill, on the south, collected there in a reservoir built under a liberal lease granted by the late Lord Panmure. The water is conveyed through the town by means of lead pipes, and the fountain-heads stand so high, that every house in the burgh, with the exception of a very few in Market Street, *might* command the water in the attics ; but in consequence of the constant drainage at the public wells, and by private dwelling-houses on a lower level, this is not the case. It is very plain, from the increase of the population, and, it may be, from the increasing cleanliness of the inhabitants, that an additional supply of water must soon be got ; and the friendly South Esk running past the Inch, which is composed of sand and shingle, offers a supply for a large well dug in the bleaching-green.

Brechin is the seat of a Presbytery. The pastoral charge of the old parish church is collegiate. Each of the ministers has now a manse and glebe. The stipend of the clergyman of the first charge is, 1 quarter 6 bushels wheat; 116 quarters 4 bushels 2 pecks 1 gallon 3-10ths pints barley; 2 quarters 6 bushels 1 gallon 3-10ths pints bear; 166 bolls 1 firlot 3-10ths pounds meal, and £29, 2s. 6¼d. in money—equal to 22 chalders, besides £10 for communion elements. The stipend of the clergyman of the second charge is 20 chalders, half meal, half barley, besides £21, 5s. 6d. from the bishop's rents, and £10 for communion elements. The communion is administered twice a-year, in May and in October, each of the established clergymen presiding alternately. A new church, containing 864 sittings, in connexion with the Establishment, was opened in the City Road in 1836. Part of the old parish was set aside, *quoad sacra*, to this church, and this section is designated the east parish; but at present there is no minister attached to it, although there is a talk of uncollegiating the parish church, redividing the parish, and placing one of the ministers in the east church, while the other remains in the cathedral. There are two Free Churches, one in Church Street, built in 1843, called the West Free Church, and the other the East Free Church, erected in 1857 at the junction of Panmure Street and Southesk Street. There is a church belonging to " the Second United Associate Congregation," re-edified in Maisondieu Lane in 1849. Another church, belonging to " the First United Associate Congregation," is in City Road, and was rebuilt in 1859. There is likewise the third congregation of the United Presbyterians, which meets in High Street in a building enlarged from the old *English* Episcopal Chapel. There are thus seven Presbyterian churches in Brechin, and there is also a Scotch Episcopal Chapel in Maisondieu Lane, called Saint Andrew's Episcopal Chapel, and ever since Episcopacy was established in Scotland there has been an Episcopal congregation in Brechin. On the opposite side of the road from the chapel, there is a library built to contain the books belonging to the Episcopal Diocese of Brechin, some of which are very valuable, and attached to the library there is a schoolroom and schoolmaster's house; but the school is in abeyance, and scarcely seems to be needed in Brechin. A few Roman Catholics belong to the parish, but there is no priest or teacher of that communion nearer than Arbroath, and the priest only visits Brechin occasionally, when he officiates in the Mason Lodge in Church Street, then converted into a temporary chapel. The different churches assemble, during winter, at eleven o'clock forenoon, and two o'clock afternoon; and during summer, at eleven o'clock in the forenoon, and a quarter after two o'clock in the afternoon, holding the summer to commence on the first Sunday of March, and winter on the first Sunday of September.

Besides the public schools in the handsome building at the junction of St Mary Street and Church Street, in which are the rector's school, the parish school, and the burgh school, there is a commodious school in Bank Street, built by the Free Church communion, under the charge of a master and a mistress; and a handsome set of schools in Montrose Street, called the Tenements Schools, built mainly at the expense of Mr Smith of Andover, in which there are a male and female teacher. There is also an infant school, which communicates with Bridge Street and Union Street, and is very commodiously situated for juveniles. There are, farther, several schools for girls merely, and several private schools for both boys and girls, one of which, in Market Street, is in the evenings converted into what is popularly known as a Ragged School. The rector of the grammar-school teaches the languages and higher branches of education, and under an arrangement with the town council, he receives a salary of £50 annually, having conveyed to them all right he has, for his lifetime, to the præceptory of Maisondieu, the funds of which are estimated as being worth about £1000. The salary of the parochial schoolmaster is £50, besides £10 in lieu of house rent. The burgh teacher has a salary of £35. None of the other teachers in the burgh has any salary. The master of the Muirland school, situated near the village of Little Brechin, about two miles northwest of Brechin, has a free house, school, and garden, and a small annual allowance from a fund mortified by Mr Johnston, minister of Brechin, about 1770. There was a mortification by the Rev. John Glendye, Dean of Cashel, who about 1690 founded a bursary in the University of St Andrews, but it was lost sight of somehow, and is now given by the patron to any one he pleases. Mr John Fyfe, minister at Navar, by a deed dated 12th May 1658, and recorded in the Presbytery Records on 17th July

1706, mortified 500 merks due by the town of Brechin, and 500 merks due by the laird of Findowrie, the interest to be applied by the Presbytery for helping to maintain " a pious young man and student at the New College of St Andrews, and whenever that occasion cannot be had of a student standing in need thereof, I appoint," says the deed, " the said annual rent to be employed for helping of some poor honest man's bairns at the school of Brechin." The Presbytery draw yearly £1, 7s. 6d. from the town of Brechin, and the like sum from the laird of Findowrie, and apply the money in educating boys at the schools in Brechin. There are other two mortifications, the one, Dakers', constituted in 1859 for the education of boys; the other, Black's, given in 1861 for the education of girls—both under the management of the town council; but they are burdened with the liferents of certain parties, and have not yet become efficient. The fees payable in the public schools are regulated by a schedule approved of by the patrons, and most of the private schools have adopted the same rates. At present there is a movement for an alteration of the fees of the public schools, and a new arrangement of the classes to be taught by each master; so we do not specify the fees, but state generally that they are very moderate. There are also Sabbath schools in different parts of the town, taught by laymen in connexion with the several Presbyterian churches; and the Episcopal clergyman generally labours most assiduously during the Sundays of the spring, summer, and autumn in catechising the young folks of his congregation.

In the town there is a parish library, consisting of above 600 volumes of a useful and religious kind; similar libraries belonging to each of the Free churches, one belonging to the Second United Associate congregation, and a library of pretty much the same description belonging to Saint Andrew's Episcopal chapel; also the extensive library belonging to the Mechanics' Institution.

A Bible Society has been long in active operation in the town, and societies in aid of those for propagating Christianity in India, and for missions, schools, and tracts, have existed for many years. The several congregations in town have likewise annual contributions for aiding in the propagation of Christianity at home and abroad; and there is a Book and Tract Society.

A dispensary for administering medicines and medical advice, gratis, to the poor, was established in 1824 ; and in 1810 a Ladies' Society for the relief of aged and indigent women was also established. These ladies distribute one shilling monthly to about sixty poor females. A coal fund, under the charge of the ladies of the burgh, has been in operation for several years, and by distributing from two to three barrels of coals in winter amongst a number of poor families, has done an immensity of good.

There are also in Brechin a curling club, having a nice pond at Brechin Castle ; a bowling club, rejoicing in a handsome green in Pearse Street; several cricket clubs, which play over the Trinity Muir market stance ; the horticultural and ornothological societies, which give displays of flowers and birds twice a year ; and last, but not least, there is the Brechin Amateur Vocal Society, which occasionally favours the public with a concert for some charitable purpose.

The Town House of Brechin is in the middle of the town, near the cross, or market place. It was built in 1789, and is a respectable edifice, containing a court-room below, with a well proportioned and neatly-finished town-hall above, *growing* too small for the increasing population of the burgh. We give a view of the Town Hall, and part of High Street and Church Street, with the Mechanics' Institution in the distance. The council-rooms communicate with the town-hall, and are immediately above the prison, a melancholy building, which originally contained a debtor's room, and two cells for criminals, all as well ventilated as a building so placed in the centre of the most crowded part of the town could be. On the establishment of a regular police, the debtor's room was converted into a police office, and the criminal cells were improved, while temporary " lock-ups " were erected in the police office. The Tolbooth of Brechin has, we believe, always stood where the present Town House stands, and we find the present site indicated about 1537 as the site of the Tolbooth. The inmates of this building, in the course of the year 1837, were twenty criminals and four debtors ; but no debtors can now be imprisoned in Brechin, nor can any criminals be detained for punishment, the jails of Forfar and Dundee being the only legalised prisons for criminals and debtors at present.

Adjoining the Court House is a property which formerly belonged to the Earl of Airlie, and of which that noble earl is still the superior or over-lord. It appears to the right in the woodcut, and good eyes may read " Baking Company" on the sign above the shop. The Airlie family were proprietors of the house in 1633, as appears from some title deeds of that date. The children of Brechin play a game, where one sets aside for him, or herself, a small space, which is termed the green, and the others trespass more or less upon this space, singing at same time, " I set my foot upon Airlie's green, and Airlie daur na catch me;" and if the occupier of the green succeeds in catching an intruder, this intruder is compelled to become "Airlie." This game is said to have reference to this property, which was exempted from the jurisdiction of the magistracy, and was solely under that of Lord Airlie, who exercised the powers of constabulary vested in that noble family, on all who intruded upon his green.

In Church Street there is a large three storey dwelling-house, known as " Lady Ballownie's House," and said to have been the town residence of the Earls of Crawford; and in it there is a draw-well of very fine water, and a large arched fire-place, confirming the theory of it having been a house of note. A dwelling-house on the north side of the Black Bull Close, with such another arched fire-place in it, now occupied by very poor tenants, was the residence of Provost Doig of Cookston, and in it was born his daughter Agnes, afterwards Lady Carnegie of Southesk.

The Swan Inn was long the principal inn of the town; but it has recently been wholly removed, and its place filled up by the City Hall in Swan Street. The Commercial Hotel in Clerk Street is now the principal inn; but there are several other highly respectable houses, amongst which may be named the Cross Guns in Market Street, the Crown Hotel in St David Street, and the Star Hotel in Southesk Street.

The former school was a neat plain building of three apartments, facing the western entrance to the town, and surmounted by a belfry and clock face. The late Lord Panmure, however, with the noble generosity of a great mind, caused to be erected on the site of the former schools a handsome building of two storeys in the Gothic style, with square-headed mullion windows, and having a front of eighty feet, with a square tower, rising in the centre to the height of eighty feet. The lower floor contains the schoolrooms for the different masters, and the second floor consists of apartments for the accommodation of the Mechanics' Institution, the lecture-room of which forms a magnificent hall, fifty-five feet by thirty feet, *growing*, like the Town Hall, too small for the burgh.

The Brechin Mechanics' Literary and Scientific Institution, instituted in 1835, with such ample accommodation as that provided by Lord Panmure, and endowed as it was by him with a gift of £1000 and a legacy of another £1000, of which, however, from circumstances only £500 have been got, an institution so endowed, has, as might have been expected, proved a decided success. The library, daily increasing, possesses above 3000 volumes; each winter some dozen of lectures are delivered on interesting subjects, and the membership, constantly increasing, numbers some 500 individuals. The inhabitants of Brechin seem, generally, to hold, with Shakespeare, that

" Ignorance is the curse of God,
Knowledge the wings wherewith we fly to heaven ;"

and we have no doubt they will continue to avail themselves of the facilities for acquiring knowledge so amply provided for them by the institution.

A gas-light company, also instituted in 1835, has thriven remarkably well, almost every house in the town and tenements being lighted with this *fluid*. The works are situated in the lower part of the town, at the Witch Den.

There is a mason lodge, a very neat building, situated in Church Street, in which the brethren of the mystic tie occasionally assemble, under the name of St James's Lodge of Masons. A friendly society, consisting of about eighty members, is connected with the lodge. The entry-money to the society varies from 5s. to £7, 15s., according to the age of the entrant, besides which, the members pay 1s. 6d. quarterly. The benefits given for these payments are, 3s. per week during the first six weeks of bad health, and 2s. per week thereafter; 1s. weekly to each member above sixty-five years of age; 20s. of 'funeral money, and 3s. quarterly to widows, or the like sum to the children, where there is no widow, till the youngest attain twelve. St Ninian's Lodge of Masons, the oldest established lodge in Brechin, is purely a lodge of masons, and keeps its character up in good style. The Old Wright Society of Brechin, to which the members contribute 1s. quarterly, gives pretty similar allowances. A benevolent society or Lodge of Odd Fellows also exists, which provides for sick members only. Some yearly societies are annually established for the same purpose. And there is an Olive Lodge of Gardeners, promising allowances to sick and to widows. Besides these, there is a society of a higher grade, styled the Merchant Society, intended to provide an annuity of £10 per annum to widows or children. An encampment of Knights Templars has been more than once established, but the camp has never been sufficiently protected, for, hitherto, it has not been able to keep its ground in Brechin. A Royal Arch Lodge, connected with the encampment, has gone with it.

Carriers have almost disappeared from the roads, and stage-coaches have gone altogether, since we last wrote—the railway having superseded carts and coaches in most directions, still there are three or four daily carters between Brechin and Montrose. Our Slateford neighbours have their two carters twice a-week to Brechin, and the Highland district of Lochlee sends down a similar conveyance each Monday, which returns north every Tuesday. Fearn and Lethnot have each their Tuesday carrier, while to Luthermuir there is a cart with goods twice a-week.

The through mails are now also carried by the railway. The hours of delivery by the letter-carriers begin from the south at 7 o'clock morning for the summer months, and 7.30 morning for the winter months; and from England and the south at 12.15 P.M. all the year round, and from the north again at the window to those having boxes at 2.30, and to the public by the letter-carriers at 6.30 P.M. On Sundays the delivery is only from the window from 1 to 2 P.M. The mail is despatched for the north, that is, for Montrose, Aberdeen, Inverness, &c., each day at 10.10 A.M. and 10 P.M., while the bags for the south close at 1 and 4.45 P.M. With one penny additional stamp, letters may be posted, in each case, five minutes later than the hours named; but letters to be registered must be presented fifteen minutes sooner. A mail gig goes to Edzell, where there is a regular post-office; the other parish posts are all carried by runners. The local despatches are all in the morning.

The *arms* of the town of Brechin are the figure of Saint Ninian sitting in a Gothic porch, with his left hand on a crucifix, bearing an image of Christ, and his right hand raised in the attitude of blessing, and below a shield with three piles upon it. There is no motto. The seal of the city is the same, with the addition of a thistle issuing from each side of the shield, and the words in black Saxon characters in a circle round the arms, " Sig: Civitatis de Brechin,"—the seal of the city of Brechin. The arms of the Bishop of Brechin are described in heraldic language, as, " Argent, Three Piles meeting in the point in base, Gules." In common language, this means: On a white shield, three red piles meeting in the point at the bottom. The " three piles" of the bishop are also in the armorial arms of the town, as already noticed. These " piles" by some are understood to represent the three nails by which Jesus Christ was fastened to the Cross. In 1848, a brass matrix was found in the Links of Montrose, showing the head of a bishop, with a hunting-horn below, and the inscription, " Sigillum Curie Officialis Brechinensis;" and amongst the documents which had belonged to the Messrs Spence, formerly town-clerks of Brechin, there were some years previously found the seal of the official of the provincial of the Dominican friars of Perth, and of Bishop David Strachan, and also the brass matrix for the seal of the chapter of the cathedral church, an elaborately executed engraving in brass. All these seals are now deposited in the museum of the Society of Antiquaries.

The *Spottiswoode Miscellany* gives this description of Brechin about 1680:—" Brechin is a royall burgh. The bishopp is provost thereof; hath the electione of a bailie. Earl Panmure hath the electione of the eldest bailie, and the toune has one. It lyes very pleasantlie upon the north syde of the water of

Southesk, which runneth by the walls thereof. The yards
thereof to the south end of the tenements thereof, where there
is a large well-built stone bridge of two arches, and where Earl
Panmure hath a considerable salmond fishing, and lykwayes
croves under the castle walls, which lyes pleasantly on the water,
and is a delicat house, fyne yards, and planting, which, with a
great estate thereabout, belonged formerly to the Earl of Marr,
and now to the Earl Panmure, and is called the Castle of Brechine. The toune is tollerablie well built, and hath a considerable trade, by reason of their vicinity to Montross, being fyve
(Scots, or eight imperial) myles distant from it; but that which
most enriches the place is their frequent faires and mercats,
which occasion a great concourse of people from all places of
the countrey, having a great faire of cattle, horse, and sheep, the
whole week after Whytsunday, and the Tuesday thereafter a
great mercat in the toune; they have a weekly mercat every
Tuesday throughout the yeare, where there is a great resort of
Highlandmen, with timber, peats, and heather, and abundance
of muirfoull, and extraordinarie good wool in its seasone. *Item*,
A great weekly mercat of cattle, from the first of October to the
first of Januare, called the Crofts Mercat. *Item*, A great horse
mercat weekly throughout all Lent. *Item*, A great horse fair,
called Palm Sunday's Fair. It is a very pleasant place, and
extraordinare good land about it. Earl of Southesk has a great
interest lykwayes in the parish. Ballnabriech, belonging to the
Laird of Balnamoone, a good house, and a considerable thing.
Cookstoune, belonging to John Carnegy, lyeth very pleasantly
at the North Port of Brechine, and is good land. The Laird of
Findourie hath a considerable interest there, the most of it in
acres about the toune; a good house, and well planted. Arrot,
belonging to the Viscount of Arbuthnot, is a fine little house,
lying upon the north syde of Southesk, with a fishing. Auldbar
hath lykwayes an interest there,—Pitforthie, Rait, Keathock,
Edgar; with a good new house, built by this present laird, Mr
Skinner, minister."

Brechin Castle, the seat of Lord Panmure, (as we generally
style that nobleman in Brechin, although he now bears the
higher title of the Earl of Dalhousie,) stands on the brink of a

perpendicular rock, above the Southesk, a little to the south of the town, from which it is separated by a continuation of the ravine behind the cathedral. This castle was besieged by the English under Edward I. in 1303, and was, for twenty days, gallantly defended by Sir Thomas Maule, then Governor in the interest of The Bruce. Sir Thomas, who was the ancestor of the family of Panmure, was slain by a stone cast from an engine placed on the opposite rising ground, upon which the castle was instantly surrendered. Part of the tower where Sir Thomas Maule was killed is still pointed out; and on the opposite rising ground, from which the fatal stone was thrown, a number of rude coffins, composed of loose stones, were lately found, in one of which was a skull with a nail driven through it, probably part of the missiles thrown from the castle. The south front of the castle, which is romantically situated above the river, has been recently rebuilt, and a square tower added. The west front forms a regular building in the style of the seventeenth century, with round towers at the flanks. Here the castle was protected by a ditch, (filled up partly when additions were made to the building in 1711, and partly at subsequent times,) while the river Esk on the south, and the ravine on the north and east, formed natural barriers against intruders; so that, originally, the castle has been pretty well protected with defences. The interior, which has been lately renovated, is handsomely and comfortably furnished, and adorned with a number of beautiful paintings, busts, and other works of art.

Brechin has given birth to several eminent men, most of whom we have already alluded to; we here enumerate them:— Bishop Gawin Douglas, author of the " Palace of Honour," and other poetical works, was born in Brechin in 1471. Alexander Scott, who wrote several poetical pieces about 1562, is understood to have been a native of Brechin. Thomas Dempster, professor successively in the colleges of Nimes, Pisa, and Bologne, is believed to have been born in Brechin in 1580. He wrote the " Ecclesiastical History of Scotland," in twenty-nine books, besides many miscellaneous works, and died at Bologne in 1625, while occupying the Greek chair of that university. Then there are the Rev. William Guthrie of Fenwick, born in 1620, author of "The Christian's Great Interest;" the Rev. John Glendye, dean of Cashel, and prebend of St Michael's, Dublin, the founder in 1690 of the Glendye bursary in the College of St Andrews; William Maitland, the author of the "Histories of London and Edinburgh," born about 1690; William Guthrie, the author of the "Geographical Grammar" which bears his name, and a variety of other works, born in 1708; David Watson, author of the "History of the Heathen Gods," &c., born in 1710; the Right Honourable George Rose, clerk of Parliament, author of "Observations on the Works of Fox," &c., born in the neighbourhood in 1744, and educated in Brechin; John Gillies, LL.D., author of the "History of Greece," and historiographer for Scotland, born in Brechin in 1746, died in 1836, in his eighty-ninth year; the Honourable Adam Gillies, one of the senators of the College of Justice under the title of Lord Gillies, born in 1766, died in 1842; a younger brother of Dr Gillies; Alexander Laing, author of "Pawkie Adam Glen," "Wayside Flowers," and many other poems, born in 1787; William Pennycook, manufacturer, and James Crabb, painter, both born about 1790, each wrote many pretty pieces of poetry, which were printed in the newspapers of the time, but neither ever published anything on his own account; Robert Lowe, teacher of dancing, an accomplished musician, author of many musical pieces, and an amateur painter of no mean powers, born in 1791; the Rev. John S. Memes, LL.D., minister of Hamilton, the author of the "Life of Canova," and a general writer on literary subjects, born in 1795; the Rev. James Martin of Edinburgh, a writer on theological subjects, born in 1803; the Rev. John Pringle Nichol, LL.D., professor of astronomy in the College of Glasgow, and author of many works on astronomy, born 30th January 1804; John Henderson, architect in Edinburgh, also born in 1804; and, finally, our *quondam* apprentice, John Hendry, Writer to the Signet, a writer on conveyancing, born on 18th Nov. 1833, and who died on 13th May 1863, at the early age of twenty-nine. All these we record amongst the dead.—Alive at the present day we may name:—The Rev. James Welsh of New Deer, a mathematician of no mean power, who, about 1810, composed a treatise on algebra, manufactured many of the types and diagrams requisite, set up the types, printed the book, and bound it, in his father's house in Blackbull Close ; Colvin Smith, Esq., R.A., a portrait-painter of fame ; the Rev. Thomas Guthrie, D.D., of Edinburgh ; the Rev. Alexander Ferrier Mitchell, professor of Hebrew and Oriental languages in the University of St Andrews ; Andrew Jervise, Esq., her Majesty's Inspector of Registrars, author of the "Memorials of Angus and Mearns," and many other works, and who can use his pencil as well as his pen ;—and if we omit others it is because our list would otherwise swell out to an unreasonable length.

APPENDIXES.

APPENDIXES.

No. I.

CHARTER BY WILLIAM I., CONFIRMING TO THE BISHOPS AND CULDEES OF BRECHIN THE RIGHT OF MARKET GRANTED BY DAVID I.

WILLELMUS, Rex Scotie, omnibus probis hominibus totius Scotie ; Salutem : Sciatis me concessisse et carta mea confirmasse Episcopis et Keldeis de ecclesia de Brechin, donationem illam quam dedit eis Rex David, avus meus, per cartam suam de foro imperpetuum habituro in villa per dies Dominicos adeo libere sicut Episcopus Sanctiandree forum habet. Testibus, Andrea, Episcopo de Catones, Nicholaio, cancellario. Apud Brechin.

Translation.

William, King of Scotland, to all honest men of the whole of Scotland, greeting : Know me to have granted, and by this my charter to have confirmed, to the bishops and Culdees of the church of Brechin that donation which King David, my grandfather, gave them by his charter, of market to be held in perpetuity in the city on the Lord's-days (or Sabbaths) as freely as the Bishop of St Andrews holds a market. Witnesses, Andrew, Bishop of Caithness, and Nicholas, the chancellor. At Brechin.

Note.—The original of this charter does not now exist, but it is copied into a *transumpt* of the principal charters of the church of Brechin, made before Robert, Bishop of Dunkeld, at the instance of John, Bishop of Brechin, on the 16th May 1433, which

transumpt is No. 54 of the charters in the charter-room of the
city of Brechin ; and it is also copied into another transumpt of
a variety of charters made at the sight of the sheriff and a number
of landed gentlemen of Forfarshire, on 21st July 1450, and which
last mentioned transumpt is No. 106 of the charters of the town.
Both transumpts are printed by the late Patrick Chalmers, Esq.,
of Aldbar, in his " Registrum Episcopatus Brechinensis," vol. i.
pages 56 and 138. The above copy is taken from the original
transumpts, and collated with Mr Chalmers's printed charters.
Mr Chalmers also prints briefly, (i. 9,) a transumpt of the same
charter, made before the Bishops of St Andrews and Dunkeld in
1318.

We stated in our first edition that Brechin was a royal burgh
in the twelfth century. This statement has since been contra-
dicted, and it has been assumed that Brechin held of an ecclesiastical superior, and that, as after the Reformation, that superiority was vested by Act of Parliament in the crown, Brechin
only became a royal burgh in the time of Charles I. in 1641. No
evidence exists that the burgh had privileges from the bishop,
although many tenements in town were held feu of him and of
the other ecclesiastics connected with the burgh ; and of the
Knights Templars ; and also of various laymen, as well as in free
burgage. In the work entitled " An Inquiry into the Rise and
Progress of Parliament," by Alexander Wight, Esq., advocate,
Edinburgh, edition 1806, page 36, we find it said, " At what precise time the erection of such corporations (royal burghs) first
took place in Scotland, cannot indeed be discovered with cer-
tainty. The oldest charters to burghs now extant, or of which
we have any knowledge from later instruments, were given by
William the Lion ; and the most, if not all, of these, are rather
to be considered as grants of particular privileges to the inhabitants, than as charters erecting them into communities or bodies
corporate, with power to choose their own magistrates," and,
in proof of this remark, Mr Wight gives a charter by James III.
to the town of Inverness, which recites *verbatim* four charters by
William the Lion and other princes, in which grants by David I.
are mentioned. Now this is exactly the case of Brechin, which
is included in the roll of the royal burghs from the earliest period.

No. II.

INQUIRY INTO THE ORIGIN OF THE WORD "BRECHIN."

Notwithstanding Mr Black's elaborate investigation into the origin of the word " Brechin," an investigation creditable alike to his research and his learning,—we think he has entirely failed in tracing the etymology of the term.

The question, like others of a similar nature, must be determined by a reference to the original inhabitants of the country, and the language they spoke. Who, then, were the aborigines of Brechin, and what was their language? At a very early period of the history of the human race, a migratory horde of Asiatics, issuing from the base of the Himmalaya Mountains in India, called in their own language " Caoilltich ; " by the Greeks, " Keltoi ; " by the Romans, " Keltae " or " Celtae ; " and in these islands, "Kelts " or " Celts," from the Celtic words *caoill*, a wood, and *tamh*, to dwell, (literally, dwellers in woods,) migrated into Asia Minor, and took possession of the coasts of Syria and adjacent territory. They worshipped Bel and Astarte, known to the Hebrews as Baal and Ashtaroth, and built temples in the midst of groves usually situated on rising eminences, at which a body of priests, denominated " Druids," officiated. In whatever country they located themselves they introduced chariots, attached to the axle-trees of which were scythes for the purpose of mowing down their opponents in battle,—and which in ages antecedent to the organisation of standing armies proved extremely formidable to barbarian infantry. In process of time, when population began to press on the means of subsistence—a crisis which occurs at an earlier stage among a pastoral than an agricultural community—detachments from this horde would in all probability have crossed the Hellespont into Europe, and settled in Greece, within sight of Italy. The word " Italy " is a compound of two Celtic words, " Edal," pasture, and " I," an island ; and though Italy is a peninsula, and not an island, yet its appearance from the coasts of Greece would naturally lead the inhabitants to suppose it was the latter. From the fertility of the Italian soil and its luxuriant vegetation, we may infer that the earlier settlers in Greece, during the summer months, when vegetation there was scorched by a powerful sun, would be attracted with their flocks and herds to the rich pasturage of Italy. Accordingly we find that when Æneas—son-in-law of Priam, king of Troy—fleeing from the wrath of the "perfidious Greeks," landed in Italy, he was opposed by numerous and warlike tribes.

The next outlet for a redundant population, pressed moreover by Greek colonists seizing on the Italian coasts, would be Gaul and Spain, which would have been entered by the Alps and Pyrenees, and from these countries Great Britain and Ireland came to be peopled. We are distinctly informed by Julius Cæsar that he found Britain thickly inhabited by a race similar in language, manners, and customs, to the Gauls.

We have now traced the aborigines of this country to the great Celtic family, who in ages involved in a hoary antiquity occupied the greater portion of Europe. A portion of this family it was, probably intermixed with a sprinkling of Shemitic blood, from whom the Abrahamidæ claimed the land of Canaan as an inheritance set apart by divine promise to them and their posterity. We know that the religious customs of the inhabitants of Canaan were very different from those of Egypt, and from the mythology which subsequently arose in Greece and Rome; and we are informed by Moses as well as by Josephus, that the Hebrews had to contend with their armed chariots, though they themselves were prohibited from using them. It is probable that the invention of the Macedonian phalanx by Philip of Macedon may have taught the Orientals the uselessness of this instrument of war as a means of charging and breaking opposing ranks, and thus led gradually to their being abandoned. Be this as it may, we learn from Cæsar's Commentaries, that chariots were used in this country, and we are informed that Boadicea the British queen, attended by her daughters, with dishevelled hair, rode round her army, exhorting them to fight the Roman invaders. And in the battle fought between the Romans and Caledonians, (Caoill-duin, men of the woods,) in the neighbourhood of Brechin, Tacitus records that by the steadiness of the imperial legions in withstanding the first charge of the Caledonians, and the weight of their assault in return, these machines were driven with great impetuosity into the ranks of their own infantry, and decided the fate of the battle in favour of the Roman general.

We think that the use of chariots in war could not have been an invention of the aborigines of this country, but must have been introduced by them from their original settlements in the East, for however suitable they might have been in the plains and table-lands of Asia, even previously to the construction of military roads, they could never have been efficient as a means of offence or defence, in a rugged and mountainous country like Scotland.

That the religious belief of the aborigines of this country was similar to that which obtained at a very early period among powerful tribes in India, and subsequently in Asia Minor, and Continental Europe, no one in the least acquainted with ancient history, —with the description of Tumuli and temples recently discovered in those countries, and with similar remains, still existing in this neighbourhood—will venture to deny; and we may also, in corroboration of this point, allude to many superstitious notions which the progress of Christianity and education have not yet wholly eradicated.

Having now shown, as we think, that the first inhabitants of this country were Celts and their language Celtic, we must necessarily refer to this language for the origin of the word " Brechin;" but, ere doing so, it may assist us in arriving at a satisfactory solution of the question that we glance at the topography of this district.

The valley extending from Montrose to Brechin bears evident traces of its having been at one period covered with the ocean. The alluvial soil, slightly mingled with boulders rounded by the action of water, demonstrate that this carse must have been produced by a process of depositation or silting, as it is usually termed,—a process still in operation, and which has contracted the Montrose basin within the memory of men still living. Nor let it be urged that the period of time intervening between the first arrival of human beings on our shores, and the origin of written history was too limited to produce so great a change; a much greater change has taken place during the last thirty centuries at the embouchure of the Nile, and other rivers. Besides, we infer from the immense forests which once abounded in this country, which cannot now be produced, and the great quantity of moss, that the internal heat of this part of the globe must then have been greater than now ; that owing to these forests a larger quantity of rain must have fallen, and thus given greater strength, volume, and velocity to the South Esk, and the rills which disembogue into it, whereby the deposit must have accumulated in a greater ratio than it has done since the cessation of these causes. We have thus no data whereby to approximate the length of time the ocean has occupied in receding to Old Montrose· The termination of the ocean we infer from the natural barrier there subsisting, to have been about Brechin Castle, the site of which would have been probably selected by the first settlers as a stronghold against the attacks of wild beasts, and in the vicinity of which, numerous habitations of men would ultimately arise.

The Celtic word "Braigh" signifies end, and "Cuan" the ocean, and the adjection and substantive being conjoined are pronounced Braighchuain, or the end of the ocean. This we feel confident is the true origin of the word Brechin. The corruption of the word must have taken place when the Scandinavians, a branch of the blue-eyed and fair-haired Teutonic race arriving from the north of Europe gradually drove the Celts beyond the Grampians, and seized on the coast-lands. It is the descendants of these Scandinavians, with a slight admixture of Celts and Saxons, who now inhabit the lowlands of Forfarshire, and who, unable to imitate or pronounce the harsh guttural tones of the Celtic, pronounce the word Brechin as they now do.

NO. III.

LIST OF THE BISHOPS OF THE SEE OF BRECHIN.

The Episcopal See of Brechin was founded and endowed by King David· I. about 1150.—*Vide,* " An Historical Catalogue of the Scottish Bishops by the Right Reverend Robert Keith," edition 1824, edited by Dr Russel of Leith, page 156. See also " History of the Bishops of Brechin," contained in a manuscript history of the Scottish bishops, in the Panmure charter-room, page 103. See likewise "The History of the Church of Scotland," by Archbishop John Spotswood, edition 1655, page 108, who states the bishoprick of "Brichen" to have been founded about 1140. See farther, "Registrum Episcopatus Brechinensis," in two quarto volumes, printed in 1856, being a second contribution by the late Patrick Chalmers, Esq., of Aldbar, to the Bannatyne Club, and in which, besides a full copy of the register, a number of charters connected with the church of Brechin, are printed from the charter-room of Brechin, from the cartulary of Arbroath, and from various private cartularies, Mr Chalmers's work is quoted as R. E. B.; and see also the preface by Cosmo Innes, Esq., to Mr Chalmers's cartulary, quoted as "Innes Preface." And finally, see in confirmation, "Vetera Monumenta Hibernorum et Scotorum Historiam Illustrantia, Quæ ex Vaticani, Neapolis ac Florentiæ Tabularijs Depromsit et Ordine Chronologico Disposuit, Augustinus Theiner, Presbyter Congregationis Oratorij Collegij Theologorum Archigymnasij Romani, Academicæ Pontificæ Archæologiæ, &c., &c.—Romæ Typis Vaticanis 1864."—Quoted as Theiner.

1. T. is the initial letter of the name of the first bishop, 1155. Keith, page 156. We have considerable doubts if there is not some mistake of dates, and whether Keith's Bishop T. of 1155 is not Turpin of 1178; the more especially as Gregory (*vide* No. 6) mentions all his other predecessors except this T. However, on the dicta of Keith, and authorities referred to by him, we have placed T. as first bishop of Brechin.

2. SAMPSON, 1157.—" Though he be not found designed bishop of this see in King David's time, yet he is bishop here in the time of King Malcolm IV.; and by a modest enough computation he might have been the first bishop preferred to the see, even by good King David himself. He, Sampson, Episcopus Brechinensis, is a witness to the charters of King Malcolm IV. to the priory of St Andrews before the year 1158." Panmure manuscript, page 103. The register of St Andrews makes Bishop *Samsone* witness to various deeds by King Malcolm and others, after 1159, see pages 128, *et seq.* His name is written *Sansane* in a charter in the archives of King's College, Aberdeen. Keith, page 560.

3. TURPIN, 1178.—" When he was invested in the bishoprick, he gave to the monks of St Thomas, of Arbroath, the churches of Old Montrose and Carcaryn, pro salute animæ suæ." Panmure MS., page 103. Keith, page 157. Mr Chalmers, in his R. E. B., vol. ii., prints, on page 255, a charter by this bishop to these monks of the " ecclesiam de veteri Munros ;" on page 256, a charter of the " ecclesiam de Cateryn ;" and on page 258, a grant of five churches, " Deo et ecclesie sancti Thome Martiris de Aber-brothoc et Monachis ibidem." Turpin is mentioned in various charters granted by his successors. There is a confirmation granted by Turpin to the Abbey of Arbroath, signed before "Hiis tertibus Hugone Episcopo Sancti Andree : *Bricio Priore Kele-deorum de Brechin,"* &c., R. E. B., vol. ii., page 269 ; and a charter granted by him to the abbey of Arbroath of a piece of land in Stracathro, signed before " Bricio Priore de Brechin, Gillefali *Kelde,* Bricio Capellano, Mathalan *Kelde,* Makbeth Maywen." R. E. B., page 270.

4. RADULPHUS, 1202.—" He confirmed to the abbey of Coupar the grants of his predecessor, Turpin, in which deed, William de Bosco, who was chancellor both to King William and his son, Alexander II., is a witness. He died anno 1218." Keith, page 158. Panmure MS., page 104. " Randulfo electo de Brechin," along with Matthew, Bishop of Aberdeen, who died in 1199, is witness to an agreement between the canons and culdees of St Andrews. See R. E. B. in confirmation, grant by this bishop to the Abbey of Arbroath of the church of Old Montrose, Vol. ii., page 255 ; and on page 257 a grant by the bishop to the same abbey of the church of " Dunnechtyn," while other charters by the same bishop are enumerated, pages 258 to 270. Bishop Randulph is also alluded to in charters granted by his successors.

5. HUGO, 1218.—He is said to have been contemporary with Robert, *elect* of Ross, regarding whose own incumbency there are considerable doubts. Hugo is also said to have been cotemporary with Adam, Bishop of Caithness, who died 1222. Keith, page 158, 206. The Panmure MS. takes no notice either of this Hugo or of Robert Mar, whom the chronicles of Aberbrothick, according to Keith, state to have been bishop of Brechin in 1219. Hugo, according to Keith's version of the chronicles of Melrose, " obijt

Episcopus Brechinen, anno 1218, cui successit Gregorius archdeaconus ejusdem episcopatus," and Gregory notices Hugo amongst his predecessors. Hence, we infer that Hugo was only a short time incumbent, and that Robert had never actually been consecrated bishop. In the R. E. B. Bishop Hugh is mentioned, vol. ii. pages 256, 259, 261, 270, and 271, in various grants by him to the abbey of Arbroath, the last deed, as well as some others, being witnessed by "Mallebryd Priore Keledeorum nostrorum." Bishop Hugh is also mentioned in charters by his successors.

6. GREGORY, 1219.—" How long he sate, or when he died, I have not been able to discover." Panmure MS., page 104. " He makes mention of Turpin, Radulphus, and Hugo, his predecessors." Keith, page 158. " He was bishop sometime after the thirty-second year of King Alexander II," or 1246 ; Nisbet's Heraldry, appendix, page 247. He, Turpin, Ralph, and Hugh, his predecessors, are all mentioned in an ordinance by his successor, Albin, R. E. B. ii. 264. He is farther alluded to, pages 256, 260, 270, and 271, and the Pope's mandate for his election is given, page 387, R. E. B. ii. This mandate is given by Theiner, page 8.

GILBERT, 1247.—" From the authority of the Chronicles of Melrose, died in the 1249." Panmure MS., page 104. Keith, page 159.

ROBERT, 1249.—Archdeacon of Brechin, succeeded Gilbert, " but died soon after." Panmure MS., page 104.

The Melrose Chronicle is the only authority for these two bishops, and from what is stated after, under the head of Albin, it is pretty plain that the Melrose Chronicle is in error. We therefore omit both Gilbert and Robert from our list.

7. ALBIN, 1247.—He " is one of the judges in a solemn arbitration betwixt the convent of Arbroath and Sir Peter de Maulia, Lord of Panmure, and Christiana de Valonijs, Lady Panmure, his wife, about the lands of Brakis and Bothmernock, lying in the lordship of Panmure, anno 1254. The bishop died in the 1269." Panmure MS., page 104. " He would appear to have been bishop here within the rein of King Alexander III., (1249–85,) since he is witness to William of Brechin, his foundation of the ' Maison de Dieu' in Brechin for the souls of William and Alexander, kings

of Scotland." Keith, page 159. This charter is printed by Mr Chalmers in his R. E. B., vol. i. page 4. Spotswood says, page 108, " Urwardus, or Edwardus, lived about the year 1260, a monk at first at Couper in Angus, a man very zealous in his calling; for it is testified of him, that he went on foot through the whole kingdom with one Eustathius, abbot of Aberbrothock, preaching the gospel wheresoever he came. Albinus, *after him*, was bishop some few years." On the margin, however, Spotswood remarks, " Since the writing of this catalogue I have found four bishops succeeding Edwardus, one after another, Turpinus, Rodolphus, Hugo, and Gregorius, but how long they sate bishops I cannot say." Spotswood gives no authority for his Urwardus, nor can we find his name in any document whatever connected with the see of Brechin at this period. Mr Chalmers prints, R. E. B., vol. ii. page 262, an agreement between Bishop Albin and his chapter and the abbot and monks of Arbroath, and an ordinance by Bishop Albinus, following thereupon, both dated, " Millesimo ducentesimo quadragesimo octavo, mense Septembris, decimo Kalendarum Octobris." In the latter of these documents the bishop enumerates his predecessors, Turpin, Ralph, Hugh, and Gregory; so it admits of grave doubts whether Gilbert or Robert were ever in the see of Brechin. This doubt is strengthened by a bull of Pope Innocent IV., (R. E. B., ii. 388,) dated at Lyons in the fourth year of the Pope's consecration, 1247, directing inquiry into the life and learning of Albinus, preceptor of the church of Brechin, who had been elected bishop by the canons of that see, but who was born of *unmarried* parents, and directing Albinus, notwithstanding, to be installed bishop if found worthy. Theiner, page 48, gives the dispensation for Albinus's illegitimacy.

8. WILLIAM DE KILCONCATH, 1269.—" Whom the Chronicle of Melross calls Lator Fratrum Predicatorum de Perth. Bishop Spotswood says he was Dean of Brechin, but from what authority I know not. He says also this prelate died going to Rome in the year 1275." Panmure MS., page 105. Spotswood, page 108. Kilconcath was alive in 1276, and is cited as testifying the authenticity of a bull of Innocent III., in Lyon's " History of St Andrew's," vol. ii. page 277. Likely, Kilconcath is the William whom Thiener, page 106, makes bishop here in 1275. Thiener,

page 109, gives, "Computus decimæ crucis in regno Scotiæ collectæ," and page 112, " Collectio decime in Episcopatu Brekynensi pro primo anno." "Summa 48, lib. 13, sol. 10 den. ob." This is in 1275.

9. EDWARD, 1276.—Spotswood is inclined to place this bishop after Sampson, but Keith introduces him after William de Kilconcath, " merely," he says, " that I may not omit him altogether," page 160. The Panmure MS. omits Edward, and Robert to be just noticed, and thus leaves a hiatus of 15 years. We, therefore, think Keith's hypothesis the correct one, and adopt Edward as the ninth bishop of Brechin, and place him in 1276, for the reason given by Mr Lyon, as above.

ROBERT, 1284.—"Robert, formerly archdeacon of this see, was bishop thereof in the year 1284." Keith, page 160. We can find no trace of such a bishop.

10. WILLIAM, 1286–1290.—"Was one of the Scotch clergy who addressed King Edward of England, that the prince, his son, might marry Margaret, the young Queen of Scotland, whereby the two crowns might be unite into one monarchy." Panmure MS., page 105. Keith, page 160. Mr Innes, in his preface to Mr Chalmers's "Registrum," says, page 8, "William, Bishop of Brechin, granted an indulgence at Durham, on 16th August 1286, and William was bishop in 1290 ; ' Rites of Durham,' page 135." In 1286, the States of Scotland sent the Bishop of Brechin, the Abbot of Jedburgh, and Geoffrey de Mowbray, as ambassadors to Edward, requesting his advice and mediation towards composing the troubles of the kingdom which had arisen during the minority of Margaret, the maiden of Norway, the granddaughter of Alexander III. Thiener, page 149, makes William bishop here in 1289.

11. NICHOLAS, 1295.—No trace of him is to be found amongst the Records of Brechin ; but Theiner, page 160, gives a bull by Pope Boniface, confirming Nicholas as bishop in the see of Brechin, dated, "vii. Kal. Februárij Pontificatus nostri anno secundo," 1296. This Pope Boniface proclaimed that " God had set him over kings and kingdoms," imprisoned his predecessor Celestine V., and laid France and Denmark under interdict.

12. JOHN DE KINNINMUND, 1298–1304.—" Of an ancient

family of that name and designation in the shire of Fife was
bishop here 22d October 1304. He is bishop before the year
1309, and in the year 1309 he is one of the bishops who, solemnly
under their seals, recognise King Robert Bruce's title to the crown
of Scotland. In the year 1311, he appends his seal, together with
Nicholas, Bishop of Dunblane, to a solemn agreement betwixt the
Abbots of Cambuskenneth and Coupar. He is bishop here in the
year 1313, also the same person is bishop anno 1321, likewise in
the 7th and 16th years of Robert I., and anno 1323, and he is
witness to King Robert's confirmation of the monastery of Aberbrothock." Keith, page 160. Panmure MS., page 105. He is a
party to an agreement with the monastery of Arbroath in 1304.
R. E. B., vol. ii. page 266. The name is sometimes written
Kinninmun*th*. He obtained from King Robert, in 1310, a charter
relieving the Church property of all secular services, R. E. B., ii. 4:
Thiener, page 164, gives a confirmation by Pope Boniface VIII. of
the election of Bishop John in 1298.

13. ADAM, 1328.—"Adam is bishop here anno 1329. Adam
was bishop here anno 1338. He is witness to King David's confirmation of the monastery of Arbroath, anno reg. 13, item anno
reg. 15, *i.e.*, anno domini 1342 and 4. Adam, Bishop of Brechin,
is witness, together with ' David de Barclay, Malcolmo de Ramsay, Vice-comite de Angus, Joanne de Straton, Waltero de
Allardes.' Now, this David Barclay seems to have been the last
laird of Brechin, who was murthered in the year 1348. Bishop
Adam was employed in several embassies into England, towards
the facilitating of King David's redemption, who had been taken
prisoner at the unfortunate battle of Durham, anno 1346.
Edward seems to have treated this bishop with more favour
than he showed to the other ambassadors, as a proof of which
we may mention that he bore his expenses when in England.
Rot. Scot., 20 : Mar. 16., Ed. III. The same prelate appears
to have been an agent in the dark negotiations of the de-
generate David II. with Edward III. See particularly, Rot.
Scotiæ, 26th Jul. 34, ed. iii." Keith, page 161. David de Barclay,
alluded to by Keith, must have been the first Barclay of Brechin,
as he left a son who was alive in 1364 ; " He died in, or about the
year 1350." Panmure MS., page 106. There is some confusion

regarding this bishop, which is by no means cleared up by the charter, dated in 1360, referred to by Dr Russell, (page 561,) said to have been granted by David II. to Bishop Leuchars; but Mr Innes, in his preface to the R. E. B., (page viii.,) says, "By a clerical error in our register a precept of David II., in the 31st year of his reign, (1359,) is made to be directed to Adam, instead of Patrick, Bishop of Brechin, *Chancellor*, and on that authority Spottiswoode has erroneously stated that Adam was Chancellor of Scotland." Mr Chalmers prints a charter granted by this bishop in 1348. R. E. B. i., 10. There is, R. E. B., ii. 389, a bull by Pope John, dated 31st October 1328, apparently confirming Bishop Adam in the see, but in reality claiming the right to nominate the bishop, and the same Pope by subsequent documents claims the same right in regard to the canons. Theiner, page 242, shows Bishop Adam to have been appointed in 1328 by this Pope John XXII. without an election of the chapter.

14. PHILIP, 1350.—He was bishop on 16th March 1350, for he of that date granted a charter to Heliscus Faucunur of certain subjects in Montrose, and this deed is No. 6 of the documents in the Brechin charter-chest, and a beautifully written little deed it is. Mr Chalmers gives a fac-simile of the charter, R. E. B., ii. 6. "Philip is in this see, 1351." Keith, page 162. Pope Clement VI. following up the practice of Pope John just alluded to, by a bull, dated 20th February 1350, *of new* appointed Philip to the office of bishop, R. E. B., ii. 393. Theiner notices this, page 292. Bishop Philip is witness, 1353, to a charter by David II. to Alexander Berkley of Wester Mathers. Spalding Miscellany, vol. v. pp. 248, 249.

15. PATRICK DE LEUCHARS, 1354.—" Descended of an ancient family in the shire of Fife, had been rector of Tinningham in East Lothian, (charta penes dominum de Cardross nunc comitem de Buchan,) was invested in the see of Brechin anno 1354, and some time after was made Lord High Chancellor of the kingdom. He was also much employed in treating about the redemption of King David II., and in adjusting the several payments of his ransom. He was both bishop and chancellor, anno reg. 29, *i.e.*, anno domini 1358, Nov. 12, *it.* Nov. 18, also anno reg. 30. He was bishop and chancellor in the thirty-first and thirty-fourth

U

years of David II. He was chancellor anno 1360, bishop and chancellor anno 1362. He was bishop anno 28 and 36, David II., and bishop and chancellor July 4, anno reg. 39, and bishop anno 40. In the year 1370, he resigned his office of chancellor, at least it is certain that he had made this resignation some time before the death of King David. He is bishop in the first, second, and third years of King Robert II., anno reg. 3, and he was bishop, and present in parliament 1373." Keith, page 162. Tytler's Hist. of Scotland, vol. ii. pp. 84, 95. "Soon after Bishop Leuchars's advancement, he was promoted to be Lord High Chancellor of Scotland, and is so designed in a confirmation to him by K. David of Walterus de Maulia, dominus de Panmure, charter of his lands of Cairncorthy, and chaplanary of Boath to the Episcopal see of Brechin, 20th Nov. 1360, which office he held for the space of sixteen years, till the 1370, he resigned the great seall, which was, by King David II., given to Dr John Carrick, chanon of Glasgow, and keeper of the privy seal, and the bishop died soon thereafter, though he had the happiness before his death to see King Robert II. peaceably settled on the throne; his death happened about the year 1375. In the 1374 he is then alive; the bishop is witness to a resignation of lands by Sir Malcolm Fleming to the Earl of Douglas." Panmure MS., page 106. There is a declaration by Bishop Leuchars regarding the number and rights of the benefices of the church of Brechin, dated in 1372. R. E. B., i. 19. Bishop Patrick is witness to a charter by David II., in 1360, to the abbey of Dunfermline, and " Patricio Epo Brechinen, cancellario nostro," is witness to a charter by David II. to the burgh of Inverness, dated at Perth, 3d March " anno regni nostri quadragesimo." Pope Clement, who is described as "a learned prelate, a generous prince, and amiable man," but who, notwithstanding seems to have been an ambitious man, by a bull, dated 17th Nov. 1352, (quoted R. E. B., ii. 394, and noticed by Theiner, page 299,) adopts, with Bishop Leuchars, the very same course he had pursued with his predecessor, Bishop Philip, no doubt thereby strengthening the power of the Church of Rome. Leuchars was one of the committee of parliament, appointed in 1369, to deliberate and give judgment upon all such judicial questions and complaints as necessarily came before parliament. Tytler's History of Scotland, vol. ii. page 155. And the Bishop was indeed an active politician during the whole reign of David II. Tytler *passim*.

16. STEPHEN, 1375.—" To Bishop Leuchars succeeded Stephen, archdean of Brechin, who sate bishop of this see anno 1384, and he discharged the office of his function till his death in 1401." Panmure MS., page 106. At request of Sir David Lindsay of Glenesk, this bishop, on 23d February 1384, erected the church of Lethnot into a prebendary, with power to the prebend thereof to be a canon of the cathedral church of Brechin, and to have a stall in the choir, and a place in the chapter. R. E. B., i. 21, *et* ii. 8. In the Spalding Miscellany, vol. v. page 319, there is an abstract of a charter before 1399 by Keith, Earl Marischall, to William Lyndesey, in which Stephen, Bishop of Brechin, is a witness.

17. WALTER FORRESTER, 1401.—" Of the family of Cardin in Stirlingshire, was first a canon of the church of Aberdeen ; next was made Secretary of State, and then promoted to the see of Brechin, in which he was a bishop as early as the year 1401. He was bishop here anno 1405 and 1408. He was bishop anno 1413, *it.* anno 8vo. 'Roberti Gubern.' As also 15th Januarij 1415." Keith, page 163. On 9th Nov. 1409, this bishop obtained from Sir John Erskine of Dun a grant of certain services payable by the church of Brechin to him, for the lands of Ecclesjohn, now called Langley Park. Cartulary of Brechin, No. 24, ratified by the Duke of Albany in 1410. R. E. B., i. 32. There is a presentation addressed to this bishop by the Earl of Crawford, by which the earl requests the bishop to examine his beloved cousin, Andrew de Ogilvy, clerk of the diocese of Dunkeld, as to his knowledge and morals, and thereafter to admit him to the prebendary of Lethnot, and to a stall in the cathedral church of Brechin, 6th December 1410. R. E. B., i. 29. On 30th June 1413, Bishop Forrester obtained a precept from Robert, Duke of Albany, addressed to the Sheriff of Kincardineshire, for the enforcement of certain "wards, reliefs and marriages, fines and escheats," from that county ; and this precept is enforced by subsequent similar writings down to 1417. R. E. B., i. 35, *et seq.* He assisted at a general council of the clergy held at Perth, 16th July 1420. R. E. B., i. 38. Dr Russell says, page 561, " He

occurs, 16th July 1420, in Reg. Eccl. Brechin, f. lxii." "How long he sate, or when his death happened no authority has occurred to me that makes it clear." Panmure MS., page 107. Mr Chalmers, R. E. B., ii. page 273, prints, from the Findowry charter-room, a charter by this bishop to "Willelmo Lam" of some property in Brechin, dated 10th May 1420, "et consecrationis nostre anno decimo."

> G., 1424.—"Dominus G. is Bishop of Brechin in the year 1424, but what name this initial letter stands for, I do not pretend to say." Keith, page 163. There is no trace of any such bishop amongst the papers belonging to the burgh of Brechin, nor does the Panmure MS. notice him, neither does Spotswood. The Right Reverend Alexander Penrose Forbes, D.C.L., present Bishop of Brechin, who has kindly revised this list, says, " G. is certainly Gualterus, and means Walter Forrester." We are quite of his opinion.

18. JOHN DE CARNOTH, 1429.—He "was bishop of this see when he accompanied Princess Margaret, daughter of King James I., into France, in order to be espoused to Lewis XI., then dauphin of that kingdom, anno 1435. John is bishop here anno 1449. John, bishop of this see, was sent into England, on an embassy with divers others, anno 1450. He is also mentioned April 18, 1451." Keith, page 163. The Cartulary of Brechin, No. 40, R. E. B., ii. 23, proves that John was bishop of this see on 4th September 1429. On 20th October of that year Walter, Palatine of Strathearn, with consent of John, Bishop of Brechin, confirms to the chapter of Brechin the right of patronage of the parish of Cortachie, R. E. B., i. 46, et ii. 24, 28. " He is styled conservator privilegiorum ecclesie Scoticane," says Dr Russel, page 561. The name of John *Crannoch*, Bishop of Brechin, occurs in a great variety of papers, connected with the burgh, down to the 17th November 1453. Brechin Cartulary No. 27. He regulates the payment to be made by each official for the maintenance of the vestments in 1435. R. E. B., ii. 40. He died August 1456, *vide* chronicles of King James II. Dr Russel says, "The following is an entry under the year 1456 in the brief chronicle of the reign of King James II. at Auchinleck. Itm yt samyn zer and moneth (August) decessit i. Brechyne mast. Jhone Crenok, Bischop of

Brechyne, yt was callit a gud actif man and all his tyme wele gouvnands."

19. GEORGE SHERSWOOD, 1454.—" Chancellour of Dunkeld and secretarie to King James II. This prelate was a son of Sherswood of Bettshiell, in Berwickshire ; being bred a churchman, his first station in the Church was rector of Cultar, anno 1449. Mr Sherswood being a learned and mettled man, King James made him first one of his clerks, and after that his secretarie. In the 1453 he was made chancellour of Dunkeld, and in the 1454 was sent upon an embassy to England; soon after his return he was promoted to be chancellour of Scotland, in the 1455, (? 1458,) and he held the office till the death of the king in 1460. How long Bishop Sherswood lived thereafter, the records of the see being defective, I cannot be positive." Panmure MS. page 108. Noticed by Keith, page 164. " In his time was the church of Fun- aven made one of the chapter." Spotswood, page 108. This scarce seems correct ; see Bishop Balfour, No. 24. Bishop Sherswood's name only occurs once in the Cartulary of Brechin, on 19th April 1458, No. 128. Dr Russel says, page 562, " George, bishop of Brechin, chancellor of Scotland, occurs 19th April 1448, in reg. eccl. Brechin, f. 99." The learned doctor is ten years wrong here, for the charter referred to above is printed, R. E. B., i. page 184, and the date is clearly 1458. There is also an instrument taken in presence of " Johannes de Schoriswod, pater germanus, Georgij Episcopi Brechinensis Cancellarij Scotie et Magister David de Guthrye de Kincaldrum Camerarij predict Domini Episcopi," and dated 28th January 1459, R. E. B., i. 188. He is mentioned as " Georgio Episcopo Brechinensis Cancellario Scotie," in 1457, in a process regarding the earldom of Mar. Spalding Miscellany, vol. v. pages 264–5. It is very evident that Keith is wrong when he introduces Robert as Bishop of Brechin in 1456, for then there was no room for Bishop Sherswood, regarding whose consecration there can be no doubt. Keith, speaking of this Bishop Robert, says, page 163, " As he is not in any former list of the bishops of this see, I can say no more of him, but that he might have died this year, and his successor been in the see in the course of the same." But it would appear this could not be, for Sherswood was appointed coadjutor in 1448, while Carnock was alive. Be-

sides, there is no mention of this Bishop Robert in the Cartulary
of Brechin, nor does the Panmure MS. take any notice of him.
Spotswood also omits him. *Robert* de Crannoch, chanter of
Brechin, on 9th October 1453, has an instrument in his favour,
most beautifully written, No. 125 Brechin Cartulary; R. E. B., ii.
94, and is witness to an obligation, granted by the chaplains of
the cathedral church of Brechin to Robert Hill on 3d Nov. 1453;
No. 126 of Brechin Cartulary, R. E. B., ii. 195. Could Sir Robert
Crannoch be the person whom Keith calls Bishop Robert? Mr
Chalmers, R. E. B., ii. 273–5, prints from the Findowry Cartulary two charters by Bishop George, dated, the first in 1457, the
second in 1461, " et consecrationes nostre anno septimo," proving
Bishop Sherswood to have been consecrated in 1454; and page
383, he gives an agreement with the town council of Montrose,
dated 13th May 1462, signed, "Georgius Brechinen," proving
Sherswood to have been then in the see.

20. PATRICK GRAHAM, 1462.—He was son to Lord Graham,
by Lady Mary Stewart, daughter to King Robert III., and hence
he was nephew to King James I. Keith, page 164. Panmure
MS., page 108. This remarkable lady gave birth to James Kennedy
who was the *last* Bishop of St Andrews, and to Patrick Graham,
who, in 1466, was made the *first Arch*-bishop of that diocese,
Lady Mary Stewart was *four* times married:—First, to the Earl
of Angus, by whom she had two sons, William and George
Douglas, who successively became Earls of Angus. Second, to Sir
James Kennedy of Dunmure, by whom she had two sons, James,
the last Bishop of St Andrews; and Gilbert, afterwards created
Lord Kennedy, the ancestor of the Marquis of Ailsa. Third, to
Lord Graham of Dundresmore, by whom she had two sons, James
Graham, the first Lord of Fintray; and Patrick Graham, the
Bishop of Brechin and Archbishop of St Andrews. And fourth, to
Sir William Edmiston of Culloden. There is in the Cartulary of
Brechin a precept addressed to Bishop Graham by King James
III., dated 2d January 1463, printed by Mr Chalmers, R. E. B.,
ii. 100, in which his Majesty enjoins the bishop to revoke the
grants of lands improperly made by his predecessors. Bishop
Graham was translated to the see of St Andrews in 1466, and, as
already said, was the first *Arch*-bishop of that diocese, having

APPENDIX. 311

procured from the Pope, Sixtus the Fourth, a bull erecting the
see of St Andrews into an archbishopric, and enjoining the
twelve bishops of Scotland to be subject to that see in all time
coming, an honour which involved Graham in difficulties pecuniary
and political. He died in 1479, in Lochleven Castle, a prisoner.
Buchanan, who is no ways favourable to the Romish clergy, gives
a long account of the persecutions to which Graham was subjected
by the King, jealous of his appointment by the Pope, to the office
of legate for Scotland, and by the clergy who feared his integrity
and strictness, and Buchanan winds up by saying, "Thus perished
a man, blameless in his life, and in learning and courage inferior
to none of his cotemporaries." B. 12, § 333–335.

21. JOHN BALFOUR, 1466.—"John, Bishop of Brechin, chancellor, occurs 6th September, a. r. Jac. III., 21 Reg, Eccl. Brechin,
f. liii., and previously John is mentioned as Bishop of Brechin,
17th February 1466–7, *ibid.* f. cxxii." Russel, page 562. He
"was bishop of this see, anno 1476, and assisted in the consecration of Bishop Livingstone of Dunkeld. He was bishop in the
year 1470, and John was also bishop in the year 1501." Keith,
page 164. Panmure MS., page 108. Amongst the records of
Brechin, there is a charter, dated 13th September 1474, by which
John, Bishop of Brechin, with consent of David, Earl of Crawford,
patron of the church of Finhaven, erects that parish church into a
prebend of Brechin. R. E. B., i. 196. There is also amongst
these records a decree of the Lords of Council and Session, 30th
June 1477, at the instance of John, Bishop of Brechin, against
George, Earl of Rothes, for the teind-duty of the earl's lands in
the Mearns. R. E. B., i. 199 *et seq. et* ii. 276. While yet only
elect, Pope Paul ii., in 1465, granted Balfour a dispensation to
hold in commendam, along with his bishopric, the parish
church of Conveth, now Laurencekirk. R. E. B. ii. 413.
About 1491, Glasgow was erected into an archbishopric, and
then Dunkeld, Dunblane, Brechin, Aberdeen, Moray, Ross, Caithness, and Orkney, were made subject to St Andrews; while Galloway, Argyle, and the Isles, were put under the jurisdiction of
Glasgow; St Andrews still retaining the primacy. Lyon's
History of St Andrews, vol. i. pages 241, 242.

22. WILLIAM MELDRUM, 1494–1500.—Keith says, "*Walter*

Meldrum, at what time he came to be bishop, or how long he sat in this see, does not as yet appear by any proper voucher that I have chanced to meet with. The chronology, however, rather requires that some person should be in this see between John Balfour and the next bishop," page 165. Dr Russel says, " William, anno 1511, omitted by Keith," page 561 ; and he adds, page 562, " William, Bishop of Brechin, previously occurs, viz., 6th May, anno 1500, and 29th June 1505, in Reg. Ec. Brechin, f. xiv., and f. xlvi." The Panmure MS. remarks, page 108, " William Meldrum ; how long he lived bishop does not appear." Amongst the Brechin papers there is an obligation by Gaspar Boncian, merchant in Florence, dated at Antwerp, 4th June 1488, to the chapter of the cathedral church of Brechin, by which he obliges "himself, in consideration of the sum of 200 ducats of Flanders, to proceed to the Court of Rome for the purpose of obtaining two bulls expede by the Pope, relating to the appointment of Sir William Meldrum, Vicar of Brechin, to the see of Brechin, in the event of the resignation or decease of John, now bishop thereof." R. E. B., ii. 124. There is also a procuratory extant, dated 6th October 1490, but altered by interlineations to 21st March 1495, R. E. B., ii. 134, by William, *Bishop of Brechin*, empowering Sir Robert Keith, professor of theology, and others, to compear before Pope Alexander VI. at Rome, and to present to him an application in name of the bishop, in order to obtain his confirmation in the see. Subsequently there are various documents in name of Bishop *William;* in 1497, regarding a dispute with John Dempster of Ouchterless ; in 1500, anent a controversy with the Laird of Pitarro; in 1505, in a charter of lands to the Church by the Duchess of Montrose ; in 1506, 1507, and 1508, in several deeds ; and finally, in 1512, in a charter by Gilbert Strachan, of certain lands to the Church, "for the safety (or good estate) of the souls of the right reverend Lord, Lord Stewart, late Archbishop of St Andrews, and also of Lord William, present bishop of Brechin," &c. R. E. B., i. 218, *et seq.*, ii. 131, *et seq.*, *item* 277. There can, consequently, be no doubt that William, and not Walter, was bishop during this period. In confirmation of all this, it may be remarked that Mr Chalmers prints, from the Findowry charter-chest, two charters by William, Bishop of Brechin, one in 1500 and the other in 1510, R. E. B., ii. 277–8 ; from the Dun charter-chest, an assedation by the same bishop, dated in 1509, page 304 ; from the Kinnaird charter-room, a deed by Bishop William in 1512, "et nostre consecrationis anno xxiiij°," page 298 ; and from the Register of the Privy Seal, page 385, a discharge granted by the same bishop, 30th May 1511 ; and again from the Carreston charter-chest in 1552, and the 31st year of his consecration. R. E. B., ii. 310. See also discharge to the Laird of Arbuthnot, dated 31st May 1511. R. E. B., ii. 385. In the folio volume of " The Acts of the Lords of Council and Session in Civil Causes for 1494," we find, page 355, under date 4th July, that the Lords decreet that "William Fresale of Durris does wrong in the detention and withholding from a reverend father in God, William, Bishop of Brechin, of the second teind of his relief of the lands of Durris, owing to the said bishop and the kirk of Brechin." We therefore put Bishop Meldrum's election to the see of Brechin in 1494, certain it had then occurred, if it had not taken place sooner.

23. JOHN HEPBURN, 1517.—He was descended of the family of Bothwell, and was one of the bishops who recognised the Earl of Arran's right to the regency in 1543. He died in the month of August 1558. Keith, page 165. Panmure MS., 108. There are documents extant in the records of Brechin, in which this bishop's name is mentioned, from the 1518 to the 1556. R. E. B. ii. 173, *et seq.* From the Findowry charter-chest, Mr Chalmers gives a charter by this bishop, granted, with consent of his chapter on 19th August 1547, " et consecrationis nostro anno vicesimo quarto," R. E. B., ii. 234, and from the Kinnaird charter-room, he gives a deed, dated 1556, " et nostre consecrationis anno xxx° tertio," R. E. B., ii. 300. This bishop therefore had been consecrated in 1523. From the Dun charter-chest, Mr Chalmers prints a deed in favour of Bishop John, dated in 1556, R. E. B., ii. 304 ; and from the Careston Cartulary, a charter, dated in 1552, R. E. B. ii. 316. He was one of the bishops who put his hand to the sentence against Patrick Hamilton in 1527. Spotswood, 63.

DONALD CAMPBELL, 1558.—" Mr Donald Campbell, a son of the family of Argyle, was destined his successor by the court here, and, no doubt, was elected by the chapter ; and therefore Bishop Leslie says, that the Abbot of Coupar did succeede Bishop Hepburn of Brechin. But his election being cass'd at Rome, in regard Mr Campbell had renounced Popery and turned Protestant, he was so modest as never to use the title of bishop, but only Abbot of Coupar, and was one of the clergy who sate in the parliament 1560, where the reformation of religion received the first legall sanction, and the Pope's authority was abolished; he died Lord Privy Seall to Queen Mary in the end of the 1562, whereupon the bishopric of Brechin was given by Queen Mary to a person who was much more acceptable to her Majesty than the other, by reason of his zeal for the Roman Catholic religion." Panmure MS., page 109. Keith, page 165. There is no trace of Campbell amongst the Brechin papers, nor does Mr Chalmers give any document bearing his name.

24. JOHN SINCLAIR, 1563.—"Mr John Sinclair, Dean of Restalrig, and a brother of the house of Roslyn, being a person learned in the civil and canon law, he was made one of the Lords of the Sessione, and after that president of the Sessione, and he continued in his office till his death in Apryle 1565." Panmure MS., page 109. Keith, page 165. Buchanan reports Sinclair as one of those who advised Queen Mary to adopt extreme measures against the reformers, B. 17, § 7. Queen Mary and Darnley were married by the Bishop of Brechin at the chapel-royal, Holyrood, on Sunday, 29th July 1565. It is said Bishop Sinclair was blind of one eye. Slaines MS. He is mentioned R. E. B., ii. 328. He died 9th April 1566, " betwixt thre and foure houris in the morning, in James Mosmanis hous in Frosteris Wynd, within Edinburgh." Diurnal of Ocurrents, page 98.

REFORMATION.

25. ALEXANDER CAMPBELL, 1566.—"This gentleman was a younger brother of James Campbell of Arkinglass, who was comptroller of Scotland in the minority of King James VI. Being educated with a view to the Church before the Reformation, he was made provost of St Giles, in Edinburgh, anno 1554, upon

the resignation of Robert Crichton, Bishop of Dunkeld. Seeing how matters went at the time of the Reformation, he turned with the times, and became a Protestant. By the recommendation of his chief, the Earl of Argyle, he had a grant of the bishopric, with a power which, I believe, was never given to any bishop of the Christian Church but himself, at least, so far as my reading has led me, which was, 'cum potestate disponendi beneficium infra totum diocesin.' Mr Campbell, seeing Episcopacy near abolished after the Reformation, he made use of that power and faculty the Queen had invested him with, and accordingly alienated most part of the lands and titles of the bishopric to his patron, the Earl of Argyle, who had got him preferred to the benefice, reserving to himself and his successors scarce so much as was a moderate enough competency for a minister at Brechin. He long while discharged the office of particular pastor at Brechin, and kept the title of bishop, though he discharged no other part of Episcopal function than what belongs to an ordinary minister in the Church, save the title, till the 1572 Episcopacy was first restored. He sate in many parliaments on the spiritual side, even when few others did as a bishop, even till the time of his death, in the beginning of the 1606." Panmure MS., pages 109, 110. Keith, page 166. The grant above referred to is given at length in R. E. B., ii. 328. On page 332 of same work, there is the licence given to this bishop, 7th May 1567, to go abroad for seven years without any danger to his benefice, and he appears to have remained abroad for the time allowed him, for in 1573 his brother, Arkinglass, gives up a rental of the bishopric, the bishop " himselff being in Geneva at the schuilis." R. E. B., ii. 428. There are amongst the records of Brechin charters granted by this bishop in January 1566, and down to the 1605, most of which prove that Bishop Campbell fully exercised the power of alienating property with which he was endowed. See also R. E. B., ii. 285–290. James VI., after the Act of Annexation of the Bishop's Temporalities to the Crown, granted those of Brechin to Campbell, R. E. B., ii. 374, who in 1603 made good his right against his Majesty's Collector-General, R. E. B., ii. 291. His wife was Helen Clephan, and they acquired the land of Monboy from George Wishart in 1583, R. E. B., ii. 292. Campbell is witness to a bond by the

Earl of Athol and others to Captain Patrick Cranstoun and his spouse of 100 merks yearly, "for the gude and thankful service done," "for the libertie and relief of our soverane, the King's Majesteis person," 31st July 1578. Spalding Miscellany, vol. v. p. 203.

26. ANDREW LAMB, 1606–1610.—Minister at Burntisland, succeeded in this see in 1606, and continued in it till the year 1619, when he was translated to Galloway on the death of Bishop Coupar. He was one of the three bishops who went by the orders of James I. into England, where he received Episcopal consecration on the 20th October 1610. Keith, page 167. Panmure MS., page 110. There is a charter by the precentor, with Bishop Andrew's consent, to the town council of Brechin in 1619. A board in the session-house, on which are recorded gifts to the church, bears, "1615, Andrew, Bishop of Brechin, gifted the hearse before the pulpit" —a brass chandelier for holding candles, of very handsome workmanship. Mr Chalmers prints a charter granted by Bishop Lamb in 1608. R. E. B., ii. 293. Lamb was a member of the first parliament summoned by Regent Moray, 15th December 1567. Tytler's History of Scotland, edition 1842, vol. vii. page 162.

27. DAVID LINDSAY, 1619.—He was son to Colonel John Lindsay, a brother of the laird of Edzel, in Angusshire. He was minister at Dundee, from whence he was translated to the see of Brechin, and consecrated at St Andrews, 23d November 1619. "He appears by his writings remaining to have been a man of good learning. By reason of his book, called 'Resolutions for Kneeling at the Sacrament,' he became very acceptable to the court, insomuch as King Charles the First was pleased to translate him to the bishopric of Edinburgh, upon Dr Forbes's death in 1634, where he continued till the 1638." Panmure MS., page 111. "The fury of the mob was like to have fallen heavy on this prelate at the first reading of the liturgy in the High Church of Edinburgh, on Sunday the 23d July 1637. He was deposed and excommunicated by the Assembly in 1638, whereupon he withdrew into England, where he died during the following troubles." Keith, page 61. Amongst the records of Brechin there is one deed with this bishop's name, in 1623. R. E. B., ii. 241.

28. THOMAS SYDSERF, 1634.—"Thomas Sydserf, afterwards better known as Bishop of Galloway and Bishop of Orkney, was

Bishop of Brechin in 1635, though omitted by Keith,"—says Mr Innes in his preface to Mr Chalmers's Work, i. 13, and he quotes Bishop Forbes's Funerals, edition 1845, page 226. Bishop Sydserf is not mentioned in any of the records of Brechin, nor would his incumbency in 1635 tally with Bishop Whiteford's consecration in September 1634, as stated in the Panmure MS. We have had it stated to us that Sydserf was bishop for a short time in 1634; and Bishop Forbes is in possession of the Episcopal seal of Thomas, Bishop of Brechin. On these authorities we rank Thomas Sydserf as a bishop of Brechin.

29. WALTER WHITEFORD, 1634.—According to Keith, page 167, he was son of James Whiteford of that ilk, by Margaret his wife, daughter of Sir James Somerville of Camnethan, and was first a minister at Monkland, and sub-dean of Glasgow, and then rector of Moffat, retaining his sub-deanery in commendam. The Panmure MS. gives the following account of this prelate :—" In the 1620, he was inaugurate doctor of divinity, and last of all he was promoted to this see upon the recommendation of the secretarie, Sir William Alexander of Menstrie, Earl of Stirling, and was consecrate in September 1634, and he held the see till the 1638, when he was outed and excommunicated by the General Assembly of Glasgow. Bishop Whiteford being very obnoxious to the fury of the incensed multitude, for being thought amongst the most forward of any of his brethren for the liturgy and book of canons, which at first set the kingdom in a flame when the troubles broke out, for the security of his person he fled into England, where he died in the 1643." Panmure MS., page 112. There are no charters extant amongst the Brechin records with this bishop's name on them, but it has been ascertained in a court of law, that "the reverend father in God, Walter, Bishop of Brechin," and the town council of Brechin, on 15th May 1637, framed a particular act regarding the multures of the mills of Brechin. In Wood's peerage, vol. i. page 753, it is stated that Bishop Whitford or Whiteford married Anne, one of the daughters of Sir John Carmichael of Carmichael. After the Glasgow Assembly of 1638 he was presented by King Charles to the living of Waldegrave, in Northamptonshire. Bridge's Northamptonshire, i. 284. On 13th April 1636, Walter, Bishop of Brechin,

and others were created burgesses of Arbroath. Burgh Record in Library at Panmure House.

30. DAVID STRACHAN, 1662.—"Upon the restauration of Episcopacy by King Charles II., his Majesty promoted to this see Mr David Strachan, parson of Fettercairn. This prelate was a branch of the antient family of Strachans of Thorntoun, in the county of Kincardine, where he was born, and had his education in the University of Saint Andrews, where he took his degrees. After that, betaking himself to the study of theologie, which he pursued with great diligence and industry, he was licensed to the ministry, and soon after settled at Fettercairn. Being a person of great and eminent loyalty, which he had manifested upon severall occasions during the usurpation, he was, upon the King's return, as the reward of his fidelity and merit, pointed out to be a bishop, and by the favour of the Earle of Middleton, who was Mr Strachan's near relation, was promoted to this see and consecrate, June 1st, anno 1662, where he exercised the office of his function till the 1671, when death translated him from this mortall life to a state of immortality." Panmure MS., page 112. Keith, page 167. The Presbytery records of Brechin, of 2d November 1671, bear that " David, Bishop of Brechin, departed this lyff, the nynth of October last." This bishop concurs with Mr John Strachan, the archdeacon, in the grant of a piece of land to the hospital of Brechin, on 11th April 1667, and this is the only time his name is found amongst the existing records of the burgh of Brechin. R. E. B., ii. 250. The session records bear that the bishop, without naming him, made his first entry to, and preached in the cathedral church, on 3d August 1662. A placard in the session-house, recording grants made to the church, states, " 1665, David, Bishop of Brechin, gifted the orlodge on the steeple," the clock in the steeple. The same board states, " 1682, Anna Barclay, relict, David B. of Brechin (gifted to the poor) £33, 6s. 8d." Mr Innes, quoting an " Account of Scotch Bishops at Slaines," says Bishop Strachan was buried in the cathedral before the pulpit.

31. ROBERT LAURIE, 1674.—He was " son of Joseph Laurie, minister at Stirling, was first appointed to the charge of a parish ; and being a celebrated preacher, and a man of moderation, he was, upon the restoration, made Dean of Edinburgh,

and then advanced to the see of Brechin ; but the benefice of this bishopric being small, he was allowed to retain his deanery, and continued to exercise a particular ministry at the church of the Holy Trinity in Edinburgh, till his death in the year 1677." Keith, page 168. From the records of the town council of 17th September 1674, it appears "that Mr John Dempster, school-master, is employed by the bishop to supply his charge as minister," because, as the margin of the council record bears, " the bishop was called to be preacher at ————," believed to be the church of the Holy Trinity in Edinburgh, which charge he held till his death. Bishop Laurie's name only occurs once amongst the Brechin charters, on 21st April 1674. R. E. B., ii. 251. There is en-grossed in the council-book a curious letter, signed " Mr Robert Laurie, Bishop of Brechin," addressed to the town council on 16th April 1675, regarding the misconduct of a Robert Strachan, kirk-officer.

32. GEORGE HALLIBURTON, 1678.—" George Halliburton, minis-ter at Coupar of Angus, was consecrated bishop of this see anno 1678, and was translated thence to the see of Aberdeen in the year 1682." Keith, page 168. Panmure MS., page 114. Some business is delayed in the session, on 2d June 1678, "till the bishop be present," and he is marked as present in the session on the 30th September that year. The head court of the burgh of Brechin, of 27th September 1678, was held " Per Reverendum in Christo Patrem Georgium Episcopum Brechinensis et Balivos ;" on 29th September 1681, this bishop, with his own hand, enters an appointment in the council-book, of " David Donaldson, younger, to continue my balzie for the ensuing year ;" and on 3d October following, this prelate, as provost, takes the lead in sign-ing the oaths to government, along with the rest of the council. There are no charters extant with his name.

33. ROBERT DOUGLAS, 1682.—" A lineal branch of Douglas of Glenbervy, in the shire of the Mearns, afterwards Earls of Angus, now Dukes of Douglas, was born anno 1626. He had his educa-tion in the King's College of Aberdeen ; was minister first at Laurencekirk, in the Mearns, then of Bothwell, Renfrew, and Hamilton, next Dean of Glasgow, from whence he was promoted to the see of Brechin anno 1682, and anno 1684, was translated

to the bishopric of Dunblane." Keith, page 168. Panmure MS.,
page 114. Robert, Bishop of Brechin, his son, Silvester Douglas,
and others, were admitted honorary burgesses of Brechin, 1st
August 1682. This bishop preached in the cathedral church only
on four occasions, twice in October in 1682, and twice in October
1683, as the session records bear.

34. ALEXANDER CAIRNCROSS, 1684.—"Though he was the
very heir of the ancient family of the Cairncrosses of Cowmislie,
yet was so low in his circumstances that he was under a necessity
to betake himself to an employment, and was a dyer in the Canon-
gate of Edinburgh, which employment he exercised for many
years, and with such success, that he was enabled to acquire some
part of the estate which had pertained to his ancestors. He was
first parson of Dumfries, until the year 1684, at which time, by
the recommendation of the Duke of Queensberry, he was promoted
to the see of Brechin, and soon thereafter to that of Glasgow,
which was ratified by the King's letters-patent, 3d December 1684.
Here he continued till the year 1686, when, having incurred the
displeasure of the Lord Chancellor, the Earl of Perth, (and deservedly, too, if all be true which Dr James Canaries, minister at
Selkirk, relates,) the King sent a letter to the privy council removing him from the archbishopric of Glasgow, of the date, January
13, 1687. A very irregular step, surely, the King should have
taken a more canonical course. He lived privately until the
Revolution in 1688, after which period he was taken notice of by
the new powers, who finding him not altogether averse to make
compliance with them, he was made Bishop of Raphoe in Ireland,
the 16th May 1693, and in that see he continued till his death,
anno 1701. He left a considerable estate to his nephew, by a
sister, George Home of Whitfield." Keith, page 269. He was
consecrated Bishop of Brechin in June or August 1684, and on
6th December following, he was presented to the archbishopric
of Glasgow. See vol. ix. of the Abstracts of the secretary's books
in the possession of the family of Mar, Nos. 39 and 40. Keith,
pages 168 and 269. Panmure MS., page 114. He is present at
the election of the magistrates of Brechin, on Monday, 29th
September 1684, and then appoints John Molison as bishop's
bailie ; and he was present at the head court of the burgh, held

4th October same year, but his name does not afterwards occur in the records of the council. Bishop Cairncross preached in the cathedral on 1st October 1684, during his visit, taking his text from Acts xx. 28. How far he acted up to his text it is not for us to judge ; but Mr Chalmers prints from the Findowry charter-chest a receipt, granted by John Spence, clerk of Brechin, and factor to Alexander, Archbishop of Glasgow, formerly Bishop of Brechin, to the Laird of Findowry, for feu-duty, dated 12th December 1685. R. E. B., ii. 298. Mr Innes says,—" After the Revolution he was made Bishop of Raphoe by King William, and held the bishopric from 1693 to 1701, the only instance of such promotion after the abolition of Episcopacy in Scotland." Preface to R. E. B., page xiv.

35. JAMES DRUMMOND, 1684.—" This gentleman was the son of Mr James Drummond, minister at Foulis, in Perthshire. Being educate with a view of serving in the Church, he was first ordained to the ministry at Achterarder, and after that was removed to the parsonage of Muthill, where he exercised his pastorall function, till the see of Brechin falling to vaick, by the translation thence of Bishop Cairncross to Glasgow, in the end of the 1684, he was preferred to this see. He was consecrate at the Abbey Church of Holyrood House the 25th December 1684. I had a very good character of Bishop Drummond from severall persons of honor and probity, who had the favor of his acquaintance, and notwithstanding the influence, it was, and might have been presumed, his chief and patron might have had with him with respect to the design of removing and taking away the laws against Popry, yet he was firm and resolved to oppose the design in his station as much as any of his brethren, the bishops, and no man was more stedfast in the Protestant religion than he, and both by his preaching and otherways, he gave ground to believe, he would have been as stanch as any man against the opening a door to let in Popry, in a parliamentary way, if it had come to the test. This piece of justice, I thought, was due to the memory of this good man, having had this account of him from a person of honour, who had access to know the bishop's sentiments of this matter, and was far from having any biass to the order of bishops, if it had not been a piece of justice to the bishop's memory. After the Revolution,

X

Bishop Drummond, being deprived with the rest of his brethren, tooke himself to a life of retirement, and lived mostly in the Countess of Errol's family, where he died in the year 1695, aged sixty-six years." Panmures MS., pages 115, 116. "It is to be said of this prelate, that though he had been promoted by the favor of his chief, the Earl of Perth, then chancellor of the kingdom, yet he always showed himself as averse to Popery as any person in the church, and it is certain there were but very few of the bishops (if any at all) who favored an alteration in religion." Keith, page 169. It appears from the records of the town of Brechin, that Bishop Drummond had not reached that burgh on 19th February 1685, as the council then appointed Alexander Rires to be doctor of the grammar-school, "provided my Lord Bishop, at his coming to the place, doe approve." The bishop is present in council on 25th September, and he preached in the cathedral church on 1st October 1685. On 18th April 1689, the Bishop preached in the Cathedral for the last time. No charters granted by him have been found. It is said he died at Slaines Castle, and was buried at Cruden.

After the Revolution, the deposed bishops continued, during their respective lifetimes, to exercise spiritual jurisdiction over such clergymen as acknowledged them in their several dioceses. But as most of these bishops were old men, it was deemed prudent to add to the number of bishops, by the election of younger men, who were received into the Episcopal college without having any particular diocese assigned to them. Dr Russel, from whom we borrow the account of the post-revolution bishops, tells us that the Rev. John Falconer, formerly one of the ministers of Cairnlice in Fife, was thus consecrated a bishop at Dundee on 28th April 1709. He is described as a man of learning, as well as of business, and of great piety and prudence. "In regard to his discharge of Episcopal offices (says Dr Russel) we find that in the year 1720, immediately after the death of Bishop Rose, (of Edinburgh,) a letter was addressed to him by a great body of the clergy in Angus and Mearns, in which they request him to assume the spiritual government and inspection of them, 'promising to acknowledge him as their proper bishop, and to pay all due and canonical obedience to him as such.' During the lifetime of

Bishop Rose, and at the request of that prelate, he had frequently officiated among them with great approbation. He, therefore, accepted this affectionate call, as he also accepted a similar one at the same time from the clergy in the presbytery of St Andrews where he had constantly resided ; and accordingly, with the consent of his brethren, he acted in these two districts as local bishop as long as he lived. But his useful life was doomed not to be long· He died in 1723." Russel, page 523. In this way then we assume into our list

36. JOHN FALCONER, 1709.—Described in the account of Scotch bishops at Slaines, as " a good and grave man, and very modest, tall, black, and stooping. He dyed at Englishmadie, July 6, 1723, and was buried at Pert."

37. ROBERT NORRIE, 1724.—Innes, preface to R. E. B. page xv.

38. MR JOHN OUCHTERLONIE, 1726.—" After the death of Bishop Rose of Edinburgh, the clergy of Fife, Angus and Mearns, appear to have had Episcopal offices performed amongst them by Bishop John Falconer. This excellent and learned man it is known to the reader died in 1723, between which date and the period of the concordate in 1731, I know not how the duties of a bishop were discharged in those extensive districts. By the articles of agreement just alluded to, it was provided that the diocese of Brechin, together with the Carse of Gowrie, the Presbyteries of Dundee, Arbroath, and Mearns, should be under the inspection of Bishop Ouchterlonie. It was on the 29th November 1726, that Mr Ouchterlonie was consecrated at Edinburgh, by the Bishops Freebairn, Duncan, and Cant, the only three, it is added, who could be prevailed on to do it. The objection to him, so far as can be gathered from the several hints, which are mystically expressed, had a reference to the Erastian notions, which, at that time, disturbed the peace of the Episcopal Church, and this candidate for the mitre appears to have relied more on his interest at the Court of St Germains than on the esteem of his brethren, or the good opinion of his superiors. Bishop Ouchterlonie died in the year 1742." Russel, pages 543, 544.

39. Mr JAMES RAIT, 1742.—" The clergy of Brechin lost no time in electing a successor to the ordinary, with whom the concordate had supplied them. They made choice of Mr Rait,

presbyter in Dundee, a highly-respected character, who was, on
the 4th of October 1742, elevated to the episcopate by the hands
of Bishops Rattray, Keith, and White, and forthwith collated to
the superintendency of Brechin.   Of this bishop, a learned corre-
spondent says, 'I know nothing more than that he possessed
strong good sense, had a very dignified manner when performing
his episcopal offices, and that he was a celebrated preacher, preaching without notes till he became a very old man.   His charges to
the youth whom he confirmed he delivered without notes and
without hesitation, long after he was eighty years of age.'   The
reader may not be displeased to peruse the following testimonials in
favour of Mr Rait, addressed, as was the practice of that period to
the Lord Bishop of Edinburgh.   'These are to testify that Mr James
Rait, son of Mr William Rait, minister of Monikie, being, by your
lordship's order, admitted to pass the preparatory trials before such
ministers in Dundee and the neighbourhood, as you appointed, in
order to his entering into the ministry, hath done the same to our
very great satisfaction, and therefore we do, with the more con-
fidence and earnestness, recommend him to your lordship to obtain
your lordship's licence for preaching, or to get him into the orders
of a deacon, as your lordship judges fit.   In witness whereof these
presents are written by our joint allowance, and ordered to be
signed by moderator and clerk, ad hunc effectum, at Dundee, the
twentieth and first day of October, 1712 years, (Signed) Robert
Norie, preses ; James Goldman, clerk.'   The venerable bishop died
in the year 1777," Russel, pages 544, 545.   The Society of Antiquaries possess the matrix of the seal of this bishop, inscribed—
" Sigillum Iacobi Rait Episcopi Brechinensis, Meliora Spero."

40.   Mr GEORGE INNES, 1778.—" This bishop was minister of a
chapel in Aberdeen, and was consecrated at Alloa, on the 13th
of August 1778, by Bishop Falconer, Bishop Rose, and Bishop
Petrie.   He was collated at .the same time to the superintendence
of the district of Brechin, but did not live long to discharge the
duties of it.   He died on the 18th of May 1781, after which date
the diocese remained some years vacant." Russel, page 545.   The
Society of Antiquaries are also possessed of the matrix of the
seal of Bishop Innes, bearing for its legend simply, " Sigillum
Georgii Episcopi Brechinensis."

41.   Dr WILLIAM ABERNETHY DRUMMOND, 1787.—" It has

been already mentioned that this distinguished man was elevated to the episcopate on the 26th of September 1787 ; that he was consecrated as Bishop of Brechin, but that almost immediately afterwards he was elected to the see of Edinburgh, where he had his pastoral charge, and that he continued to preside over the clergy of that district, till the year 1805. He was descended from the family of Abernethy of Saltoun, in the shire of Banff, and it was only upon his marriage with the heiress of Hawthornden, in the county of Mid-Lothian, that he assumed the name of Drummond. He wrote many small tracts, and was a good deal engaged in theological controversy, both with Protestants and Roman Catholics, but his intemperate manner defeated, in most cases, the benevolence of his intentions, and only irritated those whom he had wished to convince. He died on the 27th of August 1809." Russel, page 545.

42. Mr JOHN STRACHAN, 1788.—" This most respectable clergyman was sprung from the family of Strachan of Thorntoun, in the county of Kincardine, now represented by his kinsman, the gallant Admiral Sir Richard Strachan. He was consecrated at Peterhead on the same day with Dr A. Drummond, to whom, indeed, he was at that period appointed coadjutor, but the latter being, within a few months afterwards, elected by the clergy of Edinburgh, Bishop Strachan was preferred to the undivided charge of the diocese of Brechin. He lived to a very advanced age, having, however, survived for some time the powers of his mind as well as of his body, and died on the 28th of January 1810, universally beloved and regretted." Russel, pages 545, 546.

43. Dr GEORGE GLEIG, 1810.—" Seldom can it fall to the lot of a communion so small and so poor as the Episcopal Church in Scotland to enjoy the credit attached to so great a name as that of Bishop Gleig. His reputation as a scholar and philosopher is so well established by his numerous works that it is as unnecessary as it would be impertinent in me to attempt an eulogium, of which he would be the first to call in question the propriety. Having long discharged with much ability the various duties of a presbyter, he was, in the autumn of 1808, elected by the clergy of Brechin, as coadjutor to their aged bishop, and consecrated at Aberdeen, on the 30th of October the same year by Bishop Skinner, Bishop Jolly, and Bishop Torry. On the death of Bishop

Strachan, in 1810, he was preferred to the sole charge of the diocese ; and in 1816, upon the demise of Bishop Skinner, he was chosen by his brethren to fill the office of Primus, in virtue of which he presides in all the meetings of the Episcopal College." Russel, page 546.

44. DAVID MOIR, A.M., 1837.—Bishop Gleig having become unable, through the infirmities of age, to exercise his episcopal duties, being in his 85th year, the Rev. David Moir, minister of St Andrew's chapel in Brechin was elected by the clergy as his coadjutor and successor, and consecrated and collated to the superintendence of the diocese, by Bishops Walker, Skinner, and Low, at Edinburgh, on the 8th of October 1837. In August 1839, Washington College, Hartford, Connecticut, U.S., conferred the degree of Doctor of Divinity on Bishop Moir, who accepted the title, and valued it "as a token of friendly recognition and intercommunion between the Scottish Episcopal Church, and her daughter Church in America." Bishop Gleig survived till 9th March 1840, when the whole charge of the diocese devolved on Dr Moir. These duties he discharged faithfully for seven years afterwards. Bishop Moir died on 21st August 1847, as a handsome monument erected to his memory by the congregation in St Andrew's chapel bears. Dr Moir was much beloved in his congregation as a pious, zealous minister, and much esteemed in his diocese as a learned man and sound theologian.

45. ALEXANDER PENROSE FORBES, D.C.L., was consecrated on the Feast of St Simon and St Jude, 28th October 1847, by the Right Reverend William Skinner, Bishop of Aberdeen, Michael Russel, Bishop of Glasgow, and Charles Terrot, Bishop of Edinburgh. Quem Deus Conservat.

No. IV.

EXTRACTS FROM THE ACCOUNTS OF WALTER JAMESON, CHURCH MASTER OF BRECHIN, 1684. Language modernised.

Imprimis, I charge myself with one hundred merks, left over when the shoemakers gave in the money to the minister and me a little after Martinmas '83, viz., 300 merks Scots, of which there was lent to John Lowson, of Balunie, and to Alexander Watt in Brechin, his cautioner, 200 merks; the other 100 merks was ordered by the minister to be keeped for the *repairing* of the little steeple-head, and other work in the kirk, in regard I was exhausted in my last accompt, which it will clear itself according to my discharge.

Disbursements concerning the Steeple-Head, on the 16*th of May* '84.

Item, to Bailie James Allan for seventeen fathoms of towes, at 2s. 6d. fathom, is, . . .	£2	2	6
Item, to John Shirras for his workmanship, and drink money to his man, ...	31	0	0
Item, for leading the scaffolding to and again from James Moug's house, with two great stones to the steeple-head, is, ...	1	2	10
Item, for peats for melting of lead to the steeple-head,	0	6	8
Item, to James Young for five load of sand to the steeple-head, ...	0	6	8
Item, to David Brand for his help at the work at the steeple-head, ...	2	16	10
Item, to James Kinnear for his (help) to the work foresaid, ...	3	6	8
Item, at the whole occasion for meat and drink to the work, ...	6	16	10
Item, to James Low, smith, for the whole iron work to the steeple-head, ...	8	12	0
	£56	11	0

James Moug refers his payment for his workmanship done at the steeple-head, till he receives his answer from the session, for the room for ane desk begging (erecting a pew) under the stool of repentance, that was desired by him.

[In the margin of the Record there is this marking:]—Remember this is the last to the steeple-head by James Moug.

Extracts from Discharge at Martinmas 1683.

Item, to George Skinner and Thomas Langlands, by
order from the session, on the 5th July '83, 1 boll
2 firlots of oatmeal, at six lib the boll, is, . £9 0 0
Item, to John Forrest for the *Broad* in the session-
house, ... 13 6 8

Note.—Suppose that in addition to the disbursements
above given, of £56 11 0
James Moug's account, for which the favour of a pew
was expected, had been equal to John Shirras, or a
trifle more, say 31 9 0

Then we have in all, . . £88 0 0

Or equal to 14⅔ bolls of meal, at £6 the boll, the price as shown
above in 1683; so after allowing for scaffolding and iron work,
the mason work of the repairs had not extended much above the
" two great stones " brought from James Moug's house.

No. V.—ABSTRACT OF THE POPULATION OF THE PARISH OF BRECHIN, AS RETURNED BY MR DAVID PRAIN, 7TH JUNE 1841.

	Families.	Houses.			Males.	Females.	TOTAL.
		Inhabited.	Uninhabited.	Building.			
Royalty, . . .	1022	584	14	4	1757	2190	3947
Parliamentary beyond Royalty, .	478	264	5		914	1041	1955
Total Parliamentary, .	1500	848	19	4	2671	3231	5902
			871				
Country, . . .	329	315	11		832	821	1653
			326				
Totals, . . .	1829	1163	30	4	3503	4052	7555
			1197				

ABSTRACTS OF THE POPULATION OF THE CITY AND BURGH OF BRECHIN FOR 1851 AND 1861.

	WITHIN THE ROYALTY.							WITHIN THE PARLIAMENTARY BOUNDS.							TOTALS.						
	Houses.				Males.	Females.	Total.	Houses.				Males.	Females.	Total.	Houses.				Males.	Females.	Total.
	Occupiers.	Inhabited.	Uninhabited.	Building.				Occupiers.	Inhabited.	Uninhabited.	Building.				Occupiers.	Inhabited.	Uninhabited.	Building.			
31st March 1851, .	1138	525	6	4	2009	2506	4515	525	238	1		993	1130	2123	1663	763	7	4	3002	3636	6638
1861, .	1267	517	8	3	2119	2602	4721	603	253	3	8	1106	1353	2459	1870	760	11	11	3225	3955	7180
School Children, .							737							380							1117
Windowed Rooms, .	2882							1123							4005						

No. VI.

INVENTORY OF ARTICLES FOUND IN THE ROUND TOWER OF BRECHIN.

6th April 1842.—A wooden case for a trump or Jew's-harp; an iron staple ; eight buttons; a bodle, (old Scotch coin.) *7th,* A button, (Forfarshire volunteers;) fragment of a small brass fastener. *8th,* A parcel of " buckie," or periwinkle, shells ; a parcel of oyster shells ; half of a mussel shell ; small shell ; seven old nails, iron ; a piece of horn perforated ; a piece of limestone ; two teeth of animals ; four pieces of painted glass ; piece of bell metal ; four fragments of an earthenware vessel. *9th,* Oyster shells ; small shell ; bit of brownish yellow flint ; two bits of sheet lead ; bit of bell metal; bit of painted glass; two bits of verdigris ; one animal tooth ; seven old iron nails ; piece of limestone ; three fragments of an earthenware vessel. *11th,* Twelve fragments of earthenware vessels, one of them having a side ear or handle ; an old iron key; and four other pieces of iron articles, all much rusted. *12th,* Eighty fragments of earthenware vessels ; fragments of charred wood ; a leather cord ; some old iron nails ; three pieces of stained glass ; four pieces plain glass ; two pieces copper ; small circular stone ; small bit of metal ; an oval ring, apparently copper.

No. VII.
LETTER BY MR BLACK TO WILLIAM HACKETT, ESQ., MIDDLETON, COUNTY CORK, IRELAND.

BRECHIN, *13th April,* 1842.

DEAR SIR,—The obstacles alluded to in my last letter having all been removed, Mr M'Cosh and I proceeded on this day week, Wednesday, 6th April, to excavate the interior of the Round Tower of Brechin. Sir James Carnegie, Baronet, of Southesque, our principal heritor, taking an active interest in our proceedings, and Patrick Chalmers, Esquire, of Aldbar, having volunteered in the most handsome manner to pay all expenses, although, unfortunately, from his bad state of health, he is unable to witness our proceedings, and has, in consequence of continued indisposition, been obliged to resign the seat he held in Parliament for this district of burghs, a circumstance which has thrown this quarter into a fever of politics, for it will be no easy matter to find a man possessed of all Mr Chalmers's qualifications to fill his room.

The round tower of Brechin, you will recollect, has a doorway on the west side, the sill of which is six feet seven inches from the ground, and this door-way being filled up with stonework, our first proceeding was to open it. I went down on Wednesday morning by six o'clock (I wish to be minute) accompanied by David Black, carpenter in Brechin, and James Jolly, mason in Brechin, and these tradesmen, in my presence, carefully removed the stones which blocked up the doorway, leaving the arch free and uninjured, and displaying a handsome entrance into the tower. A set of wooden steps were then fitted to give access by the door, while precautions were adopted for shutting up the tower when the workmen were not there, so as to prevent any person introducing *modern antiques* for our annoyance. After removing some old wood and other lumber, recently placed there by the church officers, James Jolly was left alone, as the circle of the tower did not give scope for more workmen. He then proceeded to dig amongst the loose earth, and has been so employed till to-day, being from time to time visited by Mr M'Cosh and me. Each shovelful as dug up was carefully sifted and thrown into a heap; this sifted earth, when accumulated into a small heap was then thrown out at the door of the tower and down the wooden steps alluded to; after this the earth was put, by a spadeful at a time, into a barrow, and wheeled to a corner of the churchyard. Here again, the earth was thrown by a shovel into a cart, and then driven away. By this repeated *handling* I think it next to impossible that anything of the least consequence could have escaped observation. I directed James Jolly to keep a regular journal of his proceedings, and each evening, when he gave up work, he brought it to the British Linen Company's bank office, and left with the accountant, Mr Robert Lindsay, the articles found each day, and Mr Lindsay again labelled and marked the articles so found. David Black, the carpenter, is Mr M'Cosh's tradesman, a master workman, and an individual of undoubted character. James Jolly is a journeyman mason, a very intelligent man, and a person upon whose integrity ample reliance can be placed; and Mr Lindsay, with whom I have been acquainted through life, and who has now been with me for thirteen years continuously, is a man of the greatest probity. I am fully satisfied, therefore, that we have got a careful and correct account of everything found in the tower.

James Jolly has now dug seven feet below the door-sill, that is, he is about five inches below the external ground line and hewn basement or plinth, and has come to where the hewn work ceases, and rude, undressed stones form the building of the tower. At this depth we stop until we hear from you. We have not reached the virgin rock on which the tower is built, but we have now reached the clay, and till or sand rock, which appears to have been disturbed, as if it were what had been dug out for the foundation, and thrown into the centre of the tower. Until this depth we have dug through a fine mould, composed of decayed wood, and other vegetable matter, mixed up with a little animal matter. We found a quantity of peats, and a good deal of dross of peats, or refuse of moss ; and we also found great varieties of bones, principally sheep bones, especially jaw-bones of sheep, some bones of oxen, and a few human bones, these last being vertebræ pieces of skulls, toes, and bits of jawbones. These bones were found at all depths, but we found no bones of any size. We have likewise got a quantity of slates, a hewn stone for the top of a lancet-shaped arch ; part of the sill of a window, with the base of a mullion traced on it ; some basement stones, and others of coarser workmanship. Oyster shells, buckies, or sea shells, old nails, buttons, bits of copperas, two small lumps of bell metal, and three little bits of stained glass have also been found at different depths, and yesterday we found the remains of a key. But what will most please your pagan friends is the fact that since we were down about three feet, we have each day found various pieces of *urns* or jars. None of the pieces, although put together form a complete urn, but I think amongst the pieces I can trace out three or four distinct vessels. One appears to have been of *glazed* earthenware, and to have had little handles, as thus (*figured in the letter*), while round the inner ledge there are small round indentations; about a third of this vessel remains as marked by the dotted lines. Other two vessels are of clay, regularly baked apparently, but not glazed, and one is slightly ornamented round the edge, thus (*figured in the letter*), the indentations being evidently made by alternately pressing the thumb and forefinger horizontal, and the thumb perpendicular in the wet clay.

Now, how came all these things there? I am afraid you will set me down, not for a pagan, but for a veritable heathen, when I say that my opinion is, the slates, glass, wood, and iron, had been tossed in, at what in Scotland is called the Reformation, when our Scotch apostle, John Knox, drove your Roman apostles from what he termed their rookeries; that the bones and great part of the animal and vegetable matter had been carried to the top of the tower by the rooks and jackdaws (kaes of Scotland) for building their nests, and feeding their young, and had tumbled from thence to the bottom of the tower; that the peats and the rest of the stuff had been thrown at various times into the bottom of the tower as a general receptacle for all refuse; and that the fragments of urns or jars are just the remains of culinary articles belonging to the different kirk-officers.

After this declaration, can I expect to hear from you again, advising me what further we ought to do in regard to our round tower, which, in my eyes, remains as great a mystery as ever.

The steeple of the church of Montrose was rebuilt some eight years ago, on the site of a steeple which had existed beyond the memory of man. It was thought necessary to dig the foundation of the new tower deeper than the old had been founded, and in the course of this excavation, various skeletons were found buried amongst sand and gravel—the subsoil on which the town of Montrose stands. The fact of bodies being buried below towers and steeples then will scarce prove the erections to be either Christian or pagan.

The tracings which you sent of Cloyne Tower, represent very closely the style of building of the round tower of Brechin, especially where two or more horizontal stones are connected by a smaller perpendicular one, thus (*figured in letter*), and also where one is laid with a little toe, or thinner part of it projecting, as it were beyond itself, over another stone, as sketched above. In Brechin, too, as at Cloyne, we found it impossible to drive a nail into the joints of the doorway, while into some parts of the general masonry I have thrust my cane with ease for several inches. Sir William Gell, you remark, gives drawings of a similar mode of building in the vicinity of Rome, but is this not just a mode common to all nations in their rude state, who put up as large stones as they can find or move with ease, and bring them together by means of smaller pieces?

I was prepared to have made some remarks on Mr Windele's letters to you, but fear I have already brought sufficiency of round towers down on my head. I postpone saying anything on this subject till I see Mr Windele's book, which you are so kind as to promise me.—Believe me, dear sir, yours very truly,

D. D. BLACK.

P.S.—I have, of course, carefully preserved the urns and other relics found.

No. VIII.

LIST OF THE MAGISTRATES AND TOWN COUNCIL OF BRECHIN, FROM APRIL 1672 TO AUGUST 1864, INCLUSIVE.

In the following List from 1673 to 1715, there are letters affixed to the names of the Bailies, (P.) denoting that the Bailie was nominated by the Earl of Panmure; (E.) nominated by Mr James Erskine, as come in place of Lord Panmure; (G.) by Lord Grange, formerly Mr James Erskine; (B.) nominated by the Bishop of Brechin; and (T.) implying Town's Bailie, or the Bailie chosen by the Town Council.

1672.
George Steele, David Donaldson, yr., and David Liddell, bailies.
John Liddell, dean of guild.
David Donaldson, elder.
John Jamieson.
Laurence Skinner.
Andrew Allan.
John Fenton.
James Allan,

James Henderson.
John Skinner.
John Low.

1673.

John Liddell, (P.,) David Donaldson, yr., (B.,) and David Liddell, (T.,) bailies.
Andrew Allan, dean of guild.
John Fenton, treasurer.
James Allan, hospital master.
Geo. Steele.
D. Donaldson, elder.
Laurence Skinner.
John Jamieson.
James Henderson.
John Skinner.
John Low.

1674.

George Steele, (T.,) John Liddell, (P.,) and David Liddell, (B.,) bailies.
Dd. Donaldson, yr., dean of guild.
James Henderson, treasurer.
James Allan, hospital master.
David Donaldson, elder.
John Jamieson.
Laurence Skinner.
Andrew Allan.
John Fenton.
John Skinner.
John Low.

1675.

Dd. Donaldson, yr., (B.,) David Liddell, (T.,) and James Allan, (P.,) bailies.
Andrew Allan, dean of guild.
James Henderson, treasurer.
John Fenton, hospital master.
George Steele.
John Liddell.
John Low.
Dd. Donaldson, elder.
James Low.
John Skinner.
John Allan.

23d December.

Alexander Young, councillor, *vice* bailie John Liddell, deceased.

1676.

James Allan, (B.,) Laurence Skinner, (P.,) and Andrew Allan, (T.,) bailies.
Dd. Donaldson, yr., dean of guild.
John Skinner, treasurer.
John Fenton, hospital master.
David Liddell.
David Donaldson, elder.
John Allan.
Geo. Steele.
Alexander Young.
James Henderson.
John Baillie.

1677.

James Allan, (P.,) Laurence Skinner, (B.,) and Andrew Allan, (T.,) bailies.
Dd. Donaldson, yr., dean of guild.
Alexander Young, treasurer.
John Skinner, hospital master.
David Liddell.
John Fenton.
David Donaldson, elder.
George Steele.
James Low.
James Henderson.
James Cowie.

1678.

*George, bishop of Brechin.
James Allan, (B.,) Andrew Allan, (T.,) and John Skinner, (P.,) bailies.
Dd. Donaldson, yr., dean of guild,
James Cowie, treasurer.
David Stewart, hospital master.
Laurence Skinner.
David Donaldson, elder.
J. Jamieson.

---

* The Bishop, George Haliburton, is mentioned as sitting in council at this time, and frequently afterwards.

David Liddell.
James Henderson.
Alexander Young.
James Low.

1679.

Ja. Allan, (P.,) Lau. Skinner, (T.,)
and John Skinner, (B.,) bailies.
David Liddell, dean of guild.
James Cowie, treasurer.
David Stewart, hospital master.
Andrew Allan.
David Donaldson, yr.
J. Jamieson.
David Donaldson, elder.
James Henderson.
Alexander Young.
James Low.
        8th January, 1680.
John Fenton, councillor, *vice* Alexander Young, deceased.

1680.

John Jamieson, (P.,) Dd. Donaldson, yr., (B.,) and John Skinner,(T.,) bailies.
David Liddell, dean of guild.
James Cowie, treasurer.
David Stewart, hospital master.
James Allan.
James Henderson.
Andrew Allan.
John Fenton.
Laurence Skinner.
David Donaldson, elder.
John Gibson.
        30th June, 1681.
David Liddell, appointed to officiate as bailie in place of John Skinner, who had left Brechin.

1681.

John Jamieson, (P.,) D. Donaldson, yr., (B.,) and David Liddell, (T.,) bailies.
James Allan, dean of guild.
Francis Molison, treasurer.
David Stewart, hospital master.

Andrew Allan.
James Cowie.
James Henderson.
Laurence Skinner.
John Fenton.
David Donaldson, elder.
John Gibson.

1682.

Robert, bishop of Brechin.
John Jamieson, (P.,) Dd. Donaldson, yr., (B.,) and David Liddell, (T.,) bailies.
James Allan, dean of guild.
Alexander Dall, treasurer.
David Stewart, hospital master.
Francis Molison.
Andrew Fairweather.
John Fenton.
Laurence Skinner.
Jas. Henderson.
D. Donaldson, elder.
John Gibson.

1683.

Robert, bishop of Brechin, (subscribing provost of Brechin.)
J. Jamieson, (P.,) D. Donaldson, yr., (B.,) D. Liddell, (T.,) bailies.
James Allan, dean of guild.
Alexander Dall, treasurer.
John Hendry, hospital master.
David Stewart.
Francis Molison.
John Fenton.
Laurence Skinner.
James Henderson.
D. Donaldson, elder.
John Gibson.
        26th September 1684.
David Gray, merchant, John Low, smith, councillors, *vice* Bailie Donaldson, deceased, and John Gibson, removed.

1684.

Alexander, bishop of Brechin, (Præfectus.)

D. Liddell, (P.,) Laurence Skinner, (T.,) and Francis Molison, (B.,) bailies.
James Allan, dean of guild.
Alexander Dall, treasurer.
John Hendry, hospital master.
John Jamieson.
David Gray.
James Cowie.
David Stewart.
James Henderson.
D. Donaldson.
John Low.

1685.
James, bishop of Brechin.
James Allan, (B.,) Laurence Skinner, (T.,) and James Cowie, (P.,) bailies.
Francis Molison, dean of guild.
David Gray, treasurer.
John Hendry, hospital master.
David Liddell.
Alex. Dall.
David Stewart.
Alex. Young.
James Henderson.
Alexander Jamieson.*
John Low.

1686, 1687, and 1688.
Elections suspended by order of King and Privy Council, and former magistrates and council continued in their offices.

1689.
David Liddell, (T.,) and James Cowie, (P.,) bailies.
Francis Molison, dean of guild.
Alexander Young, treasurer.
Alex. Jamieson, hospital master.
Laurence Skinner.
William Baillie.
James Henderson.

* See 7th August 1686, *et seq.*, sometimes called "Jamie."

John Milne.
David Stewart.
David Young.
David Gray.
Andrew Knox.

1690.
Francis Molison, (P.,) and Alex. Young, (T.,) bailies.
David Liddell, dean of guild.
William Baillie, treasurer.
Alex. Jamieson, hospital master.
James Cowie.
Andrew Knox.
John Fenton.
James Low.
John Milne.
Alex. Fairweather, yr.
David Young.
James Thom.

1691.
Francis Molison, (P.,) and Alex. Young, (T.,) bailies.
David Liddell, dean of guild.
Alexander Jamieson, treasurer.
John Milne, hospital master.
William Baillie.
Andrew Knox.
James Cowie.
James Low.
John Fenton.
Alexander Fairweather.
David Young.
James Thom.
30th May 1692.
David Young, hospital master, *vice* John Milne, deceased.

1692.
Francis Molison, (P.,) and Alex. Young, (T.,) bailies.
David Liddell, dean of guild.
Alexander Jamieson, treasurer.
William Baillie, hospital master.
James Cowie.
Andrew Knox.
David Gray.

Y

James Low.
J. Sandieson.
A. Fairweather.
David Young.
James Thom.

1693.
Francis Molison, (P.,) and Alex.
Young, (T.,) bailies.
David Gray, dean of guild.
Alexander Jamieson, treasurer.
William Baillie, hospital master.
David Liddell.
Andrew Knox.
James Cowie.
James Low.
J. Sandieson.
A. Fairweather.
David Young.
James Thom.

1694.
James Cowie, (P.,) and William
Baillie, (T.,) bailies.
Alexander Young, dean of guild.
David Young, treasurer.
A. Fairweather, hospital master.
Francis Molison.
J. Sandieson.
David Gray.
Andrew Knox.
A. Jamieson.
James Low.
David Liddell.
James Thom.

1695.
Alexander Young, (T.,) and Wm.
Baillie, (P.,) bailies.
David Liddell, dean of guild.
David Young, treasurer.
A. Fairweather, hospital master.
J. Cowie.
J. Sandieson.
J. Donaldson.
John Wood.
D. Gray.
James Low.

John Spence.
James Thom.

1696.
Alexander Young, provost.
William Baillie, (P.,) and James
Cowie, (T.,) bailies.
David Gray, dean of guild.
James Thom, treasurer.
A. Fairweather, hospital master.
David Liddell.
David Young.
James Spence.
J. Donaldson.
John Wood.
John Spence.
James Low.

1697.
Alexander Young, provost.
David Liddell, (P.,) and David
Gray, (T.,) bailies.
James Cowie, dean of guild.
James Thom, treasurer.
A. Fairweather, hospital master.
William Baillie.
David Young.
Alex. Wilson.
John Doig.
James Millar.
David Robertson.
John Wood.

1698.
Alexander Young, provost.
David Gray and J. Doig, bailies.
James Cowie, dean of guild.
James Thom, treasurer.
A. Fairweather, hospital master.
David Liddell.
A. Jamieson, yr.
A. Wilson.
David Young.
James Millar.
D. Robertson.
John Wood.
NOTE.—In list of councillors
elected, William Baillie's name

is inserted by mistake for that of Alexander Wilson.

1699.
Alexander Young, provost.
Alex. Fairweather and D. Young, bailies.
William Baillie, dean of guild.
David Robertson, treasurer.
James Thom, hospital master.
John Knox, convener.
D. Gray.
James Millar.
J. Cowie.
A. Jamieson, yr.
A. Wilson.
Alex. Cobb.

1700.
John Doig, provost.
William Baillie, (P.,) and A. Fairweather, (T.,) bailies.
James Thom, dean of guild.
David Robertson, treasurer.
James Spence, hospital master.
David Gray.
Alex. Young.
A. Jamieson, yr.
Alex. Jamieson.
J. Knox, deacon convener.
Alex. Wilson.
David Myles.

1701.
John Doig, provost.
David Gray, (P.,) and A. Fairweather, (T.,) bailies.
William Baillie, dean of guild.
David Robertson, treasurer.
James Spence, hospital master.
John Donaldson, yr.
John Spence.
A. Jamieson, yr.
A. Jamieson.
J. Knox, deacon convener.
A. Wilson.
David Myles.

1702.
David Gray, provost.
William Baillie, (P.,) and Alex. Fairweather, (T.,) bailies.
Francis Molison, dean of guild.
Alexander Wilson, treasurer.
James Spence, hospital master.
John Jamieson.
A. Jamieson, (formerly yr.)
J. Liddell.
John Spence.
John Knox.
John Donaldson.
David Myles.

1703.
David Gray, provost.
A. Fairweather, (P.,) and James Spence, (T.,) bailies.
Francis Molison, dean of guild.
Alexander Wilson, treasurer.
John Spence, hospital master.
James Donaldson.
John Jamieson,
John Liddell.
A. Jamieson.
John Knox.
John Donaldson.
David Myles.

1704.
David Gray, provost.
Francis Molison, (P.,) and James Spence, (T.,) bailies.
A. Fairweather, dean of guild.
Alexander Wilson, treasurer.
John Spence, hospital master.
James Donaldson.
John Jamieson.
John Liddell.
Alex. Jamieson.
John Knox.
John Donaldson.
David Myles.

1705.
Francis Molison, (P.,) and James Spence, (T.,) bailies.

A. Fairweather, dean of guild.
James Donaldson, treasurer.
John Spence, hospital master.
David Gray.
Alexander Wilson.
John Jamieson.
John Liddell.
Alex. Jamieson.
John Knox.
John Donaldson.
David Myles.

1706.
Alexander Young, provost.
David Young, (T.,) and David
Robertson, (E.,) bailies.
James Cowie, dean of guild.
Andrew Doig, treasurer.
John Spence, hospital master.
David Gray.
John Doig.
David Myles.
A. Jamieson.
John Liddell.
John Knox.
William Clark.

1707.
Alexander Young, provost.
James Cowie, (G.,) and D. Young,
(T.,) bailies.
James Spence, dean of guild.
Andrew Doig, treasurer.
John Liddell, hospital master.
David Robertson.
David Gray.
John Knox, deacon convener.
John Doig.
David Myles.
A. Jamieson.
William Clark.
NOTE.—Jas. Cowie and David
Gray did not qualify by tak-
ing oath of abjuration.

1708.
Alexander Young, provost.

David Young, (G.,) and James
Spence, (T.,) bailies.
William Clark, dean of guild.
Robert Whyte, treasurer.
John Liddell, hospital master.
Wm. Guthrie.
A. Jamieson.
Andrew Doig.
David Robertson.
John Knox.
John Doig.
David Myles.

1709.
John Doig, provost.
James Spence, (T.,) and Andrew
Doig, (G.,) bailies.
William Clark, dean of guild.
Robert Whyte, treasurer.
John Liddell, hospital master.
Alexander Young.
David Young.
A. Jamieson.
William Guthrie.
John Knox.
David Robertson.
David Myles.

1710.
John Doig, provost.
Andrew Doig, (T.,) and William
Clark, (G.,) bailies.
James Spence, dean of guild.
Robert Whyte, treasurer.
Wm. Guthrie, hospital master.
David Young.
David Robertson.
David Myles.
A. Jamieson.
John Smith, hammerman.
John Knox.
David Windrem.

1711.
John Doig, provost.
Andrew Doig, (G.,) and William
Clark, (T.,) bailies.
James Spence, dean of guild.

John Knox, treasurer.
Wm. Guthrie, hospital master.
Robert Whyte.
James Durie.
David Myles.
D. Robertson.
John Smith.
Alex. Jamieson.
David Windrem.

1712.

John Doig, provost.
James Spence, (T.,) and Andrew
Doig, (G.,) bailies.
William Clark, dean of guild.
John Knox, treasurer.
Wm. Guthrie, hospital master.
Robert Whyte.
James Durie.
David Myles.
D. Robertson.
John Smith.
Alex. Jamieson.
David Windrem.

1713, same as 1712.

1714.

John Doig, provost.
James Spence, (T.,) and Andrew
Doig, (G.,) bailies.
William Clark, dean of guild.
John Knox, treasurer.
Wm. Guthrie, hospital master.
Robert Whyte.
James Durie.
James Smith.
D. Robertson.
John Smith.
Alexander Jamieson.
David Windrem.

1715.

James Spence, (P.,) and William
Clark, (T.,) bailies.
David Young, dean of guild.
John Knox, treasurer.
Wm. Guthrie, hospital master.

David Windrem.
Robert Allardice.
Alex. Jamieson.
John Liddell.
James Carnegy.
James M'Kenzie, yr.
John Ouchterlony.
Robert Adam.

1716.

John Doig, provost.
Andrew Doig and Robert Whyte,
bailies.
David Robertson, dean of guild.
James Durie, treasurer.
Wm. Shepherd, hospital master.
Wm. Gardener, yr.
James Cowie.
James Smith.
James Doig.
William Knox.
John Smith.
Henry Cowie.

1717, same as 1716.

1718.

John Doig, provost.
Andrew Doig and James Cowie,
bailies.
James Doig, dean of guild.
James Durie, treasurer.
Wm. Shepherd, hospital master.
Robt. Webster.
Wm. Gardener, elder.
Wm. Gardener, yr.
John Smith.
William Knox.
James Smith.
Henry Cowie.

1719.

John Doig, provost.
Andrew Doig and James Cowie,
bailies.
James Doig, dean of guild.
James Durie, treasurer.
Wm. Shepherd, hospital master.

Wm. Gardener, elder.
Robert Webster.
James Smith.
William Gardener, yr.
A. Baillie.
John Smith.
Henry Cowie.

1720.

John Doig, provost.
Andrew Doig and James Cowie,
bailies.
James Doig, dean of guild.
James Durie, treasurer.
Robert Webster, hospital master.
Alexander Moug.
David Gray.
James Smith.
W. Gardener, yr.
Alexander Baillie.
John Smith.
David Doig.

1721.

John Doig, provost.
Andrew Doig and John Knox,
bailies.
David Doig, dean of guild.
James Durie, treasurer.
Robert Webster, hospital master
James Doig.
Alexander Moug.
John Smith.
David Gray.
James Smith.
W. Gardener, yr.
Alexander Baillie.

1722.

John Doig, provost.
Andrew Doig and John Knox,
bailies.
David Doig, dean of guild.
James Durie, treasurer.
Alex. Moug, hospital master.
John Lyon.
James Doig.
John Smith.

David Gray.
James Smith.
W. Gardener, yr.
Alex. Baillie.

1723.

John Doig, provost.
Andrew Doig and David Doig,
bailies.
Alexander Moug, dean of guild.
James Durie, treasurer.
David Gray, hospital master.
John Knox.
John Lyon.
John Smith.
Henry Cowie.
James Smith.
W. Gardener, yr.
Alexander Baillie.

4th May 1724.

David Gray, H.M., appointed to
uplift town's rents, *vice* Jas.
Durie, treasurer, deceased.

1724.

John Doig, provost.
Andrew Doig and David Doig,
bailies.
Alex. Moug, dean of guild.
David Gray, treasurer.
Edward Leslie, hospital master.
Alexander Grim.
John Lyon.
John Smith.
Henry Cowie.
James Smith.
W. Gardener.
Alexander Baillie.

1725, same as 1724.

1726.

Robert Whyte, provost.
James Cowie and David Windrem,
bailies.
Alexander Moug, dean of guild.
Robert Allardice, treasurer.

John Lyon, hospital master.
John Knox.
Alexander Baillie.
Alexander Grim.
Edward Leslie.
James Smith.
Henry Cowie.
James Shiress.

1727.

Robert Whyte, provost.
James Cowie and David Windrem, bailies.
Alex. Baillie, dean of guild.
Robert Allardice, treasurer.
John Lyon, hospital master.
John Knox.
Charles Gordon.
Robert Adam.
John Duncan.
James Smith.
William Shepherd.
James Shiress.

1728.

John Knox, provost.
Robert Allardice and David Windrem, bailies.
Alex. Baillie, dean of guild.
Charles Gordon, treasurer.
John Lyon, hospital master.
John Windram.
Robert Whyte.
Robert Adam.
John Duncan.
James Smith.
John Molison.
John Adamson.

1729.

John Knox, provost.
Robert Allardice and Charles Gordon, bailies.
Alexander Baillie, dean of guild.
John Molison, treasurer.
John Lyon, hospital master.
James Knox.
John Liddell.

Robert Adam.
David Mather.
James Smith.
Thomas Hill.
John Adamson.

1730.

John Knox, provost.
Robert Allardice and Charles Gordon, bailies.
Alexander Baillie, dean of guild.
John Molison, treasurer.
John Lyon, hospital master.
James Knox.
John Liddell.
Robert Adam.
David Mather.
James Smith.
Thomas Hill.
George Davidson.

1731.

John Knox, provost.
John Molison and Charles Gordon, bailies.
Alexander Baillie, dean of guild.
James Knox, treasurer.
James Smith, hospital master.
Robert Allardice.
John Lyon.
Thomas Hill.
John Liddell.
Robert Adam.
David Mather.
George Davidson.

1732.

John Knox, provost.
John Molison and Charles Gordon, bailies.
Edward Leslie, dean of guild.
James Knox, treasurer.
David Mather, hospital master.
David Doig.
James Carnegy.
Thomas Hill.
John Low.
Robert Adam.

John Liddell.
G. Davidson.

1733.
David Doig, provost.
John Molison and Edward Leslie, bailies.
David Mather, dean of guild.
James Knox, treasurer.
John Low, hospital master.
John Knox.
David Young.
Thomas Hill.
James Carnegy.
Robert Adam.
Patrick Rennald.
George Davidson.

1734.
David Doig, provost.
John Molison and Edward Leslie, bailies.
David Mather, dean of guild.
James Knox, treasurer.
John Low, hospital master.
John Knox.
David Young.
Thomas Hill.
Alexander Grim.
Robert Adam.
Patrick Rennald.
George Davidson.

1735.
David Doig, provost.
John Molison and Edward Leslie, bailies.
David Mather, dean of guild.
James Knox, treasurer.
John Low, hospital master.
John Knox.
David Young.
Thomas Hill.
Alexander Grim.
Robert Adam.
Homer Grierson.
George Davidson.

1736.
David Doig, provost.
John Molison and David Mather, bailies.
Edward Leslie, dean of guild.
James Knox, treasurer.
John Low, hospital master.
John Knox.
Andrew Doig.
Thomas Hill.
Alexander Grim.
Robert Adam.
Homer Grierson.
George Davidson.

1737.
David Doig, provost.
John Molison and David Mather, bailies.
Homer Grierson, dean of guild.
James Knox, treasurer.
John Low, hospital master.
Edward Leslie.
John Knox.
Thomas Hill.
Andrew Doig.
Robert Adam.
Alexander Grim.
George Davidson.

1738.
David Doig, provost.
John Molison and David Mather, bailies.
Homer Grierson, dean of guild.
Andrew Doig, treasurer.
John Low, hospital master.
James Grim.
Edward Leslie.
Thomas Hill.
John Knox.
Robert Adam.
Alexander Grim.
George Davidson.

1739, same as 1738.

COUNCILLORS, 1740.
John Molison.
James Grim.
David Mather.
George Davidson.
John Low.
James Black.
John Knox.
A. Low, yr.
Thomas Hill.
D. Allardice.
Robert Adam.
James Carnegy.
John Lyon.

Persons usurping the office of Magistrates and Councillors, from Michaelmas 1740 to 1st August 1741.
David Doig, provost.
Edward Leslie and Homer Grierson, bailies.
Wm. Shepherd, dean of guild.
Andrew Doig, treasurer.
John Smith, hospital master.
Alexander Grim, elder.
George Davidson.
William Baillie.
James Doig.
Alexander Grim, yr.
David Doig, yr.
Alexander Smith.

Office-bearers, 5th Aug. 1741.
John Knox, provost.
John Molison and David Mather, bailies.
John Low, dean of guild.
Alexander Low, treasurer.
John Lyon, hospital master.

Michaelmas 1741.
John Knox, provost.
Jn. Molison and Da. Mather, bailies.
John Low, dean of guild.
Alexander Low, treasurer.
John Lyon, hospital master.
Thomas Hill.

Robert Adam.
James Black.
James Grim.
D. Allardice.
William Lowson.
James Carnegy.

1742, same as 1741.

1743.
John Knox, provost.
John Molison and David Mather, bailies.
John Low, dean of guild.
Alexander Low, treasurer.
James Carnegy, hospital master.
John Lyon.
Thomas Hill.
Robert Dorrat.
Robert Adam.
D. Allardice.
William Lowson.
James Black.

1744.
John Knox, provost.
John Molison and David Mather, bailies.
John Low, dean of guild.
Alexander Low, treasurer.
James Carnegy, hospital master.
John Lyon.
Thomas Hill.
Robert Dorrat.
Robert Adam.
James Black.
J. Molison, yr.
D. Allardice.

COUNCILLORS, 1745.
Same as last year.
Election of office-bearers interrupted by the rebels.

26th June 1747.
John Molison, provost.
John Low and David Allardice, bailies.

John Lyon, elder, dean of guild.
John Lyon, yr., treasurer.
James Duncan, hospital master.
John Knox,
John Molison, yr.,
David Mather,
Alexander Baillie,
J. Black, merchant councillors.
G. Davidson, convener, and Robert
Adam, trades' councillors.

———

Michaelmas 1747.
John Molison, provost.
John Low and David Allardice,
bailies.
Jn. Lyon, elder, dean of guild.
John Lyon, yr., treasurer.
James Duncan, hospital master.
John Knox,
John Molison, yr.,
Alex. Low,
Alex. Baillie,
Ja. Black, merchant councillors.
Rt. Dorrat, convener, and Robert
Adam, trades' councillors.

———

1748, 1749, 1750, same as 1747.

———

1751.
John Molison, provost.
Edward Leslie and David Allar-
dice, bailies.
John Lyon, elder, dean of guild.
John Lyon, yr., treasurer.
Ja. Duncan, hospital master.
John Knox,
J. Molison, yr.,
Alex. Low,
A. Baillie,
Alex. Durie, merchant councillors.
R. Dorrat, convener, and Robert
Adam, trades' councillors.

———

1752.
John Molison, provost.
E. Leslie and J. Molison, yr., bailies.
John Lyon, elder, dean of guild.
John Clark, treasurer.

James Duncan, hospital master.
David Molison,
John Knox,
Alex. Low,
A. Baillie.
Alex. Durie, merchant councillors.
Da. Shiress, convener, and Robert
Adam, trades' councillors.

———

1753, same as 1752.

———

1754.
John Molison, provost.
Edward Leslie and J. Molison, yr.,
bailies.
J. Lyon, elder, dean of guild.
John Clark, treasurer.
James Duncan, hospital master.
David Molison,
Ja. Inverarity,
Alex. Low,
Alex. Baillie,
Alex. Durie, merchant councillors.
Geo. Reid, convener, and Robert
Adam, trades' councillors.

———

1755.
John Molison, provost.
Edward Leslie and J. Molison, yr.,
bailies.
John Lyon, elder, dean of guild.
John Clark, treasurer.
Ja. Inverarity, hospital master.
James Duncan,
David Molison,
Alex. Low,
Alex. Baillie,
Alex. Durie, merchant councillors.
Geo. Reid, convener, and Robert
Adam, trades' councillors.

———

1756.
John Molison, provost.
Edward Leslie and J. Molison, yr.,
bailies.
John Lyon, elder, dean of guild.
John Clark, treasurer.
James Inverarity, hospital master.

James Duncan,
David Molison,
Alex. Low,
Alex. Baillie,
Alex. Durie, merchant councillors.
A. Wishart, convener, and Robert
Adam, trades' councillors.

1757.
John Molison, provost.
Edward Leslie and J. Molison, yr.,
bailies.
David Molison, dean of guild.
John Clark, treasurer.
Ja. Inverarity, hospital master.
John Lyon, elder,
Ja. Duncan,
Alex. Low,
Alex. Baillie,
Alex. Durie, merchant councillors.
A. Wishart, convener, and Robert
Adam, trades' councillors.

1758.
John Molison, provost.
Edward Leslie and J. Molison, yr.,
bailies.
David Molison, dean of guild.
John Clark, treasurer.
Ja. Inverarity, hospital master.
David Shiress,
James Duncan,
Alex. Low,
Alex. Baillie,
Alex. Durie, merchant councillors.
A. Wishart, convener, and Robert
Adam, trades' councillors.

1759.
John Molison, provost.
Edward Leslie and J. Molison, yr.,
bailies.
David Molison, dean of guild.
John Clark, treasurer.
Ja. Inverarity, hospital master.
David Shiress,
James Duncan,
Alex. Low,

Alex. Baillie,
Alex. Durie, merchant councillors.
J. Millar, yr., convener, and Robert
Adam, trades' councillors.

1760.
John Molison, provost.
Edward Leslie and J. Molison, yr.,
bailies.
David Molison, dean of guild.
J. Clark, treasurer.
Ja. Inverarity, hospital master.
David Shiress,
Ja. Duncan,
Alex. Low,
Alex. Baillie,
Alex. Durie, merchant councillors.
J. Millar, yr., convr., and Lauchlan
Leslie, trades' councillors.

1761.
Same as last year.

1762.
John Molison, provost.
Edward Leslie and David Molison,
bailies.
J. Molison, yr., dean of guild.
John Clark, treasurer.
J. Inverarity, hospital master.
David Shiress,
Ja. Duncan,
Alex. Low,
Geo. Reid,
Alex. Durie, merchant councillors.
R. Langlands, convr., and Lauchlan
Leslie, trades' councillors.

1763, 1764, same as 1762.

1765.
John Molison, provost.
Da. Allardice and David Molison,
bailies.
J. Molison, yr., dean of guild.
Jn. Clark, treasurer.
Ja. Inverarity, hospital master.
David Shiress,

Ja. Duncan,
Alex. Low,
Geo. Reid,
Alex. Durie, merchant councillors.
J. Millar, yr., convr., and Lauchlan
Leslie, trades' councillors.

1766.
John Molison, yr., provost.
David Allardice and David Molison, bailies.
Alexander Low, dean of guild.
John Clark, treasurer.
Ja. Inverarity, hospital master.
John Molison,
David Shiress,
Ja. Duncan,
Geo. Reid,
Alex. Durie, merchant councillors.
J. Millar, yr., convr., and Lauchlan
Leslie, trades' councillors.

1767, same as 1766.

1768.
John Molison, yr., provost.
David Allardice and David Molison, bailies.
Alexander Low, dean of guild.
John Clark, treasurer.
Ja. Inverarity, hospital master.
John Molison,
David Shiress,
James Duncan,
George Reid,
Alex. Durie, merchant councillors.
R. Langlands, convr., and Lauchlan
Leslie, trades' councillors.

1769.
John Molison, yr., provost.
David Allardice and David Molison, bailies.
Alex. Low, dean of guild.
John Clark, treasurer.
Ja. Inverarity, hospital master.
John Gourlay,
David Shiress,

James Duncan,
George Reid,
Alex. Durie, merchant councillors.
R. Langlands, convr., and Lauchlan
Leslie, trades' councillors.

1770.
John Molison, provost.
David Allardice and David Molison, bailies.
Alex. Low, dean of guild.
John Clark, treasurer.
David Shiress, hospital master.
John Mudie,
William Cay,
James Duncan,
Geo. Reid,
Alex. Durie, merchant councillors.
R. Langlands, convr., and Lauchlan
Leslie, trades' councillors.

1771.
John Molison, provost.
D. Allardice, elder, and John
Clark, bailies.
Alex. Low, dean of guild.
Alex. Durie, treasurer.
David Shiress, hospital master.
D. Allardice, yr.,
J. Duncan,
John Mudie,
Geo. Reid,
Wm. Cay, merchant councillors.
John Moug, convr., and Lauchlan
Leslie, trades' councillors.

1772, 1773, same as 1771.

1774.
John Molison, provost.
D. Allardice, elder, and John
Clark, bailies.
Alex. Low, dean of guild.
John Mudie, treasurer.
William Cay, hospital master.
A. Durie,
J. Duncan,
D. Shiress,

Geo. Reid,
D. Allardice, yr., mer. councillors.
A. Wishart, convener, and David
Lyon, trades' councillors.

1775.
John Molison, provost.
D. Allardice, elder, and John
Clark, bailies.
Alex. Low, dean of guild.
John Mudie, treasurer.
William Cay, hospital master.
A. Durie,
J. Duncan,
D. Shiress,
Geo. Reid,
D. Allardice, yr., mer. councillors.
A. Mitchell, convener, and David
Lyon, trades' councillors.

1776.
John Molison, provost.
D. Allardice, elder, and John
Clark, bailies.
Alex. Low, dean of guild.
John Mudie, treasurer.
William Cay, hospital master.
A. Durie,
J. Duncan,
D. Shiress,
Geo. Reid,
D. Allardice, yr., mer. councillors.
A. Mitchell, convr., and Lauchlan
Leslie, trades' councillors.

1777.
John Molison, provost.
D. Allardice, elder, and John
Clark, bailies.
Alex. Low, dean of guild.
John Mudie, treasurer.
William Cay, hospital master.
A. Durie,
J. Duncan,
D. Shiress,
Geo. Reid,
D. Allardice, yr., merchant coun-
cillors.

Colin Smith, convr., and Lauchlan
Leslie, trades' councillors.

1778, same as 1777.

1779.
John Molison, provost.
D. Allardice, elder, and John
Clark, bailies.
Alex. Low, dean of guild.
John Mudie, treasurer.
William Cay, hospital master.
A. Durie,
A. Durie, yr.,
D. Shiress,
Geo. Reid,
D. Allardice, yr., mer. councillors.
Colin Smith, convener, and Lauch-
lan Leslie, trades' councillors.

1780.
John Molison, provost.
D. Allardice, elder, and John
Clark, bailies.
Alex. Low, dean of guild.
John Mudie, treasurer.
William Cay, hospital master.
A. Durie,
A. Durie, yr.,
David Shiress,
George Reid,
D. Allardice, yr., mer. councillors.
J. Millar, elder, convener ; Lauch-
lan Leslie, trades' councillors.

1781, 1782, same as 1780.

1783.
John Molison, provost.
D. Allardice, elder, and John Clark,
bailies.
A. Durie, elder, dean of guild.
John Mudie, treasurer.
William Cay, hospital master.
D. Guthrie,
A. Durie, yr.,
D. Shiress,
George Reid,

D. Allardice, yr., mer. councillors.
Colin Smith, convener, and Lauchlan Leslie, trades' councillors.

1784.
John Molison, provost.
John Clark and John Smith, elder, bailies.
A. Durie, elder, dean of guild.
John Mudie, treasurer.
William Cay, hospital master.
D. Guthrie,
A. Durie, yr.,
D. Shiress,
G. Reid,
D. Allardice, yr., mer. councillors.
Colin Smith, convener, and Lauchlan Leslie, trades' councillors.

1785, same as 1784.

1786.
John Molison, provost.
John Clark and John Smith, bailies.
A. Durie, dean of guild.
John Mudie, treasurer.
William Cay, hospital master.
D. Guthrie,
A. Durie, yr.,
D. Shiress,
George Reid,
D. Allardice, mer. councillors.
J. Soutter, convener, and Lauchlan Leslie, trades' councillors.

1787, same as 1786.

1788.
John Molison, provost.
John Smith and Wm. Cay, bailies.
A. Durie, elder, dean of guild.
David Guthrie, treasurer.
James Smith, hospital master.
Thomas Molison,
A. Durie, yr.,
D. Shiress,
George Reid,

D. Allardice, mer. councillors.
Geo. Millar, convener, and Lauchlan Leslie, trades' councillors.

1789.
John Smith, provost.
Wm. Cay and Thomas Molison, bailies.
A. Durie, elder, dean of guild.
David Guthrie, treasurer.
James Smith, hospital master.
Colin Gillies,
A. Durie, yr.,
D. Shiress,
George Reid,
D. Allardice, mer. councillors.
Geo. Millar, convener, and Lauchlan Leslie, trades' councillors.

1790.
John Smith, provost.
Wm. Cay and Thomas Molison, bailies.
A. Durie, elder, dean of guild.
David Guthrie, treasurer.
James Smith, hospital master.
C. Gillies,
A. Durie, yr.,
D. Shiress,
George Reid,
Alex. Mitchell, mer. councillors.
Geo. Millar, convener, and Lauchlan Leslie, trades' councillors.

1791.
John Smith, provost.
Wm. Cay and Thomas Molison, bailies.
A. Durie, elder, dean of guild.
David Guthrie, treasurer.
James Smith, hospital master.
C. Gillies,
A. Durie, yr.,
D. Shiress,
George Reid,
Alex. Mitchell, mer. councillors.
Charles Belford, convener, and L. Leslie, trades' councillors.

1792.

John Smith, provost.
Wm. Cay and Thomas Molison, bailies.
A. Durie, yr. dean of guild.
David Guthrie, treasurer.
J. Smith, hospital master.
A. Durie, elder,
A. Mitchell,
C. Gillies,
George Reid,
D. Shiress, merchant councillors.
C. Belford, convener, Lauchlan Leslie, trades' councillors.

1793, same as 1792.

1794.

John Smith, provost.
Wm. Cay and Thomas Molison, bailies.
A. Durie, yr., dean of guild.
David Guthrie, treasurer.
Ja. Smith, hospital master.
A. Durie, elder,
A. Mitchell,
C. Gillies,
Geo. Reid,
Ja. Reid, merchant councillors.
R. Millar, convener, and Lauchlan Leslie, trades' councillors.

1795.

John Smith, provost.
Wm. Cay and Thomas Molison, bailies.
A. Durie, yr., dean of guild.
David Guthrie, treasurer.
Ja. Smith, hospital master.
A. Durie, elder,
A. Mitchell,
C. Gillies,
Geo. Reid,
J. Reid, merchant councillors.
R. Millar, convener, and James Leslie, trades' councillors.

1796, same as 1795.

1797.

John Smith, provost.
Wm. Cay and Thomas Molison, bailies.
A. Durie, dean of guild.
David Guthrie, treasurer.
James Smith, hospital master.
William Shiress,
A. Mitchell,
C. Gillies,
George Reid,
Ja. Reid, merchant councillors.
H. Millar, yr., convener, and James Leslie, trades' councillors.

1798, same as 1797.

1799.

John Smith, provost.
Thos. Molison and David Guthrie, bailies.
A. Durie, dean of guild.
James Smith, treasurer.
Alex. Mitchell, hospital master.
David Don,
J. Reid,
W. Shiress,
Geo. Reid,
C. Gillies, merchant councillors.
R. Millar, convener, and James Leslie, trades' councillors.

1800.

Thomas Molison, provost.
David Guthrie and James Smith, bailies.
A. Durie, dean of guild.
A. Mitchell, treasurer.
James Reid, hospital master.
David Don,
C. Gillies,
Ja. Watson,
George Reid,
Wm. Shiress, mer. councillors.
R. Millar, convener, and James Leslie, trades' councillors.

1801, 1802, same as 1800.

1803.

Thomas Molison, provost.
David Guthrie and Alex. Mitchell, bailies.
A. Durie, dean of guild.
David Don, treasurer.
James Reid, hospital master.
James Smith,
C. Gillies,
J. Watson,
George Reid,
Wm. Shiress, mer. councillors.
D. Mitchell, convener, and James Leslie, trades' councillors.

1804.

Thomas Molison, provost.
David Guthrie and Alex. Mitchell, bailies.
A. Durie, dean of guild.
David Don, treasurer.
James Reid, hospital master.
J. Smith,
C. Gillies,
J. Watson,
Jo. Martin,
W. Shiress, merchant councillors.
D. Mitchell, convener, and James Leslie, trades' councillors.

1805, same as 1804.

1806.

Thomas Molison, provost.
D. Guthrie and Alex. Mitchell, bailies.
A. Durie, dean of guild.
David Don, treasurer.
James Reid, hospital master.
J. Smith,
C. Gillies,
J. Watson,
John Martin,
W. Shiress, merchant councillors.
D. Shiress, convener, and James Leslie, trades' councillors.

1807, 1808, same as 1806.

1809.

Thomas Molison, provost.
D. Guthrie and Alex. Mitchell, bailies.
A. Durie, dean of guild.
David Don, treasurer.
J. Reid, hospital master.
J. Smith,
C. Gillies,
James Watson,
Jo. Martin,
W. Shiress, merchant councillors.
D. Mitchell, convener, and James Leslie, trades' councillors.

1810, 1811, same as 1809.

1812.

Thomas Molison, provost.
D. Guthrie and A. Mitchell, bailies.
A. Durie, dean of guild.
David Don, treasurer.
James Reid, hospital master.
Jo. Guthrie,
C. Gillies,
J. Watson,
Jo. Martin,
W. Shiress, merchant councillors.
G. Fotheringham, convener, and James Leslie, trades' councillors.

1813.

Thomas Molison, provost.
D. Guthrie and Alex. Mitchell, bailies.
David Don, dean of guild.
John Guthrie, treasurer.
James Reid, hospital master.
A. Durie,
C. Gillies,
J. Watson,
Jo. Martin,
W. Shiress, merchant councillors.
D. Mitchell, convener, and James Leslie, trades' councillors.

1814.
Thomas Molison, provost.
David Guthrie and Alex. Mitchell, bailies.
David Don, dean of guild.
John Guthrie, treasurer.
James Reid, hospital master.
A. Durie, yr.,
C. Gillies,
J. Watson,
Jo. Martin,
W. Shiress, merchant councillors.
G. Fotheringham, convener, and James Leslie, trades' councillors.

1815.
David Guthrie, provost.
Alex. Mitchell and David Don, bailies.
Colin Gillies, dean of guild.
John Guthrie, treasurer.
James Speid, hospital master.
James Reid,
W. Shiress,
A. Durie, yr.,
Jo. Martin,
J. Watson, merchant councillors.
G. Fotheringham, convener, and James Leslie, trades' councillors.

1816.
David Guthrie, provost.
A. Mitchell and Dav. Don, bailies.
Colin Gillies, dean of guild.
John Guthrie, treasurer.
James Speid, hospital master.
James Reid,
W. Shiress,
D. Guthrie, yr.,
Jo. Martin,
J. Watson, merchant councillors.
D. Mitchell, convener, and James Leslie, trades' councillors.

1817, same as 1816.

1818.
David Guthrie, provost.

David Don and Jas. Speid, bailies.
Colin Gillies, dean of guild.
John Guthrie, treasurer.
Jo. Martin, hospital master.
A. Mitchell,
J. Watson,
J. Reid,
W. Shiress,
D. Guthrie, yr., merchant councillors.
D. Mitchell, convener, and James Leslie, trades' councillors.

1819.
David Guthrie, provost.
James Speid and David Reid bailies.
Colin Gillies, dean of guild.
John Guthrie, treasurer.
John Martin, hospital master.
A. Mitchell,
John Smith,
David Don,
Ja. Reid,
D. Guthrie, yr., merchant councillors.
J. Mathers, convener, and James Leslie, trades' councillors.

1820.
Colin Gillies, provost.
James Speid and John Guthrie, bailies.
William Baillie, dean of guild.
David Guthrie, treasurer.
John Smith, hospital master.
J. Martin.
James Pennycook.
Alex. Guthrie.
William Robb.
Charles Fettes.
John Mathers, deacon convener.
David Shiress, trades' councillor.

1821, same as 1820.

1822.
Colin Gillies, provost.

Z

James Speid and John Guthrie, bailies.
Colin Rickard, dean of guild.
David Guthrie, treasurer.
John Smith, hospital master.
John Martin.
Alex. Guthrie.
J. Pennycook.
William Robb.
Charles Fettes.
James Low, deacon convener.
Wm. Grim, trades' councillor.

1823.
James Speid, provost.
John Guthrie and Alex. Mitchell, bailies.
Colin Rickard, dean of guild.
David Guthrie, treasurer.
John Smith, hospital master.
Jo. Martin.
Alex. Guthrie.
J. Pennycook.
William Robb.
Charles Fettes.
James Low, deacon convener.
Wm. Grim, trades' councillor.

1824.
James Speid, provost.
Jo. Guthrie and Alex. Mitchell, bailies.
David M'Kenzie, dean of guild.
David Guthrie, treasurer.
John Smith, hospital master.
Jo. Martin.
Alexander Guthrie.
J. Pennycook.
William Robb.
Charles Fettes.
James Low, deacon convener.
Robert Craig, trades' councillor.

1825.
James Speid, provost.
John Guthrie and A. Mitchell, bailies.
David M'Kenzie, dean of guild.

David Guthrie, treasurer.
John Smith, hospital master.
John Martin.
Charles Fettes.
David Ogilvy.
David Dakers.
Alexander Guthrie.
Ja. Ramsay, jun., deacon convener.
Robert Craig, trades' councillor.

1826.
James Speid, provost.
John Guthrie and David Ogilvy, bailies.
Alex. M'Kinlay, dean of guild.
David Guthrie, treasurer.
John Smith, hospital master.
A. Mitchell.
Jo. Martin.
Alex. Guthrie.
Charles Fettes.
David Dakers.
Ja. Ramsay, jun., deacon convener.
John Mathers, trades' councillor.

1827, same as 1826.

1828.
James Speid, provost.
David Ogilvy and David Guthrie, bailies.
James Watson, jun., dean of guild.
Alex. M'Kinlay, treasurer.
Jo. Smith, hospital master.
Alex. Mitchell.
John Martin.
Alex. Guthrie.
Charles Fettes.
James Douglas.
James Low, deacon convener.
Alex. Craig, trades' councillor.

1829.
James Speid, provost.
David Ogilvy and David Guthrie, bailies.
Ja. Watson, jun., dean of guild.
Alex. M'Kinlay, treasurer.

Jo. Smith, hospital master.
Alex. Mitchell.
John Martin.
Alex. Guthrie.
Charles Fettes.
James Douglas.
James Low, deacon convener.
John Todd, trades' councillor.
8th July 1830.
David Shepherd, councillor, *vice*
A. Mitchell, deceased.

Michaelmas 1830.
James Speid, provost.
David Guthrie and John Smith,
bailies.
David Dakers, dean of guild.
Alex. M'Kinlay, treasurer.
Alex. Guthrie, hospital master.
John Martin.
Charles Fettes.
Ja. Douglas.
D. Shepherd.
J. Watson, jun.
William Grim, deacon convener.
John Todd, trades' councillor.
29th April 1831.
Alexander Black, councillor, *vice*
C. Fettes, deceased.

Michaelmas 1831.
James Speid, provost.
David Guthrie and John Smith,
bailies.
David Dakers, dean of guild.
Alex. M'Kinlay, treasurer.
Alex. Guthrie, hospital master.
John Martin.
James Douglas.
Da. Shepherd.
J. Watson, jun.
Alexander Black.
Wm. Grim, deacon convener.
Ja. Belford, trades' councillor.

1832.
James Speid, provost.

David Guthrie and John Smith,
bailies.
David Lamb, dean of guild.
Alex. M'Kinlay, treasurer.
Alex. Guthrie, hospital master.
John Martin.
James Douglas.
Da. Shepherd.
J. Watson, jun.
Alexander Black.
Wm. Grim, deacon convener.
Ja. Belford, trades' councillor

November 1833.
James Speid, provost.
David Dakers and Wm. Sharpe,
bailies.
Thos. Ogilvy, dean of guild.
James Millar, treasurer.
R. M'Kenzie, hospital master.
David Guthrie.
James Laing.
Wm. Shiress.
David Lamb.
Alex. Guthrie.
David Craig.
Alexander Mather.

1834.
James Speid, provost.
David Dakers and Wm. Sharpe,
bailies.
Thomas Ogilvy, dean of guild.
James Millar, treasurer.
Robert M'Kenzie, hospital master.
David Guthrie.
James Laing.
Wm. Shiress.
David Lamb.
Alex. Guthrie.
David Craig.
James Baxter.

1835.
James Speid, provost.
David Guthrie and Wm. Sharpe,
bailies.
David Lamb, dean of guild.

James Millar, treasurer.
Robert M'Kenzie, hospital master.
James Laing.
Alexander Guthrie.
David Craig.
James Baxter.
William Gordon.
David Mitchell.
Robert Don.

6th June 1836.

James Hood, John Speid, councillors, *vice* James Speid and James Laing, resigned; David Guthrie, provost.

13th June.

David Lamb, senior bailie.

20th June.

James Baxter, dean of guild.

___

November 1836.

David Guthrie, provost.
David Lamb and Wm. Sharpe, bailies.
James Baxter, dean of guild.
James Millar, treasurer.
R. M'Kenzie, hospital master.
Alex. Guthrie.
David Craig.
Wm. Gordon.
David Mitchell.
Robert Don.
James Hood.
John Speid.

8th May 1837.

Robert Welsh, David Guthrie, jun., councillors, *vice* David Lamb and William Sharpe.
James Millar and Robert Welsh, bailies.

13th May.

David Craig, treasurer.

___

November 1837.

David Guthrie, provost.
James Millar and Robert Welsh, bailies.
James Baxter, dean of guild.
David Craig, treasurer.

Alex. Guthrie, hospital master.
Wm. Gordon.
David Mitchell.
Robert Don.
James Hood.
John Speid.
D. Guthrie, jun.
Alex. Mather.

___

1838.

David Guthrie, provost.
James Millar and Robert Welsh, bailies.
James Baxter, dean of guild.
David Craig, treasurer.
Alex. Guthrie, hospital master.
Ja. Hood.
John Speid.
D. Guthrie, jun.
Wm. Duncan.
David Mitchell.
Robert Don.
William Gordon.

___

1839.

David Guthrie, provost.
James Hood and Robert Welsh, bailies.
William Duncan, dean of guild.
David Craig, treasurer.
Alex. Guthrie, hospital master.
David Guthrie, yr.
David Mitchell.
Robert Don.
William Gordon.
James Shepherd.
James Baxter.
Colin Rickard.

___

1840.

David Guthrie, provost.
James Hood and Robert Welsh, bailies.
William Duncan, dean of guild.
David Craig, treasurer.
Alex. Guthrie, hospital master.
David Mitchell.
Robert Don.

William Gordon.
James Shepherd.
James Baxter.
Colin Rickard.
David Guthrie, yr.

1841.

David Guthrie, provost.
James Hood and Robert Welsh, bailies.
William Duncan, dean of guild.
David Craig, treasurer.
Alex. Guthrie, hospital master.
James Shepherd.
James Baxter.
Colin Rickard.
David Guthrie, yr.
David Mitchell.
William Gordon.
Robert Don.

1842.

David Guthrie, provost.
James Hood and Robert Welsh, bailies.
William Duncan, dean of guild.
David Craig, treasurer.
Alex. Guthrie, hospital master.
David Guthrie, yr.
William Gordon.
Robert Don.
David Mitchell.
Patrick Guthrie.
James Baxter.
James Scott.

1843.

David Guthrie, provost.
James Hood and William Duncan, bailies.
James Scott, dean of guild.
David Craig, treasurer.
Alex. Guthrie, hospital master.
David Guthrie, yr.
William Gordon.
Robert Don.
David Mitchell.
Patrick Guthrie.

James Baxter.
George Reid.

1844.

David Guthrie, provost.
James Hood and Wm. Duncan, bailies.
James Scott, dean of guild.
David Craig, treasurer.
Alex. Guthrie, hospital master.
David Guthrie, yr.
William Gordon.
Robert Don.
Patrick Guthrie.
James Baxter.
George Reid.
John Don.

1845.

David Guthrie, provost.
James Hood and William Duncan, bailies.
James Scott, dean of guild.
David Craig, treasurer.
Alex. Guthrie, hospital master.
David Guthrie, yr.
William Gordon.
Robert Don.
George Reid.
John Don.
Patrick Guthrie.
James Baxter.

1846.

David Guthrie, provost.
Wm. Duncan and David Craig, bailies.
James Scott, dean of guild.
George Reid, treasurer.
Alex. Guthrie, hospital master.
William Gordon.
Robert Don.
John Don.
Patrick Guthrie.
James Baxter.
David Guthrie, yr.
George Anderson.

1847.

David Guthrie, provost.
Wm. Duncan and David Craig, bailies.
James Scott, dean of guild.
George Reid, treasurer.
Alex. Guthrie, hospital master.
Patrick Guthrie.
James Baxter.
David Guthrie, yr.
George Anderson.
William Gordon.
Robert Don.
John Don.

1848.

David Guthrie, provost.
W. Duncan and D. Craig, bailies.
David Guthrie, yr., dean of guild.
George Reid, treasurer.
Alex. Guthrie, hospital master.
George Anderson.
William Gordon.
Robert Don.
John Don.
Patrick Guthrie.
James Scott.
Charles Mitchell.

1849.

David Guthrie, provost.
David Craig and George Reid, bailies.
David Guthrie, yr., dean of guild.
John Don, treasurer.
Alex. Guthrie, hospital master.
William Gordon.
Robert Don.
Patrick Guthrie.
James Scott.
Chas. Mitchell.
William Blackhall.
John Wilson.

1850.

David Guthrie, provost.
David Craig and George Reid, bailies.

David Guthrie, yr., dean of guild.
John Don, treasurer.
Alex. Guthrie, hospital master.
William Gordon.
Robert Don.
Patrick Guthrie.
James Scott.
Chas. Mitchell.
William Blackhall.
John Wilson.

1851.

David Guthrie, provost.
David Craig and George Reid, bailies.
David Guthrie, yr., dean of guild.
John Don, treasurer.
Alex. Guthrie, hospital master.
William Gordon.
Robert Don.
William Blackhall.
John Wilson.
Patrick Guthrie.
James Scott.
Michael Ferrier.

1852.

David Guthrie, provost.
David Craig and George Reid, bailies.
David Guthrie, yr., dean of guild.
John Don, treasurer.
Alex. Guthrie, hospital master.
William Gordon.
Robert Don.
John Wilson.
Patrick Guthrie.
James Scott.
Michael Ferrier.
James Greig.

1853.

David Guthrie, provost.
David Craig and George Reid, bailies.
David Guthrie, yr., dean of guild.
John Don, treasurer.
Alex. Guthrie, hospital master.

Patrick Guthrie.
James Scott.
Michael Ferrier.
James Greig.
William Black.
William Gordon.
James P. Jack.

1854.
David Guthrie, provost.
Wm. Duncan and George Reid, bailies.
James P. Jack, dean of guild.
John Don, treasurer.
James Greig, hospital master.
William Black.
William Gordon.
Michael Ferrier.
Charles Will.
James Fairweather.
William Anderson.
Alex. Guthrie.

1855.
David Guthrie, provost.
Wm. Duncan and Wm. Anderson, bailies.
James P. Jack, dean of guild.
John Don, treasurer.
Charles Will, hospital master.
William Black.
William Gordon.
Michael Ferrier.
James Fairweather.
Alex. Guthrie.
William Davidson.
Joseph Hendry.

1856.
David Guthrie, provost.
Wm. Duncan and Wm. Anderson, bailies.
William Davidson, dean of guild.
John Don, treasurer.
Chas. Will, hospital master.
Michael Ferrier.
James Fairweather.
Alex. Guthrie.

Joseph Hendry.
William Black.
James L. Gordon.
David Scott.

1857.
David Guthrie, provost.
Wm. Duncan and Wm. Anderson, bailies.
William Davidson, dean of guild.
John Don, treasurer.
Charles Will, hospital master.
Alex. Guthrie.
Joseph Hendry.
William Black.
James L. Gordon.
David Scott.
Michael Ferrier.
James Fairweather.

1858.
David Guthrie, provost.
Wm. Duncan and Wm. Anderson, bailies.
William Davidson, dean of guild.
John Don, treasurer.
Charles Will, hospital master.
William Black.
James L. Gordon.
David Scott.
Michael Ferrier.
James Fairweather.
Charles Mitchell, jr.
Hunter Mather.

1859.
David Guthrie, provost.
Wm. Duncan and Jo. Don, bailies.
William Davidson, dean of guild.
Charles Will, treasurer.
Hunter Mather, hospital master.
Michael Ferrier.
James Fairweather.
Charles Mitchell, jr.
James L. Gordon.
James Guthrie.
George C. Scott.
William Black.

1860.
David Guthrie, provost.
William Duncan and John Don, bailies.
William Davidson, dean of guild.
Charles Will, treasurer.
Hunter Mather, hospital master.
Charles Mitchell, jr.
James L. Gordon.
James Guthrie.
George C. Scott.
William Black.
John Lamb.
James Middleton.

1861.
David Guthrie, provost.
William Duncan and John Don, bailies.
William Davidson, dean of guild.
Charles Will, treasurer.
Hunter Mather, hospital master.
James L. Gordon.
James Guthrie.
George C. Scott.
William Black.
John Lamb.
James Middleton.
Charles Mitchell, jr.

1862.
David Guthrie, provost.
Charles Will and Wm. Davidson, bailies.
James L. Gordon, dean of guild.
James Middleton, treasurer.
Hunter Mather, hospital master.
John Lamb.
Charles Mitchell, jr.
James Guthrie.
David Scott.

David Craig.
William Whitson.
John Davidson.

1863.
David Guthrie, provost.
Wm. Whitson and Wm. Davidson, bailies.
James L. Gordon, dean of guild.
James Middleton, treasurer.
Hunter Mather, hospital master.
Charles Mitchell, jr.
James Guthrie.
David Scott.
David Craig.
John Guthrie.
John Lamb.
William Black.

13th July 1864.
Alexander Guthrie, elected provost, in room of David Guthrie, resigned.
David Craig, bailie, in room of William Whitson, resigned.
William Black, dean of guild, in room of J. L. Gordon, resigned.

17th August.
Charles Mitchell, elected junior Bailie, in room of William Davidson, resigned.
John Guthrie, town treasurer, in room of James Middleton, resigned.
John Dakers, hospital master, in room of Hunter Mather, resigned.

31st August.
John Burnett, elected bailie, in room of Charles Mitchell, who declined to accept the office.

No. IX.

TABLE of the WAGES of the LABOURING CLASSES in the PARISH of BRECHIN, on Averages of Ten Years from 1780 to 1837 inclusive, with instances in Good and Bad Seasons; constructed by the late DAVID LEIGHTON, Esq. of Bearhill, from information collected by the Committee on the State of the Poor, 1838.

YEARS.	Masons per Day.		Wrights per Day.		Labourers per Day.		Shoemakers per Week.		Ploughmen per Year.	Women in the House per annum.	Men for Harvest.	Women for Harvest.	Spinning per Spindle.	
	s.	*d.*	*s.*	*d.*	*s.*	*d.*	*s.*	*d.*			*s.* *s.*	*s.* *s.*	*s.*	*d.*
1780—1789	1	$5\frac{8}{9}$	0	$9\frac{6}{9}$	0	$9\frac{7}{9}$	...		£6 10*s.*	£3 15*s.*	25 to 35	25	0	11
1790—1799	1	9^{8}	1	$3\frac{4}{9}$	1	3^{4}	7	0	£8 to 10	£4 to £5	40 to 60	30 to 50	1	6
1800—1809	2	8^{9}	1	$11\frac{1}{6}$	1	7^{8}	10	6	£10 to 24	£5 to £6 10	40 to 60	30 to 50	1	1
1810—1819	2	9	2	$6\frac{4}{9}$	1	9^{4}	9	0	£14 to 20	£6 to £7	35 to 50	30 to 40	0	$11\frac{1}{2}$
1820—1829	2	8^{9}	2	$1\frac{1}{6}$	1	8^{8}	9	0	£8 to 14	£5 to £6	℔ threave	℔ threave	0	$8\frac{3}{4}$
1830—1837	2	7	2	$0\frac{2}{5}$	1	8^{2}	9	0	£9 to 15	£7 to £10	℔ do.	do.		
Good crops 1798	2	0	1	4	1	6								
Good crops 1822	2	9	2	0	1	8								
Bad crops 1800	2	2	1	8	1	2								
Bad crops 1826	2	3	2	0	1	10								

TABLE of the FIARS PRICES of OATMEAL in the COUNTY of FORFAR, compared with the WAGES of LABOUR in the PARISH of BRECHIN, on Averages of Periods of Ten Years, from 1780 to 1837 inclusive, with Instances of Good and Bad Crops, constructed by the late DAVID LEIGHTON, Esq. of Bearhill, from Tables of Fiars Prices framed by the late Mr DAVID DAKERS of Brechin, and information as to Wages, gathered from various sources, by the Committee appointed to Examine into and Report on the State of the Poor in Brechin Parish, 1838.

YEARS.	Boll of Oatmeal.		EQUAL TO DAY'S WAGES OF		
			Masons.	Wrights.	Labourers.
	s.	*d.*			
1780—1789	14	0^{2}	9·401	17·309	17·210
1790—1799	17	4^{7}	9·568	13·506	13·444
1800—1809	23	5^{4}	8·551	12·144	14·289
1810—1819	22	5^{11}	8·179	8·866	12·622
1820—1829	17	10^{11}	6·532	8·539	10·332
1830—1837	16	2^{2}	6·266	7·957	9·614
Good Crops 1798	15	2^{9}	7·606	11·422	10·852
Good Crops 1822	14	3	5·181	7·125	8·55
Bad Crops 1800	43	0	19·846	28·666	36·857
Bad Crops 1826	27	5	12·185	12·185	14·954

Corrigendum: Since pages 56 and 57 were thrown off, the Right Honourable the Earl of Southesk has ascertained that his predecessor Earl James died in 1730 ; so that it was not Sir John Carnegie, who then became head of the family, but Sir James Carnegie, the son of Sir John.

INDEX.

Abe, John, 5.
Aberdeen, 6, 30, 38, 52, 60, 164.
Aberlemno, 12, 258.
Abernethy, 240, 248.
Adam, Bishop of Brechin, 19.
Adicate, 29.
Advertiser, Brechin, 197, 221, 270.
Æsica, 13.
African Company, 110.
Agricola, 13.
Agricultural Association, 187.
Agriculture of Parish, 258.
Airlie, Lord, 71, 282.
Airlie Street, 264.
Airlie's Green, 282.
Albert, Prince, 228.
Albin, Bishop of Brechin, 17.
Aldbar, 49, 78, 133, 163, 221.
Ale, Ordinary, to be drunk, 120.
Alexander II., 5, 17.
Alexander III., 17.
Alexander, George, 184, 227.
Algerine Prisoners, 99.
Allardice, James, 148.
Andrews, Saint, 56.
Anglesey, Island of, 8.
Angus Burghs, 30.
Ann, Saint, 50.
Ann, Queen, 150.
Arbroath, 5, 19, 30, 41, 46, 57, 76, 84, 88, 125, 204.
Arbroath Road, 199, 216.
Arbuthnot, 88.
Arbuthnott, Carnegy. *See* Carnegy.
Ardmore, Tower of, 251.
Ardoch, 29.
Ardovie, 254.
Argyle, Earl, 39; Marquis, 66.
Arms of Warfare, 94, 97, 101, 172.
  „   Heraldic, 124, 285.
Arrat, 50.

Asylum, Montrose Lunatic, 164.
Assessments on Burgh, 30, 37, 276.
  „   Parochial, 226.
Athole, Earl of, 22.
Augustinian Monks, 6.
Authors, 134, 137, 288.

Bailie Court. *See* Courts.
Bailies, Mode of Electing, 61, 65, 82, 92, 112, 127.
Baillie, General, 67.
Bakers, 58, 60, 97.
Balbegno, 96.
Balbirnie, 32.
Balfeich, 51.
Baliol, King, 19.
Ballownie's House, 282.
Balloon Tytler, 175.
Balls, Dancing, 199.
Balnabriech, 32.
Balnamoon, 26, 28, 147. *See* Carnegy.
Balyeordie, 26, 64, 126.
Bank Street, 221, 279; School, 221.
Banking Establishments, 158, 168, 269.
Bannatyne, John, 50.
Banns, Proclamation of, 183.
Barley Flour, 269.
Barrelwell, 9, 14, 258.
Barrie's Burn, 266.
Baths, 226.
Battledikes, 13.
Battles, 12, 13, 27, 56, 94, 105, 146.
Baxter, John, 238.
Bede House, 43.
Beggars, 69, 196.
Bells, 24, 64, 119, 161, 165, 183, 190, 217.
Bellie, Thomas, Trial of, 53.
Benevolent Societies, 281.
Berkley, Alexander de, 19; David de, 20; stall, 51.

Bible Society, 280.
Bible for Church, 128.
Billings, R. W., 237, 238.
Bishops. *See* Church and Appendix III.
Bishop's Close, 25, 42, 132, 156, 172, 253.
Black Bull Close, 50, 282, 289.
Black's Mortification, 280.
Blacksmith, Lindsay, hereditary, 32.
Blair, Rev. Mr, 148, 152.
Blawart Lap, 14.
Bleachfield, 113, 137, 180, 204, 222, 271, 277.
Bleaching-greens, 204.
Board of Health, 199.
Bœce, Hector, 3.
Bogdike, 34.
Bonnetmakers, 56.
Bonnyton, 40.
Bothers, 24, 29.
Bothwell Bridge, Battle of, 94.
Boundaries, Parliamentary, 265.
Bourd of Brechin, 47.
Bow Butts, 120.
Bowick, James, 192, 196.
Bowl, Punch, 163.
Bowling Club, 228, 281.
Boys, Dress of, 167.
Books, Price of, 76.
Brachtullo, 16.
Branks, witches, 76.
Bread, 269.
Brechin Advertiser, 197, 221, 270.
Brechin in 1680, 285.
　„　　Burgh, description of, 263.
　„　　Burning of, 11, 87.
　„　　Castle, 8, 18, 19, 47, 54, 69, 108, 158, 286.
　„　　City Boundaries, Parliamentary, 265.
　„　　Sir David de, 19.
　„　　Derivation of name, 8.
　„　　Henry de, 16, 17.
　„　　Little, 137.
　„　　Lordship of, 37.
　„　　Origin of, 1.
　„　　Parish, 258.
　„　　See of, 6, 41. *Vide* Church.
　„　　William de, 16, 17, 255.
Brecon, in Wales, 11.
Breich, in county of Linlithgow, 11.
Brewers, 274.
Bridge of Brechin, 69, 98, 164.
　„　　Cemetery, 226.
　„　　Finhaven, 161.
　„　　Idvie, 99.

Bridge of Montrose, 167.
　„　　Prossin, 99.
　„　　Stannochy, 192.
　„　　Water Esk, 99.
　„　　Street, 206, 208, 263, 279.
British Linen Company Bank, 168, 269.
Broichan, a Druid, 8.
Broomley, Lands of, 21.
Brougham, Lord, 205.
Bruce, King Robert, 172.
Buchan, 12.
Buchanan, George, 13, 18, 44.
Buckler Stane, 14.
Building Warrants, 193.
Burgage-holding, 265.
Burgesses, 96, 276.
Burgess-tickets, 138.
Burghs, Royal Constitution of, 1.
　„　　Convention of, 2.
　„　　Courts, 120, 277.
Burgh Reform, 188, 204.
　„　　School, 201.
　„　　Session, 72.
Burghill, Burkhill, or Buttergill, 10, 32, 48, 158, 258.
　„　　Fountains, 222, 224, 227.
Burns, David, 221.
　„　　Robert, 227.
Burness, Baker Poet, 176.
Burning of Brechin, 11, 87.
Bursary, 81, 104, 279, 280.
Butcher Trade, 198.
　„　　Market, 132, 156, 269.
Butter, 269.
　„　　Market, 235.
Burying Places, 50, 124, 261.

Cadger Hillock, 203, 263.
　„　　Wynd, 205, 263.
Cairnbank, 24, 27.
Cairncross, Bishop, 96, 320.
Caithness, See of, 6.
Caldhame, 50, 52, 226, 264, 266.
Caledonia, 9, 13.
Cambridge, Duke of, 228.
Camus and Camiston Cross, 12.
Campbell, Alex., Bishop, 314.
Campbell, Donald, Bishop, 313.
Canals, 159.
Canute of Denmark, 12.
Carcary, 31. House, 185.
Carnegie, Lands of, 66.
Carnegy Arbuthnott, of Balnamoon, 27, 145, 147, 160.
Carnegy, of Cookston, 109, 110.
　„　　Sir David, 164, 168, 170, 173.
　„　　Sir James, 217, 220.
　„　　James, Poet, 134.
　„　　Lady, 220.

Carnegy, of Kinnaird. *See* Southesk.
„ of Pitarrow, 56.
Carnoustie, 12.
Carnoth, John, Bishop, 23, 25, 50, 253, 308.
Captains of Town, 102.
Careston, 87, 258.
Carpenters, 190, 268.
Carriers, 284.
Carron, 159.
Castle. *See* Brechin Castle.
Castle Street, 264.
Caterthun, 9, 14, 25.
Cathedral. *See* Church.
Cattiscors, 49.
Cattle Markets. *See* Markets.
Causewayed Streets, 208.
Cemetery, 220, 226, 226, 227, 270.
Census, 216, 261, 266, 329.
Chalmers, Sheriff, 163.
„ Patrick, 197, 217, 225, 249.
„ Rev. Dr, 214.
Chapels, 17.
Chanonry House, 83.
„ Wynd, 257.
Chanter's Manse, 43.
Chaplains. *See* Church.
Chaplainries, 48, 50.
Chapmen of Angus, 275.
Chapter of Cathedral, 48, 49.
Charles I., 63, 65, 68, 69.
„ II., 77, 91, 92, 93, 94, 95.
Charles, Prince, 141.
Carters, 1, 2, 6, 10, 16, 17, 19, 20, 21, 23, 27, 30, 32, 41, 42, 43, 48, 56, 112, 125.
Cheese, 269.
Chester, John, Earl of, 17.
Chews, 269.
Chickens, 269.
Cholera, 119, 221.
Christopher, Saint, 51.
Church Matters, 219.
„ Roman Catholic, 1, 5, 6, 7, 16, 19, 37, 42, 48, 101, 254.
„ Reformed Presbyterian, 7, 37, 76, 114, 138, 152, 164, 183, 211, 217, 226, 277, 278.
„ Episcopalian, 7, 39, 59, 63, 64, 74, 77, 84, 85, 89, 93, 95, 102, 134, 149, 169, 217, 226.
„ United Presbyterian. *See* United.
„ Free. *See* Free.
„ Bible, 128.
„ Clock, 77.
„ Seats, 64, 124.
„ Street, 155, 185, 206, 208, 212, 264, 278, 279, 281, 282, 283.
„ Yard, 71, 82, 124, 220.

Church of Brechin, 1, 4, 6, 7, 16, 17, 21, 26, 29, 31, 32, 36, 45, 48, 59, 61, 63, 64, 74, 77, 81, 100, 123, 133, 152, 162, 182, 215, 219, 229, 230, 253.
Cists, 207.
Circuit Court, Dundee, 27.
City Cross. *See* Cross.
City Guard, 97.
City of Glasgow Bank, 269.
City Hall, 283.
City Nursery, 274.
City Road Church, 227.
City Road, 193, 224, 264, 278.
Claverhouse, Graham of, 105.
Cleansers, 70.
Clement VI., Pope, 19.
Clergy in Brechin, 277.
Clerk Street, 52, 194, 203, 210, 264, 282.
Climate, 261.
Clocks of Church, 77 ; Town, 137, 165.
Close, Bishop's. *See* Bishop's Close.
Clothing Society, 217.
Cloyne, Round Tower of, 251.
Coaches, 200, 221.
Coals, 268, 269.
Coal Fund, 228, 281.
Coffins, ancient, 254.
Collace, John de, 26, 28.
„ Thomas, 27.
College of Justice, 37.
„ Yard, 5.
„ Well, 5.
Collison, Mr, 245, 247.
Cologne Cathedral, 221.
Columba, Saint, 4, 7.
Colmeallie, 7.
Commercial Hotel, 282.
Commissary Court, 77, 78.
Common Muir, Cognition of, 33. *See* Muir.
Common Den. *See* Den.
Connor, de of Ballybriken, 10.
Constable. *See* Justiciar and Constable.
Constables, 65, 94, 198.
Convener of Trades, 92, 132 ; Court, 58.
Conventicles and Covenanters, 63, 66, 93, 96.
Convention of Royal Burghs, 2, 18, 61, 83, 106, 112, 189.
Cookston, 109, 110, 158, 222, 254, 264, 266, 267.
Corn Crops, deficient, 31, 91.
„ Laws, 215, 219.
„ Mill, 222.
Corduroy, 167.
Corporation. *See* Municipal.
Cotton Mill, 272.
Council and Session, Lords of, 36.
Council. *See* Town Council.

Council, First Election of, 84.
„   Meetings, 208.
„   Room, 281.
Coupar, 41.
Courts, 44, 85, 120, 227.
Court-room, 226.
Covenanters. See Conventicles.
Crabb, James, 216, 288.
Crafts. See Trades.
Craig, 87.
Crawford, Earl of, 21, 27, 29, 49, 56, 282.
Cricket Club, 221, 228, 281.
Crimean War, 225.
Crofts, 51, 52, 194, 203. See Markets.
Cromwell, Oliver, 37, 66, 78.
Cross, Holy, 50 ; of Burgh, 112, 138, 159.
Cross Guns Tavern, 282.
Crown Inn, 256, 282.
Cruik, 26.
Cruizin, 192.
Culdees, 1, 4, 8.
Culloden, Battle of, 142, 146.
Cumberland, Duke of, 119, 124, 140, 149.
Cupar, 99.
Curling, 226, 281.
Currency Laws, 220.
Customs, Local, 180, 184, 187, 276.
„   Right of, 30.
„   on Foreign Goods, 38.

Dakers' Mortification, 280.
Dalgety, 17, 256.
Dalhousie, Lord, 55.
„   Fox, Earl of, 224, 226, 286.
Dam Acre, 108.
Danes, 3, 11.
Darien Scheme, 110.
David I., 1, 2, 4, 6, 19.
„   II., 19, 20.
Davie, John, 130.
Deacon, Convener, 132.
Dear Years, 31, 39, 171, 181, 188, 217.
Defiance Coach, 221.
Dempster, Walter, 29 ; William, 33 ; Matthew, 33 ; Thomas, 79.
„   of Carreston, 50.
Den, 112, 120, 183, 186.
Den Burn, 108, 265, 272.
Den Nursery, 186, 228, 264, 265, 274.
Desks in Church, 64, 100, 124.
Denmark, 12, 37.
Derivation of Name of Brechin, 8.
Dick, Dr, 217.
Dickson and Turnbull, 256, 274.
Dispensary, 191, 281.
Disruption of Kirk of Scotland in 1843, 214.

Distilleries, 139, 273.
Distillery Lane, 210, 264.
Doig, David, 140 ; Dr David, 177 ; John, 122, 126, 128, 129, 140 ; Agnes, Lady Carnegie, 282.
Donald I., 5.
Donaldson, David, 71, 85, 93, 95.
Donations to Church, 77, 80.
Douglas, Gawin, 287.
„   Robert, Bishop, 96, 319.
Dove Wells, 158, 184, 185, 193.
Dovertie, Wm., 158, 184, 185.
Dress of Boys, 167 ; Men, 185.
Dreuse in Gaul, 9.
Drinking Habits, 186.
Druids, 6, 8, 14.
Drumcairn, 29.
Drum, John of, 49.
Drums, Middle, 41 ; West, 49.
Drumlachlan, Ireland, 245.
Drummond, James, Bishop, 102, 114, 321.
Drummond, John, 165.
Drumsleed, 99.
Duchad O'Brian, 244.
Dumblane, See of, 6.
Dun, 21, 36, 87, 258.
Duncan, John, 162.
Dundee, 3, 21, 26, 30, 50, 51, 60, 66 67, 77, 84, 88, 99.
„   Bank, 158.
„   Viscount, 105.
Dunfermline, 4.
Ducklings, 269.
Dung on Streets, 180.
Dunkeld, See of, 6.
Dunlappy, 13, 264.
Dunnottar, 38.
Duthoc, St, Altarage of, 52.

Eaglesjohn, 21.
East India Company, 111.
East Church, 213, 214, 217.
„   Free Church, 226.
„   Mill, 272.
Ecclesiatics in Town, 277. See Church.
Edinburgh, City, 3, 66 ; Council Records, 38 ; University, 169.
Educational Institution of Free Church, 221.
Educational Society, 222.
Edward I., King, 18, 287 ; Edward II., 172.
Edzell, 5, 7, 87, 214.
Eggs, 269 ; Markets, 225.
Elder, Ruling, 138, 169.
Election, Poll, 105.
„   of Council, 64, 82, 84, 105, 122.
„   „   in 1832, 204.

Election of Trades, 194.
„ of M.P., 197, 201.
Eminent Men of Brechin, 287.
Erick, the Dane, 12.
Episcopacy, 6, 63, 76, 87, 93.
Episcopal, Chapel, 278.
Erskine of Brechin, 37, 45.
„ of Dun, 21, 36, 37, 41.
Esk River, 72, 160.
Excise, 92, 95, 268.
Exercise, Church, 87.
Exports, 54, 78.

Fairs. *See* Markets.
Falconer of Newton, 107, 108.
Fancy Fair, 220.
Farming of Parish, 258.
Farnell, 87, 258.
Feal, 120.
Fearn, 9, 34, 87.
Feeing Markets, 275. *See* Markets.
Fenton, James, of Ogil, 33.
Ferrier, David, merchant, 145.
Ferriers of Kintrocket, 255.
Feu-duties, Bishop's Grant of, 108, 109.
„ Holding, 265.
Feus of Muir, 137.
Findowrie, 28, 41, 68, 280.
Finhaven, 24, 28, 49, 161.
Forbes, Bishop, 227.
Foote, Rev. A. L. R., 218.
Foot Soldiers, 66.
Forfar, 30, 68.
Fires, 87, 191, 192, 218.
Fire-engine, 218.
Fish, 269.
Fleshers, 56, 156.
Fleshmarket, 128, 132, 156, 225.
Fletcher of Saltoun, 110.
Flodden Battle, 56.
Floods, 197, 220, 224.
Flour, 269.
Food, 267, 269.
Fordmouth, 197.
Fordyce, Rev. James, 149, 152.
Forfar, 13, 17, 30, 68.
Forked Acre, 21, 32.
Free Church, 138, 214, 217, 218, 221, 226, 278, 279.
French Invasion, Threatened, 172.
Friars, Red, 51.
Friendly Societies, 283.
Fuel, 154, 269.
Funerals, 190.
„ Fine for non-attendance at, 59.
Fyfe's Mortification, 279.

Gainshot, 137.
Galgacus, 13.
Gallowgate, 113.

Gallowhill, 91, 139, 264.
Garioch, Earl of, 16.
Gas, 205, 267, 283.
Gate Penny, 60.
Geddes, Janet, 63, 93.
General Assembly, 226.
George I., 125, 134; George II., 137; George III., 154; George IV., 187, 191, 197.
George, Saint, 52.
Gibson, James, 218.
Gillies, Adam, 169, 179, 288.
„ Colin, 173, 177, 179.
„ Dr John, 178, 288.
Gilfumman, in Glenesk, 7.
Gifts to Church, 77, 80.
Gin as a Drink, 166.
Glammis, 13.
Glasgow, 99, 159 ; See of, 6.
Glebe, 215, 277.
Glenbervie, 47, 49.
Glencadam, 265, 274.
Glendey, Rev. John, 104, 288.
Glenesk, 7, 29, 49.
Glovers, 58.
Gold's Yards, 264.
Gordon, Earl Huntly, 27.
Gordon, J. L., town-clerk, 229.
Gough, Richard, 239, 245, 247.
Governors of Brechin, 128.
Grain Markets, 274.
Graham, Patrick, Archbishop, 29.
„ Patrick, Bishop, 29, 310.
„ of Claverhouse, 105.
„ of Leuchland, 79.
Grammar School, 89, 157, 184, 201.
Grampians, 7.
Grants to Church. *See* Church.
Graves, Ancient, 207.
Grave-stones, Ancient, 254.
Gray's Acre, 186.
Greenhill, David, 220.
Great Britain, United Kingdom of, 111, 121.
Grose, Mr, 237.
Guard, City, 97.
Guildhall, 165.
Guildry, 60, 85, 111, 123, 132, 157, 165, 169, 188, 276.
Guild Sister, 86.
Gun, Willie, 216.
Guthrie, Benefice of, 48.
„ David, 224.
„ Gideon, 127, 129.
„ John, Kincraig, 119.
„ Thomas, Rev. Dr, 289.
„ William, Rev., Pitforthy, 80, 287.
„ William, author, 135, 288.
Gypsies, 167.

Habits, &c., of People, 267.
Hackett, Wm. Ireland, 250.
Hair Cairn, 27.
Haliburton, George, Bishop, 93, 319.
Hall, Town, and Prisons, 164, 281.
Hammermen Trade, 44, 58, 60, 113.
  See Trades; Records, 59.
Handsell Monday, 190.
Harris, Mr, of Ireland, 245.
Harbour of Montrose, 207.
Harold, the Dane, 12.
Haugh of Brechin, 32.
Haughmuir, 188.
Hazard Sloop of War, 145, 150.
Head Court of Burgh, 85.
  „ Stones in Churchyard, 124.
Health, Board of, 199.
Hens, 269.
Henderson, George, 160, 228, 238.
  „ John, Nurseryman, 186.
  „ „ architect, 288.
  „ & Sons, 274.
Hendry de Brechin, 16, 17.
Hendry, Charles, 215.
  „ John, 288.
Henry de Lichton, 248.
Hepburn, John, Bishop, 35, 313.
Herd, Town's, 113.
Herzeld, 31.
Heritors of Brechin Parish, 262.
High Street, 179, 206, 208, 212, 253, 263, 264, 278, 281.
Highlanders in Brechin, 142.
Hiring markets, 275.
Hog, Alexander, preceptor of Maisondieu, 256.
Holidays, 226.
Holy Cross, 50, 52.
Holy Writ, Act anent, 35.
Honorius, Pope, 6.
Horse Markets, 275.
Horse, Regiment of, 66.
Horticultural Society, 214.
Hospital of Brechin, 43, 171, 265.
Hospitium of Knight Templars, 256.
Hotels, 282.
Houses and Rents, 267.
Huddleston, Mr, 9.
Hume, Joseph, M.P., 197, 219, 220.
Huntington, Earl of, 16.
Huntly, Alex. Gordon, Earl of, 27, 56.
Huntlyhill, 27.
Hurry, General, 67.
Hurricane in October 1838, 214.
Husbandry of Parish, 259.
Huts for Plague Patients, 71.
Hutton, James, Town-officer, 174.

Improvements, 179, 206, 207, 217.

Inch, 153, 203, 220, 222, 224, 226, 271, 277.
Income of Burgh, 276.
Incorporations, 276.
Incorporated Trades, 56, 97, 140.
Indigent Ladies' Society, 281.
Infant School, 205, 220.
Inglis, Meg, 186.
Inns, 282.
Innes, Cosmo, 2, 5, 6.
Innocent, Pope, 20.
Institution, Mechanics, 205, 283.
Insurance Companies, 269.
Invasion, Threatened, 172.
Ireland, 9.
Ireland, James, 273.

Jack, Charles, 170.
Jacobites of Forfarshire, 148.
Jail, 45, 90, 96, 112, 206, 215, 218, 228, 281.
James I., 21, 23, 120; II., 21, 26, 27, 29, 56; III., 29, 30; IV., 27, 38, 56; V., 3, 32, 37; VI., 38, 42, 43, 46, 53, 56, 73, 125; VII., 54, 60, 96, 100, 105; VIII., 54, 125, 130, 147, 150.
James, The Pretender, 130.
James, St, The Apostle, 60.
James Place, 264.
Jamieson, Thomas, 272.
Jedburgh, 41.
Jervise, Andrew, 11, 238, 289.
Jesu Nomine, Chaplainry of, 51.
Jews, 167.
John, The Pope, 19.
John, St, of Jerusalem, 24.
John, St, The Evangelist, 51.
Johnston, Rev. John, 140.
Jolly, James, 249, 250.
Juliana, Mother of William de Brechin, 17.
July Fair, 214.
Justice Hall, 216.
Justice of Peace Courts, 277.
Justiciary and Constable, 65, 106, 123, 127.
Justiciary, High Court of, 53.
Juvenile Society, 186.

Katherin, St, Virgin, 51.
Keithock, 13, 24, 34, 160.
Keldeis or Culdees, 1, 4, 8.
Kenneth III., 3, 4.
Kettle, The First Tea, in Brechin, 140.
Kildare, Round Tower of, 239.
Kilgarry or Kilgerre, The Forest and Hermitage of, 25, 27.
Kilkenny, Round Tower of, 239.
Killiecrankie, Battle of, 105.
Killivair, 14.

Kilmoir, 41, 43, 49.
„ Manse of, 257.
Kinbrocket, 32.
Kincraig, 32.
Kinnaird, 17, 56, 73, 87, 130, 222, 254.
Kinnimond, John de, Bishop, 17, 303.
Kirk Den, 16.
Kirk Door Keys, Lands of, 52.
Kirk-sessions, 64, 72, 74, 76, 81, 86, 90,
  92, 96, 100, 109, 118, 126, 128, 133,
  188, 196.
„ Records, 111.
Kirkyard Burn, 264.
Kirriemuir, 60.
Kistaveens, 207.
Knights Templars, 256, 284.
Knox, Provost, 139, 141.
Kuldees, Kyldees, or Culdees, 1, 4, 8.

Labourers, 268.
Lady, Altarage of Our, 51.
Lady Day formerly commenced year,
  53.
Ladies' Coal Fund, 228.
Laing, James, 211.
„ Alexander, 227, 288.
Lammas Muir Market, 109, 203, 275.
Lamps, 222.
Landward Session, 70, 72, 115, 118.
Langhaugh, 14.
Langley Park, Lands of, 21.
Latch Lands, 266.
„ Road, 193, 264.
Laurence, St, 51.
Lawrie, Robert, Bishop, 318.
Leighton, Sir David, 228.
Leightonhill Muir, 7.
Leod, Abbot, 4, 5.
„ Donald, his Grandson, 5.
Lethnot, 24, 26, 49, 87, 264.
Leuchars, Patrick de, Bishop, 21, 305.
Leuchland, 32, 65.
Libraries, 280, 283.
Lichton, Henry de, of Lethnot, 248, 249.
Liddell, Bailie, 85.
Lindsay, Sir David, of Glenesk, 49.
„ David, Bishop, 63, 316.
„ Heritable Smith, 32.
Linen Trade, 124, 153, 270.
Linton, Rev. William, 201, 255.
Lion, William the, 1.
Little Brechin, 137, 279.
Little Carcary, 31.
Little Mill, 40, 50, 137.
„ Stairs, 108.
Little Steeple, 96, 104. See Round
  Tower.
Livingston Parish, 11.
Loan of Cookston, 109.
Local Militia, 173, 182.

Lochleven, 5, 29.
Lochty, 34.
Locomotion on Roads, 199, 200.
Loft in Church, 86, 162.
Logiepert, 147.
Logie, Peter, 146.
Low, Alexander, of Swan Inn, 148.
Low, Andrew, 163.
Low, Bishop David, 225.
Lowe, Robert, 288.
Lower Wynd, 155, 185. See Church
  Street.
Lower Tenements, 197. See River
  Street.
Loyalty Fund, 170.
Lyall, Rev. Mr, 151.

Magdalene, St Mary, 50, 52.
„ Chapel, 50, 261.
Magistrates, 276.
Maidlen Chapel, 50.
Mails, 284.
Maisondieu Chapel, 16, 17, 51, 192,
  255.
„ Præceptory, 89, 256, 279.
„ Farm of, 256, 258, 266.
„ Land, 278.
„ Vennel, 255.
Maitland, William, 152, 287.
Malcolm II., 3, 11; IV., 6.
„ Alexander, 195.
Malise, 5.
Malt, 44.
Maltmen, 61, 95.
Manse, 139, 215, 267. Offices, 183.
Manufactures, 78, 229, 270.
Mar, Earl of, 45, 125, 126, 131.
Mar's Year, 125.
Marches, 107, 109, 137, 228.
Margaret of Norway, 18.
Marionettes, 209.
Markets, 1, 17, 20, 30, 31, 107, 108, 109,
  138, 156, 174, 181, 190, 194, 204, 214,
  222, 274.
Market Street, 51, 179, 194, 208, 210,
  256, 263, 264, 279, 282.
Marwick, J. D., City-clerk of Edin-
  burgh, 3.
Marriages, 100.
Martin, Rev. James, 288.
Mary, Virgin, Chapel of, 17. Stall, 51.
Mary, Queen, 36, 46.
Mary, St, Street, 179, 210, 264, 279.
Maryton, 26, 87.
Masons, 226, 268.
Mason Lodge, St James, 279, 283.
„ Knight Templars, 284.
„ St Ninian's, 284.
Mass, 63.
Mather, Bailie, 143.

2 A

Maule, Hon. Fóx, 224.
„ Harry, of Kelly, 54, 108.
„ Hon. Lauderdale, 225.
„ Panmure Family, 54, 64, 201.
„ Sir Thomas, 18, 287.
„ Hon. William, 201, 223.
Meal, 91, 164, 171, 188.
Mealhill, 108.
Meal-market, 131, 164.
Meal-mills, 180.
Meal-mob, 188.
Meal Wynd, 91, 131.
Measures and Weights, 24, 160.
Mechanics' Institution, 205, 208, 217, 220, 224, 280, 281, 283.
Meetings of Council, 208.
Meldrum, William, Bishop, 52, 311.
Melville, Rev. Henry, 213.
Member of Parliament, 121, 125, 187, 197, 201, 220, 265.
Memes, Dr John, 227, 288.
Menmuir, 10, 25, 26, 71, 76, 126, 258, 264, 266.
Merchants, 61.
Merchant Society, 284.
Michael Den Burn, 264.
Middle Drums, 41.
Militia, 94, 173, 183.
Mill, John, kirk-officer, 69, 77.
Mills of Brechin, 17, 40, 45, 105, 108, 113, 128, 180, 191, 222.
Mill Stairs, 51, 108, 137, 206, 228, 265.
Millar, David, Arbroath, 5.
Minister, Choosing a, 74.
Minister of Brechin, Second, 183.
Ministers' Stipends, 276, 277.
Mistletoe of the Oak, 7.
Mitchell, Alexander, 225.
Mitchell, Rev. A. F., 289.
Mitchell, Convener David, 15.
Mitchell & Young, seedsmen, 274.
Moir, Bishop David, 220, 326.
Molison, Provost, 141, 151, 187.
Monroumonth Muir, 73.
Montboy, 34.
Montrose Burgh, 11, 15, 20, 24, 30, 31, 38, 51, 57, 66, 71, 76, 84, 87, 88, 141, 164, 165, 167, 187, 207.
Montrose Bridge, 167.
Montrose Harbour, 207.
Montrose, Marquis of, 67, 69, 84.
Montrose Review Newspaper, 217.
Montrose Street, 218, 224, 263, 265, 266, 279.
Mornan, Thane of Brechin, 12.
Moss of Brechin, 75.
Morton, Regent, 43, 46.
Mortifications for education 81, 104, 279, 280.

Muir of Brechin, 26, 33, 83, 137, 159, 160, 206, 219.
Muirfauld, 34, 159, 219.
Muirland School, 279.
Municipal Corporation, 1.
Murlingden, 71.
Murray, Lord George, 142.
Murray, Regent, 39.
Murray, See of, 6.
Macalpine, Kenneth, 3, 4, 52.
Macarthur, William, town-officer, 174.
M'Cosh, Rev. Dr James, 213.
M'Gregor of Crofts, 194.
„ Street, 203.

Navar, 30, 37, 45, 54, 87, 104, 201, 264, 279.
Navy, Men to serve in the, 170.
Negroes, none in parish, 167.
Nether Tenements, 148, 263. *See* River Street.
Nether Wynd. *See* Lower Wynd.
Newspaper, Local, 197, 221, 270.
Newton, Falconer of, 107, 108.
Nero, Emperor, 69.
Nicol, Dr John P., 288.
Nicolas, Saint, Altarage of, 52.
Ninian, Saint, Altarage of, 52.
Ninian, Saint, masons, 284.
Noble families connected with Brechin, 54.
Nomine Jesu, Chaplainry of, 51.
Noran, River, 73.
Norval, Rev. Mr, 213.
Norsemen, 7.
North Port, 91, 95, 139, 263, 265, 274.
North Port Distillery, 273.
Northern Lights, 131.
North-water-bridge Market, 107.
Norway Dikes, 12.
Nurseries, 113, 226, 274.
Nursery, Den, 186, 228.

Oak, Misletoe on, 7.
Oaths to Government, 95, 100.
Oathlaw, 13, 87.
Oatmeal, 269.
Obelisk at Carnoustie, 12.
Odd Fellow Society, 284.
Officer, Captain, 102.
Officers, Town, 174, 190.
Ogil, Laird of, 145.
Ogilvy, John, of Little Brechin, 137.
Ogilvy, Lord, 145.
Olave, the Dane, 12.
Orange, Prince of, 100.
Ordinary Ale to be drunk, 120.
Origin of Brechin, 1.
Ormiston, William, 238.

Oswalds, Guthries, and Craig, 222.

Packmen, 275.
Palatine of Strathearn, 22, 51.
Panbride, 12.
Panmure, Family of, 54, 55, 64, 106, 126, 160, 201, 256, 265.
   ,,   Lord, 185, 201, 205, 208, 209, 217, 222, 223, 282.
   ,,   Street, 52, 194, 203, 210, 264, 278.
Paper-mill, 105, 222, 272.
Parish School, 184, 187, 201.
Parliament, Member of, 88, 93, 121, 125, 197, 220.
Parliamentary Boundaries, 265, 266.
   ,,   Electors, 201, 265.
   ,,   Reform, 188.
Parochial Board, 226.
   ,,   Lodging-house, 224.
Pasturage of Trinity Muir, 188.
Paterson, William, 110.
Path Head, 169.
Path Wynd, 205, 208.   *See* Bridge St.
Path Road, 190, 228.
Patriotic Fund, 225.
Patter, Tibbie, 155.
Patrick, Bishop, 248.
Paviour, 60.
Pawnbrokers, 268.
Pearse Street, 264.
Perambulation of Muirs, 219.
Peats, 269.
Pennant, Mr, 244.
Peel, Sir Robert, 221.
Pennycook, William, 288.
Pettintoscall, 32.
Petrie, Dr George, 251.
Pews in Church, 60, 100.
Pewter Dishes, 167.
Philip, Bishop, of Brechin, 19, 305.
Pictavia, 9.
Picts, or Peghts, 3, 247.
Pigs, 269.
Piper, 90.
Pitarrow, 56.
Pitforthie, 9, 29, 81, 266.
Pitpullox, 9, 32, 140.
Pittendriech, 9, 32, 258.
Pittengardner, 51.
Plague, or Pestilence, 52, 60, 70, 255.
Plan of Brechin, by Wood, 191.
   ,,   Trinity Muir, by Henderson, 160.
Players, Stage, 175, 221.
Pob, 154.
Police, 198, 277.
   ,,   Act, 221, 222, 225, 226, 228, 270, 276.
   ,,   Office, 206, 281.

Poll Election, 105, 128.
Poor, 171, 181, 187, 188, 196, 216, 226, 270.
Poor-House, 224.
Pork, 269.
Population, 216, 223, 260, 266, 329.
Pope Clement, 19.
   ,,   Innocent, 19.
   ,,   John, 19.
Ports of Burgh, 95, 138, 153.
Posting-master, 84.
Post-Office, 270, 284.
Potatoes, 269.
Poultry, 269.
Powbridge, 83.
Power Looms, 229, 271.
Prain, David, 198, 216.
Præceptory of Maisondieu, 89, 201.
Precentor, 183.
Precedence in Council, 162.
Prentice Neuk, 208.
Presbyterianism, 63, 76, 87, 93, 114.
Presbytery of Brechin, 277.
   ,,   Records, 87, 98, 115, 127, 149, 279.
Pretender, James, 130.
Prince Regent, 187.
Prince of Wales, 217, 228.
Printing Establishment, 125, 197.
Privy Council, 90.
Privy Seal Records, 40, 46.
Prior of the Culdees, 5.
Prison, 45, 90, 96, 112, 206, 215, 218, 228, 281.
Proclamation of Banns, 183.
Procurator before Sheriff, 45.
Professional Men, 218, 269.
Properties, Tenure of, in Burgh, 265.
Property of the Burgh, 276.
Protestantism, 37.
Provisions, Price of, 269.
Provost First Elected, 111.
Public Affairs, 187, 197, 220, 221, 267.
   ,,   Records, 1.
Punch-bowl, 263.

Qualochty, 34.
Quarries, 268.

Ragged School, 222, 291.
Railways, 190, 192, 205, 214, 216, 218, 219, 221, 259, 284.
Randolph de Strathphetham, 16.
Reading Rooms, 224, 225.
Rebellion in 1715, 108, 125.
   ,,   1745, 82, 91, 119, 141, 146.
Red Friars, 51.
Redhall, 51.
Redhead, 12

Reeves, Dr, 4.
Reform, Political, 170, 188, 215.
Reform Acts, 93, 123, 157, 189.
Reformation, 37, 39.
Refreshment Rooms, 224.
Regiments of Horse and Foot, 66.
Registrar of Births, &c., 270.
Registrum Episcopatus Brechinensis, 6, 30.
Restennet, 41.
Richard of Cirencester, 13.
Rifle Corps, 227, 228.
River Street, 148, 197, 220, 224, 263, 265, 266.
Roads, 17, 160, 165, 174, 199, 200, 201, 204, 216, 262, 268.
Robert I., 17, 172.
   „   II., 20, 22, 29.
   „   Bishop of St Andrews, 5.
Roman Catholics, 37, 167.
Roman Camps, 12, 13.
Rome, Church of, 4.
Rose, George, 178, 288.
Ross, See of, 6.
Ross of Rossie, 197.
Round Tower, 24, 46, 96, 104, 219, 230, 234, 252.
Royal Burghs, Constitution of, 1.
Royal Bank, 269.
Royal Proclamation, 169.
Royal Tribunal of Druids, 9.
Royalty of Burgh, 259, 266.
Ruling Elder, 130, 169, 226.
Russian Gun, 225.
Ruxton, Robert, 188.

Sabbath Alliance, 220.
   „   Observance of, 59.
   „   Schools, 152, 280.
Saint Andrews, Bishop of, his Right of Market, 1 ; Canon of, 5 ; See of, 6.
Saint David Street, 179, 199, 210, 256, 264, 282.
Saint John of Jerusalem, Hospital of, 24.
Saint Mary Street, 179, 210, 264, 279.
Saint Sebastian, 52.
Saltoun, Lady, 166.
Savings Banks, 198, 269.
Samson, Culdee, 5.
Sansane, Bishop, 6, 299.
Sawmill, 272.
Scales Acre, 52, 203.
   „   Lane, 203.
Schools, 45, 89, 112, 140, 157, 160, 181, 184, 187, 201, 208, 215, 222, 226, 227, 279, 282.
School Fees, 158, 181, 202, 288.
   „   House, 112, 160.
   „   Infant, 205.

School Loft in Church, 183.
   „   Master, 45, 89.
   „   Mistress, 131.
Scott, Alexander, 47, 287.
Scott, Sir Walter, 14, 244.
Scots Acts, 2.
Seats in Church, 64, 100, 124.
Sebastian, Saint, Altarage of, 52.
Secession Churches, 217.
Sessions, Kirk, 72 ; Lords of, 36.
Sett of the Burgh, 122.
Sewing-machines, 225.
Shambles, 276.
Sharp, William, 107.
Sharpe, Archbishop, 94.
Shanks, Rev. William, 139.
Sheriff-courts, 33, 45, 207.
Sherwood, Arms of Bishop, 223.
Shiress, William, slater, 250.
   „   „   writer, 211.
Shoemakers, 58.
Shuffle Katie, 209.
Sievewright, Norman, 178.
Simpson, Deacon, precentor, 183.
Simpson of Ogil, 176.
Simpson, Thomas, at Abernethy, 240, 241, 242.
Sinclair of Roslin, 36.
Skinner, Laurence, 74, 81, 89, 103, 114, 129.
   „   John, 103, 114, 117, 118.
Skinner's Burn, 264, 265.
Skinner trade, 265.
Slateford, 13.
Slavery, 99.
Small, Dr Abernethy, 243, 245, 246, 247.
Small Debt Court, 207.
Smith, Lindsay, hereditary blacksmith, 32.
Smith, Charles, author, 245.
   „   Colvin, 184, 289.
   „   John, of Andover, 226.
Smugglers, 273.
Snow in Summer, 222.
Societies, 280, 281.
Soil of Parish, 258.
Soldiers, 66, 94.
Soup Kitchen, 72.
Southesk, Family of, 31, 56, 73, 126, 164, 168, 170, 173, 197, 217, 220, 265.
Southesk River, 10, 72, 160, 197, 222, 258, 263, 264, 265, 277, 286.
Southesk Street, 112, 194, 203, 210, 218, 220, 264, 278, 282.
South Port, 50, 169, 206, 264.
Spalding Club Miscellany, 19, 82.
Special Constables, 198.
Speid of Ardovie, 254.

Spences, Town-clerks, 44, 82.
Spence, Bailie, 125, 127, 129.
Spinning-mill, 222, 272.
Spring Tryst, 275.
Stamp Masters, 124.
Standing Stones, 7, 12.
Stannachy, 72, 192, 201, 263.
Star Hotel, 282.
State Taxes, 2, 30, 37;
Statute Labour Roads, 174.
Steeples, 24, 46, 82, 96, 104, 219, 223, 230, 252.
Stelites, Simon, 245.
Stennis, in Orkney, 7.
Stewart, Charles Edward, 142.
Stewart, James, Lord of Brechin, 30.
  ,,   Walter,   ,,   22, 51.
Stone, Curious Carved, in Churchyard, 254.
Stone Coffins, 254.
Stonehenge, 7.
Stracathro, 10, 87, 99, 130, 258.
Strachan, 16.
Strachan, Alexander, writer, 228.
Strachan, David, bishop, 77, 318.
Strachan, Robert, kirk-officer, 89.
Strangers, Act against, 84.
Strathmore Railway, 192, 218.
Strathphetham, 16.
Streets of Burgh, 91, 131, 229, 263, 264, 282.
Streets, Repaired, 169, 214; Renamed, 218.
Sueno of Denmark, 12.
Surgeons, 218, 269.
Swan Inn, 91, 148, 282.
Swan Street Improved, 229.
Swine, 269.
Symmer of Balzordie, 79.

Tailors, 58, 155, 225 ; Trade Election, 195.
Tanners, 265.
Tarnty Market, 275.
Taxations on Burgh, 30, 37.
Tay, 13, 20.
Tayock, Bridge, 76, 165.
Tea-kettle, The First, 140.
Temperance Society, 200.
Templars, Knights, 256.
Templehill of Bothers, 24, 257.
Tenements Schools, 226, 227, 279.
Tents in Markets, 165.
Test Oaths, 100.
Threephaugh Ford, 26.
Thomson, Thomas, advocate, 1.
Thomas, Saint, Altar of, 51.
Thursday Sermon, 86.
Tickets, Burgess, 138.
Tilbury Fort, 147, 150.

Timber Market, 179.
Tings of the Norseman, 7.
Tobacco Works, 267.
Toddshouses on Muir, 34.
Toland, 9.
Tolbooth, 42, 45, 90, 96, 112, 164, 206, 215, 218, 281.
Tolling Bells, 119.
Toll Roads, 160.
Torfechyn, Magister de, 24; Earl of, 256.
Tower, Round, 24, 234. *See* Round Tower.
Town's accounts, 171.
Town-Clerk, 82, 229, 270.
  ,,   Hall, 164, 206, 226, 264.
  ,,   Herd, 113.
  ,,   House, 281.
  ,,   Officers, 174, 190.
  ,,   Parks, 188.
  ,,   Vassals, 191.
Trades Election, 194.
  ,,   Incorporated, 58, 92, 97, 113, 123, 132, 140, 155, 156, 188, 190, 198.
  ,,   in Town, 268.
Treasurer, Lord High, Books of, 38.
Trinitarians, Order of, 51.
Trinity Markets, 97, 159, 275.
  ,,   Stance, 156, 221, 281.
  ,,   Muir, 33, 137, 159, 160, 181, 188, 190, 275.
  ,,   Village, 206, 217.
Tryst Market, 190.
Turkish Captives, 99.
Turnpike Roads, 262.
Tytler, Dr, 174.
  ,,   James, 175.

Umbrellas, first in Brechin, 166.
Uninhabited Houses, 266.
Union Bank, 164, 269.
Union of England and Scotland, 53, 111, 121.
Union Street, 206, 210, 224, 263, 279.
United Presbyterian Church, 227, 278.
University of Edinburgh, 169.
Unthank, 52, 266.
  ,,   David Ferrier, tenant of, 145.
Upper Wynd, 179. *See* St David Street.
  ,,   Tenements, 263. *See* Montrose Street.

Vaccination, 261.
Vagrants, 70, 84.
Valuators of Properties, 191.
Vane of Fearn, 9.
Vassals of Town, 191.
Vennel, 193. *See* City Road.
Vespasiana, 13.

Victoria I., 207, 209, 216, 219.
Virgin Mary, Chapel of, 17.
Vocal Society, 281.
Volunteers, 172, 173, 182.
Voters, Parliamentary, 201.

Wages of Tradesmen, 267.
Wales, Prince of, 217, 228.
Walker, David, 199.
Warden, town-officer, 141.
Warnings of Tenants, 186.
Washing-house, 203, 228, 276.
Washing-mills, 180.
Water, 158, 214, 222, 224, 227, 276, 277.
Water to Private Houses, 214.
Waterstone, David, 33.
Watson, David, 134, 287.
Watson, James, 139.
Waulk Mill, 40, 108.
Way, Albert, 238.
Weavers, 58, 271.
Wedgwood Ware, 167.
Weigh-house, 45, 128, 180, 276.
Weighing-machine, 187.
Weights and Measures, 44, 169.

Wellington, Duke of, 224.
Wells, 158, 193, 222.
Welsh, Rev. James, 288.
Western Bank, 227.
Whisky, Manufacture of, 267, 273, 274.
William the Lion, 1.
    ,,   IV., 197, 198, 207.
    ,,   Prince of Orange, 100.
Willison, Rev. John, 115.
Wilson, Dr Daniel, 252.
Windell, Mr, Ireland, 251.
Wishart, John, of Pitarrow, 51.
Witches, 73, 75.
Witch Branks, 76.
Witchden, 76, 283.
Witchden Mill, 272.
Wood's Plan of Brechin, 191.
Wool Fair, 222.
Wright, Elisha, 24, 248.
Wright Trade, 190; Society, 284.
Wrights in Brechin, 268.
Writers in Brechin, 218, 226, 269.

Years, Dear, 30.
York Building Company, 55, 57.

THE END.

BALLANTYNE AND COMPANY, PRINTERS, EDINBURGH.

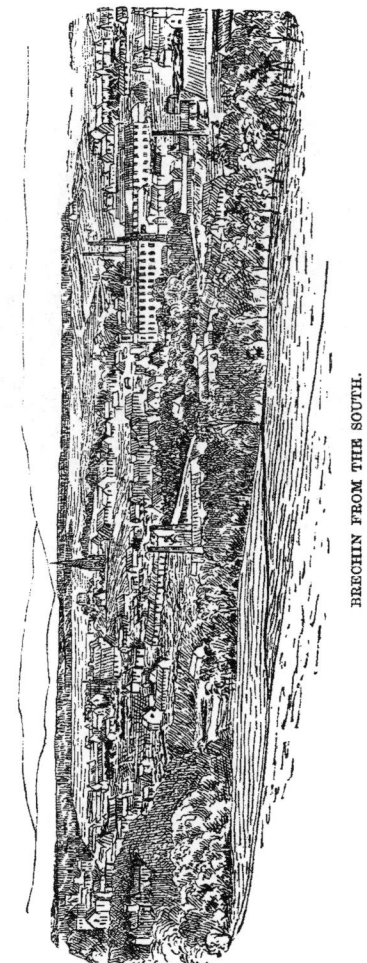

BRECHIN FROM THE SOUTH.

BRECHIN CATHEDRAL FROM THE WEST.

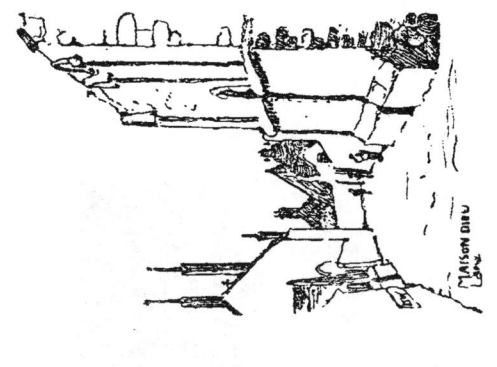

BRECHIN IN 1600.

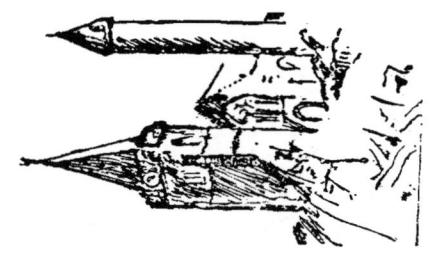

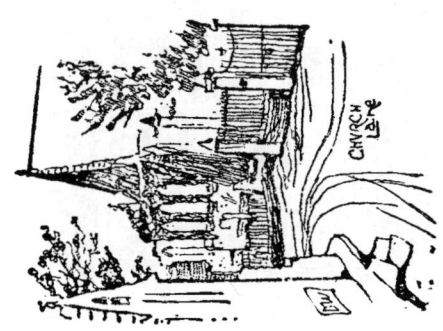

CHURCH LANE

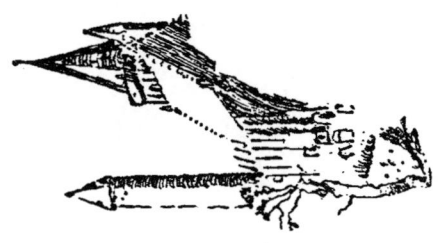

BRECHIN CATHEDRAL—RUINS OF OLD CHANCEL.

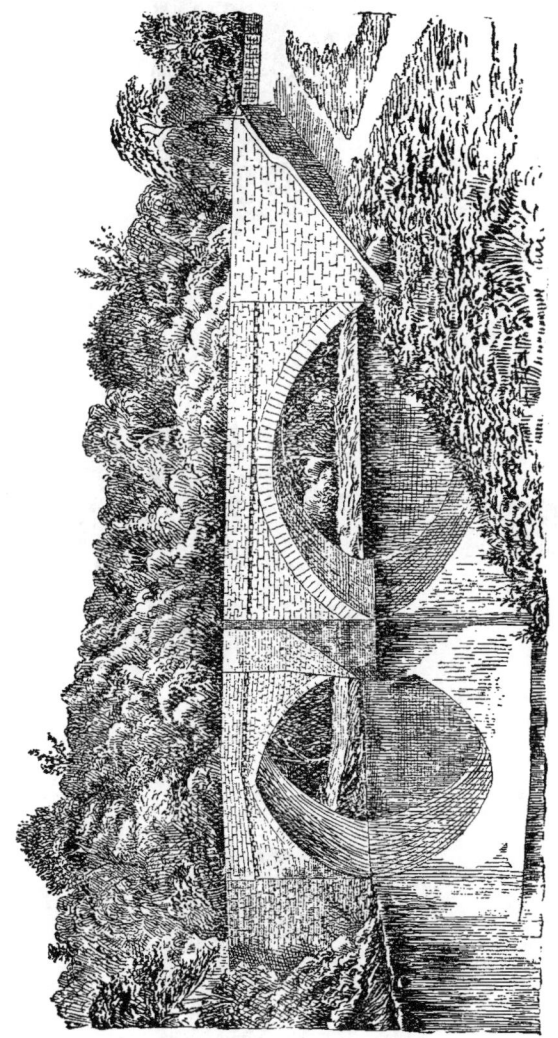

BRECHIN BRIDGE.

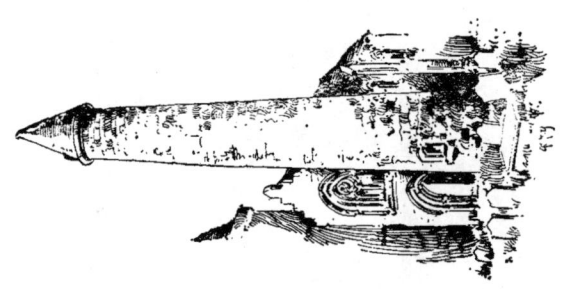

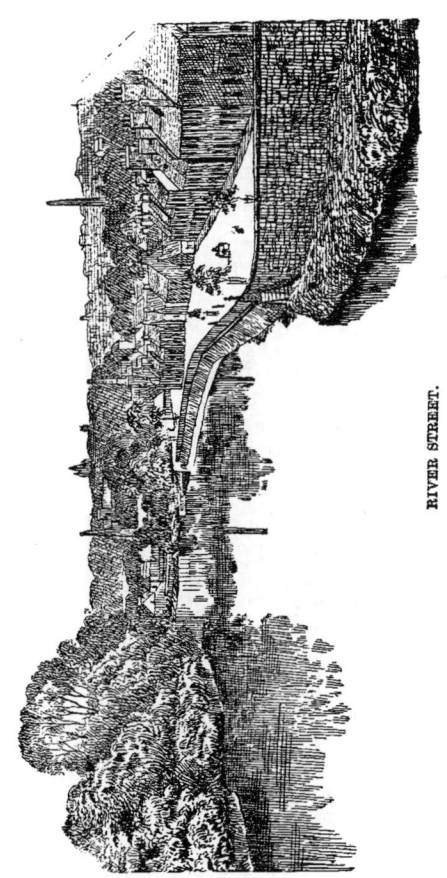

RIVER STREET.

ST NINIAN'S SQUARE.

Market St.
Brechin

High St.

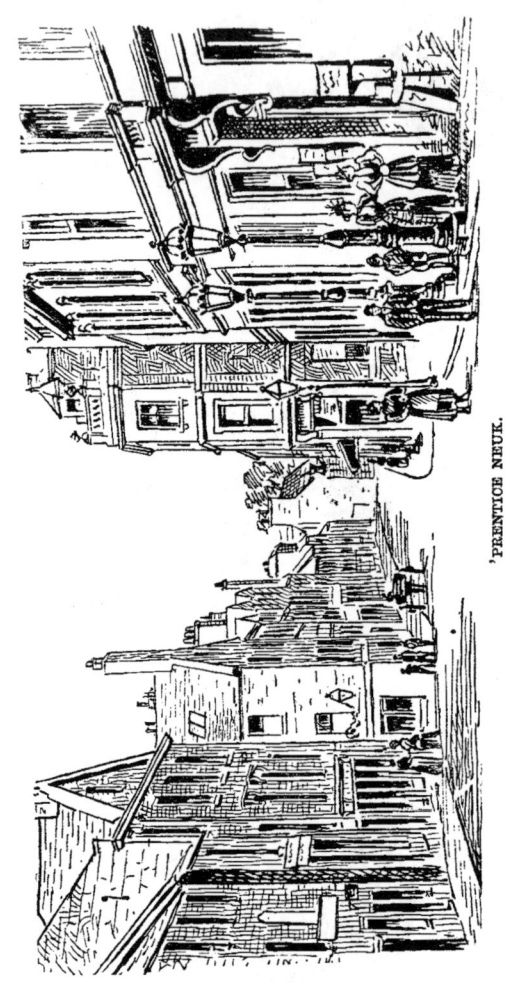

'PRENTICE NEUK.

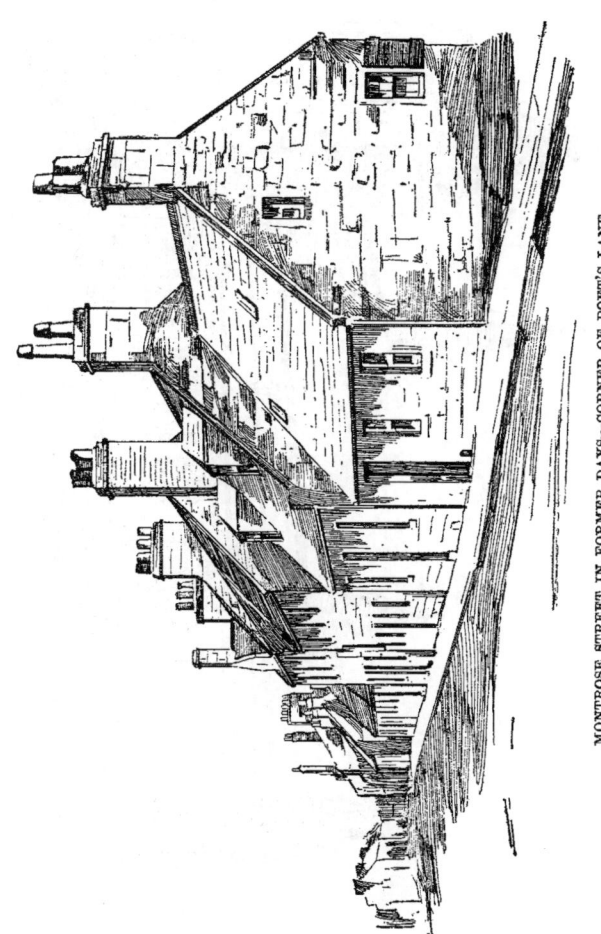

MONTROSE STREET IN FORMER DAYS—CORNER OF POET'S LANE.

BRECHIN CATHEDRAL (RESTORED).

BRECHIN CATHEDRAL—NEW AISLE.

DEN BURN WORKS, BRECHIN (D. & R. DUKE).
ESTABLISHED 1851.

S. ANDREW'S EPISCOPAL CHURCH.

GARDNER MEMORIAL PARISH CHURCH.
(ERECTED 1898.)

CHURCH OF THE HOLY TRINITY.

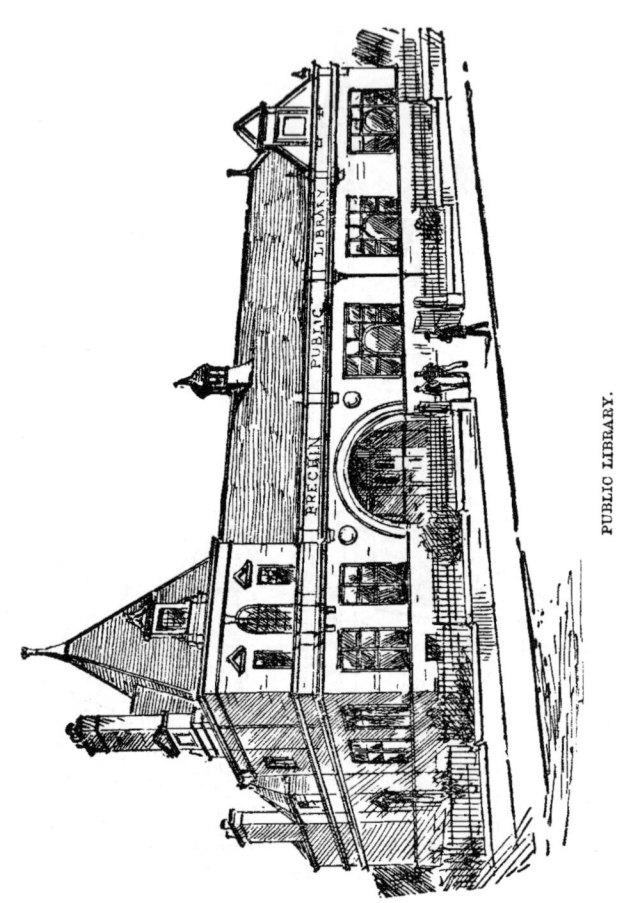

PUBLIC LIBRARY.